CHILDREN OF AUSTERITY

Children of Austerity

Impact of the Great Recession on Child Poverty in Rich Countries

Edited by

BEA CANTILLON, YEKATERINA CHZHEN,
SUDHANSHU HANDA, AND BRIAN NOLAN

Published by The United Nations Children's Fund
and Oxford University Press

unicef

OXFORD
UNIVERSITY PRESS

OXFORD
UNIVERSITY PRESS

Great Clarendon Street, Oxford, OX2 6DP,
United Kingdom

Oxford University Press is a department of the University of Oxford. It furthers the University's objective of excellence in research, scholarship, and education by publishing worldwide. Oxford is a registered trade mark of Oxford University Press in the UK and in certain other countries

First Edition published in 2017

Impression: 1

Published in the United States of America by Oxford University Press
198 Madison Avenue, New York, NY 10016, United States of America

British Library Cataloguing in Publication Data
Data available

Library of Congress Control Number: 2016950867

ISBN 978–0–19–879796–8

Printed in Great Britain by
Clays Ltd, St Ives plc

Contents

List of Figures

List of Tables

List of Contributors

Aya K. Abe holds a PhD from the Fletcher School of Law and Diplomacy, Tufts University. In 1999 she took a position at the National Institute of Population and Social Security Research, which is a research arm of the Ministry of Health, Labour, and Welfare. She has participated and led many research projects on poverty and inequality in Japan and has published numerous books and articles on poverty issues in Japan. Her 2008 book entitled *Child Poverty : Re-examining Japan's Inequality* is widely acclaimed to be the first book in Japan which focuses on child poverty in the country. She serves on numerous committees of national and local government on poverty and social assistance issues. In 2015, she left her previous position to take up a professorship at the Tokyo Metropolitan University.

Sara Ayllón is an Associate Professor at the Department of Economics at the Universitat de Girona (Spain). She obtained her PhD at the Applied Economics Department at the Autonomous University of Barcelona (UAB) in 2009. She previously graduated with an MSc in European Social Policy at the London School of Economics, and she has a BSc in economics and another in journalism. Most of her research focuses on the economics of poverty and inequality, economics of the family, labour economics, health economics, and applied microeconometrics. Her recent list of publications includes a book analysing the effects of the Great Recession on child poverty in Spain (*Childhood, poverty and the economic crisis*, Social Studies Collection No. 40, 'La Caixa' Foundation) and several peer-reviewed articles for international journals such as the *Review of Income and Wealth*, *Social Indicators Research*, *Economics and Human Biology*, *Economics Letters*, and *Demographic Research*. Sara is currently the principal investigator in Spain of the EU-funded Horizon 2020 project 'NEGOTIATE—Negotiating early job-insecurity and labour market exclusion in Europe'.

Thomas Bahle is a lecturer in sociology at the University of Mannheim (Germany) and project director at the *Mannheimer Zentrum für Europäische Sozialforschung* (MZES). His main research areas are comparative welfare state, family policies, social services, and minimum income protection.

Jonathan Bradshaw is Emeritus Professor of Social Policy at the University of York, UK. His research interests cover living standards, social security policy, family policy, child well-being, and comparisons of welfare states. His most recent book is *The Well-being of Children in the UK* (Policy Press, 2016). *Jonathan Bradshaw on Social Policy: Selected writings 1972–2011* was published in 2013. He is the UK coordinator of the European Social Policy Network. He is a Fellow of the British Academy, a member of the Board of the Child Poverty Action Group and an Honorary Fellow of UNICEF, UK.

Bea Cantillon is Professor of Social Policy and Director of the Herman Deleeck Centre for Social Policy at the University of Antwerp, Belgium. She has published on issues relating to poverty, social policy, social security, the welfare state, and gender. She has acted as a consultant to, among others, the OECD, the European Commission, and the Belgian government. Books she has co-edited include *Social Indicators: The EU and Social Inclusion* with T. Atkinson, E. Marler, and B. Nolan: *Reconciling Work and Poverty Reduction* with F. Vandenbroucke, both from Oxford University Press.

Yekaterina Chzhen is a social and economic policy specialist at the UNICEF Office of Research—Innocenti. She specializes in comparative social policy, focusing on the interplay between government policies and individual level outcomes, such as poverty, deprivation, and labour market participation. She currently leads UNICEF's Innocenti Report Card series on child well-being in OECD countries and is also part of the team studying multidimensional child poverty. She joined UNICEF in February 2013 after two and a half years as a post-doctoral fellow in quantitative methods in social and political sciences at Nuffield College, Oxford. She completed her PhD in social policy and economics at the University of York in 2010.

András Gábos has a PhD in sociology and is senior researcher at Tárki Social Research Institute, Budapest. His main research fields are poverty, child poverty and well-being, and fertility effects of family policies. He coordinated the 'Study on child poverty' project for the Employment directorate-general of the European Commission (2009). He has recently been involved in several comparative research projects on poverty and social exclusion, including Poverty Reduction in Europe: Social Policy and Innovation (ImPRovE), Integrating Expertise in Inclusive Growth (InGRID), and Strategic Transitions for Youth Labour in Europe (STYLE).

Sudhanshu Handa is Professor of Public Policy at the University of North Carolina at Chapel Hill. Between 2013 and 2016 he served as Chief of Social and Economic Policy at UNICEF's Office of Research, Florence, Italy. During that period he was part of the research team that produced the Innocenti Report Card, which assesses the status of child poverty and well-being in OECD countries. Over the last seven years he has also led five large-scale evaluations of national cash transfer programmes in sub-Saharan Africa as part of the Transfer Project. His previous positions include lecturer at the University of the West Indies, Jamaica, professor of agricultural economics at the Eduardo Mondlane University, Maputo, Mozambique, and social development specialist,

Inter-American Development Bank. He received his PhD in Economics from the University of Toronto in 1993.

Jan O. Jonsson is Official Fellow of Nuffield College, Oxford, Professor of Sociology at the Swedish Institute for Social Research, and affiliated with the Institute for Futures Studies. Among his research interests are social stratification, the welfare and living conditions of children and youth, and ethnic integration.

Peter Krause is senior researcher at the German Socio-Economic Panel (SOEP) in the German Institute for Economic Research (DIW Berlin). His main research interests are income distribution and dynamics, social inequality and deprivation, and capabilities and quality of life.

Gill Main is a University Academic Fellow in the School of Education at the University of Leeds. Her research focuses on child and youth poverty, social exclusion, and well-being. She has investigated the links between child poverty and subjective well-being, and how incorporating children's own perspectives of their needs can elucidate these links. She has recently worked on the 2012 UK Poverty and Social Exclusion Study and the Children's Worlds study. She is currently working on a study of child poverty and social exclusion in Australia.

Bertrand Maître is a senior research officer at the Economic and Social Research Institute in Dublin. His main research interests focus on multidimensional approaches to poverty, social exclusion, and quality of life. He is particularly interested in the development and the use of instruments comprising not only indirect but also direct measures of deprivation, ranging from durable goods to participation in social life, through to housing and environmental conditions. His recent work appears in *Social Indicators Research*, *Journal of Family and Economic Issues*, *Longitudinal and Life Course Studies*, and *The Economic and Social Review*.

Manos Matsaganis is associate professor of public finance at Politecnico di Milano. He was trained as an economist in Greece (AUEB) and in England (MSc York; PhD Bristol). He has worked at the London School of Economics (1990–3), the Greek Prime Minister's Office (1997–2001), the University of Crete (1996–9 and 2001–4), and the Athens University of Economics and Business (2004–16), where he continues to coordinate the Policy Analysis Research Unit. In 2014–15 he visited the United States as a Fulbright Scholar (winter term: Center for European Studies, Harvard; spring term: Center for Equitable Growth, UC Berkeley). His current research focuses on the distributional implications of the Eurozone crisis, the political economy of austerity in Southern Europe, and the effects of the minimum wage on employment, earnings, and poverty.

Carina Mood is professor of sociology at the Swedish Institute for Social Research, and at the Institute for Futures Studies. Her research interests include poverty, inequality, children's resources, and intergenerational transmission of advantage.

Luisa Natali is currently a social policy consultant at the UNICEF Office of Research—Innocenti—in Florence. She holds a Master's in Development Economics as well as being a PhD candidate in development economics at the University of Sussex. She has previously worked as a research consultant for the Institute of Development Studies, the Overseas Development Institute, the UK Department for International Development, and the American Institutes for Research. She has gained international work experience in Bangladesh, South Africa, and Zambia. Her main research fields are development economics and policy impact evaluation; her research interests lie in social policy and social protection, and in particular in the evaluation of cash transfer programmes, child well-being, poverty and vulnerability analysis, and the economics of gender.

Brian Nolan is director of the Employment, Equity, and Growth Programme at the Institute for New Economic Thinking, Oxford Martin School, professor of social policy at the Department of Social Policy and Intervention, and senior research fellow at Nuffield College, Oxford. His main areas of research are income inequality, poverty, and the economics of social policy. His publications include *The Handbook of Economic Inequality* (2008) co-edited with W. Salverda and T. Smeeding, *Poverty and Deprivation in Europe* (2011) co-authored with C. T. Whelan, *The Great Recession and the Distribution of Household Income* (2013), co-edited with S. Jenkins, A. Brandolini, and J. Micklewright, and two co-edited volumes with W. Salverda et al., *Changing Inequalities in Rich Countries: Analytical and Comparative Perspectives* and *Changing Inequalities and Societal Impacts in Rich Countries: Thirty Countries' Experiences*, all from Oxford University Press.

Chiara Saraceno, former professor of sociology at the University of Turin and research professor at the WZB in Berlin, is presently honorary fellow at the Collegio Carlo Alberto, Turin. In 1999–2001 she chaired the Italian Poverty Comission. Among her recent publications are *Il lavoro non basta: La povertà in Europa negli anni della crisi* (Feltrinelli, 2015) and, in English , 'A Critical Look to the Social Investment Approach from a Gender Perspective', *Social Politics*, 22 (2015); and 'Trends and Tensions within the Italian Family', in *The Oxford Handbook of Italian Politics*, ed. E. Jones and G. Pasquino (Oxford University Press, 2015).

Timothy M. (Tim) Smeeding is the Lee Rainwater Distinguished Professor of Public Affairs and Economics at the University of Wisconsin-Madison and former director of the Institute for Research on Poverty (IRP). He was the founding director of the Luxembourg Income Study (LIS) from 1983 to 2006. His recent work has been on child poverty and mobility across generations, as well as inequality, wealth, and poverty in a national and cross-national context. Books he has co-edited include *Persistence, Privilege and Parenting: The Comparative Study of Intergenerational Mobility* (Russell Sage Foundation, 2011); *From Parents to Children: The Intergenerational Transmission of Advantage* (Russell Sage Foundation, in press); and *The Handbook of Economic Inequality* (Oxford University Press, 2009); and he is co-author of *Poor Kids in a Rich Country: America's Children in Comparative Perspective* (Russell Sage Foundation, 2003); and *The American Welfare State: Laggard or Leader?* (Oxford University Press, 2010).

István György Tóth has a PhD in sociology and is director of Tárki Social Research Institute, Budapest. He directed and co-directed a number of comparative research projects on social structure and inequalities in Europe, recently including Growing Inequalities Impacts (GINI), Poverty Reduction in Europe: Social Policy and Innovation (ImPRovE), and Inclusive Growth Research Infrastructure Diffusion (InGRID). He is a member of the advisory board to the Luxembourg Income Study. He was co-editor of *Changing Inequalities and Societal Impacts in Rich Countries: Thirty Countries' Experiences* (Oxford University Press, 2014) and co-authored the chapter 'Cross-country Evidence of the Multiple Causes of Inequality Changes in the OECD Area' in A. Atkinson and F. Bourguignon's *Handbook of Income Distribution* (Elsevier, 2014).

Wim Van Lancker is a multimedia specialist turned social scientist, holding a bachelor's degree in multimedia and communication technology (University College West-Flanders), a master's degree in political sciences (Ghent University), and a PhD from the University of Antwerp. Currently he works as a post-doctoral research fellow of the Research Foundation Flanders (FWO) and as a lecturer in social policy, affiliated with the Herman Deleeck Centre for Social Policy at the University of Antwerp. His main research topics are family policy and its social distribution, child poverty and social inequality, the design and effectiveness of social policy, and the social investment state.

Julie Vinck holds a master's degree in social and economic sciences (University of Antwerp) and social policy analysis (KU Leuven). Currently, she works as a PhD fellow of the Research Foundation of Flanders (FWO), affiliated with the Herman Deleeck Centre for Social Policy at the University of Antwerp, investigating 'The poverty-care nexus in the social investment state: an empirical examination of childhood disability, child poverty and parental employment in Belgium'. Her research interests include child poverty, childhood disability, family policy, the selectivity in social policy, the work-care dilemma, and how social policy could respond to this.

Christopher Wimer is co-director of the Center on Poverty and Social Policy at Columbia University and research scientist at the Columbia Population Research Center. His research interests include poverty measurement, how low-income families cope with poverty and hardship, and the role of social policies in promoting the wellbeing of disadvantaged populations.

1

Introduction: Scope and Methods

Yekaterina Chzhen, Sudhanshu Handa, Bea Cantillon, and Brian Nolan

1.1. INTRODUCTION

The 2008 financial crisis triggered the first contraction of the world economy in the post-war era. Although the global economy recovered by 2010, many industrialized countries remained in a cycle of low and uneven growth. By 2011, several countries were also facing a sovereign debt crisis. During the recession, amid falling wages and increasing unemployment, government capacity to address worsening social conditions was often constrained by mounting deficits. Following an initial round of expansionary counter-cyclical policy, the crisis itself put pressure on many governments to implement austerity measures. Thus social protection systems were under threat when they were most needed.

Children and young people were some of the main victims of the crisis and ensuing austerity in advanced economies. The majority of forty-one countries in the European Union (EU) and/or the Organization for Economic Co-operation and Development (OECD) saw increases in child poverty between 2008 and 2012, with 2.6 million more children living in poverty by the end of this period (UNICEF Office of Research, 2014). By 2013, nearly a million more young people aged 15 to 24 were not in employment, education, or training across the EU. The countries most severely affected by the financial and economic crisis recorded some of the largest increases in child poverty. However, children in rich countries were at a greater risk of poverty than the population as a whole long before the outbreak of the crisis. The lack of progress in protecting children in the pre-crisis years highlights the existence of structural constraints, against which many of the rich welfare states have proved powerless.

1.2. SCOPE AND MOTIVATION OF THE BOOK

The impact of the crisis and austerity on children varied widely across the rich world. Countries differed in their 'initial conditions' at the outset, with respect both to the extent and nature of child poverty and to the capacity of the welfare state to protect children from the effects of an economic downturn. The severity and length of the economic crisis and countries' capacity to respond to it, given their existing fiscal space and external constraints (e.g. from the financial markets or the bailout programmes), also differed greatly.

Bearing in mind the reasons why the impact of the crisis on children would vary across countries, this book sets out to describe the processes that occurred in a diverse group of countries during the period between 2007–8 and 2013–14—processes that resulted in large increases in child poverty. It also highlights instances where child poverty rates did not go up as much in spite of a severe economic downturn. In doing so, the volume aims to draw attention to the situation of children, challenging the thinking around what recessions and austerity can do to vulnerable groups. Offering an analysis of material child well-being in industrialized countries during the crisis and its aftermath, the study poses the following key research questions: 1) what happened to child poverty during this tumultuous time? 2) what was the policy response, especially as it related to families with children? and 3) what could countries have done differently to protect children? These questions are addressed through a set of in-depth analyses of the impact of the economic crisis and its aftermath on children in eleven OECD countries that span a wide range in terms of their initial conditions, the extent of the economic shock, and their responses to it. These include Belgium, Germany, Greece, Hungary, Ireland, Italy, Japan, Spain, Sweden, the United Kingdom, and the United States.

This is the first comparative study to analyse the medium-term effects of the recent global economic crisis, as well as government responses to it (including both fiscal stimulus and fiscal consolidation measures), with an explicit emphasis on children. It builds on, complements, and makes a substantial contribution to two recent publications that also investigated the impact of the crisis on household incomes in rich countries: *The Great Recession and the Distribution of Household Income* (Jenkins et al., 2013) and 'Children of the Recession: the Impact of the Economic Crisis on Child Well-Being in Rich Countries' (UNICEF Office of Research, 2014). However, Jenkins et al. did not focus on children, drew on a smaller sample of country case studies (Germany, Ireland, Italy, Sweden, the UK, and the US), and dealt with a shorter time period (up to 2011). Indeed, they found little change in household income distribution two years after the start of the economic crisis, but predicted that there would be a greater impact from the fiscal consolidation measures being put in place. Meanwhile, the UNICEF study documented a substantial worsening in the living conditions of children between 2008 and 2012–13 in the majority of forty-one countries of the EU and/or the OECD, but largely missed the nuances of impacts within countries, particularly as regards regional variation. We fill this research gap by focusing on children and by providing details of the experiences of a diverse sample of eleven rich countries between 2007 and 2014 (the latest year for which comparable data were available at the time of writing).

The volume is organized as follows. Chapter 2 gives an overview of how the crisis affected industrialized economies and fed through to social spending and to key indicators of child poverty and material deprivation. This serves to set the context for the in-depth case studies of eleven of these countries presented in the rest of the volume. These country case studies tell the story of the economic crisis in terms of the impact on children—including particularly vulnerable groups (and regions)—and the country-level policy response. A concluding chapter (Chapter 14) then draws out the key impacts and responses, highlights the lessons learned in terms of how to protect children during crises, and provides guidance on what countries can do in the future to ensure that families with children are protected from economic shocks.

This is the product of an international collaboration between the UNICEF Office of Research—Innocenti and teams of national academics in eleven OECD countries. As the Innocenti Report Card 12, entitled 'Children of the Recession', raised awareness of the adverse impacts of the crisis and the recession on children in rich countries, it was imperative to continue to highlight the plight of children by telling more in-depth stories of what happened in different countries, and by providing positive constructive recommendations to governments on how to protect children during future crises.

1.3. CASE STUDIES

The eleven case countries are a diverse sample in terms of their initial conditions and the way in which the crisis played out. By focusing on their experiences in depth, we draw attention to the varied impacts of the crisis and to how different countries responded to it, while providing important lessons to other advanced economies. The eleven countries are also a genuinely diverse set, with two non-EU countries (Japan and the US) and three EU countries outside the monetary union (Hungary, Sweden, and the UK).

The US is included because it is the largest economy in the world, was the epicentre of the global financial crisis, and is home to almost one-third of all children in the OECD. We selected three Mediterranean countries that were hit hard by the economic crisis and austerity—Greece, Italy, and Spain—as well as two non-Mediterranean countries that were also hit hard but recovered more quickly (Ireland and the UK). Meanwhile, Belgium, Germany, and

Sweden are EU economies that weathered the crisis reasonably well, while Hungary represents the newer EU Member States. Finally, Japan offers a perspective of a non-European country that lived through two decades of low growth, following a longer period of rapid economic development.

In 2008, child poverty rates ranged from a low of 13–18 per cent in Belgium, Germany, Ireland, and Sweden to a high of 27–30 per cent in Spain and the USA, with the rest of the countries falling in the 20–25 per cent range (UNICEF Office of Research, 2014).[1] At the same time, working-age unemployment (25–64) varied from just 4 per cent in Japan to 10 per cent in Spain, while female (25–54) activity rates ranged from a low of 65 per cent in Italy to a high of 88 per cent in Sweden. The countries also differed in average levels of income per person and social spending, both key to their initial capacity to cope with the economic shock. The level of social spending as a share of GDP at the onset of the crisis was lowest in Japan and the US, followed by Greece, Hungary, Ireland, and Spain; and highest in Belgium, Germany, Italy, Sweden, and the UK. Average income per person, measured as GDP per capita adjusted for differences in purchasing power, was lowest in Greece, Hungary, and Japan and highest in Ireland, Sweden, and the US. All eleven economies had been growing on the eve of the crisis in 2007, with annual GDP growth ranging from 0.5 per cent in Hungary, 1–2 per cent in Italy, Japan, and the US, around 3 per cent in Belgium, Germany, Sweden, and the UK, to 4–5 per cent in Greece, Ireland, and Spain.

The extent and nature of the ensuing economic shock varied greatly. As the next chapter outlines in more detail, four of the case-study countries experienced economic contractions in excess of 9 per cent, based on changes in real GDP per capita between the highest pre-crisis level in 2006–8 ('peak') and the lowest post-crisis level in 2009–14 ('trough'): Spain (9 per cent), Ireland (12 per cent), Italy (13 per cent), and Greece (26 per cent). The rest of the countries saw sizeable peak-to-trough contractions of 5–7 per cent, except Belgium, which experienced a more moderate contraction of 3 per cent. The speed and scale of recovery, if any, also differed across the eleven countries. Germany returned to strong and sustained growth by 2010–11; another four economies recovered by 2014, but not quite as robustly: Hungary, Japan, Sweden, and the US. At the same time, Belgium, Ireland, and the UK came close to reaching their pre-crisis level of GDP per capita in real terms by 2014. By contrast, Italy and Spain have been on a steady downward trajectory, with barely any sign of improvement, while Greece saw the longest and deepest contraction of all, with economic output levelling out in 2013 at 75 per cent of its 2007 value in real terms. Almost a decade since the start of the global financial crisis, Greece is still locked in a cycle of austerity and economic stagnation.

[1] Child poverty rates are measured as the proportion of children living in households with disposable incomes below 60 per cent of the national median.

Thus, although all eleven economies suffered in 2008–9, they can be classified into three groups, based on the size of contraction and the speed of recovery: 1) those that were severely hit by the crisis and experienced a slow and uneven recovery: Greece, Italy, and Spain; 2) those that were severely hit but returned to growth reasonably fast, if not always reaching their pre-crisis level of per capita national income: Ireland, Hungary, the UK, and the US; and 3) those that were moderately hit and recovered rapidly, if not fully: Belgium, Germany, Japan, and Sweden.

The countries in the first two groups are undoubtedly key to discussion of the effects of the economic crisis on children's material well-being in OECD countries; but the inclusion of the third group perhaps deserves further justification. Thus, although Sweden came out of the recent economic crisis relatively unscathed, it did experience a deep economic downturn in the early 1990s that, in terms of its severity, was comparable to the 'Great Recession' in the US. Offering a longer-term perspective than most other chapters, Sweden illustrates the long-run impact of a deep recession on children's living conditions, offering lessons to countries that suffered most in the recent crisis. Belgium and Germany sustained high rates of child poverty before the onset of the crisis, despite their being sophisticated welfare states, with poverty highly concentrated among groups with low attachment to the labour market. Japan is notable for its fragmented social protection system and low benefit coverage of working-age households.

Finally, several of the case-study countries experienced major political shifts during the period under analysis, which affected their response to the ongoing economic crisis. A change of government in the UK brought about a reversal in policy, with a move towards deep cuts in social spending on working-age transfers. A new US president helped design and implement the American Recovery and Reinvestment Act 2009, which had some positive impact on the nation's poor. A new government in Japan scaled back a short-lived expansion in child benefit generosity and coverage. In Hungary, a new government shifted focus away from family allowances to family tax benefits, while cutting social assistance. Thus we draw on a broad range of institutional settings and contexts in learning lessons about how best to protect children across the developed world in subsequent crises.

All the case-study chapters follow the same structure. First, they briefly describe the macroeconomic nature of the crisis and the main transmission channels through which it affected households with children. Then they analyse key trends in child poverty rates, profile, and composition both before and during the crisis, using standard and comparable measures of child poverty based on nationally representative household surveys. As far as possible, identical definitions of key child poverty predictors are used (e.g. very low work-intensity household, lone-parent family, large family, migrant household). Regional divides are discussed where pertinent (e.g. Belgium and

Italy). Although, for reasons of data availability, most of the indicators focus on households with children, rather than on children themselves, several chapters also employ direct measures of children's deprivation from national surveys (e.g. Italy, Sweden, and the UK). Each chapter then discusses the prevailing policy regime at the start of the crisis and government responses to the recession, including both stimulus and austerity measures, with respect to their capacity to protect children during an economic downturn. Several chapters explicitly place the discussion of policy responses in the context of changing political priorities, broader government policy, and public discourses on poverty (e.g. Japan and the UK). Key messages and lessons learned are then drawn at the end of each chapter.

1.4. SUMMARY AND CONCLUSIONS

The central purpose of this volume is to add to the debate on the impact of economic downturns and austerity policies on children on the basis of empirical data, highlighting key policy lessons and strategies. Although it is still early for a full reckoning of the human cost of the crisis, the analysis of experiences of a diverse sample of eleven OECD countries highlights several key messages. The final chapter in this volume brings this evidence together in a detailed discussion of how the crisis affected children, how the countries responded, and what lessons can be drawn to protect children more effectively in future crises.

First, both automatic stabilizers and anti-cyclical stimulus measures were extremely important at the macroeconomic level as the crisis struck. Second, the labour market has been central to the transmission of the impact of the crisis to households with children. In many of the countries studied, increasing child poverty was closely linked to an increase in the proportion of low work-intensity households. In many countries, this meant that the crisis disproportionately increased poverty among specific risk groups that already faced exceptionally high rates of poverty and low attachment to the labour market: notably those with low levels of education, single parents, and those of migrant background. Third, social transfers played a central role in cushioning the immediate impact of the crisis through the labour market on household disposable incomes and on child poverty, but the income protection system was much more robust and effective in some countries than in others. Finally, as the crisis unfolded, both the severity of the initial shock and the external pressures (e.g. from the financial markets and bailout programmes) affected countries' ability to continue protecting the incomes of households with children. Although the necessity and the scale of adjustment pursued by many countries in the aftermath of the crisis is still debated in the absence of a counterfactual ('what would have happened if a different course had been pursued?'), we often see evidence of an unequal distribution of the austerity burden. Children and working-age households were the main victims of fiscal consolidation, while pensioners were largely protected.

Chapter 2 gives an overview of how the crisis affected forty-one industrialized economies of the EU and OECD, and how it fed through to social spending and to key indicators of child poverty and material deprivation. This serves to set the context for the in-depth case studies of eleven of these countries presented in the rest of this volume.

REFERENCES

Jenkins, Stephen P., Andrea Brandolini, John Micklewright, and Brian Nolan (eds) (2013). *The Great Recession and the Distribution of Household Income* (Oxford: Oxford University Press).

UNICEF Office of Research (2014). 'Children of the Recession: The Impact of the Economic Crisis on Child Well-being in Rich Countries'. *Innocenti Report Card 12* (Florence: UNICEF Office of Research—Innocenti).

2

Impact of the Economic Crisis on Children in Rich Countries

Yekaterina Chzhen, Brian Nolan, Bea Cantillon, and Sudhanshu Handa

2.1. INTRODUCTION

The global financial crisis of 2007–8 originated in the banking sector in the US, quickly spread to the rest of the world and pushed it into recession in 2009. The economic crisis affected households in developed countries through three main channels: the labour market, the financial market, and the public sector (Natali et al., 2014). Falling demand for goods and services lead to a worsening in labour market conditions, including job losses, reduced hiring and promotion, stunted wage growth, and an increased reliance on temporary contracts. Turbulence in the financial markets resulted in dwindling asset values and restricted access to credit. As governments intervened by bailing out financial institutions and stimulating the economy in the earlier phase of the crisis, and as social transfers increased automatically with rising unemployment, while tax revenues fell, public debt soared, and government finances came under increased pressure from international markets. Five Eurozone countries—Cyprus, Greece, Ireland, Portugal, and Spain—were unable to repay or refinance their government debt and requested assistance from the International Monetary Fund, the European Commission, and the European Central Bank ('the Troika'). In the second phase of the crisis, roughly from 2011 onwards, many governments were implementing austerity policies by tightening access to benefits, reducing social transfers, cutting spending on services and increasing taxes such as VAT (OECD, 2014).

Economic crisis can affect children through all three channels, by hitting household incomes from employment, investment, and social transfers. This, in turn, poses longer term risks to child well-being through reduced family investment in child nutrition, health, education, and leisure and social activities

(UNICEF Office of Research, 2014). Financial insecurity can tax family relationships, affect the quality of parental engagement and care, and even lead to child maltreatment (Brooks-Gunn, Schneider and Waldfogel, 2013).

This chapter provides an overview of how the Great Recession affected the economies of the industrialized world and fed through to social spending and to key indicators of child poverty and material deprivation. This serves to set the context for the in-depth case studies of eleven of these countries presented in the rest of this volume. The study period includes both the global economic crisis of 2009 and the ensuing muted and uneven recovery, based on comparable data up to 2014.

Section 2.2 describes macro-economic and labour market trends and section 2.3 reviews changes in child poverty and material deprivation rates between 2008 and 2014. Section 2.4 analyses changes in social spending and the value of cash transfers for families with children.

2.2. NATURE OF THE CRISIS AND RECOVERY ACROSS FORTY-ONE COUNTRIES

2.2.1. Macroeconomic Trends

In 2009, the OECD area saw the first fall in GDP per capita in the post-war period, but the size of the contraction varied substantially across countries (Figure 2.1). In Korea and Poland real GDP per capita continued to grow year on year between 2007 and 2014 in spite of hitting the brakes in 2009 and again in 2012. Meanwhile, Estonia, Latvia, and Lithuania saw a double-digit contraction in 2009, followed by a swift, if shallow, recovery.

Across the eleven case study countries included in the following chapters, the size of the contraction at the height of the global recession in 2009 ranged from 3 per cent in Belgium to 7 per cent in Ireland.[1] However, GDP contraction in Greece did not reach its trough until 2011, while Spain experienced year-on-year falls in output between 2008 and 2013. Meanwhile, Belgium, Germany, Hungary, Ireland, Italy, Japan, Sweden, and the UK recovered briefly and saw another halt in GDP growth around 2012–13. Yet, only in Italy did the second fall in GDP per capita amount to more than 1 per cent. Meanwhile, the US economy continued to recover, albeit slowly, from 2010 onwards.

[1] Note that annual GDP per capita estimates from the World Development Indicators Database analysed in this chapter may differ from national sources used in the rest of the volume.

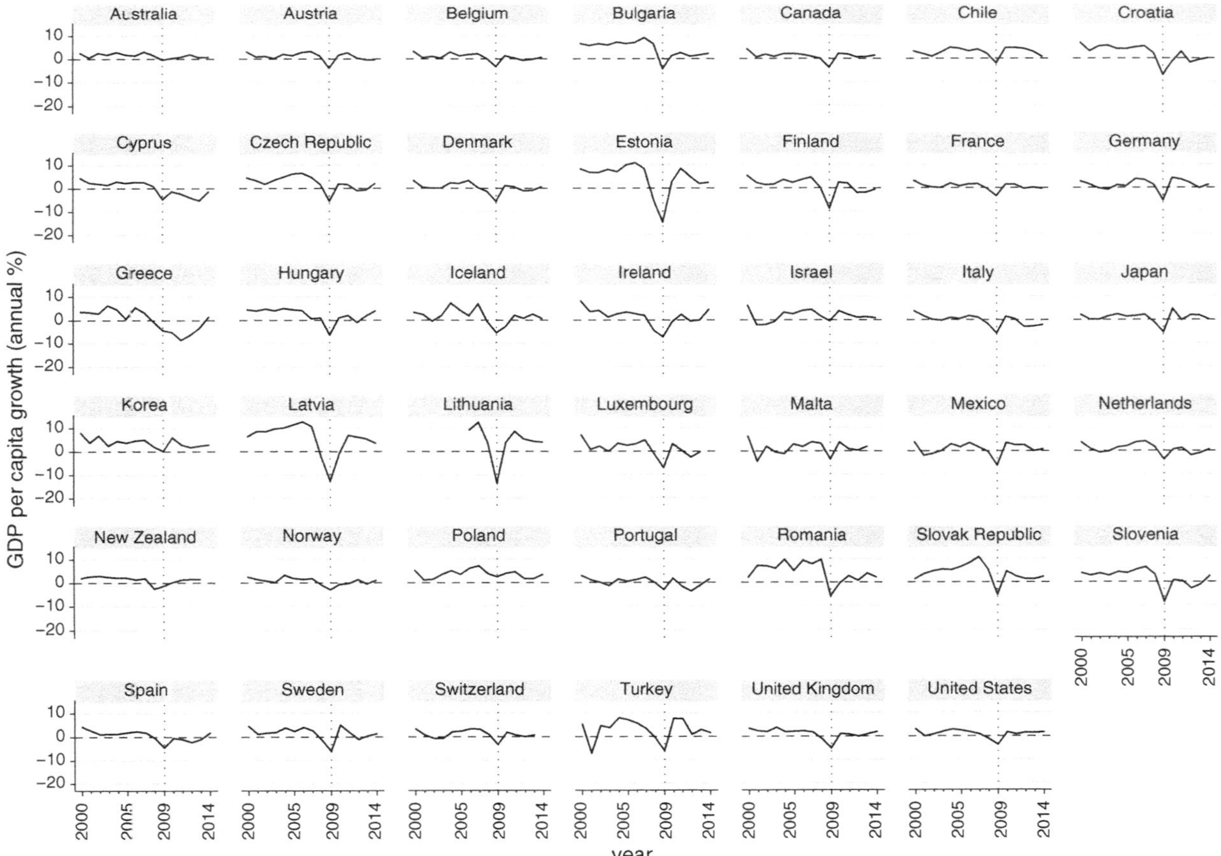

Figure 2.1. Annual economic growth (real GDP per capita, annual %)

Source: World Development Indicators, last update 14 October 2015. Data are in constant local currency.

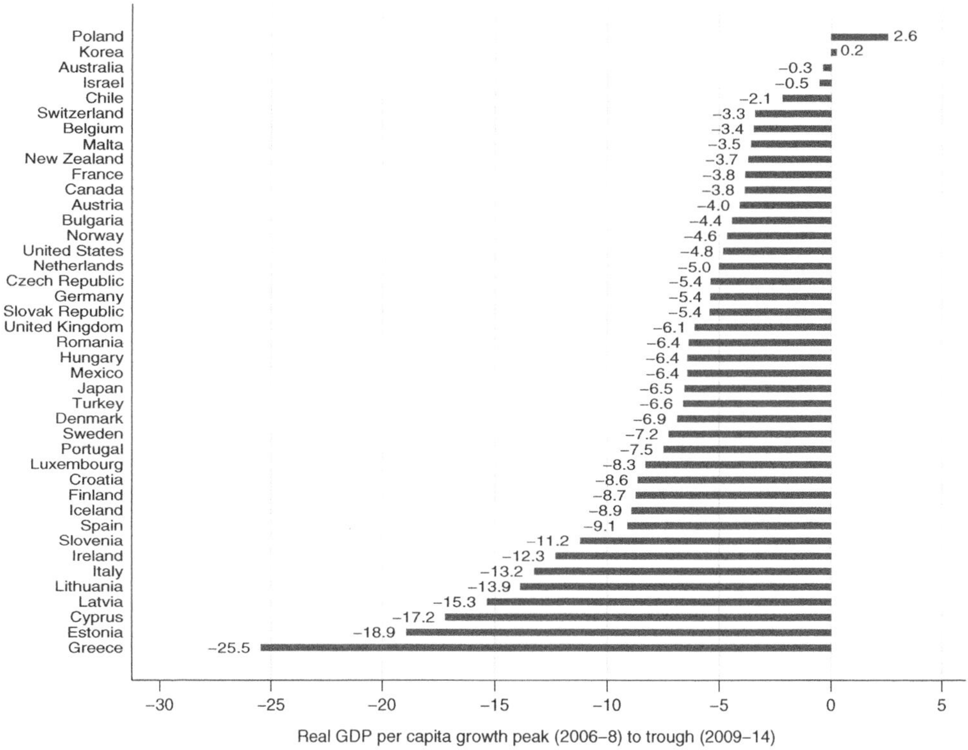

Figure 2.2. Real GDP per capita growth (%) peak to trough (2007–2014)

Source: World Development Indicators, last update 14 October 2015. Data are in constant local currency.

Since the exact timing of the contraction in economic output differed across the forty-one countries, Figure 2.2 plots growth in real GDP per capita between its highest pre-crisis level in 2006–8 ('peak') and its lowest post-crisis level in 2009–14 ('trough'). Poland stands out as the only country that experienced notable economic growth (of nearly 3 per cent), while Australia, Israel, and Korea stayed within 1 percentage point from peak to trough. The majority of the countries, including most of the case study countries, experienced peak-to-trough falls in GDP per capita of between 2 per cent and 9 per cent. Eight countries saw double digit reductions, ranging from 11–13 per cent in Ireland, Italy, and Slovenia to 25 per cent in Greece. Thus, the eleven case study countries are a diverse group in terms of fall in GDP: while Belgium was only moderately affected by the crisis based on this measure, Ireland, Italy, Greece, and Spain were some of the most severely hit.

The timing and scale of economic recovery, if any, also varies considerably across all forty-one countries as well as the eleven case studies. Figure 2.3 plots real GDP per capita between 2007 and 2014, indexed to the level of 2007. The majority of the countries, twenty-three out of forty-one, saw their economies

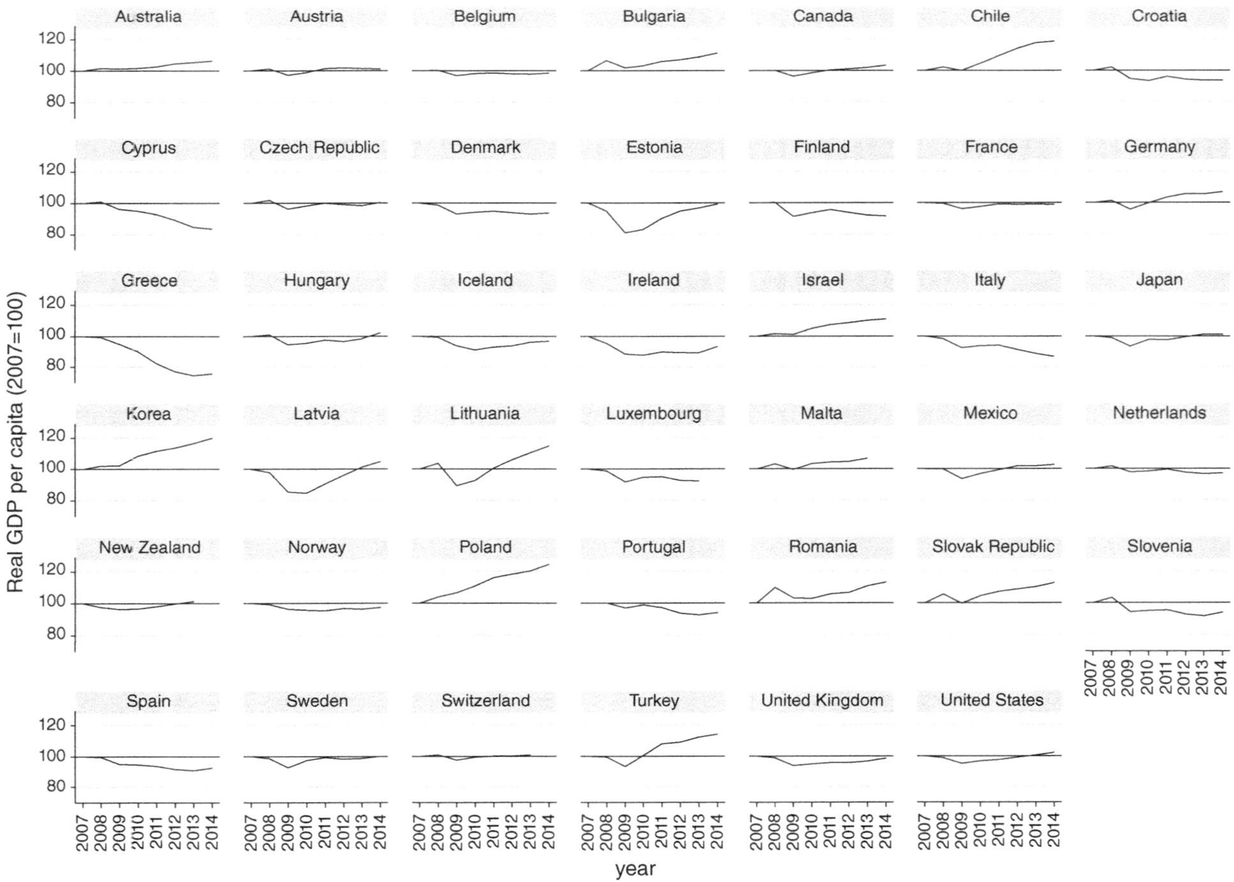

Figure 2.3. Real GDP per capita (2007=100)

Source: World Development Indicators, last update 14 October 2015. Data are in constant local currency.

exceed the 2007 level in the post-crisis period, while the remaining eighteen countries had not recovered by 2014. The economies of Korea and Poland, which had not had a contraction in the first place, exceeded their pre-crisis levels by the largest margin, but it was Chile, Lithuania, and Turkey that saw the strongest recovery from economic shock.

Among the eleven case studies, Germany had by far the swiftest and strongest recovery, as GDP per capita reached its pre-crisis level in 2010 and exceeded it in 2011. Another four countries—Hungary, Japan, Sweden and the US—recovered by 2014 but not quite as robustly. The other six had not made a full recovery by this time, although Belgium and the UK came within a whisker of reaching the 2007 level of GDP per capita in real terms. Meanwhile, Irish GDP per capita hovered around the 90 per cent mark. The Italian and Spanish economies were on a steady downward trajectory until 2013, with barely a sign of improvement by 2014. Greece saw the longest and deepest contraction of all, with economic output levelling out in 2013 at 75 per cent of its 2007 value in real terms.

2.2.2. Labour Market Trends

The global financial crisis spilled over into the real economy by reducing demand for labour and driving unemployment up, especially among 15 to 24-year-olds. Record numbers of young people were out of work, education, or training during the crisis (OECD, 2013, 2014; Chzhen and Richardson, 2014). Youth unemployment exceeds that of prime-age adults even in periods of economic growth and tends to go up faster during recessions (see Scarpetta, Sonnet and Manfredi, 2010 for the period 1996–2007). This is also the case during the crisis: a 1 percentage point fall in a country's economic output is associated with greater increases in unemployment for those under 25 than for 25 to 64-year-olds.[2]

Figure 2.4 plots the level and direction of change in youth (15–25) and prime-age (25–64) unemployment between 2007 and 2014. The vast majority of countries saw an increase in the unemployment rate for both age groups, but youth unemployment often increased by a greater absolute margin. Youth unemployment went up by 18–35 percentage points in six Southern European countries that were hit hard by the crisis (Croatia, Cyprus, Greece, Italy, Portugal, and Spain), with at least one in three young job-seekers out of work in 2014. Meanwhile, a minority of countries—Germany, Chile, Malta,

[2] For example, between 2007 and 2014, a 1 ppt increase in a country's real per capita annual GDP growth is associated with a 0.41 ppt lower youth unemployment rate and a 0.14 lower prime-age unemployment rate, both statistically significant at $p<0.001$ in a fixed effects panel regression model.

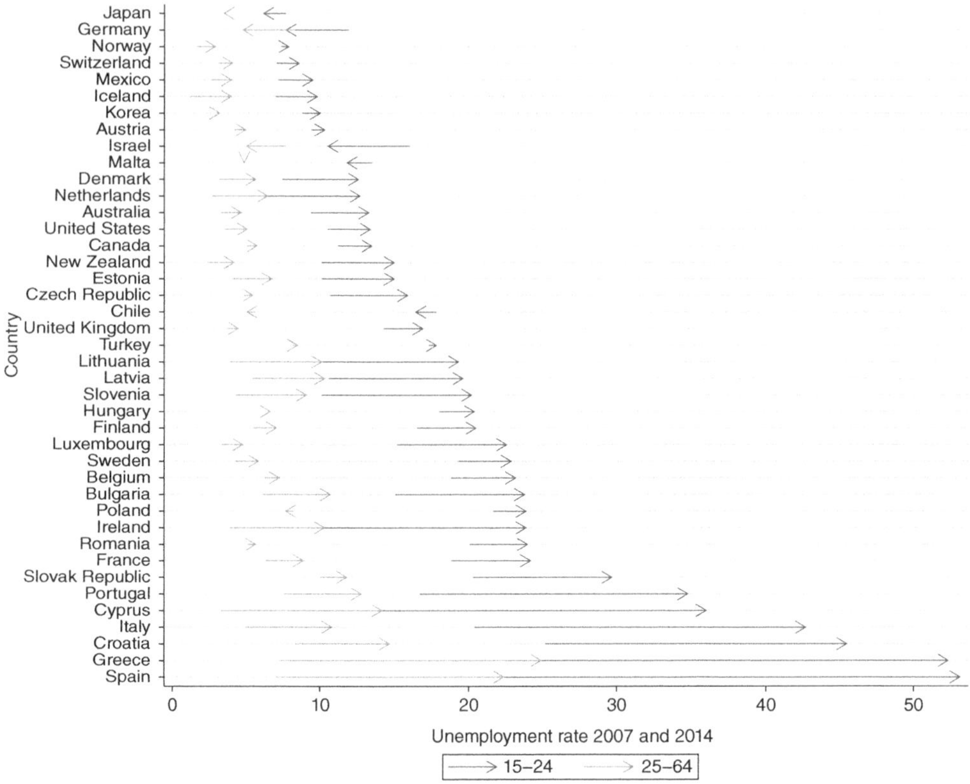

Figure 2.4. Unemployment rates (2007–2014)

Source: Eurostat, last update 2 December 2015; data for Australia, Chile, Israel, Japan, Mexico, New Zealand, Turkey and the United States from OECD.Stat.

Japan, and Israel—managed a decline in youth unemployment, but suffered some of the least severe economic slowdowns in the comparison.

Although youth unemployment tended to increase by a greater absolute margin than prime-age unemployment, there is not enough evidence to suggest that the *relative* situation of young people necessarily worsened. The negative impact of the crisis on young people in the labour market was one of degree rather than kind. The ratio of youth to adult unemployment remained stable, suggesting that the substantial structural barriers faced by young people in the labour market remained broadly the same. In Greece, where both youth and prime-age unemployment skyrocketed, the relative increase was greater for adults, and the ratio of youth to prime-age unemployment went down from 3.3 in 2007 to 2.1 in 2014.

However, unemployment upon entry to the labour market can have long-term consequences for young people's future employability and earnings (Bell and Blanchflower, 2011). Even those who held on to work during the crisis were often in precarious employment, with the number of 15 to 24-year-olds in involuntary part-time work tripling between 2008 and 2013 in EU countries more exposed to the economic crisis (UNICEF Office of Research, 2014). According to OECD estimates,[3] the share of young people in temporary employment (of all dependent employment) ranged from under 10 per cent in Australia, Latvia, Lithuania, and Romania to 70 per cent or more in Poland, Slovenia, and Spain by 2014. Temporary employment was far less prevalent among workers aged 25–54, ranging from under 5 per cent in Bulgaria, Romania, the Baltic countries, and the UK to around one-quarter in Chile, Poland, and Spain. These labour market trends suggest that children in households with prime-age workers may have been less exposed to the negative effects of the economic crisis through the labour market, but the transition from school to work for older children and youth was compromised in many countries.

2.3. CHILDREN IN CRISIS

This section describes changes in children's living conditions between 2008 and the latest year for which cross-country comparable statistics are available. It focuses on trends in child poverty rates, material deprivation rates, and shares of children living in very low work intensity households. Some of the analysis is limited to countries included in the European System of Social Indicators (ESSI)—the EU member states plus Iceland, Norway, and Switzerland. The remaining ten countries do not publish fully comparable statistics, but Chapters 9 and 13 give a detailed account of children's material circumstances during the crisis in Japan and the US respectively.

Advanced economies tend to measure income poverty using a relative threshold, such as 50 per cent (e.g. OECD) or 60 per cent (e.g. EU) of the national median disposable income adjusted for household size and composition. The US does not use a comparable relative definition of poverty: its official poverty line is around 30 per cent of the median (see Chapter 13). However, an analysis of trends in relative poverty may be misleading at times of sudden changes in the standards of living of the whole population. Instead of allowing the poverty line to fluctuate with median incomes, holding the poverty line constant in real terms over time, or 'anchoring' it in a base year, helps compare like with like. For example, if the national median income falls during the crisis, the relative poverty line measured as a percentage of the median would also decrease, and the resulting poverty rate would likely be

[3] OECD.Stat 'LFS—Employment by Permanency' (downloaded on 21 April 2016).

lower than if the poverty line were anchored. Thus, it is important to use both an anchored and a moving poverty line, as well as non-monetary indicators of material deprivation, to paint a fuller picture of changes in children's living conditions during the crisis.

According to UNICEF's report on the impact of the crisis in rich countries (UNICEF Office of Research, 2014), the share of children living in income poor households increased in 23 out of 41 countries between 2008 and 2012. The largest absolute increases of 10 percentage points (ppt) or more were reported in Ireland, Croatia, Latvia, Greece, and Iceland. Among the non-EU countries, only Mexico (5 ppt) and the US (2 ppt) saw an increase in child poverty, while Australia, Canada, Chile, Japan, Korea, and Turkey observed a decrease of at least 2 percentage points. The comparison used a relative poverty line of 60 per cent of the national median income in 2008, adjusted for inflation in 2012.

Using more recent data, Figure 2.5 plots the magnitude and direction of change in child poverty between 2008 and 2014 in thirty-one European countries. Anchored child poverty escalated in two-thirds of these countries, with increases of over 10 percentage points in Cyprus (16 ppt), Iceland (15 ppt) and Greece (29 ppt). There were sizeable increases (7–9 ppt) in Hungary, Italy, Ireland, and Spain. Germany and the UK saw modest increases (1–2 ppt), while Belgium and Sweden managed decreases of around 1 percentage point. However, based on 60 per cent of the contemporary median, by 2014 the highest child poverty rates (of at least 30 per cent) were in Bulgaria, Romania, and Spain. The choice of a poverty line (anchored or moving) made the biggest difference in Greece, Iceland, and Ireland, where median incomes fell in real terms, and the share of children in households with incomes below 60 per cent of the 2008 median increased substantially.[4]

Figure 2.6 shows the relative poverty rates (at 60 per cent of the median) for households that contain dependent children and *working* adults for thirty-one European countries. The in-work poverty rate is considerably lower than the total poverty rate for households with children in every country in the comparison, suggesting that work is an effective pathway out of poverty. However, in-work poverty is still prevalent and sometimes rising. Between 2008 and 2014, the rates of in-work poverty increased by 3 percentage points or more in Bulgaria, Estonia, Luxembourg, and Romania. Among the case study countries, Italy, Hungary, Germany, Sweden, and the UK saw increases of around 1 ppt, Belgium observed no change, while Greece, Ireland, and Spain saw decreases of 1–3 ppt. Meanwhile, evidence for the US also suggests that low wages are a

[4] Although the choice of a relative poverty line (anchored vs contemporary) can make a large difference to the estimates of aggregate child poverty rates, individual-level risks associated with key household-level predictors of poverty tend to be similar for the two poverty thresholds (Chzhen, 2016).

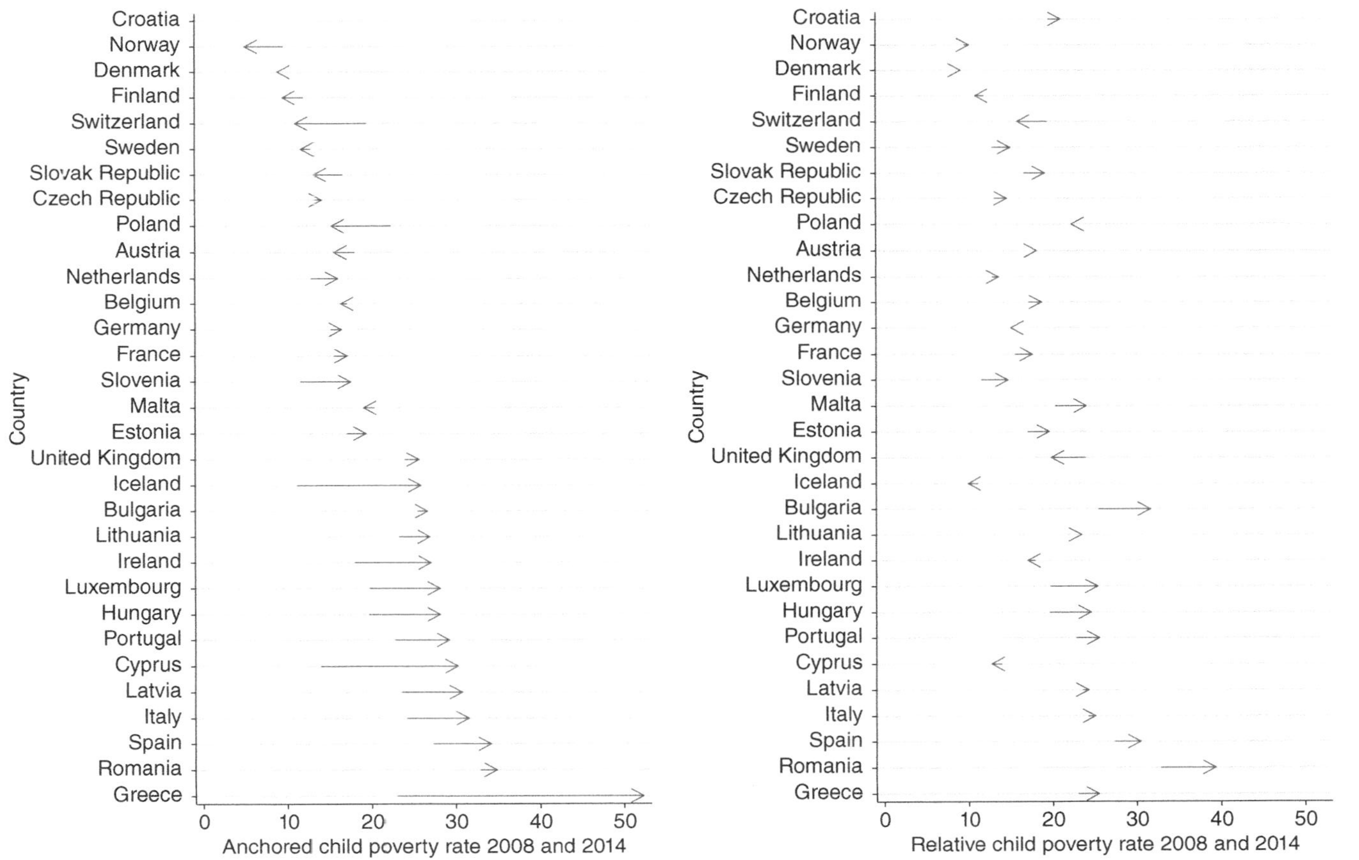

Figure 2.5. Child poverty rates (2008–2014) in 31 European countries

Source: Eurostat, last update 17 December 2015. Break in the series for Austria, Denmark, Estonia, Spain, and the UK. The period 2010–14 is used for Croatia and 2008–13 for Switzerland. Countries sorted by the value of anchored child poverty in 2014.

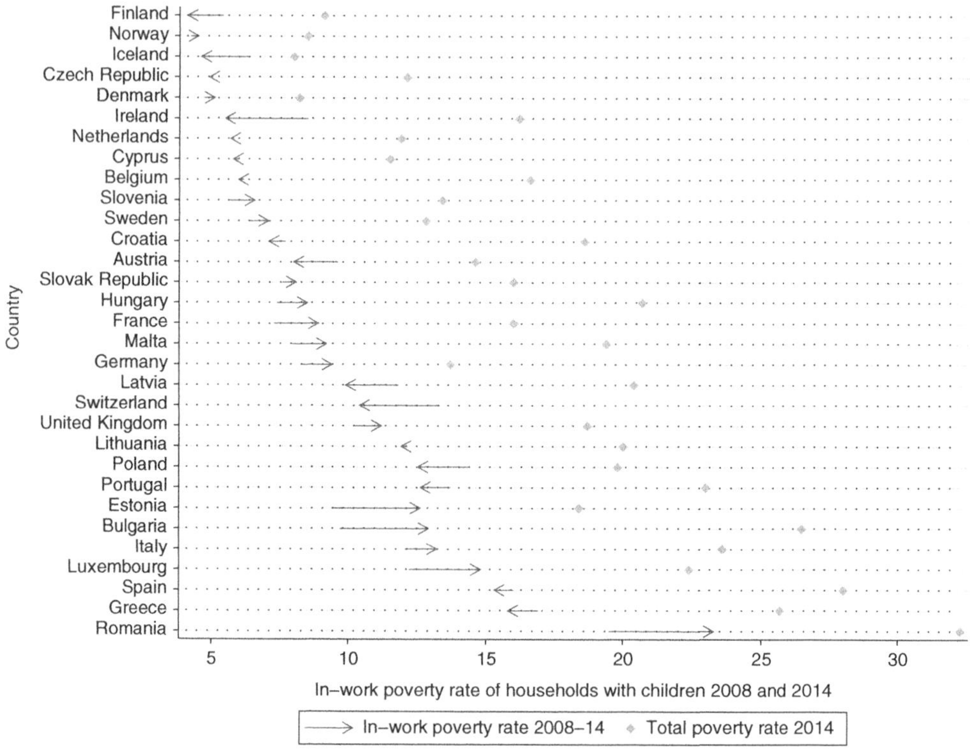

Figure 2.6. In-work poverty rates among households with children (2008–2014) in 31 European countries

Source: Eurostat, last update 17 December 2015. Break in the series for Austria, Denmark, Estonia, Spain, and the UK. The period 2010–14 is used for Croatia and 2008–13 for Switzerland. Countries sorted by the value of in-work poverty rate in 2014.

serious problem, as one-third of families of frontline manufacturing production workers were relying on one or more social assistance programmes each year between 2011 and 2014 (Jacobs et al., 2016).

Yet low work intensity is still associated with increased child poverty risks. In twenty-seven out of thirty-one European countries, more than half of children living in very low work intensity households were poor in 2014. Eurostat defines very low work intensity as 'the ratio of the total number of months that all working-age household members have worked during the income reference year and the total number of months the same household members theoretically could have worked in the same period' below 20 per cent.[5] Unlike current labour market activity of the household reference

[5] <http://ec.europa.eu/eurostat/statistics-explained/index.php/Glossary:Persons_living_in_households_with_low_work_intensity> (accessed on 12 January 2016).

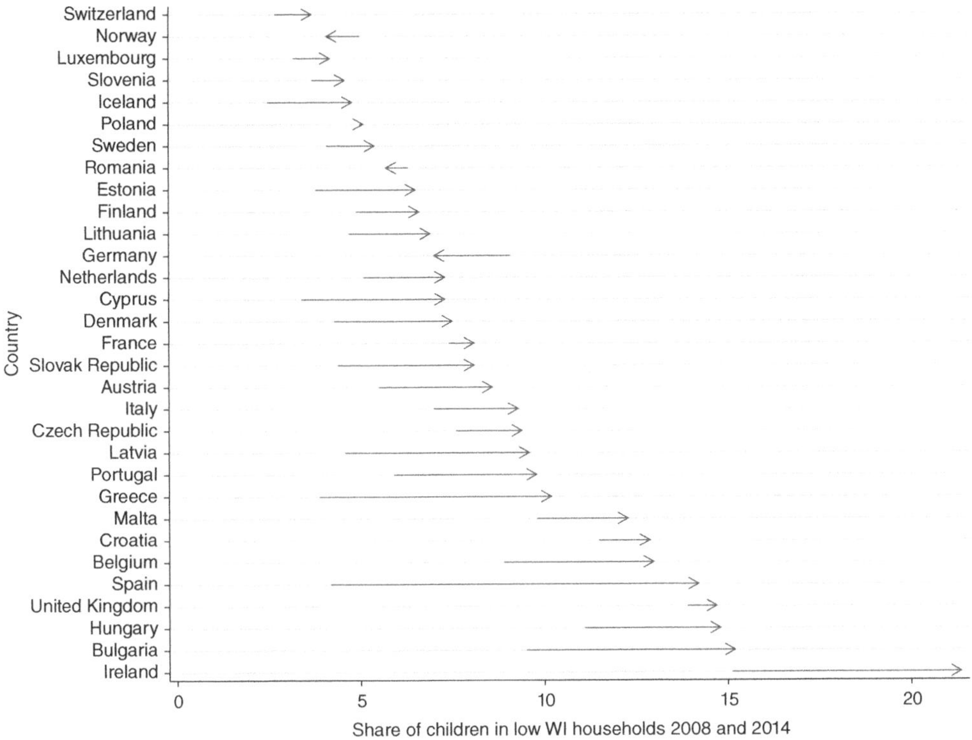

Figure 2.7. Proportion of children living in low work intensity households (2008–2014) in 31 European countries

Source: Eurostat, last update 17 December 2015. Break in the series for Austria, Denmark, Estonia, Spain, and the UK. The period 2010–14 is used for Croatia and 2008–13 for Switzerland. Countries sorted by the value of low WI rate in 2014.

person, work intensity measures labour supply of all adult household members (aged 18–59) over the same income reference period as household income.[6] The share of children living in very low work intensity households increased by one point or more in the majority of the European countries studied (Figure 2.7). The greatest increases of 6–10 ppt were recorded in Ireland, Greece and Spain, some of the hardest hit countries. Meanwhile, Germany is the only country reporting a decrease in the share of children in low work intensity households of at least 1 ppt. By 2014, this share ranged from 4 per cent in Switzerland to 22 per cent in Ireland. Overall, the percentage of children living in very low work intensity households in Europe tends to be lower in countries with higher working-age (25–54) female labour force

[6] The income reference period in the EU Statistics on Income and Living Conditions is the calendar or tax year before the interview in all ESSI countries except Ireland (where it is 12 months before the interview) and the UK (where it is the current year).

participation,[7] suggesting that barriers to maternal employment are an important driver of low household work intensity and, therefore, child poverty.

To complement monetary measures of household resources with a more direct indicator of living standards, Figure 2.8 traces changes and levels of the share of children living in materially deprived households between 2008 and 2014. Households are considered deprived if they cannot afford three or more out of nine items considered necessary for a decent standard of living in the EU: 1) to face unexpected expenses; 2) to afford a one-week annual holiday away from home; 3) to avoid arrears in rent, mortgage, utility bills, or hire purchase instalments; 4) to have a meal with meat, chicken, fish (or vegetarian equivalent) every second day; 5) to keep the home adequately heated; 6) to have a washing machine; 7) to have a colour TV; 8) to have a telephone; 9) to have a personal car (Guio, 2009). Child material deprivation rates increased in fifteen out of thirty-one countries. Six of the eleven case study countries recorded some of the greatest increases in the comparison: the UK (5 ppt), Spain (7 ppt), Italy (8 ppt), Hungary (9 ppt), Ireland (11 ppt), and Greece (23 ppt). After a relentless increase in the share of children in deprived households between 2008 and 2014, Greece has the fourth highest rate in the comparison, behind only Bulgaria, Romania, and Hungary.

Although the share of children in materially deprived households is a useful indicator of living standards of households with children, on which the EU collects comparable data annually, it does not measure deprivation at the level of the child. All nine standard deprivation items are measured at the household level and refer to households as a whole. Yet children do not necessarily get a fair share of household resources and they usually do not have an equal say in consumption decisions (Chzhen and Ferrone, 2016). However, the EU Statistics on Income and Living Conditions (EU-SILC) collected information on access to twelve child-specific deprivation items[8] for all children aged 1 to 15 in the household as a group in an ad hoc module in 2009 and 2014. Although 2009 cannot be considered a pre-crisis year and most European countries were recovering from the crisis by 2014, there is likely to be a lag in the crisis affecting children's items. The share of children lacking an item for any reason (including non-affordability) increased most for 'some new (not

[7] Across thirty European countries, the correlation between the share of children under 18 living in very low work intensity households and the share of women aged 25–54 in the labour force increased in absolute terms from −0.38 ($p<0.05$) in 2008 to −0.43 in 2014 ($p<0.05$), based on OECD and Eurostat labour market statistics.

[8] 'Some new (not second-hand) clothes', 'Two pairs of properly fitting shoes', 'Fruits and vegetables once a day', 'One meal with meat, chicken or fish (or vegetarian equivalent) at least once a day', 'Books at home suitable for their age', 'Outdoor leisure equipment', 'Indoor games', 'Regular leisure activity', 'Celebrations on special occasions', 'Invite friends around to play or eat from time to time', 'Participate in school trips and school events that cost money', 'Suitable place to study or do homework'.

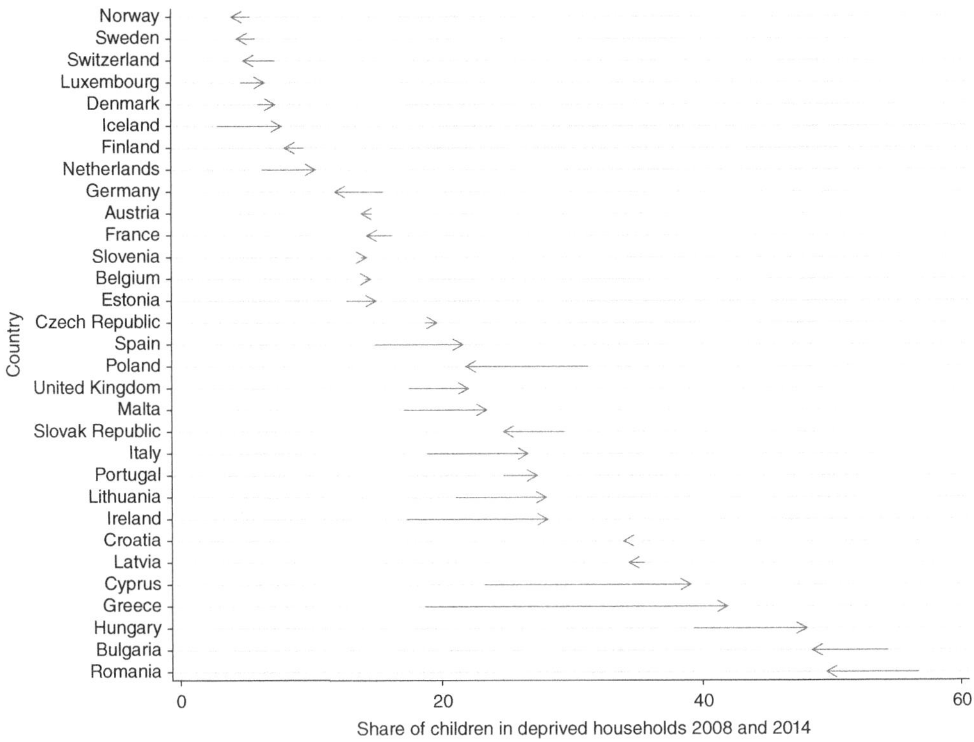

Figure 2.8. Proportion of children living in materially deprived households (2008–2014) in 31 European countries

Source: Eurostat, last update 17 December 2015. Break in the series for Austria, Denmark, Estonia, Spain, and the UK. The period 2010–14 is used for Croatia and 2008–13 for Switzerland. Countries sorted by the value of material deprivation rate in 2014.

second-hand) clothes', 'celebrations on special occasions', and 'invite friends around to play or eat from time to time'. Lacking access to these items is likely to affect the quality of children's peer relationships negatively. Figure 2.9 shows the share of children not being able to invite friends over in 2009 and 2014. The largest absolute increases were in Cyprus (12 points) and the UK (19 points), although the highest deprivation levels in 2014 were observed in Hungary (44 per cent) and Romania (49 per cent).

2.4. SOCIAL SPENDING

As the economic crisis drove up unemployment, putting pressure on income-tested benefits, spending on social protection benefits increased at first but as

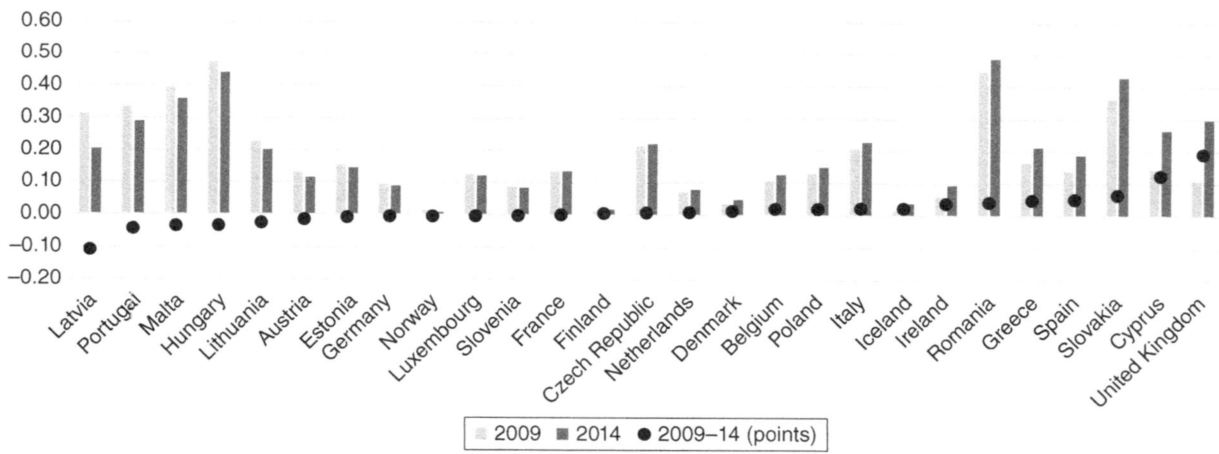

Figure 2.9. Share of children who cannot invite friends round to play from time to time (2009 and 2014) in 27 European countries

Source: EU-SILC User Database 2009 and 2014. No valid data for 2009 for Bulgaria, Croatia, and Sweden and no data for 2014 for Switzerland. Sorted by magnitude of absolute change between 2009 and 2014.

Statistically significant differences between 2009 and 2014 (at $p<0.05$) in all countries except the Czech Republic, Germany, France, Malta, Norway, and Slovenia.

austerity policies came into force it levelled off or decreased. Expenditure on social protection benefits as a share of GDP increased in thirty-four out of forty-one countries between 2005 and 2013 (Figure 2.10). However, in most of these countries the increase took place between 2005 and 2009, while only fourteen countries saw an increase of 1 ppt or more between 2009 and 2013, with the greatest rise in spending in Ireland (5 ppt). Meanwhile, social spending fell in nine countries, with the greatest decreases in Lithuania (6 ppt) and Estonia (4 ppt).

Austerity hit family benefits particularly hard. Figure 2.11 shows changes in spending on child and family related benefits as a share of total social protection spending in thirty-one ISSI countries and Turkey between 2005 and 2013. Although the majority of these countries spent a stable share on family related benefits, five countries saw an increase of 1–5 ppt between 2005 and 2010—Hungary, Poland, Lithuania, Bulgaria, and the UK—most of it before 2009. Four countries—Romania, Ireland, Latvia, and Cyprus—recorded a 2–4 ppt fall in family benefits spending between 2005 and 2010 and a further decrease between 2010 and 2013. Ten countries decreased the share of family benefits spending by at least 1 ppt, and not a single country increased it during the austerity period (2010–13).

While spending on family benefits shrank in absolute terms in many European countries during the economic crisis and austerity, spending on pensioners increased. Per capita spending on family benefits fell in real terms between 2008 and 2013 in twenty countries (Figure 2.12), while spending on old age benefits increased in all thirty-two countries. In only three countries—Bulgaria, Germany, and Switzerland—did spending on family benefits increase faster than old age spending, but it is only because relative increases tend to be larger for smaller starting values. An emerging body of research suggests that children were the main victims of austerity compared with pensioners across Europe, as poverty rose faster for under-18s than for over-65s, and policy reforms tended to favour pensioners (see Bradshaw and Chzhen, 2015; Hills et al., 2014).

Indeed, social transfers were far more successful in alleviating pensioner poverty than child poverty over the period 2008–14. Figure 2.13 shows changes in the effectiveness of transfers in reducing poverty for children and the elderly. The effectiveness of social transfers is measured as the difference between pre- and post-transfer poverty rates. It is a crude indicator that does not tell us what the world would look like if all benefits were suddenly withdrawn or if they had not existed in the first place. Moreover, absolute changes in this indicator over time do not necessarily reflect changes in the structure or generosity of cash transfer systems, as they may also be driven by the amount of poverty to be reduced. When many people lose their jobs and start receiving unemployment or social assistance benefits, it may appear that transfers become more effective in reducing poverty even if the social protection

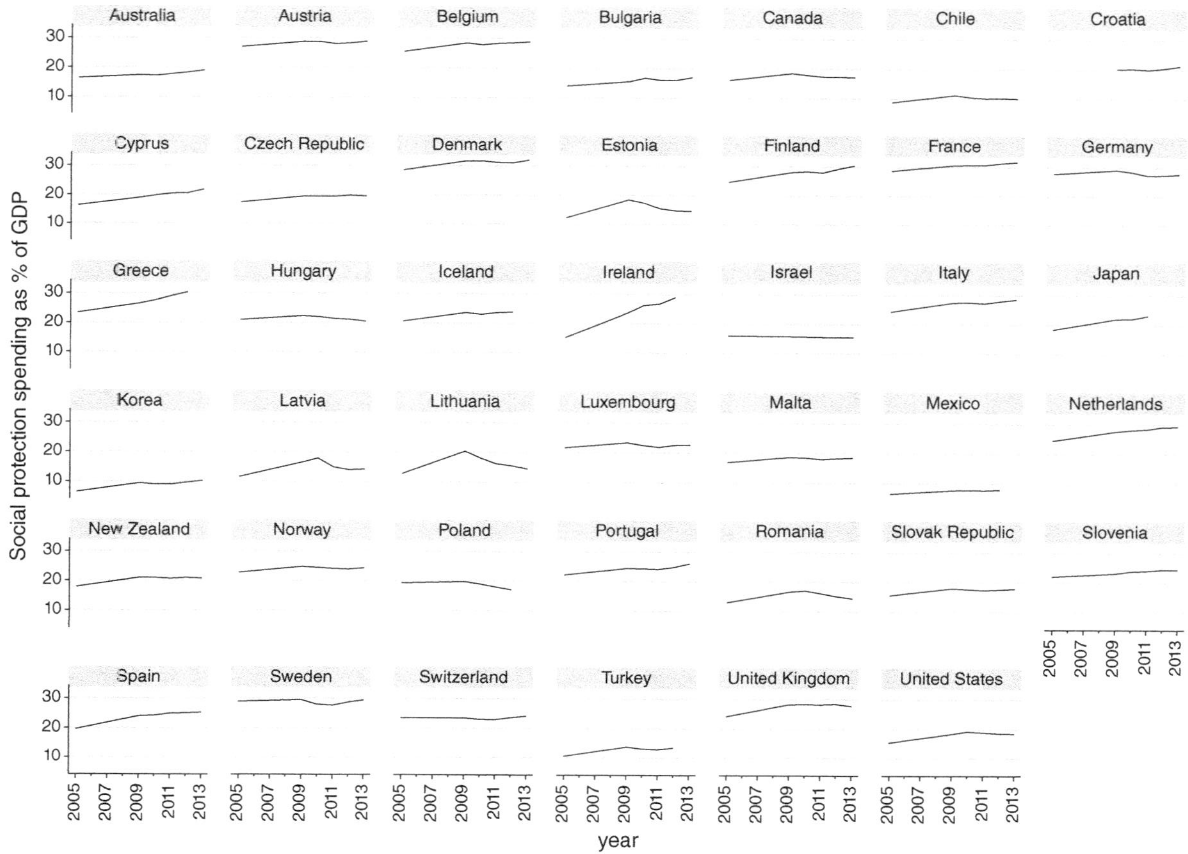

Figure 2.10. Social protection benefits spending as a share of GDP (2005–2013) in 41 countries

Source: Eurostat, last update 11 January 2016; data for Australia, Chile, Israel, Japan, Mexico, New Zealand, and the United States from OECD.Stat.

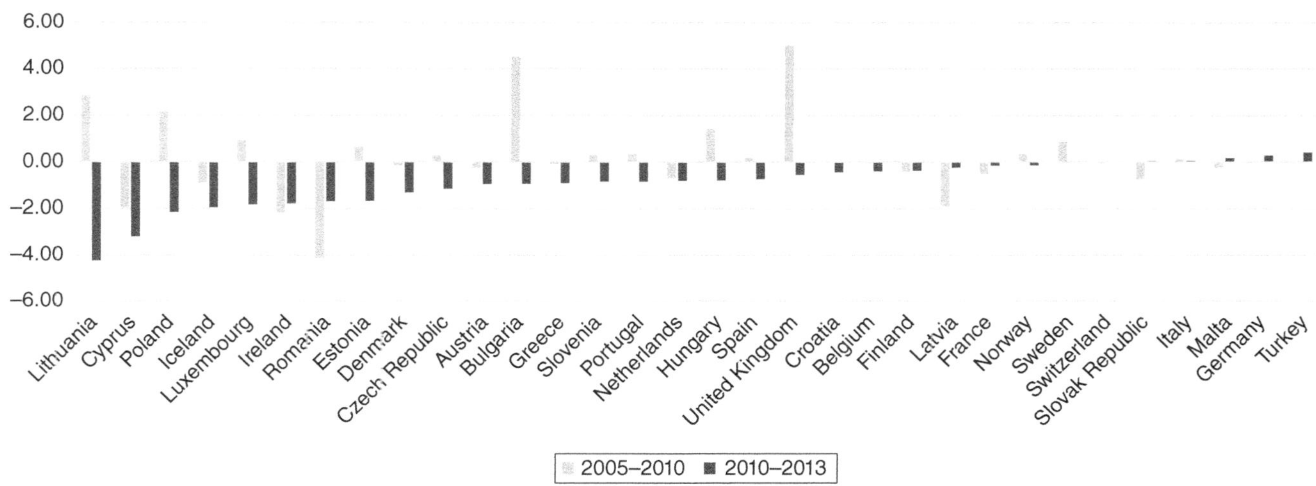

Figure 2.11. Changes in spending on family related benefits as a share of total social protection spending (2005–2013) in 32 countries

Source: Eurostat, last update 11 January 2016. Data for 2012 used for Poland, Ireland, Iceland, and Greece and 2010 for Turkey.

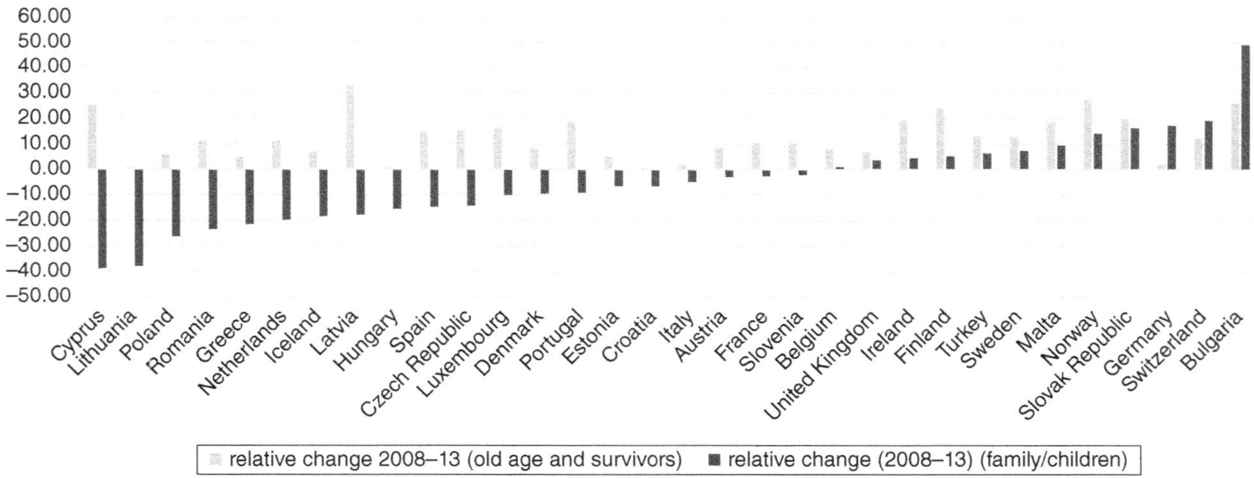

Figure 2.12. Per cent changes in real per capita spending on old age and family benefits (2008–2013) in 32 countries

Source: Eurostat, last update 11 January 2016. Data for 2012 used for Poland, Ireland, Iceland, and Greece and 2010 for Turkey.

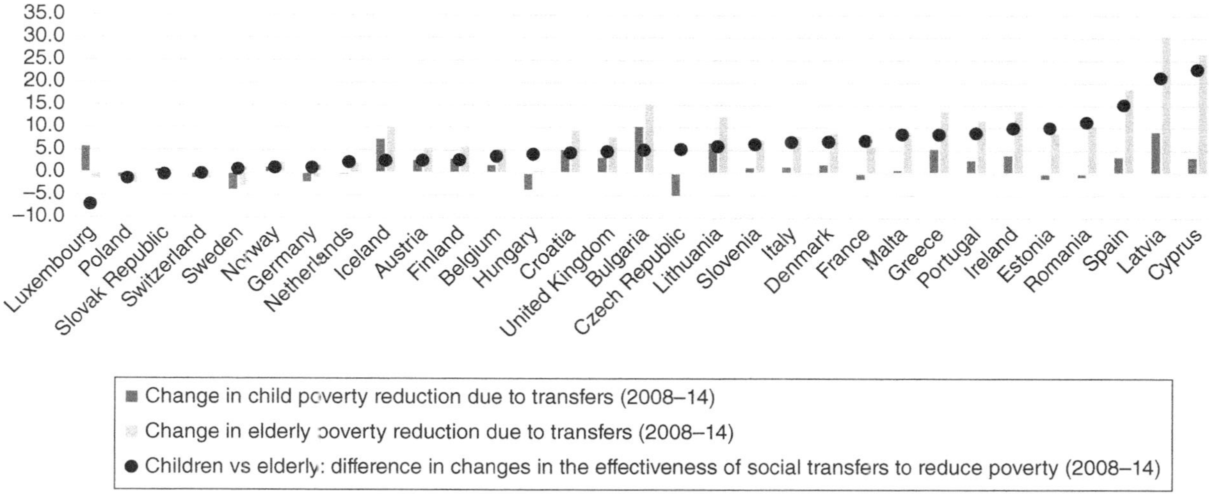

Figure 2.13. Changes in effectiveness of social transfers to reduce child and elderly poverty (2008–2014) in 31 countries

Source: Eurostat, last update 18 December 2015.

system remains the same. In spite of these caveats, there is a clear trend in favour of the elderly. Although social transfers, which include pension benefits, always make more of a difference to post-transfer elderly poverty rates, their effectiveness increased faster or fell more slowly for the elderly than for children in nearly every European country. The only exceptions are Luxembourg and Poland, where the changes favoured children, and the Slovak Republic and Switzerland, where there are no differences at all.

2.5. CONCLUSION

This chapter shows that the countries to be studied in depth in the rest of this book cover a broad span in terms of the extent and nature of the macroeconomic impact of the crisis, their initial levels of economic output per head and of child poverty and deprivation, and the increases in child poverty observed during the recession. Thus Greece, Italy, and Spain were severely hit by the crisis and went through a protracted fiscal consolidation and slow recovery. Their fragmented social protection systems were not able to protect the incomes of households with children at the time when unemployment soared, resulting in some of the largest increases in child poverty and deprivation between 2008 and 2014.

Meanwhile, Ireland, Hungary, the UK, and the US were hit hard at an initial stage of the crisis, largely due to their exposure to turmoil in the financial markets, but returned to growth relatively quickly, even if not always to the pre-crisis levels in absolute terms. Their existing social protection systems and extra fiscal stimulus managed to cushion the impact of the crisis at the outset, although not sufficiently to arrest growth in child poverty rates. Among the four countries, Ireland suffered the deepest recession and most extensive fiscal consolidation (imposed by the 'bailout' programme), with anchored child poverty increasing by 11 percentage points between 2008 and 2013. The remaining four countries, Belgium, Germany, Japan, and Sweden, were moderately hit and recovered fast, with barely an increase in anchored child poverty by 2013. This diversity provides us with ample scope to learn from their varying experiences.

REFERENCES

Bell, David N. F., and David G. Blanchflower (2011). 'Young People and the Great Recession', *Oxford Review of Economic Policy 27*, no. 2: pp. 241–67.

Bradshaw, Jonathan, and Yekaterina Chzhen (2015). 'The Outcomes of the Crisis for Pensioners and Children'. *Belgisch Tijdschrift voor Sociale Zekerheid 1*: pp. 39–50.

Brooks-Gunn, Jeanne, William Schneider, and Jane Waldfogel (2013). 'The Great Recession and the Risk for Child Maltreatment'. *Child Abuse and Neglect 37*, no. 10: pp. 721–29.

Chzhen, Yekaterina (2016). 'Unemployment, Social Protection Spending and Child Poverty in the European Union during the Great Recession'. *Journal of European Social Policy*. doi: https://doi.org/10.1177/0958928716676549.

Chzhen, Yekaterina and Lucia Ferrone (2016). 'Multidimensional Child Deprivation and Poverty Measurement: Case Study of Bosnia and Herzegovina'. *Social Indicators Research*. doi:10.1007/s11205-016-1291-8.

Chzhen, Yekaterina and Dominic Richardson (2014). 'Young People (not) in the Labour Market in Rich Countries during the Great Recession'. *UNICEF Office of Research Working Paper 2014-12* (Florence: UNICEF Office of Research—Innocenti).

Guio, Anne-Catherine (2009). 'What Can Be Learned from Deprivation Indicators in Europe' 2009 edn. *Eurostat Methodologies and Working Papers* (Luxembourg: Office for Official Publications of the European Communities).

Hills, John, Alari Paulus, Holly Sutherland, and Iva Tasseva (2014). 'A Lost Decade?: Decomposing the Effect of 2001–11 Tax-benefit Policy Changes on the Income Distribution in EU Countries'. *ImPRovE Discussion Paper No. 14/03* (Antwerp).

Jacobs, Ken, Zohar Perla, Ian Perry, and Dave Graham-Squire (2016). 'Producing Poverty: The Public Cost of Low-Wage Production Jobs in Manufacturing'. (Berkeley, CA: UC Berkeley Center for Labor Research and Education).

Natali, Luisa, Bruno Martorano, Sudhanshu Handa, Goran Holmqvist, and Yekaterina Chzhen (2014). 'Trends in Child Wellbeing in European Union Countries during the Great Recession: A Cross-country Comparative Perspective'. *Office of Research Working Paper No. 2014–10* (Florence: UNICEF Office of Research).

OECD (2013). *Education at a Glance 2013: OECD Indicators* (Paris: OECD Publishing).

OECD (2014). *Society at a Glance 2014: OECD Social Indicators: The Crisis and its Aftermath* (Paris: OECD Publishing).

Scarpetta, Stefano, Anne Sonnet, and Thomas Manfredi (2010). 'Rising Youth Unemployment during the Crisis: How to Prevent Negative Long-term Consequences on a Generation?' *OECD Social, Employment and Migration Working Papers 106* (Paris: OECD).

UNICEF Office of Research (2014). 'Children of the Recession: The Impact of the Economic Crisis on Child Well-being in Rich Countries'. *Innocenti Report Card 12* (Florence: UNICEF Office of Research—Innocenti).

3

Belgium: Creeping Vulnerability of Children

Julie Vinck, Wim Van Lancker, and Bea Cantillon

3.1. INTRODUCTION

Belgium is one of the most advanced welfare states in the world. It has a highly developed social security system, high levels of social spending, and low levels of income inequality, which have remained fairly stable over the past few decades. Moreover, the country fared pretty well during the Great Recession that followed the worldwide 2007–8 financial crisis (Jenkins et al., 2013). The impact in terms of job loss and gross domestic product (GDP) contraction was rather modest, and the Belgian economy quickly regained its pre-crisis levels. The Organization for Economic Co-operation and Development (OECD) and the European Commission have both hailed the role of the Belgian safety net in safeguarding the welfare of the majority of citizens (European Commission, 2010; OECD, 2011).

Despite these achievements, however, the Belgian welfare state has been plagued by comparatively high levels of child poverty, and by a creeping, yet significant, increase in child poverty that started in the good years before the crisis. This suggests structural shortcomings in the way that children are protected against the risk of living in poverty. In Belgium, the share of jobless households is relatively high; meanwhile the redistributive impact of social policies on poverty rates has declined since the 1990s, in consequence of a declining benefit adequacy for vulnerable families and a shift from working-age cash spending to pensions, healthcare, and working-age in-kind spending (Cantillon and Vandenbroucke, 2014).

In this chapter we discuss how children fared before, during, and after the Great Recession in Belgium. We focus on the nature of the crisis in Belgium, discuss trends in child poverty and its determinants, and examine whether the crisis has had an impact on pre-existing child poverty trends—and if so, how. Finally, we discuss how social and fiscal policies should be recalibrated in order to improve the living conditions of Belgian children.

3.2. THE 'GREAT RECESSION' AND ITS AFTERMATH

In the pre-crisis period between 2004 and 2008, Belgium experienced a spell of weak but stable economic growth of 0.7 per cent on average. When the crisis struck in the third quarter of 2008, GDP fell by about 4 per cent (Figure 3.1), and GDP growth was negative for four successive quarters. In the third quarter of 2009 GDP growth was again positive, and by mid-2010 GDP was back to its pre-crisis levels. The global financial and economic crisis hit Belgium mainly through two channels. First, with its small, open economy, Belgium suffered from the drop in global trade, which affected consumption and economic activity (European Commission, 2010). Second, the sustainability of Belgian banks was highly dependent on the international financial system, and the collapse of Lehman Brothers triggered government intervention to sustain all major banks, affecting public debt ratios (IMF, 2009). From 2011 to 2013 Belgium experienced a period of stagnation, including a brief period of negative growth (a so-called 'double dip'). From the second quarter of 2013 onward, economic growth was restored, albeit at a slow rate of less than 0.5 per cent. In this chapter, we focus on the first phase of the crisis.

Although the impact of the crisis in terms of economic growth was rather modest—certainly in comparison to other countries discussed in this book (e.g. Ireland, the United Kingdom, Spain, Greece)—the decline in GDP was the strongest since the Second World War (De Mulder and Druant, 2011).

The initial response of the Belgian government to the crisis was to prevent job loss as much as possible. In doing so, on the one hand it encouraged employers to make use of the existing scheme of so-called 'temporary unemployment' for blue-collar workers, while on the other hand it introduced a number of crisis measures for white-collar workers (see section 3.4). Figure 3.2 shows the unemployment rate over time for Belgium and three neighbouring countries: Germany, the Netherlands, and France. During the pre-crisis period of economic growth, which was almost identical to the French experience, the unemployment rate declined from 8.6 per cent in 2005 to 6.3 per cent in the second quarter of 2008, at which point the crisis kicked in. The unemployment rate peaked again at 8.7 per cent in the third quarter of 2010. In contrast to what happened in France and the Netherlands, Belgian unemployment rates declined again to 6.6 per cent in 2011. The German labour market was hardly affected by the crisis (see Chapter 4). In the fourth quarter of 2015, unemployment reached a peak of 8.7 per cent—still 1.9 percentage points (ppt) lower than France, and 2.6 ppt lower than the average for the Eurozone.

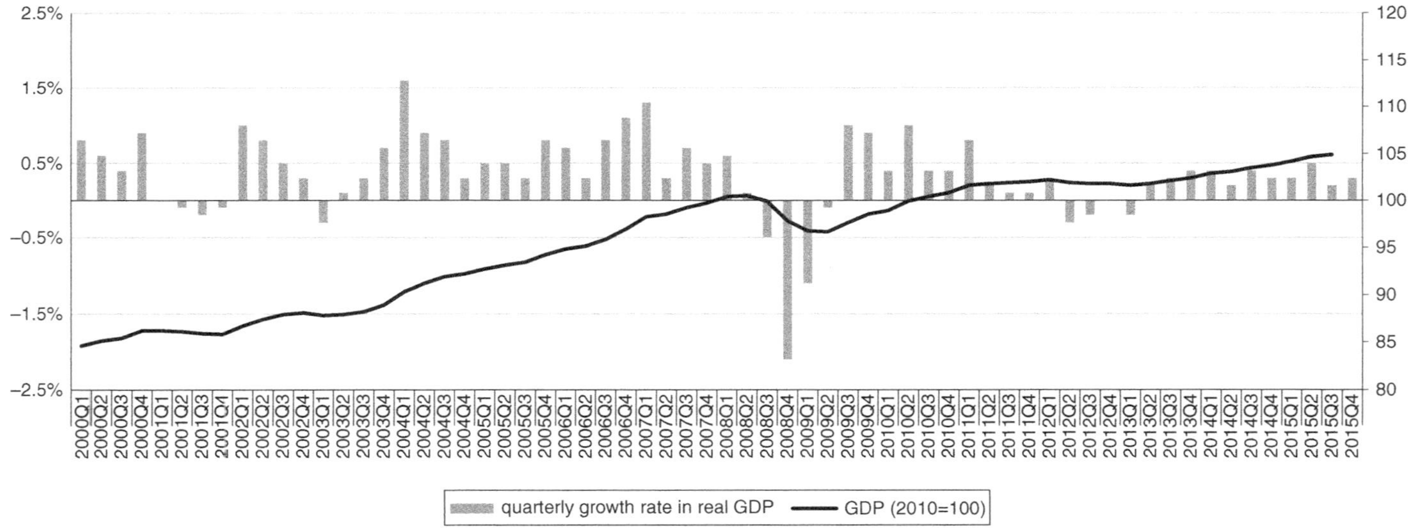

Figure 3.1. Quarterly GDP growth rate (left axis) and GDP relative to 2010 level (right axis), Belgium (2000–2015)

Note: GDP adjusted for seasonal cycles and adjusted by working days.

Source: NBB. Eurostat.

Figure 3.2. Quarterly unemployment rate, Belgium and neighbouring countries (2005–2015)

Note: Unemployment according to ILO definition.

Source: Eurostat.

In sum, compared to what happened in France and the Netherlands the Belgian labour market recovered rather quickly in the first phase of the crisis, and employment losses were limited (see Figure 3.3). Although initial employment rates were low (62.4 per cent versus 64.9 per cent in France, 70.1 per cent in Germany, and 77.2 per cent in the Netherlands), the total employment rate declined by only 0.4 ppt. In Germany, employment rates continued to grow, while in France (–0.9 ppt) and in particular in the Netherlands (–2.5 ppt) employment losses were much more tangible.

However, the burden of the crisis was not shared equally. As in the neighbouring countries, young workers were hit hardest: while the employment rate for older workers (aged 55–64) increased by almost 3 ppt, the employment rate of young workers (15–24) declined by more than 2 ppt. In particular, industry, construction, the financial sector, administrative and support services, and the information and communication sector suffered job losses (Bulté and Struyven, 2013). As a consequence, and in contrast to the neighbouring countries, it was not the low-skilled, but rather the high- and medium-skilled groups that experienced the biggest setbacks in employment rates.

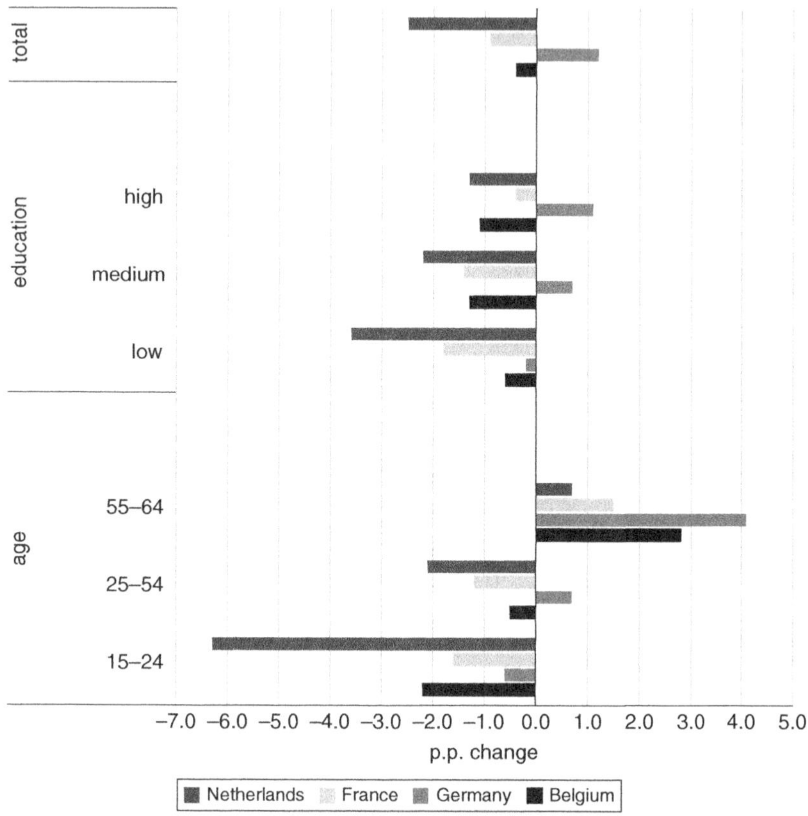

Figure 3.3. Percentage point change in employment rates by age and education, Belgium and neighbouring countries (2008–2010)

Source: Eurostat.

3.3. CHILD POVERTY BEFORE, DURING AND AFTER THE CRISIS

3.3.1. Trends in Living Conditions of Children in Belgium

In this section we analyse child poverty trends from 2005 to 2013, drawing on the European Union (EU) portfolio of primary indicators of social inclusion. Figures 3.4 and 3.5 show poverty trends for different age groups before, during, and after the crisis, using both a relative (Figure 3.4) and a more absolute poverty threshold 'anchored' in 2008 (Figure 3.5). The poverty threshold corresponds to 60 per cent of median equivalized household income. These monetary indicators are complemented by a measure of severe material deprivation (SMD) in Figure 3.6. SMD represents the share of the

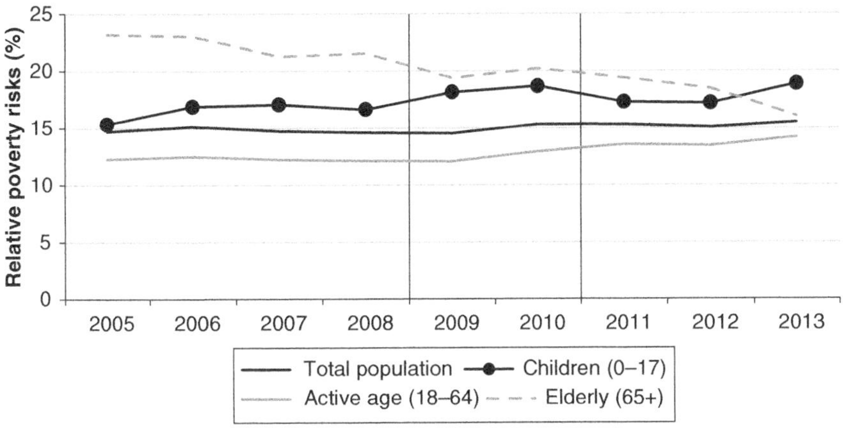

Figure 3.4. Relative poverty risk in Belgium, before, during, and after the crisis (income years 2005–2013)

Notes: Income years instead of survey years. The two vertical black lines mark the first phase of the crisis, in which the Belgian labour market was affected.

Source: Authors' calculations using the EU Statistics on Income and Living Conditions (EU-SILC) 2006–14.

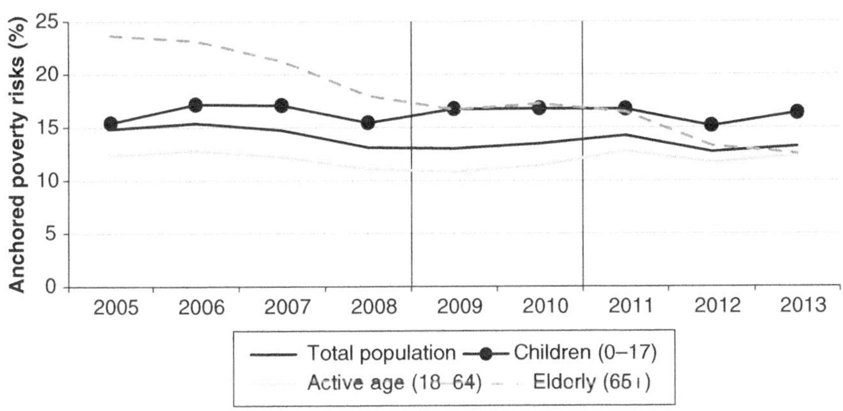

Figure 3.5. Anchored poverty risk in Belgium, before, during, and after the crisis (income years 2005–2013)

Notes: See Figure 3.4. The fixed threshold anchors the poverty threshold at the 2008 (income year 2007) level.

Source: Authors' calculations using EU-SILC 2006–14.

population who report that they cannot afford at least four out of nine items or activities deemed important for maintaining a decent standard of living. See Nolan and Whelan (2011) for more information.

Unlike those countries hit hard by the recession, in Belgium median incomes continued to grow throughout the period, and the relative poverty risk of the population remained stable at around 15 per cent. Figure 3.4 shows, however, that this pattern of stability disguises a shift in the relative poverty risk from the elderly to children (and the active-age population to a lesser extent). This intergenerational shift is observable in many other countries (see Chapter 2) though with important cross-country and temporal variations.

In 2005, the relative poverty rate of children (aged under 18) was 15 per cent—below the European average, but well above the neighbouring countries of France, Germany, and the Netherlands in terms of child poverty risk. Figure 3.4 illustrates the fact that child poverty went up to 17 per cent in 2008, and increased further to 19 per cent during the crisis period. Afterwards the rate fluctuated somewhat, but was back at 19 per cent in 2013. The rate for active-age adults remained stable at about 12 per cent until 2009, and rose to 14 per cent in 2013. The poverty rate for the elderly (aged 65 and over) fell sharply over the whole period, from 23 per cent in 2005 to 16 per cent in 2013.

The anchored poverty measure in Figure 3.5 shows similar (albeit less marked) developments. Child poverty fluctuated around 15 per cent, went up to 17 per cent during the crisis, and fluctuated around 16 per cent after the crisis. Elderly poverty declined strongly, while the poverty rate for active-age adults went up during the crisis.

Figure 3.6 shows the evolution of SMD rates for different age groups in Belgium. It is clear that the deprivation rate for children has been consistently higher than for pensioners. The rate of deprivation dropped from 10 per cent to about 7 per cent before the crisis, went up again at the peak of the crisis, after which it fluctuated around 8 per cent. The SMD for children dropped sharply in 2013. Corroborating the decline in monetary poverty, SMD rates among the elderly are low and exhibit a downward trend. For other age groups, trends in SMD (if any) have been much less prominent.

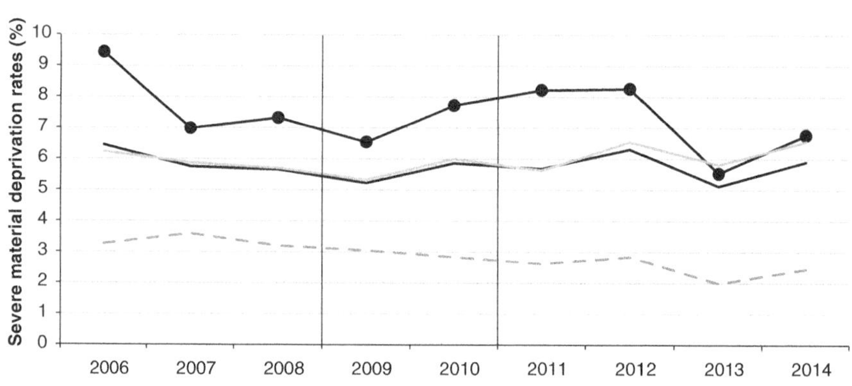

Figure 3.6. Severe material deprivation in Belgium, before, during, and after the crisis (survey years 2006–2014)

Notes: The horizontal axis represents the EU-SILC survey years 2006–14. The two vertical black lines show the crisis years.

Source: Authors' calculations using EU-SILC 2006–14.

Table 3.1. Share of children and share of poor children living in a household that cannot afford child-specific material deprivation items, Belgium, 2009 and 2014 (per cent)

	Share children			Share poor children		
	2009	2014	*t-test*	2009	2014	*t-test*
Some new clothes	6.2	8.5	*	18.7	27.8	*
Two pairs of properly fitting shoes	3.7	3.8		7.5	14.4	*
Fresh fruit and vegetables once a day	1.7	2.2		6.8	8.6	
One meal with meat, chicken, fish, or vegetarian equivalent at least once a day	3.1	2.7		13.5	8.7	
Books at home suitable for their age	3.9	4.3		10.3	16.4	
Outdoor leisure equipment	3.8	4.2		14.2	14.4	
Indoor games	2.1	2.5		9.8	9.0	
Regular leisure activity	7.8	8.7		28.0	30.7	
Celebrations on special occasions	3.1	5.7	***	10.4	16.7	*
Invite friends round to play and eat from time to time	2.9	6.1	***	12.7	23.4	**
Participate in school trips and school events that cost money	3.0	4.2		7.9	14.2	*
Suitable place to study or do homework	7.9	11.6	**	21.1	32.1	**
Lacks at least one item	18.6	19.3		53.2	54.8	

Note: The child-specific material deprivation items are asked of the household head for children aged 1–15, though the proportions in this table are for (poor) children aged below 18. *= significant at 0.10 level; **= significant at 0.05 level; ***= significant at 0.01 level.

Source: Authors' calculations using EU-SILC 2009 and 2014.

The SMD indicator captures material deprivation of the household in which children live, rather than material deprivation of children themselves. An EU-SILC ad hoc module carried out in 2009 and from 2013 onwards includes a series of questions that refer directly to the lives of children by including child-relevant items and activities on the list. This allows us to gain more insight into the living conditions of children and how these have changed over time. Although it is not possible to estimate the impact of the crisis, the data provide detailed information on how children's living standards evolved in the post-crisis period. Table 3.1 shows the share of children (aged under 18) and the share of poor children (aged under 18) living in households that were not able to afford these child-specific items in 2009, and again in 2014.

In Belgium, 19 per cent of children lack at least one of the child-specific material deprivation items. This is strongly related to income poverty: 54 per cent of poor children lack at least one item. Items or activities that children lack the most are having a suitable place in which to do homework, being able to participate in regular leisure activities, and getting some new clothes. One child in ten has no suitable place to study, a proportion that for poor children rises to one-third. In addition, Table 3.1 shows a significant increase over the past few years in the number of poor children unable to participate in school trips, to invite friends, or to celebrate on special occasions, and who lack two pairs of properly fitting shoes. It is not the case that more poor children became materially deprived between 2009 and 2014, but those that were deprived of at least one item saw their situation deteriorate even further.

Finally, it is important to acknowledge that marked differences in child poverty rates and living standards prevail across the three Belgian regions (Guio et al., 2015; Vandenbroucke and Vinck, 2015). In the mid-2000s, 10 per cent of Flemish children lived in relative poverty, compared with 20 per cent in Wallonia and even, in Brussels, around 30 per cent. During the crisis, these regional differences were reinforced: the child poverty rate increased to 25 per cent in Wallonia and to almost 40 per cent in Brussels, while remaining stable in Flanders. After the crisis, child poverty rates tended to converge somewhat: they declined in Wallonia (−5 ppt), remained stable in Brussels (−1 ppt), and increased in Flanders (+3 ppt) (Guio, 2016).

3.3.2. The Role of the Labour Market

Since relative income poverty is measured at the household level, it is necessary to take the labour market attainment of parents into account, in order to appreciate the impact of the recession on child poverty. The extent to which parents are able to earn income from paid labour largely determines the poverty risk of their children. As a corollary, job loss might be the driving force underlying the increase in the child poverty rate during the recession. In this section, we examine how child poverty is related to the work intensity of parents; in the next, we discuss whether the impact of the crisis on the labour market can account for the increase in child poverty during that period.

Parental labour market attainment is measured by the household work-intensity indicator, representing the ratio between the total number of months worked by working-age household members and the total number of months that they could, in theory, have worked. In very low work-intensity (VLWI) households, parents work for less than 20 per cent of their potential and have only loose ties to the labour market—the typical example being jobless households with no or only little income from paid work. In contrast, in high work-intensity (HWI) or very high work-intensity (VHWI) households parents work for more than 55 per cent of their potential, and have strong ties to the labour market—a typical example being a two-earner family. Low work-intensity (LWI) and medium work-intensity (MWI) households work for between 20 per cent and 55 per cent of their potential, for instance breadwinner families or single parents working part time (Corluy and Vandenbroucke, 2014).

Figure 3.7 shows that the poverty risk of children is basically an inverted picture of the work intensity of the household in which they live. Merely

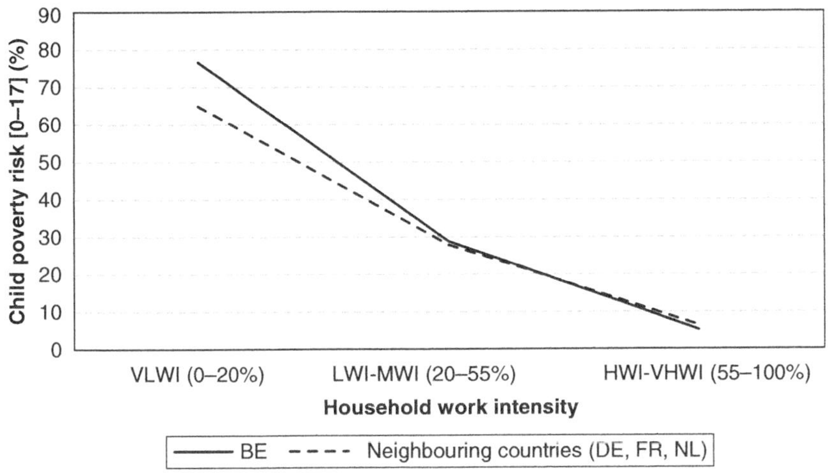

Figure 3.7. Child poverty risk by household work intensity, Belgium and neighbouring countries (income year 2013)

Notes: The dashed line refers to the unweighted average of the three main neighbouring countries (Germany, France, and the Netherlands). Working-age household members are defined as all individuals between 18 and 59, except students between 18 and 24. The difference in the poverty risk between VLWI households in Belgium and VLWI households in neighbouring countries is statistically significant ($p < 0.05$).

Source: Authors' calculation using EU-SILC 2014.

5 per cent of children living in HWI-VHWI households are at risk of being poor in Belgium, while for VLWI households the figure is 77 per cent. This is significantly higher than the poverty risk of children living in VLWI households in the neighbouring countries. Moreover, in 2014, 13 per cent of children and 53 per cent of poor children lived in VLWI households; only crisis-struck Ireland reported higher levels. Hence one piece of the Belgian child poverty puzzle: a high share of children live in VLWI households, and those children run a particularly great risk of being poor (see Vandenbroucke and Vinck, 2015, for further reading).

3.3.3. Gauging the Impact of the Crisis

Figure 3.4 showed that child poverty in Belgium started increasing well before the onset of the crisis, but that during the crisis period child poverty rates increased at an even faster rate. The question now is whether this pattern can be attributed (at least partially) to the impact of the crisis on the labour market. This will be answered by means of decomposition analysis (Corluy and Vandenbroucke, 2014; Vandenbroucke and Vinck, 2015). Such analysis allows us to estimate the extent to which 1) changes in the share of children living in households with different work-intensity levels and 2) changes in the poverty risk of those children contribute to changes in the child poverty rate, and how the role of these factors changed before, during, and after the crisis.

Since the recession in Belgium translated into job losses but not into a fall in median incomes, one impact of the crisis would be that changes in the child poverty rates during that period are explained by changes in the share of children living in VLWI households, and not by changes in the poverty risk of these children.

Table 3.2 shows that before the crisis, the increase in child poverty of 1.3 ppt can be explained by an increase in the poverty risk of children living in VLWI households (+0.9 ppt) and of children living in households with higher work-intensity levels (+1.9 ppt), while a declining share of children living in VLWI households mitigated these trends (−1.4 ppt). During the crisis period, child poverty rates increased by 2.0 ppt. This can be wholly attributed to an increase in the share of children living in VLWI households (+2.0 ppt), while the poverty risk of children living in VLWI (+0.2 ppt) and in other households (−0.3 ppt) remained fairly stable. After the crisis, the child poverty rate persisted at about the same level, because the effect of a declining share of children living in VLWI households (−0.5 ppt) and a decreasing poverty risk of these children (−0.6 ppt) was undone by an increase in the poverty risk of children living in other households (+1.5 ppt).

These results suggest, first, that the crisis was indeed a catalyst for increasing child poverty rates, due to its impact on the labour market; and second, that the employment recovery after the crisis has not translated into lower poverty rates, suggesting that labour market participation as such has become less of a protection against poverty. Even though the impact of the crisis was short-lived in Belgium, previous research suggests that even short spells of living in poverty

Table 3.2. Decomposition of changes in Belgian child poverty rates on the basis of household work intensity, before, during, and after the crisis

	Child poverty	Explanatory factors			Child poverty change	Change explained by		
		Share of children (VLWI)	Child poverty risk (VLWI)	Child poverty risk (other WI)		Share of children (VLWI)	Child poverty risk (VLWI)	Child poverty risk (other WI)
2005	15.3%	13.1%	72.2%	6.7%				
2008	16.6%	11.0%	79.5%	8.8%	1.3	−1.4	0.9	1.9
2010	18.7%	13.8%	81.0%	8.5%	2.0	2.0	0.2	−0.3
2013	18.8%	13.0%	76.6%	10.1%	0.2	−0.5	−0.6	1.5

Note: 2005, 2008, 2010, and 2013 refer to income years.

Source: Authors' calculations using EU-SILC 2006, 2009, 2011, and 2014.

have a scarring effect on the future life opportunities of children, in that they increase the likelihood of future poverty spells (Fouarge and Layte, 2005).

3.3.4. Sociodemographic Characteristics

The risk of being poor is not randomly distributed among children, but is tied to the sociodemographic characteristics of the household in which poor children live—characteristics such as parental education, family structure, and migration status. In turn, these characteristics impact on the opportunities for parents to earn sufficient income in the labour market. Figure 3.8 shows the share of children and the share of poor children by sociodemographic characteristics of the household.

It is clear that poor children are overrepresented in single-parent families (34 per cent of poor children), in families with at least one parent born outside the EU (45 per cent of poor children), and in families with poorly educated parents (34 per cent of poor children). Poor children are also slightly over represented in large families (three or more children), but this is less prominent than the aforementioned characteristics. Therefore, living in a large family is not included as a separate characteristic in the following analyses. While having low qualifications is an important determinant of living in poverty and a strong predictor of occupational success (Troger and Verwiebe, 2015; Gesthuizen and Scheepers, 2010), it is important to note that 45 per cent of poor children live in a household with at least one medium-skilled parent, and 20 per cent live in a household where at least one parent is highly educated. Child poverty is clearly not to be reduced to lack of educational qualifications. In the same vein, while family structure and migration status are important factors underlying child poverty, a fair number of poor children live in families that do not share these characteristics.

This is confirmed by Table 3.3, in which the overlap between family structure, migration status, and level of education for poor children is shown. First of all, 32 per cent of poor children live in 'other' households, and less than a third of these children have low-skilled parents. Second, the overlap between single parents and non-EU families is limited to 10 per cent of poor children. Third, while the children of highly skilled single parents are hardly at risk of being poor, for children living in migrant families that risk is much more tangible. The relationship between parental educational qualifications and child poverty differs for different types of household.

All in all, the sociodemographic characteristics of poor children's families reveal a second piece of the Belgian puzzle. About 68 per cent of poor children grow up in a single-parent or a migrant family—the highest proportion (alongside Austria and Sweden) for any European country (analyses not shown). Yet, while poor children are overrepresented in families with low-skilled parents, the majority of the parents of poor children living in a single-parent or a migrant family are *not* low-skilled.

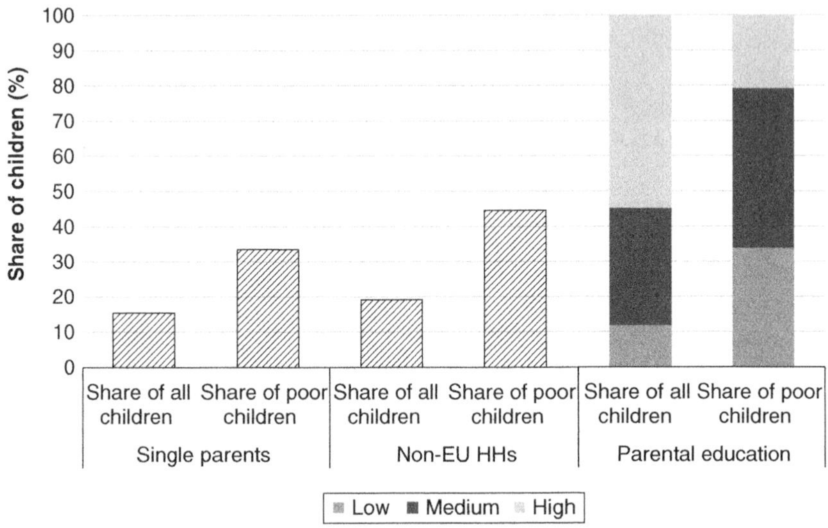

Figure 3.8. Share of children and share of poor children by family characteristics: single parents, non-EU household, and highest educational level of the parents, Belgium (2014)

Notes: Non-EU households are defined as households where at least one parent was born outside the EU; the highest educational level observed among the parents is taken as the educational level of the household (dominance criterion).

Source: Authors' calculations using EU-SILC 2014.

Table 3.3. Overlap between family characteristics for poor children, Belgium, income year 2013

Poor children	Low educated	Medium educated	Highly educated	Total
Single parent	8.6%	12.8%	2.4%	23.8%
Non-EU HH	10.7%	13.3%	10.5%	34.5%
Both single parent and non-EU	6.0%	3.0%	1.2%	10.2%
Other	8.9%	15.9%	6.8%	31.6%
Total	34.1%	45.0%	20.8%	100%

Note: Non-EU households are defined as households where at least one parent is born outside the EU; the highest educational level obtained by the parents is taken as the household educational level.

Source: Authors' calculations using EU SILC 2014.

3.3.5. Work Intensity and Sociodemographic Characteristics

In the previous sections, it was shown that child poverty in Belgium is related to the work intensity of the household on the one hand and to sociodemographic characteristics on the other. In this section, these two pieces of the puzzle will be fitted together. Figure 3.9 shows the relationship between child poverty, household work intensity, and the two types of households in which poor children are overrepresented: single parents (left panel) and migrant households (right panel).

The relationship between child poverty and household work intensity differs between single parents and migrant families. The distribution of children living in single-parent families over work intensity takes the form of a U-shape: single parents tend to be either strongly or weakly attached to the labour market. The share of children living in migrant families is much more equally distributed over work-intensity categories. Importantly, the figure provides further evidence that attaining paid work is not a sufficient condition for combating child poverty: 22 per cent of children living in HWI-VHWI single-parent families and 13 per cent of children living in HWI-VHWI migrant families are at risk of being poor, versus only 6 per cent of all children. Interestingly enough, 67 per cent of children living in VLWI single-parent families and 86 per cent of VLWI migrant families are living in poverty, versus 77 per cent of all children. In sum, non-working single parents are somewhat better protected against poverty than are non-working migrant families, while working migrant families are somewhat better protected against poverty than working single parents. This is related to the structure of the household: single parents are single earners (by definition), and it is increasingly difficult to maintain a sufficient living standard on only one income (Van Lancker et al., 2015; Daly, 2005).

Figure 3.10, finally, shows the relationship between child poverty, parental education, and work intensity of the household. Three observations can be made. First, there is almost no difference in the child poverty risk over work intensity between low and medium-educated households. Being highly skilled, however, is consistently associated with a lower child poverty risk. Second, here, too, the results show that having paid employment as such is not enough; respectively 9 per cent and 17 per cent of children living with low- and medium-skilled parents with high levels of work intensity are poor. Since the majority of children with low- and medium-skilled parents live in HWI-VHWI households, these are no trivial numbers. Third, the picture confirms that attaining a high level of education is an insufficient condition to avoid poverty as well: 15 per cent of children with highly educated parents live in VLWI or LWI-MWI households with child poverty rates of 62 per cent and 18 per cent, respectively.

In sum, educational policies will not help to combat child poverty if high qualifications do not lead to high levels of work intensity, while policies that focus on employment will not deliver, if even high levels of work intensity are inadequate to steer clear of poverty. This calls for a renewed emphasis on income protection, for jobless and working families with children alike.

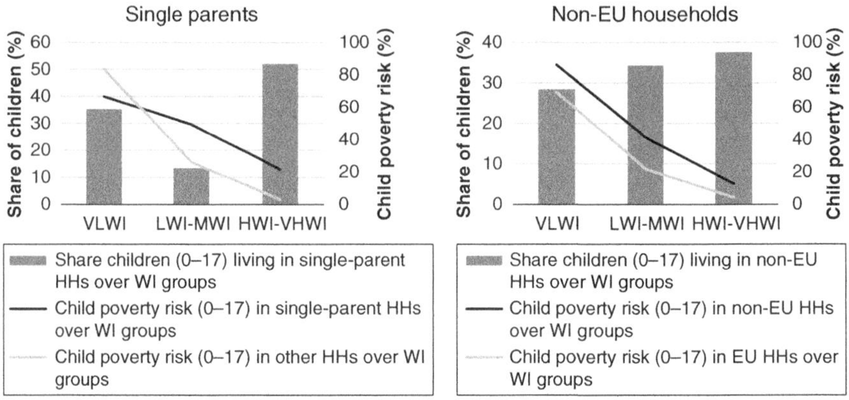

Figure 3.9. Children living in single-parent households (left panel) and non-EU households (right panel): share and poverty risks over household work intensity, Belgium (income year 2013)

Note: Non-EU households are defined as households where at least one parent is born outside the EU.

Source: Authors' calculations using EU-SILC 2014.

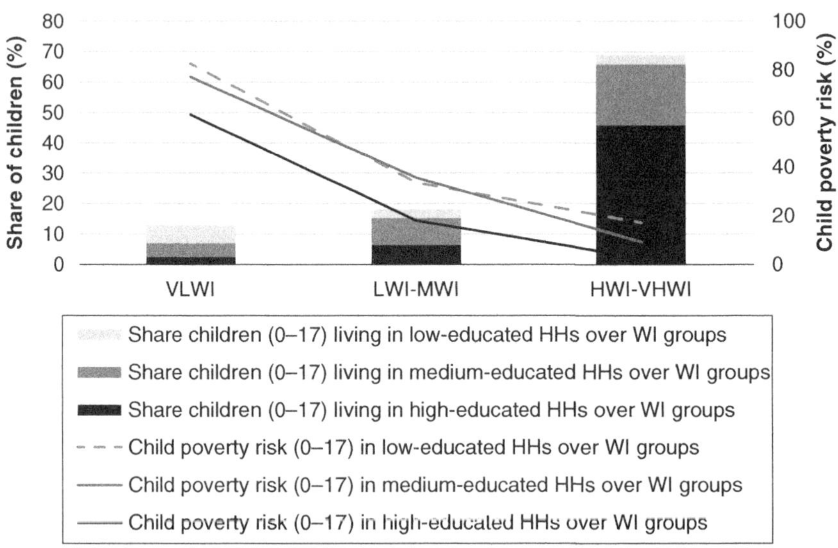

Figure 3.10. Children living in households with low, medium, or high-skilled parents: share and poverty risk over work intensity, Belgium (2013)

Note: The highest educational level obtained by the parents is taken as the household educational level.

Source: Authors' calculations using EU-SILC 2014.

3.4. POLICIES

3.4.1. Policies before the Crisis

Belgium's policy response to the great economic, social, and demographic transitions of the 1970s and 1980s has been depicted as a prime example of 'welfare without work' (Esping-Andersen, 1996). In that period, Belgium was characterized by low employment rates, a high level of social expenditure, a strong social safety net, and low (and stable) poverty rates (Cantillon, 1999). Since the second half of the 1990s, haunted by historically high levels of public debt (reaching a peak of 135 per cent of GDP in 1993) and pressured by the obligation to reduce public debt under the Maastricht Treaty, successive Belgian governments slowly contributed to a process of policy reorientation, in order to achieve budgetary restraint, employment growth, and equality.

In hindsight, that process of reorientation can be interpreted as a 'social investment turn' in policy making (Hemerijck, 2012). The ambition was for higher employment rates to translate into lower poverty rates and reduced social spending on 'passive' cash transfers, thus creating budgetary room to invest in more 'productive' activation policies and human capital policies (childcare, higher education). This in turn was projected as supporting higher levels of labour market participation. On the face of it, the strategy seems to have delivered. Employment rates started to rise; and while overall social spending remained steady at a high level, there was a shift in the nature of spending (Figure 3.11): spending on elderly care, childcare, career breaks,

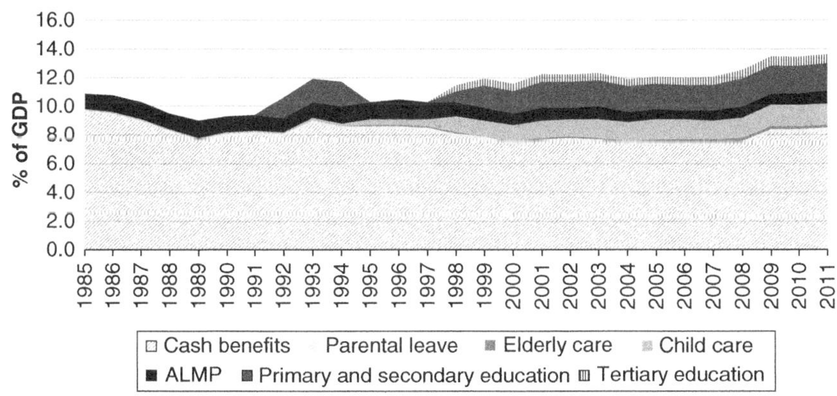

Figure 3.11. Social spending on active-age persons (under 65) as a percentage of GDP, functional distribution, Belgium (1985–2011)

Note: Spending on 'cash benefits' includes spending on unemployment benefits, sickness and disability benefits, and child benefits.

Source: Calculations by Linde Buysse and Annemie Nys, based on Meeusen and Nys (2014).

education, and active labour market policies increased from 1.3 per cent of GDP in 1985 to 5.1 per cent of GDP in 2008, while spending on cash benefits for the active-age population declined from 9.6 per cent of GDP in 1985 to 7.4 per cent in 2008 (Cantillon and Vandenbroucke, 2014).

However, the 'social investment turn' largely failed to deliver on its promise to reduce poverty. Although the design of many individual tax-benefit policies were pro-poor (Decoster et al., 2015), below the radar there was a creeping vulnerability of children (Vandenbroucke and Vinck, 2015). The analyses of child poverty presented in this chapter have demonstrated that a policy paradigm focusing on human capital investment, including expansion of childcare and higher education, and labour market activation falls short of reducing child poverty. Four reasons can be discerned. First, employment growth has benefited VLWI households much less than it has benefited households with higher levels of work intensity (Corluy and Vandenbroucke, 2014). Second, as a consequence, government investment in policies that are grafted onto labour market participation (such as childcare services) have also mainly benefited work-rich households (Van Lancker, 2013). Third, access to higher education remains socially stratified (OECD, 2014). Fourth, despite continuous upwards adjustments of social benefits in the period before the crisis, cash benefits for the active aged (minimum unemployment benefits, social assistance, child benefits) became less adequate in protecting these families from poverty (see section 3.4.4).

3.4.2. Policies during the Crisis

During the Great Recession, the Belgian government implemented a number of crisis measures to prevent job losses. First, before the crisis struck, a temporary lay-off scheme that allowed employers to partially or fully suspend the employment contract of blue-collar workers in case of severe economic or natural circumstances (bad weather, strikes, economic downturns) was already in place. This 'temporary unemployment' scheme grants affected workers (partial) unemployment benefit, even though they retain a contractual bond with their employer; while employers save the costs associated with dismissal (Van Gyes, 2010). Employers resorted to this measure in high numbers: in the first quarter of 2009, some 279,643 workers were temporarily unemployed for at least a day, a 75 per cent increase over the first quarter of 2008.

Second, in April 2009 the government and the social partners agreed on crisis measures for white-collar workers, with the explicit aim of keeping job losses and dismissals at bay. Three provisions were implemented: a so-called short-time work arrangement (STWA) scheme, meant to facilitate a temporary reduction in working time at the company level; the extension of the temporary unemployment scheme to white-collar workers; and a specific crisis-related extension of the existing time credit scheme at the individual level (Van Gyes, 2009).

Finally, as part of the crisis measures, the Belgian government increased the levels of social assistance benefits and levels of temporary unemployment benefits by 2 per cent above price indexation (Marchal et al., 2014). This seems to be in line with initial European Commission recommendations to increase transfers to the poor, since these are likely to be spent immediately and hence will contribute to improving aggregate demand (Commission of the European Communities, 2008).

As a consequence of the increase in unemployment, the compensation for reduction in working hours, and the slight increase in some benefits for the unemployed, spending on unemployment benefits went up by 0.5 ppt of GDP. Belgium's public debt ratio again increased to 97 per cent of GDP in 2010, and surpassed 100 per cent of GDP in 2012. Successive Belgian governments had reduced the public debt ratio quite successfully to 84 per cent in 2007, from its peak in the 1990s. The crisis hence halted two decades of falling public debt ratio (IMF, 2011).

From 2012 onwards, following a general trend among European welfare states, the Belgian government started following a more austerity-guided policy agenda, including a focus on fiscal consolidation through the reduction of social expenditure and the implementation of cost-cutting measures. This has been partially fuelled by fears of increasing public debt ratios and a looming impact of ageing, two evolutions that have been designated as potential threats to the long-term fiscal sustainability of Belgium by the European Commission.[1] At the federal level, these measures (decided upon or implemented by the Di Rupo government from 2011 until 2014, and by the Michel government thereafter) included imposing stricter conditions on unemployment benefit entitlement, a sharper decrease in levels of unemployment benefit over time (while not imposing a formal time limit on benefit entitlement), and first limiting and subsequently scrapping an activation allowance (*wachtuitkering*) covering unemployed people who did not qualify for regular unemployment benefits (mostly higher-education graduates who had not yet found a job). Other austerity measures included an across-the-board cut of 10 per cent in the public wage bill and cost-reducing measures in healthcare. In an attempt to reduce the tax burden on wages still further, in 2014 it was decided to have an across-the-board reduction in labour costs (by reducing employers' social security contributions) and a one-off 'skipping' of automatic wage indexation in 2015. At the same time, and under European impetus, the federal and regional governments implemented a Youth Guarantee Plan that focused on integrating (early) school

[1] Under the Stability and Growth Pact (SGP), see e.g. European Commission (2016).

leavers into the labour market. Hitherto, no evaluation studies have been carried out.

Austerity measures have also been taken at the regional level. For example, in Flanders the Bourgeois government (2014–19) has decided on various measures that will raise the prices paid by families for water and electricity: the free quotas of water and electricity are being abolished, an energy tax (*Turteltaks*) is being introduced, and the VAT rate on electricity is again being increased to 21 per cent (having been reduced to 6 per cent by the second Peeters administration (2011–14)). Moreover, childcare becomes more expensive: the minimum price is raised from €1.56 to €5 per day, and the child discount (applicable to the second and any subsequent child) is limited to children under the age of 12.

3.4.3. Policy Discourse

It should be noted that before, during, and after the crisis, poverty has always been high on the policy agenda in Belgium and its regions. Various 'action plans' to eradicate poverty have been adopted, often with a clear focus on child poverty. At the federal level, the most recent plan was adopted in 2012 (and a new plan was recently announced); at the Flemish level in 2015; in Brussels in 2012; and in 2015 for the first time also in Wallonia. In Flanders, moreover, a clear target to halve the child poverty rate by 2020 was adopted in 2010 (Pact 2020 Strategy). These plans lack real bite, however, and are focused on supporting local initiatives and small projects (cheap or free meals, crowdfunding initiatives, parental support programmes), without defining long-term policy initiatives to ensure a structural improvement in the income and labour market position of poor families.

In line with other countries, and encouraged by the European Commission and international organizations such as the World Bank and the OECD, over the past decade the policy focus of anti-poverty programmes has shifted towards early childhood (Vandenbroeck et al., 2012). The result, however, is that policy makers increasingly focus on children aged 0–3, emphasizing childcare use and parental support programmes; not necessarily the kind of public measures needed to strengthen the social safety net. A focus on the earliest years to combat child poverty carries with it the risk that structural policies that actually matter will be disregarded.

3.4.4. The Way Forward

Despite the introduction of tax deductions on low wages (*werkbonus*) and the uprating of many benefits in the late 2000s before the crisis, at the structural level the net minimum wage, social assistance, and unemployment benefit levels are well below the poverty threshold for families with children (Van Mechelen and Marchal, 2013; Cantillon et al., 2016). Added to that, the policy focus on employment as a fast track to social inclusion (which Belgium shares with other European countries) and the post-crisis austerity measures in the unemployment insurance system mentioned above have made unemployed families with children even more vulnerable to living in poverty. The stricter conditions for entering unemployment insurance that have been imposed on school leavers, for instance, have led to a surge in young people claiming social assistance benefits (POD MI, 2014), while microsimulation studies have demonstrated that the changes in the benefit levels for the longer-term unemployed will lead to a significant surge in the poverty risk among these families (Centrale Raad voor het Bedrijfsleven, 2014).

In the previous section, we showed that child poverty in Belgium is concentrated in single-parent families on the one hand and in non-EU families on the other. These families are more often low-skilled than other families: the prevalence of lone parenthood is related to social class and educational attainment (Pintelon et al., 2013). Corluy and Verbist (2014) have shown that lower educational levels, larger families, and the region they live in explain, at least in part, the low labour market attachment of non-EU-born immigrants. Corluy (2014) has documented extensively how Belgium has the worst track record of the EU-15 countries when it comes to the labour market integration of non-EU migrants. This means that policies must focus on enabling non-working single parents and non-EU migrants to get a foothold in the labour market.

However, many non-EU migrant families and lone parents *are* connected to the labour market, yet still face above-average poverty risks. This means that strengthening the safety net should not be limited to non-working families. In that respect, child benefits could play an important role. Research has shown that child cash benefits are a potentially powerful weapon to combat child poverty (Van Lancker and Van Mechelen, 2015) and single-mother poverty (Maldonado and Nieuwenhuis, 2015; Van Lancker et al., 2015).

Figure 3.12 shows the impact of child cash benefits and other cash transfers on reducing child poverty among work-poor households across European welfare states. Belgium stands out as having only a small impact due to transfers. In absolute terms, all cash transfers taken together reduce child poverty by 21 ppt, of which child benefits account for 12.5 ppt.

The Belgian child benefit system is universal in nature, meaning that child benefits are for the most part allocated to families with children, irrespective of the income level of the parents (Van Lancker and Van Mechelen, 2015). Only a marginal share of the child benefit budget is selectively allocated to certain types of low-income families, such as the long-term unemployed and single

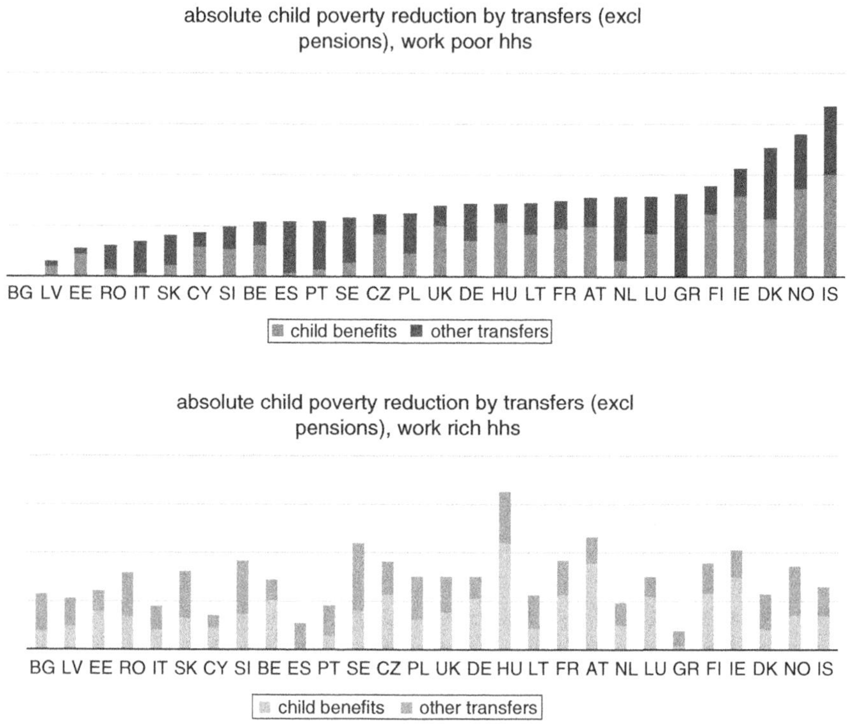

Figure 3.12. Absolute child poverty reduction by transfers (excluding pensions), VLWI households, Belgium (income year 2009), per cent

Source: Authors' calculations using EU-SILC 2010.

parents.[2] Microsimulation exercises have shown that redressing the balance between selectivity and universality would yield significant gains in terms of child poverty reduction (Hufkens et al., 2013), and hence would contribute to strengthening the safety net for vulnerable families with children, even if they are engaged in paid employment.

Belgium has been rather slow to adopt the 'activation turn' in social policy, but since 2004 activation policies have been implemented for the unemployed, starting with the youngest age groups. Cockx et al. (2011) and Cockx and Baert (2015) show that the activation turn has been quite successful, though there are limits to what activation can achieve, since much depends on the profile of the unemployed and the availability of jobs. As the majority of low-educated

[2] Since the sixth state reform enacted in 2015, however, competency for child benefits changed from the federal level to the regions. The fact that regions bear full competencies for operating and designing their child benefit systems opens a window of opportunity for reforms. Yet, it could also lead to interregional divergence in terms of entitlements and benefit levels.

parents have no or only marginal attachment to the labour market, it is crucial to create jobs at the lower end of the labour market. Yet, to be effective in reducing child poverty, these jobs have to be adequately paid. Given the profound transitions in the labour market currently faced by developed economies (Goos et al., 2009), with declining opportunities for low-skilled persons to attain decent jobs (Salverda, 2016), this will require greater government involvement through subsidies for lower-end jobs, public employment, and tax credits (Atkinson, 2015).

A precondition for successfully integrating families with children into the labour market is to make sure that formal childcare facilities are available, accessible, and affordable. Here, too, progress can be made. In Belgium, childcare has been the responsibility of the regions since the 1980 state reform. Responsibility for monitoring care for the under-3s is entrusted to a public organization, while the actual provision of services is performed by semi-private organizations. Those childcare centres and childminders that are subsidized by the regional government have income-related parental fees and have to give some priority to vulnerable groups; but given the supply shortage, in practice priority is often given to working parents. It has to be noted here that there is no legal entitlement to a place in childcare. Earlier research has clearly shown that the lack of places in childcare is detrimental for low-skilled and low-income parents. Disadvantaged families are rarely able to plan their childcare needs well in advance, since they often find themselves in precarious and flexible forms of employment, if they are employed at all (Vandenbroeck et al., 2008). As a consequence, childcare use is highly biased in favour of work-rich and higher-income families (Van Lancker and Ghysels, 2012).

3.5. CONCLUSION

Before the crisis, the Belgian welfare state was plagued by comparatively high levels of child poverty, and by a creeping, yet significant, increase in child poverty. This is related to the relatively high share of jobless households and a decline in the redistributive impact of social policies on poverty rates. Although the impact of the crisis in terms of job loss and GDP contraction was rather modest, and although unemployment affected those with a low level of education less than those with a high level, our analyses show that it has had an impact on the child poverty risk, by increasing the number of children living in work-poor households. This has translated into deteriorating material living conditions among children since the Great Recession.

In Belgium, the majority of poor children grow up in a single-parent or a migrant family. Yet, it is important to acknowledge that while poor children are overrepresented in families with low-skilled parents, the majority of the parents of poor children living in single-parent or migrant families are *not* low-skilled. Moreover, while a high share of children live in households with only a marginal attachment to the labour market, and while those children run a particularly high risk of being poor, many poor children are living in households with higher levels of work intensity. Child poverty is neither simply a problem of being poorly qualified nor one of having no work.

In policy terms, first it is crucial to integrate workless families with children into the labour market. To achieve this, successful activation, making work pay for the low-skilled, and structural labour market reforms are needed, while childcare services should be more readily available, accessible, and affordable. Second, though expensive, it is not impossible to guarantee a decent minimum income in general, and adequate child benefit packages in particular—provided the policy design is efficient. Child benefit reforms are a potentially powerful weapon in this respect. In general, in Belgium the poverty-reducing capacity of social spending should be reinforced.

Although the Belgian safety net in general is still going strong, with high levels of social spending, the now prevailing policy paradigm—with its focus on human capital investment and employment—has failed to address the creeping vulnerability of children. The crisis has had an amplifying effect on these evolutions, but did not cause them. The main unresolved issues of the Belgian welfare state are the high numbers of jobless households (especially among migrant families and single parents), the extremely high poverty risk of children growing up in these households, and benefits that are inadequate to shield families with children from poverty, whether or not they work. A focus on education and work will not be sufficient to solve these structural problems.

REFERENCES

Atkinson, Anthony B. (2015). *Inequality: What Can be Done?* (Cambridge, MA: Harvard University Press).

Bulté, Steven and Ludo Struyven (2013). 'De Belgische arbeidsmarkt na 5 jaar crisis: nooit eerder werden minder nieuwe jobs gecreëerd'. *DynaM Analyse*, December (Leuven: HIVA).

Cantillon, Bea (1999). *De welvaartsstaat in de kering* (Kapellen: Pelckmans).

Cantillon, Bea, Sarah Marchal, and Chris Luigjes (forthcoming). 'Decent Incomes for the Poor: Which Role for Europe?'. *Journal of Common Market Studies.*

Cantillon, Bea and Frank Vandenbroucke (2014). *Reconciling Work and Poverty Reduction: How Successful are European Welfare States?* (Oxford: Oxford University Press).

Centrale Raad voor het Bedrijfsleven (2014). 'De versterkte degressiviteit van de Belgische werkloosheidsuitkeringen; Effecten op de financiële vallen in de werkloosheid en op de inkomenspositie van de werklozen'. *Documentatienota, CRB 2014-0264* (Brussels: Centrale Raad voor het Bedrijfsleven).

Cockx, Bart and Stijn Baert (2015). 'Uitbesteding van verplichte begeleidings-en opleidingstrajecten voor langdurig werklozen: profit, nonprofit, of behoud de overheidsdienst?'. *Over.Werk 25*, no. 4: pp. 126–36.

Cockx, Bart, Muriel Dejemeppe, and Bruno Van der Linden (2011). 'L'activation du comportement de recherche d'emploi favorise-t-elle un retour plus rapide à l'emploi?'. *Regards économiques 85*: pp. 1–14.

Commission of the European Communities (2008). 'Communication from the Commission: From Financial Crisis to Recovery: A European Framework For Action'. COM/2008/0706 final (Brussels: Commission of the European Communities).

Corluy, Vincent (2014). 'Labour Market Outcomes and Trajectories of Immigrants in Belgium', doctoral thesis, University of Antwerp, Faculty of Political and Social Sciences, Department of Sociology.

Corluy, Vincent and Frank Vandenbroucke (2014). 'Individual Employment, Household Employment, and Risk of Poverty in the European Union: A Decomposition Analysis'. In Bea Cantillon and Frank Vandenbroucke (eds), *Reconciling Work and Poverty Reduction: How Successful are European Welfare States?* (Oxford: Oxford University Press).

Corluy, Vincent and Gerlinde Verbist (2014). 'Can Education Bridge the Gap? Education and the Employment Position of Immigrants in Belgium'. *ImPRovE Discussion Paper No. 14/02* (Antwerp: Herman Deleeck Centre for Social Policy).

Daly, Mary (2005). 'Gender Mainstreaming in Theory and Practice'. *Social Politics 12*, no. 3: pp. 433–50.

De Mulder, J. and M. Druant (2011). 'The Belgian Labour Market during and after the Crisis'. *[National Bank of Belgium]Economic Review*, issue i: pp. 89–104.

Decoster, André, Sergio Perelman, Dieter Vandelannoote, Toon Vanheukelom, and Gerlinde Verbist (2015). 'A Bird's Eye View on 20 Years of Tax-Benefit Reforms in Belgium'. *KU Leuven Discussion Paper Series DPS15.07* (Leuven: KU Leuven).

Esping-Andersen, Gøsta (1996). 'Welfare States without Work: The Impasse of Labour Shedding and Familialism in Continental European Social Policy'. In Gøsta Esping-Andersen (ed.), *Welfare States in Transition: National Adaptations in Global Economies* (London: Sage).

European Commission (2010). 'European Economic Forecast: Spring 2010'. *European Economy* 2/2010 (Luxembourg: Publications Office of the European Union).

European Commission (2016). Commission Staff Working Document 'Country Report Belgium 2016'. SWD(2016) 71 final (Brussels: European Commission).

Fouarge, Didier and Richard Layte (2005). 'Welfare Regimes and Poverty Dynamics: The Duration and Recurrence of Poverty Spells in Europe'. *Journal of Social Policy 34*, no. 3: pp. 407–26.

Gesthuizen, Maurice and Peer Scheepers (2010). 'Economic Vulnerability among Low-educated Europeans: Resource, Composition, Labour Market and Welfare State Influences'. *Acta Sociologica 53*, no. 3: pp. 247–67.

Goos, Maarten, Alan Manning, and Anna Salomons (2009). 'The Polarization of the European Labor Market'. *American Economic Review Papers and Proceedings 99*, no. 2: pp. 58–63.

Guio, Anne-Catherine (2016). 'La structure globale des revenus de la population et la lutte contre la pauvreté', presented at the seminar 'De socio-economische rol van de kinderbijslag: een instrument in de strijd tegen de armoede', FAMIFED, Brussels, 26 May 2016.

Guio, Anne-Catherine, Frank Vandenbroucke, and Julie Vinck (2015). 'Kinderarmoede hoger op de politieke agenda plaatsen: enkele cijfers om beter te begrijpen wat er op het spel staat', in Isabelle Pannecoucke, Willy Lahaye, Jan Vrancken, and Ronan Van Rossem (eds), *Armoede in België: Jaarboek 2015* (Ghent: Academia Press): pp. 113–40.

Hemerijck, Anton (2012). *Changing Welfare States* (Oxford: Oxford University Press).

Hufkens, Tine, Dieter Vandelannoote, Wim Van Lancker, and Gerlinde Verbist (2013). 'Hervorming van de Vlaamse kinderbijslag en armoedebestrijding: een simulatie van alternatieven'. *CSB Berichten 11* (Antwerp: Centrum voor Sociaal Beleid Herman Deleeck).

International Monetary Fund (IMF) (2009). 'Belgium: 2008 Article IV Consultation—Staff Report; Staff Supplement; and Public Information Notice on the Executive Board Discussion'. *IMF Country Report No. 09/87* (Washington, DC: IMF).

International Monetary Fund (IMF) (2011). 'Belgium: Selected Issues Paper'. *IMF Country Report No. 11/82* (Washington, DC: IMF).

Jenkins, Stephen P., Andrea Brandolini, John Micklewright, and Brian Nolan (eds) (2013). *The Great Recession and the Distribution of Household Income* (Oxford: Oxford University Press).

Maldonado, Laurie C. and Rense Nieuwenhuis (2015). 'Family Policies and Single Parent Poverty in 18 OECD Countries, 1978–2008'. *Community, Work and Family 18*, no. 4: pp. 395–415.

Marchal, Sarah, Ive Marx, and Natascha Van Mechelen (2014). 'The Great Wake-Up Call? Social Citizenship and Minimum Income Provisions in Europe in Times of Crisis'. *Journal of Social Policy 43*, no. 2: pp. 247–67.

Meeusen, Leen and Annemie Nys (2014). 'The Evolution of Public Social Spending 1985–2009'. In Bea Cantillon and Frank Vandenbroucke (eds), *Reconciling Work and Poverty Reduction: How Successful are European Welfare States?* (Oxford: Oxford University Press).

Nolan, Brian and Christopher T. Whelan (2011). *Poverty and Deprivation in Europe* (Oxford: Oxford University Press).

Organisation for Economic Co-operation and Development (OECD) (2011). *Economic Surveys: Belgium 2011* (Paris: OECD).

Organization for Economic Co-operation and Development (OECD) (2014). *Education at a Glance 2014: OECD Indicators* (Paris: OECD Publishing).

Pintelon, Olivier, Bea Cantillon, Karel Van den Bosch, and Christopher T. Whelan (2013). 'The Social Stratification of Social Risks: The Relevance of Class for Social Investment Strategies'. *Journal of European Social Policy 23*, no. 1: pp. 52–67.

Programmatorische Overheidsdienst Maatschappelijke Integratie (POD MI) (2014). 'RVA-sanctie en doorstroom naar de OCMW's'. *Focusnota 8* (Brussels: POD MI).

Salverda, Wiemer (2016). 'The Tsunamis of Educational Attainment and Part-time Employment, and the Change of the Labour Force 1960–2010: What can be Learned About Self-reinforcing Labour-market Inequality from the Case of the Netherlands, in International Comparison?'. *ImPRovE Working Paper No. 16/04* (Antwerp: Herman Deleeck Centre for Social Policy).

Troger, Tobias and Roland Verwiebe (2015). 'The Role of Education for Poverty Risks Revisited: Couples, Employment and Profits from Work–Family Policies'. *Journal of European Social Policy 25*, no. 3: pp. 286–302.

Van Gyes, Guy (2009). 'Reducing Working Time as Anti-crisis Measure'. Eurofound (27 July 2009). <http://www.eurofound.europa.eu/observatories/eurwork/articles/reducing-working-time-as-anti-crisis-measure>.

Van Gyes, Guy (2010). 'Crisis in Social Dialogue Due to Anti-crisis Measures'. Eurofound (8 April 2010). <http://www.eurofound.europa.eu/observatories/eurwork/articles/industrial-relations/crisis-in-social-dialogue-due-to-anti-crisis-measures>.

Van Lancker, Wim (2013). 'Putting the Child-centred Investment Strategy to the Test: Evidence for the EU27'. *European Journal of Social Security 15*, no. 1: pp. 4–27.

Van Lancker, Wim and Joris Ghysels (2012). 'Who Benefits? The Social Distribution of Subsidized Childcare in Sweden and Flanders'. *Acta Sociologica 55*, no. 2: pp. 125–42.

Van Lancker, Wim, Joris Ghysels, and Bea Cantillon (2015). 'The Impact of Child Benefits on Single Mother Poverty: Exploring the Role of Targeting in 15 European Countries'. *International Journal of Social Welfare 24*, no. 3: pp. 210–22.

Van Lancker, Wim and Natascha Van Mechelen (2015). 'Universalism under Siege? Exploring the Association between Targeting, Child Benefits and Child Poverty across 26 Countries'. *Social Science Research 50*, no. 1: pp. 60–75.

Van Mechelen, Natascha and Sarah Marchal (2013). 'Struggle for Life: Social Assistance Benefits, 1992–2009'. In Ive Marx and Kenneth Nelson (eds), *Minimum Income Protection in Flux* (Basingstoke: Palgrave Macmillan).

Vandenbroeck, Michel, Sven De Visscher, Karen Van Nuffel, and Johan Ferla (2008). 'Mothers' Search for Infant Child Care: The Dynamic Relationship between Availability and Desirability in a Continental European Welfare State'. *Early Childhood Research Quarterly 23*, no. 2: pp. 245–58.

Vandenbroeck, Michel, Griet Roets, and Rudi Roose (2012). 'Why the Evidence-based Paradigm in Early Childhood Education and Care is Anything but Evident'. *European Early Childhood Education Research Journal 20*, no. 4: pp. 537–52.

Vandenbroucke, Frank and Julie Vinck (2015). 'Child Poverty Risks in Belgium, Wallonia and Flanders: Accounting for a Worrying Performance'. *Belgisch Tijdschrift voor Sociale Zekerheid 57*, no. 1: 51–98.

4

Child Poverty during the Recession in Germany

Thomas Bahle and Peter Krause

4.1. INTRODUCTION

In Germany, child poverty was hardly affected by the crisis, because the crisis did not have any profound negative or long-lasting impact on employment. The labour market proved robust, and economic growth soon recovered after the initial shock of 2008/9. Moreover, social benefits were not cut during the crisis. Family policies were actually developed further and benefits were increased. Hence, at first sight the German story of the crisis and child poverty would appear to be rather short and simple. However, below this surface of relative success lingers a research puzzle: why did child poverty increase even during the years before the crisis, and why did it not decline after the quick recovery from the crisis? This puzzle leads to two perhaps discomforting questions: what is going wrong if a country with a stable economy and quite high spending on family policies is unable to solve the problem of child poverty adequately? And what could this mean for future crisis scenarios with perhaps less favourable macroeconomic conditions? It is the country's relative success in coping with the crisis, together with its failure to solve the problem of child poverty, that points to some unresolved structural problems in the German welfare system.

This chapter seeks to unravel this puzzle. The next section analyses why the crisis did not have a negative impact on the labour market—hence, why it did not have a strong effect on child poverty. This finding is confirmed by data presented in section 4.3, showing the main trends and structures in child poverty during the crisis. Section 4.4 looks at how various policies have tackled child poverty in recent years. The focus is on family policies and minimum income protection, because these are most relevant for families at risk of poverty. The analysis highlights policy deficits that are at the root of structural problems leading to child poverty. Some of these policies were changed during the crisis, but not necessarily because of the crisis. Another important point is that significant reforms in both family policy and minimum income protection occurred some years before the crisis, in the early 2000s, mainly in response to the deep structural problems in the German economy and on the labour market at the time. One can thus argue that the lack of policy reforms during the crisis is partly due to the fact that the system had already been adapted to another, earlier, crisis context.

4.2. THE IMPACT OF THE CRISIS

In order to understand the overall economic development in Germany before, during, and after the recession, one should identify four periods:

- 2001–5: Before the recession—economic stagnation
- 2006–8: Before the recession—economic growth
- 2009–10: Great Recession—economic decline and recovery
- 2011–13: After the recession—economic growth at lower rates

The Great Recession came to Germany at a time of economic growth, which had followed a period of stagnation and crisis. In a longitudinal perspective 2005, rather than 2009, was the most critical year in the German economy for decades. Unemployment in 2005 reached an all-time peak, and total government debt climbed to its highest level. From the time of reunification in the 1990s until 2005, real incomes had stagnated for the bulk of the population, while inequality in earnings and disposable income had increased substantially (Biewen and Juhasz, 2012; Goebel et al., 2015; Krause, 2015). Only the richest income groups gained in real terms, while poverty rates increased. This stagnation period was related to an ongoing increase in inequality in market incomes, to high public deficits, high unemployment, and the further convergence between eastern and western Germany. Many indicators show a lower economic performance in the first half of the 2000s than during the recession. Germany clearly was on a path of growth when, in autumn 2008, suddenly the financial crisis struck. After a strong initial fall in gross domestic product (GDP) in 2009, the economy very soon returned to growth in 2010 (Figure 4.1), and in 2011 the pre-crisis level of 2007 was exceeded. Since then growth has continued, though at a lower rate.

The recession had a relatively modest and short-lived social impact, compared to most other European and Organization for Economic Co-operation and Development (OECD) countries (OECD, 2015). A small decline in employment during the recession affected mainly employees in manufacturing, the metal, and the electrical industries, and in subcontract work. Overall

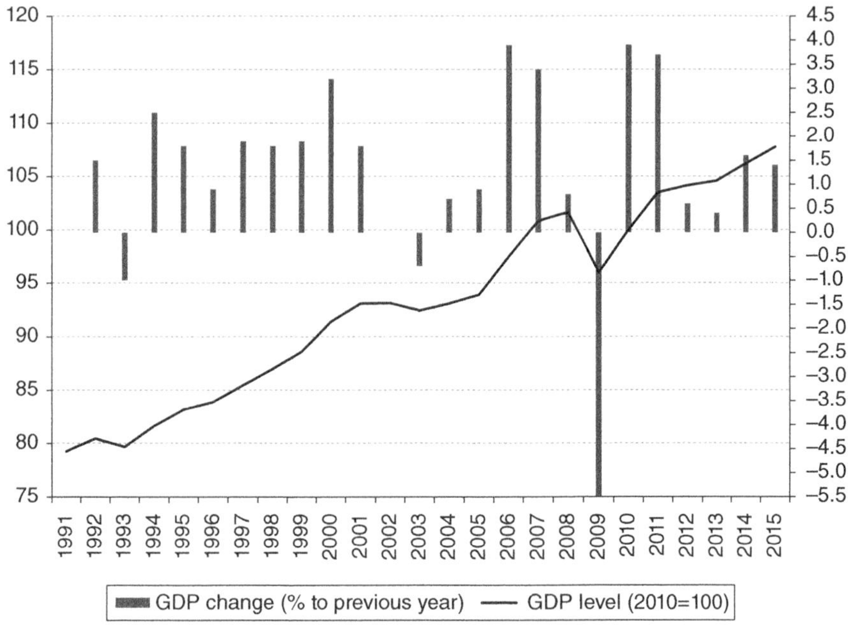

Figure 4.1. Changes in GDP, Germany (1991–2015)
Source: Statistisches Bundesamt (2016).

labour force participation declined only marginally during the recession. Therefore the decline in unemployment, which started in the second half of the 2000s, was only briefly interrupted, and unemployment was hardly affected by the crisis. It peaked in 2005, declined thereafter, and went up only slightly in 2009. Then it returned to its previous declining path (Figure 4.2).

The long-term unemployment rate (measured as a percentage of the labour force) also declined significantly after 2005, but the share of the long-term unemployed among all unemployed persons has remained high. As a response to the severe crisis before the recession, in 2003–5 far-reaching social reforms were enacted. Social protection for the unemployed was cut, activation policies were implemented, and labour market governance was relaxed (see section 4.4). The labour market had already improved significantly from 2005 until the most recent crisis hit (Figure 4.2).

Social expenditure likewise remained remarkably stable over the crisis: from 2005 until 2008, it grew less than GDP. In 2009, it went up a little and remained stable thereafter. There were no significant cuts during the crisis. The proportion of social expenditure as a percentage of GDP hovered around 30 per cent (Figure 4.3). The only longer-lasting direct impact of the crisis was a huge and permanent increase in overall public debt (Figure 4.3).

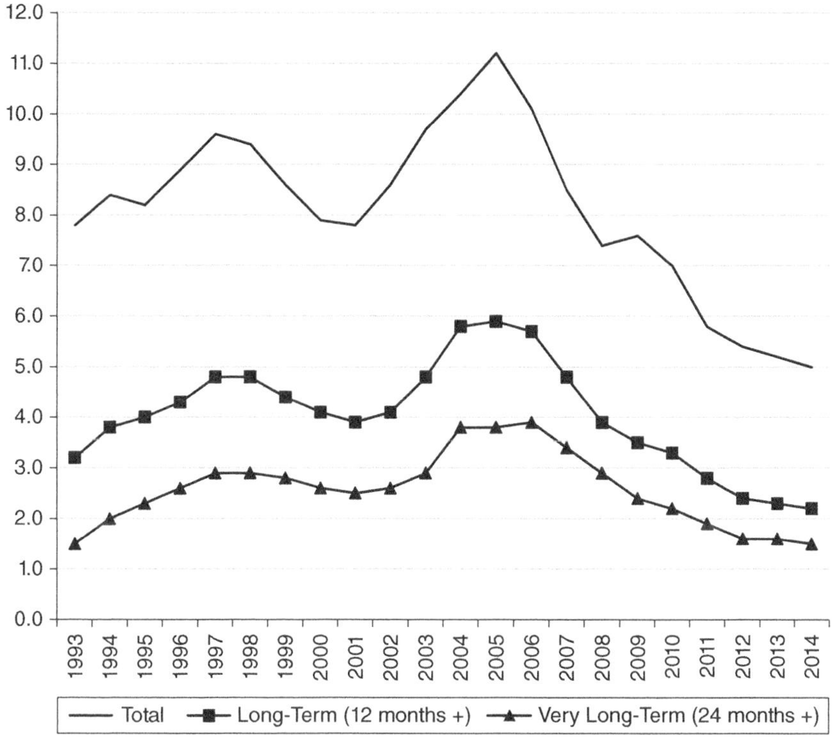

Figure 4.2. Unemployment rates, Germany (1993–2014)
Source: EUROSTAT (2015); Statistisches Bundesamt (2015).

The fact that the German economy was not negatively affected by the recession for a longer period can be explained by its relatively robust state after the severe crisis of 2005 and by the relatively successful response to the recession by government and social partners (Bosch, 2011). The political conditions for the implementation of these measures were favourable at that time. The government was formed by a 'grand coalition' of Christian Democrats and Social Democrats, which made consensus building in the German federal system much easier. In addition, trade unions and employer organizations were heavily involved in crisis consultations. Social partnership in Germany had been declining for years, but during the crisis it could be revived, because the old institutional procedures were still intact. Eichhorst and Weishaupt (2013) argue that the social partners still had strong formal and informal communication channels, mainly at the sectoral level. They were able to extend these channels to the central level at the onset of the crisis, because the strategic players in the metal and automobile industries were crucial for the national pact. Thus the social partners were able to develop a common

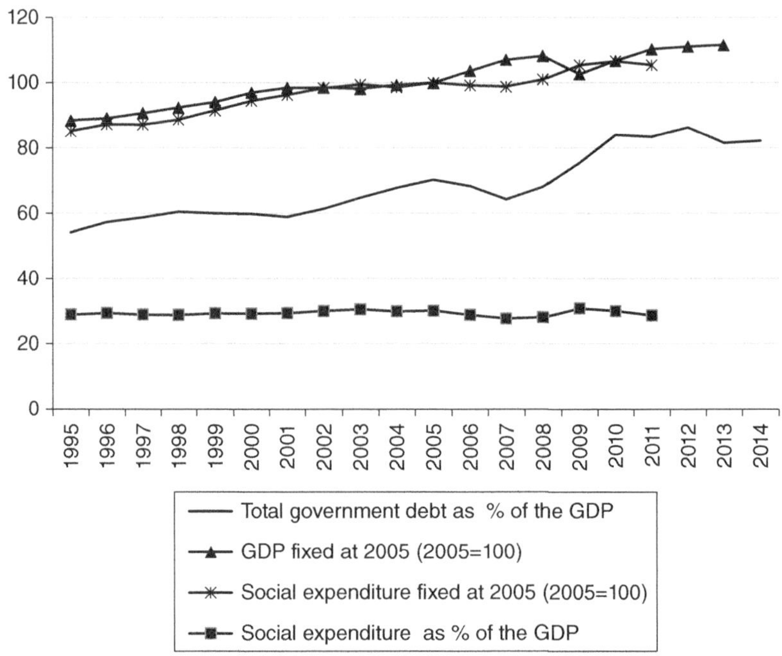

Figure 4.3. GDP, government debt, and social expenditure, Germany (1995–2014)
Source: EUROSTAT (2015); Statistisches Bundesamt (2015).

understanding of the crisis situation and establish a fair exchange of interests, with wage and employment stabilization as key instruments, supported by social policies.

The direct responses to the crisis can be divided into three parts (for the following description cf. Schelkle, 2012 and Eichhorst and Weishaupt, 2013). The first and immediate response aimed at stabilizing financial markets and preventing a domino effect after the collapse of Lehman Brothers in early September 2008. The second response aimed at stabilizing macroeconomic demand, and the third at preventing a rise in unemployment. The stabilization programmes were substantial and had wide coverage, including the core workforce and average families. It seems that these measures were successful in preventing a deep recession and a rise in unemployment. Yet they were not targeted at those most in need.

The first and immediate crisis response was a peculiar combination of two actions that could not be more different. A first technocratic step was to set up a huge fund to stabilize banks in crisis or invest in public ownership of banks. Banks in crisis were not in fact nationalized, but were bought by the state. This policy was effective, but also highly expensive for the state in the long run. A domino effect was thereby prevented, at the cost of a huge increase in public debt. The second action was a public statement of guarantee, by which the dramatic nature of the crisis became obvious to everyone. On 5 October 2008 Chancellor Merkel (Christian Democratic Union—CDU) and Minister of Finance Steinbrück (Social Democratic Party—SPD) declared on television that the state would guarantee all bank deposits in Germany held by private households. This was both an alarming and a calming announcement. It made it dramatically clear how severe the situation actually was, and at the same time promised security. In the end, it turned out that the public accepted the promise and the alarming news did not lead to a run on the banks.

The second direct response to the crisis was stabilization of macroeconomic demand. This aim was realized by three consecutive stimulus packages that combined tax relief and public spending programmes. These measures were targeted at key industries and the core workforce. Altogether, public expenditure on the three packages amounted to around €70 billion, which was about 2.8 per cent of GDP in 2010 (Statistisches Bundesamt, 2011). The stabilization fund for banks is not included in this figure. A prominent feature of the stimulus package was a subsidy for scrapping older cars and replacing them with new, more ecological ones. A premium of €2,500 was paid to individuals for each car replaced. The car-scrapping scheme was negotiated between state, employers, and trade unions. The stimulus package also included tax reliefs for firms and families, as well as a single flat-rate payment of €100 for each child. Aid to families was substantial, but not targeted at those most in need.

The third response aimed at stabilizing employment. The main instrument used for this was the short-work programme (*Kurzarbeit*) which had long been in existence. In the past, this programme had allowed firms that were in temporary economic difficulties to reduce the working time of their staff, and thereby also the wage bill, for a specified period. The loss in wages was then partly compensated for by a temporary short-work payment by the public employment office, at a rate of 60 per cent for persons without children and 67 per cent for those with. The programme was attractive to both employers and the state: the former could keep their core workforce, while the latter could prevent an immediate rise in unemployment. During the crisis, entitlement to this programme was relaxed and coverage widely extended. The possible payment period was prolonged to twenty-four months in 2009, but reduced again to eighteen months in 2010, once the situation had begun to improve. Before the crisis, the regular payment period was six months. Data show how significant this programme was in preventing a rise in unemployment (Figure 4.4). In 2009, around 1.2 million workers on average participated in the programme, and in 2010 the figure was still around 500,000. In 2011, then, under improved economic conditions, the number fell to pre-crisis levels of around 100,000 workers. Overall, the estimate is that the programme helped to stabilize around 500,000 full-time jobs during the crisis (Schelkle, 2012).

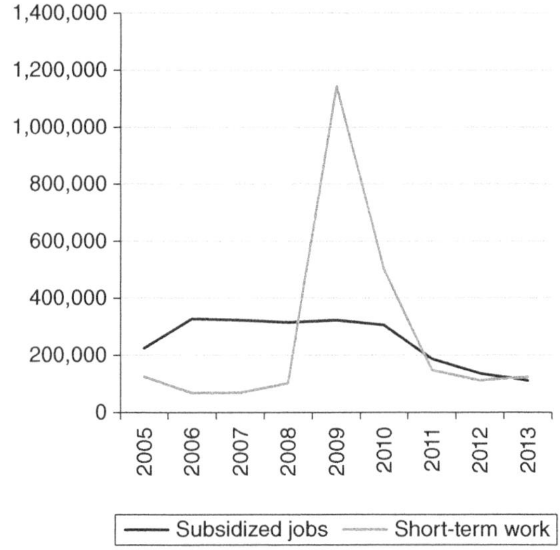

Figure 4.4. Impact of short-term work programme, Germany (2005–2013)
Source: Bundesagentur für Arbeit: Arbeitsmarkt in Deutschland—Zeitreihen bis 2013, S. 62.

4.3. CHILD POVERTY BEFORE, DURING, AND AFTER THE GREAT RECESSION

Inequality in household market incomes steadily increased in Germany from the beginning of the 1990s until 2005. Inequality in disposable incomes and poverty rates also increased in the first half of the 1990s, then decreased and stabilized during the second half of the 1990s, thanks to social policy interventions (an increase in child allowances and in the tax-free minimum subsistence income, both initiated by the German Federal Constitutional Court).

The following empirical analyses are based on the German Socio-Economic Panel (SOEPv30l).[1] This is a representative longitudinal survey of individuals and households, which started in 1984 in West Germany and was extended to eastern Germany in June 1990, even before the formal reunification (Wagner et al., 2007; 2008). The database has been permanently refreshed with new sub-samples. The analyses for the years 2001 to 2013 are based on almost 20,000 individual observations per year for the entire population of Germany.

With the ongoing increase in inequality of market incomes at the beginning of the new millennium, we observe a corresponding increase of inequality in

[1] For continuous information on material deprivation, data from the EU Statistics on Income and Living Conditions (EU-SILC) have additionally been considered.

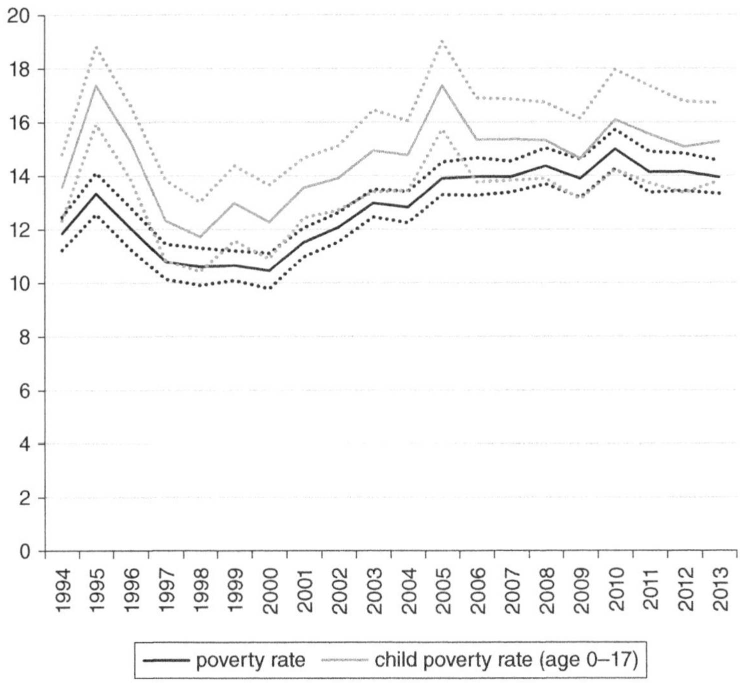

Figure 4.5. Poverty rates, Germany (1994–2013)

Source: Authors' calculations using the German Socio-Economic Panel (SOEP) v30l.

disposable incomes and poverty rates. Developments in child poverty followed the same trends at higher levels until 2005 (Figure 4.5), with a reduction in child poverty during the second half of the 1990s (as families with children benefited from the social policy changes), and a big new increase in child poverty rates afterwards, at the beginning of the new millennium.

4.3.1. Development of Inequality and Poverty

Figure 4.6 (a–d) summarizes the main trends in the development of income distribution from 2001 to 2013 in four periods before, during, and after the Great Recession, according to an income stratification based on disposable household income.[2] The population figures (Figure 4.6a) indicate a decline in

[2] This income stratification uses equal relative income thresholds (instead of equal population shares, like the quantiles)—each category includes income gains up to 30 per cent, starting from the median (Krause, 2016).

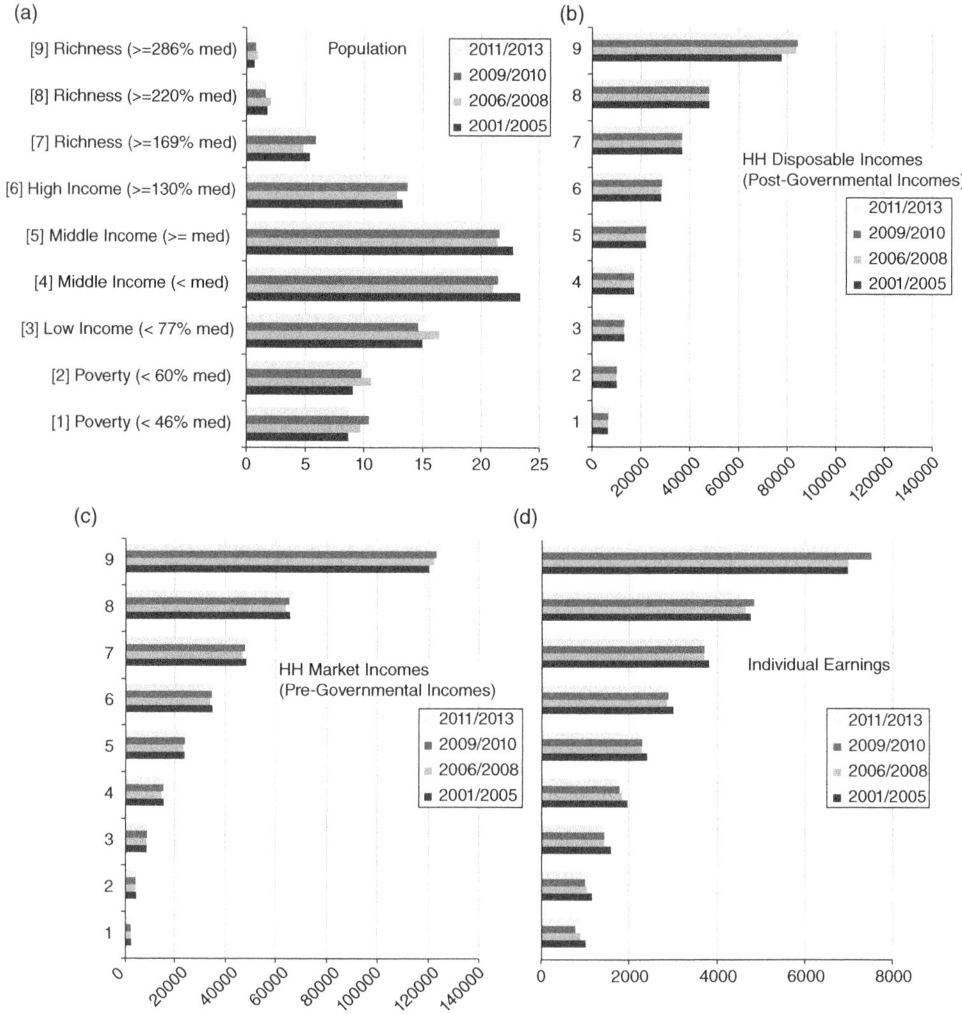

Figure 4.6. (a-d). Trends in income distribution in Germany before, during, and after the Great Recession

Source: Authors' calculations using SOEP.

middle incomes after the first period. It appears that the share of the very poor increased up until the recession, and declined thereafter. The size of post-tax, post-transfer income (i.e. disposable income) (Figure 4.6b) remained remarkably stable throughout the decade—with almost no real gains at any level, apart from for the richest (whose incomes increased further after 2005 as well, but at a lower rate). Pre-tax, pre-transfer household gross income (i.e. household market income) (Figure 4.6c) is much more unevenly distributed in

Germany, with lower income values for the poor and higher values for the wealthy. However, the development during the recession is quite similar to that of the post-governmental figures. Finally, individual earnings (Figure 4.6d) indicate diminishing income in real terms, especially at lower- and middle-income levels—not just during the recession period.

Figure 4.7 summarizes for the same periods the trends in median disposable income and poverty rates from a life-cycle perspective. The periodic means indicate that real income levels remained almost the same until 2010, and increased thereafter; meanwhile poverty levels increased before the recession period and remained high afterwards. The differentiations according to age reveal an increase in median income levels for young age groups also, even during the recession period. The poverty rates for younger ages decreased correspondingly, but the poverty rate for prime-age adults remained even lower through the period of the crisis. These figures illustrate that the German response to the crisis focused on safeguarding the prime-age labour force, with positive effects for (young) children living in the household.

In line with long-term economic development, we observe an increase in income poverty until 2005. After that, the poverty rates remained stable at a higher level, with a brief and modest increase at the time of the recession (Figure 4.5). Child poverty rates show almost the same development at a higher level, with a peak in 2005. After 2005, the child poverty rate approached the poverty rate for the population as a whole, thereafter remaining only marginally higher.[3] Again, there was a short-term spike at the time of the recession. Poverty gaps increased further at the time of the recession and declined afterwards. Poverty gaps for children were significantly higher than those for the population as a whole until 2005, but thereafter they declined to a level marginally below—with another spike in the years of recession (Figure 4.8). The development of child poverty in Germany over these periods may be summarized as a decline from higher levels to more or less the same as the (increased) overall poverty rate for the entire population. The brief (and small) spike at the time of the recession seems to be somewhat stronger for child poverty—especially in terms of the poverty gap.

[3] These analyses refer to SOEPv30l (1984–2013). Later data versions (SOEPv31l, 1984–2014) include further samples for households with children and migrants and include also further differentiations of the weighting scheme for the migrant population. Analyses on poverty and child poverty show therefore in 2014 slightly higher rates, though the overall long-term trend remains the same.

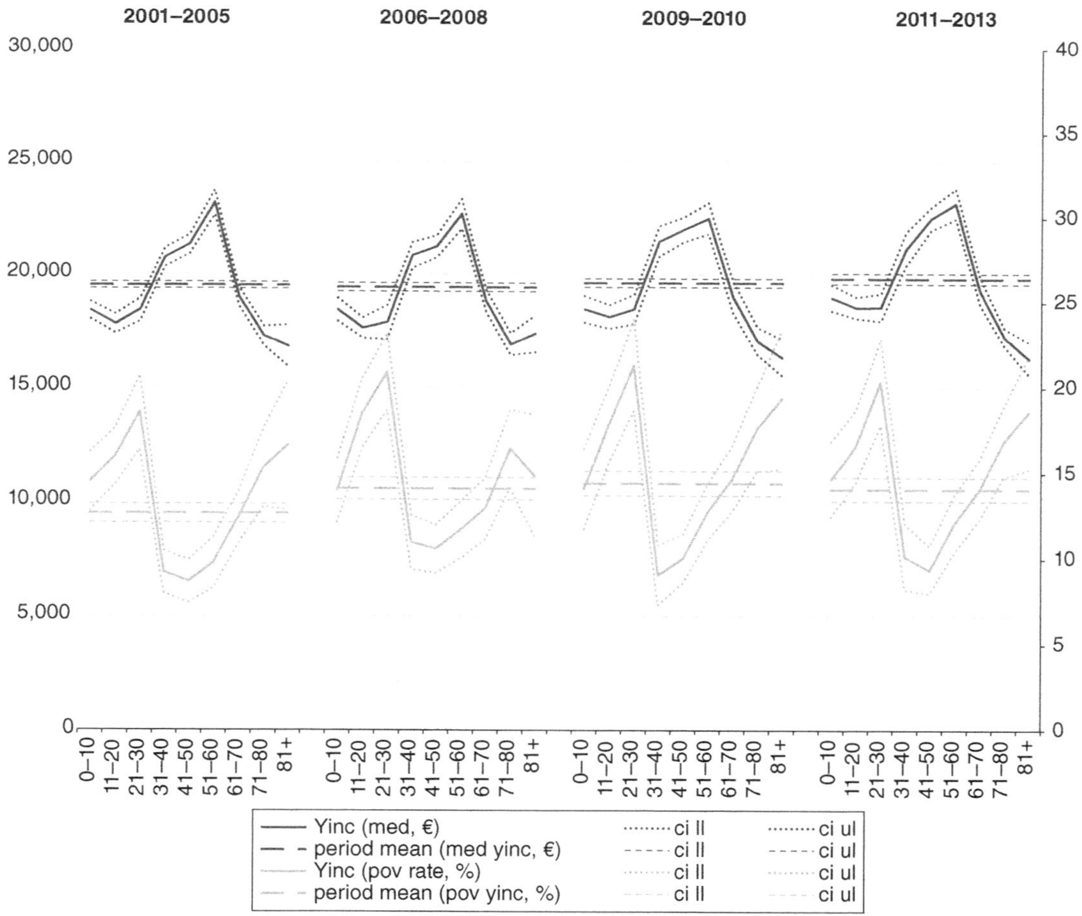

Figure 4.7. Trends in median disposable income and poverty rates, Germany (2001–2013)

Source: Authors' calculations using SOEP.

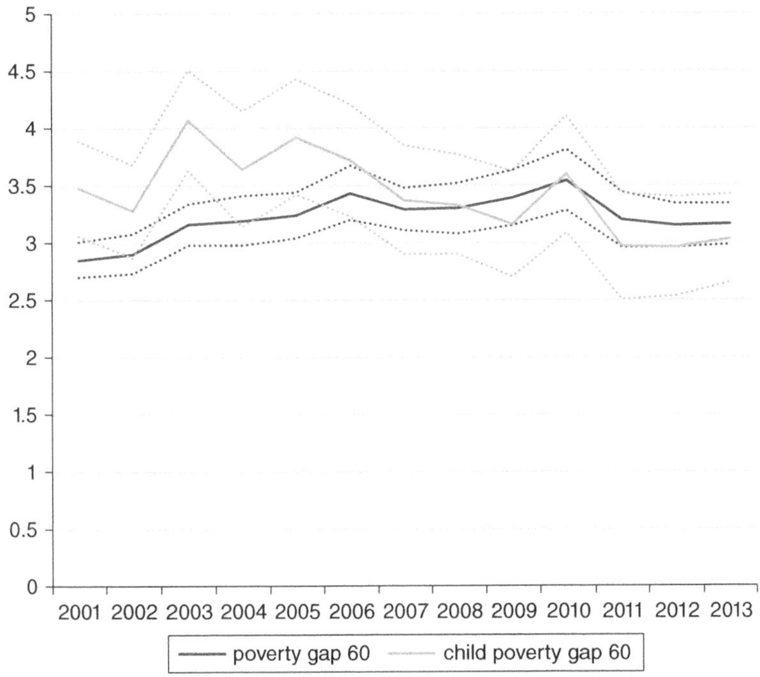

Figure 4.8. Poverty gaps, Germany (2001–2013)
Source: Authors' calculations using SOEP.

4.3.2. Children: Economic Well-being, Risks of Poverty, and Social Policy Impacts

In a long-term perspective, children have usually experienced lower levels of material well-being and higher risks of poverty than the overall population. This discrepancy has been more or less eliminated in Germany since the millennium. The short spikes in the poverty rates at the time of the recession did not change this overall trend. Nevertheless the equivalized mean and median values of pre- and post-governmental incomes are lower for children than for the total population—which also reflects the different stages in income development during the life-cycle for parents with young children (Table 4.1). Indicators of inequality, such as the Gini coefficient and the Palma ratio,[4] confirm consistently high levels of inequality and a strong social policy impact due to the quite high differences between pre- and post-governmental

[4] The Palma ratio has been adapted as an indicator of inequality from the newly established Social Development Goals (SDG, indicator 10.1). It reflects here the income ratio of the richest 10 per cent to the poorest 40 per cent.

Table 4.1. Indicators on income, inequality, and poverty for children in Germany before, during, and after the recession

	2001–2005		2006–2008		2009–2010		2011–2013	
	total	age 0–17	total	age 0–17	total	age 0–17	total	age 0–17
Annual disposable household income (mean, €, 2013)	21848	19691	22239	20278	22424	20583	22883	21218
Household market income (Mean, €, 2013)	23614	23787	23609	23759	24074	24209	24753	25439
Annual disposable household income (median, €, 2013)	19494	18032	19402	18139	19567	18387	19794	18833
Household market income (median, €, 2013)	20290	21567	19641	21275	20310	21748	20627	22092
Palma ratio (household disposable income)	0.929	0.844	1.044	0.935	1.024	0.895	1.035	0.928
Palma ratio (household market income)	3.037	1.551	3.412	1.824	3.057	1.647	3.105	1.740
Gini (household disposable income)	0.265	0.245	0.286	0.263	0.284	0.257	0.286	0.264
Gini (household market income)	0.489	0.368	0.508	0.396	0.495	0.381	0.498	0.390
Redistribution rate (excl. pensions)	*0.458*	*0.334*	*0.437*	*0.336*	*0.426*	*0.325*	*0.426*	*0.323*
Poverty rate (household disposable income)	12.7	14.9	14.1	15.3	14.4	15.4	14.1	15.3
Poverty rate (household market income)	33.9	21.4	35.5	23.9	34.5	22.5	34.2	22.1
Redistribution rate (excl. pensions)	*0.625*	*0.304*	*0.603*	*0.360*	*0.583*	*0.316*	*0.588*	*0.308*
Poverty rate (anchored 2008)	[13.0]	[15.2]	[14.6]	[15.8]	14.5	15.6	13.7	14.6
Poverty gap (fgt1*100)	3.070	3.675	3.342	3.478	3.465	3.379	3.171	2.988
Poverty rate at 50% of median	7.2	8.5	7.9	8.4	8.3	8.1	7.7	7.5
Poverty gap at 50% of median (fgt1*100)	1.718	2.084	1.808	1.788	1.902	1.796	1.664	1.369
Long-term poverty rate	7.1	8.1	8.2	8.4	8.4	7.1	8.4	8.1
Material deprivation (Ind[4/9], SOEP)	8.9	12.6	12.3	17.0	-	-	9.1	10.2
Material deprivation (Ind[3/8], EU-SILC)	9.4	9.7	10.9	12.5	10.2	10.9	10.3	10.0
Multidimensional poverty rate (AF,33—Ind[5])	12.6	12.9	13.9	13.1	13.7	13.0	14.0	12.6
mfgt1[*100] (AF,33—Ind[5])	3.457	3.620	3.776	3.405	3.760	3.301	3.700	2.983
mfgt2[*100] (AF,33—Ind[5])	1.434	1.528	1.533	1.338	1.526	1.293	1.480	1.104
Multidimensional poverty rate (CSPI,TH2—Ind[5])	10.5	10.7	11.6	10.8	11.5	10.2	11.7	10.3
mfgt1[*100] (CSPI,TH2—Ind[5])	2.587	2.601	2.864	2.395	2.864	2.224	2.808	2.071
mfgt2[*100] (CSPI,TH2—Ind[5])	1.091	1.094	1.188	0.927	1.184	0.868	1.145	0.756

Source: Authors' calculations using SOEP.

incomes. According to the Gini coefficient, the comparatively high inequality in pre-tax, pre-transfer incomes in Germany is reduced by social policy impacts: by more than 40 per cent for the total population and by more than 30 per cent for children (the rate is lower, as parents of younger children have higher labour market participation rates, and therefore usually higher market incomes). Similarly poverty rates are reduced by about 60 per cent for the entire population and by about 30 per cent for children.[5]

The overall mean and median income values do not indicate any systematic negative impact on the economic well-being of children from the recession in general (Table 4.1). However, the more differentiated indicators on income poverty and deprivation show at least some peaks—referring to the vulnerability of children's economic conditions in a period of crisis. The income decrease during the crisis affected higher incomes as well. Therefore in the recession, inequality in market incomes was lower than in the boom period before. Accordingly, pre-governmental poverty was somewhat lower during the recession.

The massive (social) policy efforts to overcome the crisis do not show up in conventional pre-to-post-governmental income measures. Nevertheless they worked. The anchored poverty line (here fixed at the survey year 2008, when annual incomes showed the highest value) indicates marginally higher poverty rates for the recession period and lower values afterwards. Indicators of poverty using stronger poverty lines[6] (50 per cent median) show ongoing (and increasingly) high levels of poverty rates and poverty gaps, with a decrease after the crisis for the total population; for children, however, the poverty rates and gaps decreased after 2005. Long-term poverty rates also increased after 2005 and remained high during and after the recession for the total population, but show more ups and downs for children. Material deprivation rates[7] were at their highest after 2005 and decreased thereafter—for the population as a whole and for children.

Multidimensional income poverty measures provide further robust insights into the development of poverty risks, as modifications to incomes (with imputed rent, after housing costs, monthly income screener)[8] are considered

[5] Poverty rates for pre-governmental income (market income) are based on the same poverty lines as the post-governmental income (disposable income).

[6] These poverty measures are also discussed in the context of SDG indicators (Kroll, 2015).

[7] Material deprivation measures for the SOEP refer to the years 2001, 2003, 2005, 2007, 2011, 2013 considering nine items, five of them identical to EU-SILC. For EU-SILC, measures for all years from 2005 to 2013 are available for eight items. Deprivation scores are treated as 1 if at least a third of the items are indicated as lacking (in case of the SOEP, four out of nine, and three out of eight for EU-SILC), and as 0 otherwise (following the usual dual cut-off threshold of 33 per cent for multidimensional poverty applications).

[8] The multidimensional measures of income poverty are related to five alternative household income measures (annual incomes for the previous year, current monthly incomes, annual incomes including imputed rent, annual incomes after housing costs, and monthly incomes

together with the single-item-based view of poverty. Multidimensional measures are applied here for ordinal and cardinal cases (MFGT0,1,2),[9] based on two alternative approaches—the Dual Cut-off method, according to the Alkire–Foster (AF) approach (Alkire and Foster 2011a; 2011b; Alkire et al. 2015), and the Correlation Sensitive Poverty Index (CSPI), developed by Rippin (2012; 2014). Both measurement approaches indicate an increase in multidimensional income poverty after 2005 for the total population, followed by an almost stable trend thereafter; meanwhile the rates for children remained almost the same according to the AF approach, or declined according to the CSPI approach. The ordinal poverty rates for children almost converged with those of the entire population, while the cardinal rates of poverty gaps for children (MFGT1,2) after 2005 are even lower than the corresponding values for the entire population.

Similar findings show up if we consider individual characteristics for all adult members of households with young children.[10] Regarding labour market performance, we observe a small increase in rates for low earnings for the total population and for households with children after 2005, and a decline after the recession (Table 4.2). High dependency ratios[11] declined marginally for the total population and remained almost stable for households with children at the time of the recession. The employment-to population ratio[12] increased after 2001 and the low-employment-to-population ratio declined for households with children during and after the recession. The work-intensity rates[13]

after housing costs). The poverty thresholds refer in each case to 60 per cent of equivalent median incomes for the total population.

[9] MFGT refers to the multidimensional version of the well-established poverty measure by Foster, Greer, and Thorbecke (1984; 2010) indicating the incidence, intensity, and inequality of poverty.

[10] In this grouping of 'Households with children' the parents and other adult household members are also considered in order to indicate the social and economic background for the living conditions of children.

[11] Dependency ratios are here adapted as household ratios—the sum of the number of young and elderly people at an age when both groups are generally economically inactive (i.e. under 15 years of age and aged 65 and over), compared to the number of people of working age (i.e. 15–64).

[12] Employment-to-population ratio—OECD indicator, here adapted as a household ratio. The household (HH) employment-to-population ratio is defined as the proportion of the household's working-age population that is employed: number of employed persons (main activity status) of working age (15–64) in the household/total number of persons of working age (15–64) in the household.

[13] Work intensity is measured at the household level according to the EU-SILC methodology, with consideration of part-time work. EU-SILC: 18–64, without dependent children, part-time weight—based on the main activity status in the previous year. Activity status refers to the number of months in the previous year which the person has given information about (the 'workable' months) and the number of months in the previous year for which the person has been classified as 'at work' (paid employment, full time, or part time; paid apprenticeship or training under special schemes related to employment; self-employment (with or without employees, including unpaid work in family enterprise). Working time (hours/week) for part-time work and mini-jobs are in SOEP operationalized as a proportion of yearly mean values for at least six months of work in the previous year relative to full employed (thirty-five hours/week).

Table 4.2. Indicators on earnings, work, and subjective well-being for households in Germany with children before, during, and after the recession

	2001–2005		2006–2008		2009–2010		2011–2013	
	total	hh.child < 18	total	hh.child < 18	total	hh.child < 18	total	hh.child < 18
Individual earnings (mean, €, 2013)	2649	2643	2563	2552	2578	2543	2540	2559
Individual wages/h (mean, €, 2013)	17.0	17.4	16.5	16.9	17.0	17.2	16.6	17.2
Individual earnings (median, €, 2013)	2387	2358	2262	2200	2263	2136	2255	2132
Individual wages/h (median, €, 2013)	15.0	15.4	14.5	15.0	14.5	14.9	14.2	14.7
Low earnings (<66% median)	29.9	32.9	31.4	35.4	31.9	35.8	30.6	32.9
Low wages/h (<66% median)	23.5	23.3	25.4	24.6	24.9	24.4	23.6	22.1
Household dependency ratio (total) %	53.9	93.5	50.7	93.0	47.9	93.0	48.6	94.0
Household dependency Ratio (child) %	46.0	92.9	43.2	92.9	40.1	92.5	40.7	93.3
Household dependency ratio (old age) %	7.9	0.6	7.6	0.7	7.8	0.5	7.9	0.7
Household high dependency ratio (>0.5)	*10.3*	*19.0*	*9.4*	*18.4*	*9.0*	*18.9*	*9.0*	*18.6*
Household employment-to-population ratio	68.8	69.7	70.9	71.9	74.4	76.1	75.4	76.0
Household low employment-to-population ratio (<0.5)	20.2	16.7	19.1	16.1	17.0	14.1	16.2	13.6
Household work intensity	67.3	71.1	67.7	69.9	69.9	72.5	71.1	73.9
Household low work intensity (<=0.2)	10.4	6.3	10.4	7.7	9.1	6.1	9.1	6.5
Satisfaction with life (mean 0–10)	6.9	7.0	6.8	7.0	6.9	7.0	7.0	7.2
Satisfaction with household income (mean 0–10)	6.2	6.0	6.0	6.0	6.2	6.2	6.5	6.5
Satisfaction with labour/work (mean 0–10)	6.8	6.9	6.7	6.8	6.7	6.8	6.9	7.0
Worries financial situation (% big worries)	22.9	28.2	25.0	30.1	24.0	27.9	18.8	20.9
Worries economic development (% big worries)	43.0	41.1	32.1	31.9	40.7	38.1	20.8	19.7

Source: Authors' calculations using SOEP.

increased almost steadily from 2001 until 2010 for the total population and for households with children. As a consequence, there were very few households with low work intensity at the time of the recession—indicating the high affinity to the labour market of households with children in periods of economic crisis.

Subjective indicators of life satisfaction, as well as of satisfaction with work and household income, indicate an increase after the recession for the population as a whole, as well as for those living in households with young children. Worries on the own financial situation were higher for members of households with young children, but declined after the recession—as they did for the population as a whole. Major concerns for overall economic development differed less between the population as a whole and those living in households with young children—these rates of overall economic worries declined from 40 per cent to 20 per cent after the recession, an impressive indicator for the end of the subjective financial burden after the crisis.

4.3.3. Sociodemographic Characteristics of Children in Poverty

Poverty rates for young children have converged with those for the entire population since the beginning of the new millennium, whereas the poverty rates of young adults have increased. Further sociodemographic differentiations indicate how the recession has affected child poverty in different groups (Table 4.3).

The youngest children, up to the age of 11, show the lowest poverty rates within the young under-30 population. Young adults endured the highest poverty rates of all age groups until 2010. After 2010, when the overall poverty rates remained high, we also observe a surge in poverty risks for the elderly. People with a background of direct and indirect migration are at higher risk of poverty, but do not show much variation over time since 2005. People living in eastern Germany have a higher risk of poverty, but they seem to have been even less affected by the recession than those living in western Germany. Urban and rural areas differ in poverty risks, but showed no further differences during the recession. The poverty risks of individuals without a certificate of education, of unskilled workers, and of the unemployed further increased during the recession. In general, the poverty risks for the working population remained almost stable, but increased for non-working individuals in the recession period. Young single households and single-parent households with two or more children also experienced an increase in poverty risks since the recession, but the poverty risks of single-parent households with one child decreased again after the recession. A decrease in poverty rates after the recession can also be observed for post-family households (with the youngest child aged 18 or over)—it seems that

Table 4.3. Socio-demographic characteristics of child poverty in Germany before, during, and after the recession

Poverty line at 60% of median	*% of population*	Germany (total)			*% of population*	Households with children		
		Poverty rate				Poverty rate		
	2011–13	2005–8	2009–10	2011–13	*2011–13*	2005–8	2009–10	2011–13
Total population	*100.0*	14.1	14.4	14.1	*100.0*	14.6	14.1	13.9
Sex								
Male	*49.2*	12.6	12.8	13.0	*48.8*	12.9	12.8	12.8
Female	*50.8*	15.5	16.1	15.2	*51.2*	16.2	15.5	15.0
Age groups								
0–17	*15.4*	15.9	15.4	15.3	*43.3*	15.6	15.3	15.1
18–30	*14.8*	21.1	20.9	19.9	*10.7*	23.3	25.0	22.8
31–44	*18.0*	10.9	9.3	9.7	*30.0*	11.5	9.8	10.8
45–59	*23.8*	10.8	11.4	10.9	*15.6*	10.6	10.5	10.5
60–74	*18.8*	13.1	14.4	14.6	*0.4*	–	–	–
75+	*9.3*	16.2	20.9	18.3	*0.0*	–	–	–
Age groups in young population								
0–5	*12.8*	14.9	15.4	15.1	*19.9*	14.7	15.5	15.1
6–11	*17.7*	14.4	13.0	14.5	*28.0*	14.3	12.9	14.2
12–17	*20.4*	17.9	17.5	16.1	*32.3*	17.5	17.4	15.9
18–24	*24.8*	23.1	22.3	20.1	*11.3*	24.3	21.0	22.5
25–30	*24.3*	18.8	19.4	19.6	*8.5*	22.2	29.8	23.2
Migration background								
Without	*76.2*	12.2	12.6	12.5	*68.9*	12.6	12.0	11.8
Direct	*10.9*	24.1	25.5	22.8	*11.3*	21.2	21.8	19.9
Indirect	*12.9*	17.2	16.9	15.6	*19.8*	18.7	18.6	17.6
Region								
North-west	*42.5*	13.4	14.4	13.2	*44.4*	14.1	12.0	12.7
South-west	*34.2*	11.8	12.2	11.9	*35.1*	10.5	13.6	12.0
city state	*6.4*	16.8	15.2	16.0	*4.7*	23.8	22.2	15.7
East	*17.0*	19.3	18.9	19.8	*15.8*	23.0	18.8	21.0
Region type								
Urban	*68.1*	13.6	13.8	13.2	*68.5*	13.8	13.1	12.8
Rural	*31.9*	15.1	15.9	15.9	*31.6*	16.2	16.4	16.3
Municipality size (in thousands)								
<2	*6.0*	12.3	13.4	15.8	*6.4*	11.9	15.0	18.8
2–20	*33.8*	12.9	12.6	11.7	*34.5*	13.9	11.8	10.3
20–100	*28.2*	13.7	16.0	13.9	*31.1*	13.5	15.6	13.8
100–500	*15.3*	17.4	16.3	18.6	*13.6*	18.5	15.5	20.0
>500	*16.7*	14.4	14.1	14.5	*14.4*	15.8	14.6	14.8

(continued)

Table 4.3. Continued

Poverty line at 60% of median	*% of population*	Germany (total)			*% of population*	Households with children		
		Poverty rate				Poverty rate		
	2011–13	2005–8	2009–10	2011–13	*2011–13*	2005–8	2009–10	2011–13
Home ownership								
Owner	*50.0*	5.9	6.2	6.2	*51.9*	4.3	4.2	5.0
Tenant	*50.0*	21.3	22.4	21.9	*48.2*	24.5	24.8	23.5
Marital status								
Married, living together	*51.0*	8.7	9.1	8.7	*66.2*	8.2	8.3	8.2
Married, separated	*2.3*	24.4	18.7	21.3	*2.1*	34.9	32.8	30.4
Single	*29.6*	19.4	18.1	18.1	*25.8*	23.7	21.2	20.6
Divorced	*9.4*	23.8	25.2	25.0	*5.2*	32.8	35.4	32.9
Widowed	*7.7*	14.7	21.3	17.8	*0.6*	–	–	–
Education								
Without certificate	*9.1*	28.8	32.6	32.8	*7.1*	33.6	37.4	37.3
Uncompleted secondary school	*3.6*	15.3	14.9	17.6	*4.0*	19.4	20.4	26.5
Completed general secondary school	*24.4*	12.1	13.7	14.1	*16.0*	14.7	15.0	14.3
Completed intermediate secondary school	*24.4*	10.1	10.4	9.9	*28.3*	10.5	11.1	10.2
Completed grammar school	*9.7*	13.9	12.7	12.7	*10.2*	6.8	4.2	5.9
Other	*6.2*	24.5	26.7	24.4	*7.2*	23.3	25.5	24.7
College or university degree	*20.4*	5.0	5.3	5.0	*20.8*	5.4	4.2	3.7
In education/ training	*2.3*	18.2	15.1	14.7	*6.4*	18.0	14.8	16.2
Working status								
Full time	*38.8*	4.1	4.0	3.9	*45.7*	5.4	5.5	6.0
Part time	*17.9*	12.6	12.6	12.5	*29.6*	10.8	9.7	9.7
Unemployed	*5.7*	47.6	49.7	55.0	*7.0*	51.6	55.9	56.4
In education/ training	*3.9*	25.1	25.8	26.5	*5.0*	20.1	16.1	25.5
Not working	*33.7*	15.7	18.1	17.6	*12.7*	17.1	16.9	17.2

Occupation position								
Unskilled worker	*13.4*	16.1	19.1	16.7	*12.5*	19.2	21.5	20.2
Skilled worker, foreman	*13.0*	5.1	5.0	5.2	*12.9*	5.9	7.1	8.4
Self-employed	*10.1*	5.8	7.0	6.6	*9.6*	7.4	5.6	8.5
Apprentice, trainee	*4.1*	21.3	18.0	19.1	*3.9*	17.3	16.3	15.0
Employee with simple tasks	*14.4*	10.6	11.4	12.8	*15.5*	10.9	12.6	14.0
Qualified Professional	*24.2*	3.5	2.8	3.3	*23.7*	4.5	3.2	3.9
Managerial	*14.6*	1.4	1.7	1.7	*15.0*	0.9	0.7	0.9
Low/middle-level civil service	*1.9*	0.8	0.4	2.6	*2.2*	1.1	0.8	4.4
High-level civil service	*4.3*	1.0	1.6	1.7	*4.6*	0.9	0.7	0.4
Household size								
1	*20.3*	23.0	25.5	26.0				
2	*34.1*	11.7	11.9	11.0	*5.0*	45.4	45.6	36.2
3	*18.6*	13.3	12.7	10.0	*30.3*	16.3	15.3	12.2
4	*18.1*	8.2	7.8	8.8	*42.8*	8.3	8.7	9.6
5+	*8.9*	18.1	16.8	18.1	*22.0*	17.7	16.4	19.6
Head of household age								
16–34	*14.3*	23.2	24.3	22.7	*17.8*	22.2	25.7	22.1
35–54	*45.6*	11.8	10.8	10.9	*78.1*	12.6	11.4	12.1
55–74	*29.7*	12.6	14.1	13.7	*4.1*	14.4	14.2	13.7
75+	*10.4*	15.7	19.8	17.4	*0.01*	–	–	–
Household members								
Head (m|f)	*53.4*	16.0	16.8	16.5	*30.8*	16.0	15.6	14.6
Partner (m|f)	*22.8*	9.1	9.3	8.7	*19.8*	9.7	9.3	9.1
Child < 18	*15.2*	15.6	15.3	15.1	*43.2*	15.6	15.3	15.1
Child >=18	*8.1*	13.2	12.3	11.0	*6.0*	17.7	13.8	18.0
Others	*0.5*	–	–	–	*0.1*	–	–	–
Household type								
Single	*20.3*	23.0	25.5	26.0				
Partner	*30.5*	9.0	9.3	9.0				
Family	*30.7*	10.2	9.4	9.7	*87.4*	10.2	9.4	9.7
Single-parent	*4.4*	45.4	47.3	43.3	*12.6*	45.4	47.3	43.3
Post-parent	*13.7*	10.7	10.6	8.0				
Other	*0.4*	–	–	–				

(*continued*)

Table 4.3. Continued

Poverty line at 60% of median	*% of population*	Germany (total)			*% of population*	Households with children		
		Poverty rate				Poverty rate		
	2011–13	2005–8	2009–10	2011–13	*2011–13*	2005–8	2009–10	2011–13
Household type, detail								
Single, <35	*4.2*	35.5	37.1	37.2				
Single, 35–54	*5.3*	16.9	15.5	17.6				
Partner, <35	*3.7*	11.9	6.7	7.4				
Partner, 35–54	*6.1*	4.4	3.5	2.9				
Family, 1 child	*13.3*	9.6	8.8	7.7	*37.8*	9.6	8.8	7.7
Family, 2 children	*12.8*	8.3	7.6	8.9	*36.5*	8.3	7.6	8.9
Family, 3+ children	*4.6*	16.9	16.0	17.8	*13.1*	16.9	16.0	17.8
Family, adult child(ren)	*10.7*	7.7	6.6	5.1				
Single-parent, 1 child	*2.4*	44.9	43.0	35.6	*6.8*	44.9	43.0	35.6
Single-parent, 2+ children	*2.0*	46.0	52.3	52.4	*5.8*	46.0	52.3	52.4
Single-parent, adult child (ren)	*3.0*	21.4	24.1	18.6				
Partner, 55–74	*15.2*	9.5	10.8	10.9				
Partner, 75+	*5.5*	11.9	14.6	11.6				
Single, 55–74	*6.7*	21.9	25.5	25.3				
Single, 75+	*4.2*	20.7	27.6	26.5				
Single + others	*0.4*	–	–	–				

Source: Authors' calculations using SOEP.

during the recession more young adults remained in (or went back to) the parental home in order to share and reduce living expenses.

4.4. POLICIES AND DEBATES

In Germany, the policies that were enacted during the crisis should be seen in a longer-term perspective. There are, first, long-term institutional features of the German welfare system that are responsible for a number of structural problems related to child poverty. These conditions continue to have a profound impact, even if some significant policy reforms took place before the crisis. There is, second, the impact of the reforms enacted in the early

2000s in three major fields that are very relevant to our study: labour market governance, minimum income protection, and family policy. Reforms in the first two areas were closely connected to each other. Both responded to a crisis on the labour market, where there were high unemployment rates and very high long-term unemployment rates. This 'crisis before the crisis' culminated in 2004–5 in the highest unemployment rates measured since the 1950s. In the third area, family policy, significant reforms began in the early 2000s. These reforms supported a dual-earner model, after a long time in which the male-breadwinner model had been the *Leitbild* of German family policy.

As in Sweden, perhaps, it was the experience of an earlier crisis that helped to mitigate the impact of the most recent crisis. In contrast to Sweden, however, the new policies did not have time to change the existing welfare and labour model, because the period of time between the two crises was too short. Therefore, despite these reforms, the long-term institutional conditions of the German welfare system continued to have a strong impact on the structural problems related to child poverty. As shown in the previous section, child poverty was barely affected by the recent crisis; but nor did it decline when the economic conditions began to improve. The reasons for this 'stickiness' are rooted in two fundamental institutional conditions that characterize the Germany welfare system: the Bismarckian type of social insurance, with earnings-related benefits (Bosch, 2015) and a male-breadwinner model in which female partners, especially mothers, are often regarded as secondary earners (Pfau-Effinger, 2004). In social life, both conditions have seen some erosion over recent decades, but their institutional underpinnings are still partly in place. At the same time, the number of jobs for the low-qualified workforce has declined (especially in industry) and wages for this group have been low (especially in services). Assortative mating has further enforced the polarization between households with different qualifications. The social insurance system has little to offer families that suffer from these problems. As a consequence, the German labour market has a comparatively high share of long-term unemployed persons, in spite of declining overall unemployment since 2005; this means that the share of persons who have been unemployed for more than twelve months has remained relatively stable. There is also a growing share of low-paid earners (Holst and Dörre, 2013). For both long-term unemployed and working poor there is mainly the minimum income protection system (Bahle et al., 2011). However, it grants benefits that are below the relative income poverty threshold. The number of recipients in this scheme peaked in 2006 at more than 7.2 million people aged 20–65 (11.3 per cent of the age group), and since then has declined. Expenditure also peaked in that year at about 1.0 per cent of GDP, or 3.7 per cent of total social expenditure (Bahle et al., 2011: 170, 183). In addition, the male-breadwinner model has also been eroding (Trappe et al., 2015). Still in 2013, however, only 15 per cent of couples with children below 18 had both partners working full time; in 45 per cent of cases, one partner worked full time and the other part time; and in 30 per cent of cases, only one of the partners worked[14] (OECD Family Database). This is still a very traditional division of labour. Though the proportion of dual-income earners has grown, women (especially mothers) still face huge difficulties in entering employment and earning an adequate income. This is the case because the policy changes started only recently, and therefore have not yet solved the strong structural problems related to full-time work for mothers. These difficulties are greatest for large families and single-mother families, rather than for single fathers. Single parenthood is not the real issue; single motherhood is (Chzhen and Bradshaw, 2012).

The erosion of industrial employment and the decline of the male-breadwinner model have gone hand in hand and have resulted in structural problems, especially (but not exclusively) for low-qualified parents and single mothers. Low-qualified workers (including many migrant families) and single mothers (with few migrants) are the groups that are most at risk of poverty (Geißler, 2014; Goebel and Krause, 2016). These problems can analytically be located at three stages: difficult integration into work, low earnings, and inadequate social protection. In the following part of the chapter, those policies that focus on these problems are analysed, taking into account developments during the crisis and their potential impact on child poverty. Two policy areas are analysed in more detail: family policies and minimum income protection (see Bahle, 2008, and Bahle et al., 2010, for comparative-international overviews of these areas).

4.4.1. Difficult Integration into Work

The first locus of problems is integration into work. Low work intensity is usually strongly related to poverty (Graaf-Zijl and Nolan, 2011). This problem is manifested in persistent long-term unemployment and part-time work. Germany is characterized by both a high share of long-term unemployed and a high proportion of part-time jobs, of which many have few working hours (so-called mini-jobs). Low-qualified persons are mainly affected by the first; mothers with children by the second. Therefore children living in these households have a high risk of poverty. Mothers still face difficulties in combining childcare and paid work. Lack of childcare facilities and short school hours often allow only part-time work.

[14] In addition, in around 5% of couples both partners do not work and in another 5% other working constellations exist, for example part-time/part-time.

Table 4.4 therefore illustrates how the interaction of low work intensity and poverty, in association with low earnings and low wages, has affected households with children during the period of recession. As shown before, the poverty rates, as well as the rates for low earnings and low wages, remained almost unchanged after 2005 during the crisis—for the total population, as well as for households with children. Low work-intensity rates decreased for households with children during the crisis, indicating greater pressure for labour market participation during the recession period. Correspondingly, during the recession period we observe an increase in poverty rates among households with children that have low earnings or low wages. The same can be observed for low work-intensity rates—these rates also show a sharp increase for households with children in poverty, with low earnings, or with low wages in the period of recession. Households with children are clearly quite sensitive to labour market conditions, and the interrelationship between work intensity, low earnings, low wages, and poverty increased in the crisis period.

Long-term unemployment is addressed by qualification and activation policies, which have been extended since 2005 (Dingeldey, 2011; Heidenreich and Aurich-Beerheide, 2014). These policies were implemented as part of a reform package that fundamentally changed labour market governance in Germany. In 2001, the so-called Job-AQTIV Law (in force since 1 January 2002) intensified assistance for unemployed persons through a broad range of measures, including counselling, training, employment assistance, and personal assistance. In 2002, the labour market was significantly deregulated (in force since January and April 2003). In particular, new forms of small part-time jobs were created, each endowed with low social security rights: the so-called mini- and midi-jobs, and a new form of self-employment subsidized by the state (so-called 'Ich-AG'). The idea of these new jobs was that they would become a springboard for the unemployed on their way (back) onto the labour market. Parallel to these measures, the conditions for unemployment insurance benefits were tightened up, in particular the obligation to take another job (requiring fewer qualifications and offering less pay) and the duration of benefits.

These reforms had resulted in a new, more flexible system of labour market governance before the crisis occurred. Despite some success since then, however, inactivity and unemployment rates are still disproportionally high among low-qualified persons. Activation has aimed primarily at bringing the unemployed into work, rather than at offering them qualifications. This policy has also resulted in more low-paid jobs. As a consequence, the poverty problem has partly been shifted from unemployment to low-paid work (Marx and Nolan, 2014). In contrast to countries like the UK, Germany has no strong support for low-income earners. There is no tax credit scheme, and social insurance contributions (proportional to wages) often place considerable pressure on low-earners.

Table 4.4. Poverty rates and low work intensity rates for households in Germany with children before, during, and after the recession

	2001–2005		2006–2008		2009–2010		2011–2013	
	total	hh.child < 18	total	hh.child < 18	total	hh.child < 18	total	hh.child < 18
Total rates								
Poverty rate (60% median)	12.7	14.9	14.1	15.3	14.4	15.4	14.1	15.3
Low earnings (< 66% median)	29.9	32.9	31.4	35.4	31.9	35.8	30.6	32.9
Low wages/h (< 66% median)	23.5	23.3	25.4	24.6	24.9	24.4	23.6	22.1
Household low work intensity (< =0.2)	10.4	6.3	10.4	7.7	9.1	6.1	9.1	6.5
Household poverty rates for individuals/households with								
low earnings (< 66% median)	75.2	70.2	76.7	68.9	79.9	73.2	75.8	66.6
Low wages/h (< 66% median)	64.9	58.2	68.5	58.2	67.6	65.2	63.4	55.3
HH low work intensity (< =0.2)	33.4	31.5	35.0	32.4	31.3	28.5	31.0	26.4
Low household work intensity rates for individuals/households with								
Poverty (60% median)	40.6	66.2	47.6	59.6	49.8	66.7	48.3	56.9
Low earnings (< 66% median)	60.5	73.7	64.4	82.6	66.9	84.5	63.4	78.7
Low wages/h (< 66% median)	57.1	64.3	60.1	59.4	49.7	80.1	57.7	64.9

Source: Authors' calculations using SOEP.

Part-time work is mainly a female risk, rooted in a traditional view of motherhood and its sticky institutional underpinnings. Tax law and the social security system still offer privileges to parents who follow a traditional gender role model (for an overview of existing benefits, see Prognos, 2014). The married couples' tax-splitting scheme is highly attractive to couples (with or without children) whose income differentials are high. A non-working partner has statutory healthcare and long-term care insurance without the payment of extra premiums. If the marriage is dissolved, the pension credits accumulated by both partners during marriage are usually split equally, which protects a non-working partner. If a working partner dies, the survivor receives a proportion of the deceased's pension. The strong male-breadwinner model with a non-working partner is on the retreat, but many couples with children still have one partner, usually the mother, who works part time (see above). This arrangement often functions well, because it is supported by policies; but problems often arise if the partnership is dissolved. Non-working mothers then often face huge problems if they want to return to the labour market. Lack of childcare is just one element; another is loss of work experience during the interruption to the career. It is therefore no surprise that in Germany more than a third of single mothers are unemployed (living on minimum income protection), and another third have only low earnings, on account of part-time work. In both cases, relative poverty is almost certain.

Single parenthood—or to be more precise, single motherhood—is an unresolved issue in the German welfare system. The share of single-parent families increased from 13.8 per cent in 1996 to 19.4 per cent in 2010 (Achatz et al., 2013). Single mothers are highly overrepresented among recipients of minimum income protection: around 40 per cent of single mothers depend on these benefits. The poverty rate of children living in such families is exceptionally high. Single mothers also remain in minimum income protection for a long time: the average duration of a spell of benefit receipt (not counting multiple spells) is 2.5 years (Achatz et al., 2013). Single parents who depend on minimum income protection differ from other single parents in certain respects. On average, they have more children, lower qualifications, and more health problems. Yet even highly qualified single parents face huge difficulties in finding a well-paid job. Not surprisingly, in 2008 some 92.0 per cent of single parents with low qualifications were either unemployed or low-wage earners (i.e. on less than two-thirds of median earnings); but even 40.3 per cent of highly qualified single parents are in the same situation (Bahle et al., 2015). These figures demonstrate that the main issue is not poor qualifications, but single-parenthood status, which is not adequately addressed in the German welfare system.

Lack of childcare also remains a problem, although several policy reforms since the early 2000s have significantly extended the number of childcare places. In 2004, a federal law required 230,000 additional places to be created in childcare facilities or family day care (*Tagesmütter*) by 2010. In 2008, another federal law established a legal right for a childcare place in a facility or in family day care for all children from the age of 1, with effect from 1 August 2013. To this end, the federal state provided €5.4 billion to the states (Länder) until 2014, and about €800 million per annum from 2015. The Länder (which have legal responsibility in this area) should cascade the federal funds down to local communities, which (together with non-profit organizations) are responsible for organizing the services. Thanks to these reforms and to the high investment in this area, childcare facilities have expanded in recent years, yet the gap between supply and demand remains a large one. In 2007, the federal state, the Länder, and the local communities agreed to increase childcare coverage for children under the age of 3 to 35 per cent by 2013 (Statistische Ämter des Bundes und der Länder, 2014). The increase needed to hit this target was 750,000 places, and at the time it was assumed that this would meet anticipated demand. Today, it is acknowledged that more places are needed, adding up to a coverage rate of about 40 per cent. The actual figures still fall a long way short of this threshold, however. Regional differences are still enormous and most places are available only part time. In March 2014, for example, the coverage rate for children below the age of 3 was 32.3 per cent for Germany (27.4 per cent in the western part, 52.0 per cent in the eastern). The total coverage rate for full-day places was only 17.5 per cent (12.0 per cent in the western part, 40 per cent in the eastern).

Coverage rates for children aged 3–6 have long been much higher, but again for this age group most places are provided part time. In March 2014, the coverage rate for this age group was 93.5 per cent in Germany, with no strong regional differences. The full-day coverage rate, however, was only 41.7 per cent, and again there were major regional differences: 34.1 per cent in the western part of the country and 72.6 per cent in the eastern. The problem of inadequate childcare is not confined to children below compulsory school age, however. In most primary schools (children aged 6–10), hours are only part time. Though more and more schools offer full-day hours, this process has only begun. Meanwhile most Länder and local communities support (and often require) the extension of full-day school hours. The major aim behind this policy is to improve the educational chances and integration prospects of disadvantaged children (Müller et al., 2014). Yet–partly as a side effect—the compatibility of school hours and parents' work arrangements is thereby also improved.

4.4.2. Low Earnings

The conditions for integration into work have been improved, but a structural problem remains, especially for low-qualified persons and single mothers. Yet even if integration into work is achieved, that does not mean that poverty is always overcome. Even with full-time employment, wages are often not high enough to prevent poverty among families (Marx and Nolan, 2014). The issue of low earnings is complex, however. In Germany, it has a lot to do with part-time work, mainly among women; but in recent years another problem has surfaced: low hourly wages. The shift from industrial to service-sector employment has widened the wage distribution and opened up a growing segment of low-paid work (Bosch, 2015). Moreover, privatization in the public sector has contributed strongly to the growth of low-paid work. Many low-paid, temporary, and part-time jobs revolve around the public sector, which has undergone fundamental change in recent years. The state itself is one of the main drivers of these problems. A third reason for the growth in low earnings is the eroding system of collective bargaining in Germany (Lohmann, 2009; Visser, 2010). Over the years, membership of trade unions has declined sharply, especially in the new states (Ebbinghaus and Göbel, 2014). Membership of firms in employers' associations has also declined, but still the organization rate is higher among employers than among employees. Paradoxically, it is actually the high membership rate of firms that ensures a high coverage rate of collective agreements: around 60 per cent of the labour force (Brandl, 2013). Nonetheless, the decline of collective agreements contributes to the growth of low pay in some sectors and regions of the economy, in particular in services and in the former German Democratic Republic (East Germany). Public services are being hollowed out by privatization, and private services are losing collectively binding wage agreements.

The issues of low earnings and working poverty were intensively debated before and during the crisis. For several years, the Social Democrats campaigned for a statutory minimum wage—something that was strongly opposed by the Christian Democrats. Trade unions themselves were long against a statutory minimum wage, because they feared losing power and influence. Recently most trade union officials have changed their opinion: they tend to think now that a statutory minimum wage can serve as a useful baseline for additional collective agreements above this level. Moreover, such a legal limit can prevent dumping wages in those sectors of the economy that are not covered by collective agreements. Finally, the minimum wage was included in the coalition agreement between the Christian Democrats and the Social Democrats and became law in 2014 (with effect from 2015). The minimum wage has not resulted in massive job losses, as critics feared, but there has also been no massive reduction in working poverty, as proponents had hoped. The design of the measure is simply oriented at individual wages, and cannot solve all the problems of low income for families with children. The level of the minimum wage is currently set at €8.50 per hour. This may lift a full-time working individual above the poverty line, but it definitely does not solve the problem of part-time work for single mothers and the problem of additional costs of children.

Unlike the UK, Germany has no effective tax credits for working families to lift them out of poverty. There is only a modest measure (introduced years before the crisis) which supports low-income families. This child benefit supplement (*Kindergeldzuschlag*) is paid to parents who earn at least €900 (couples) or €600 (single parents) per month, but would still be entitled to minimum income protection solely because they have children. The maximum amount of the child benefit supplement is €140 per month per child. The benefit cannot be combined with minimum income protection benefits. The maximum income limit for entitlement is equal to the minimum income protection entitlement for parents plus housing costs plus the child benefit supplement. Hence, within a small band of incomes, the benefit prevents working families from becoming dependent on minimum income protection due to the presence of children. In 2008, entitlement conditions and income assessment were relaxed. As a result, the number of children for whom the benefit was paid climbed from around 30,000 in 2007 to 130,000 in 2008 and 210,000 in 2010 (Bundesagentur für Arbeit, 2015). Compared to the number of children who depend on minimum income protection, this is still a very small number.

4.4.3. Inadequate Social Protection

Social transfers play a significant role in the income of families at risk. Family benefits and minimum income protection are the most relevant policies here, but they have to be seen in combination with other social benefits (Cantillon et al., 2014). However, for reasons of space the following description is limited to these two areas.

During the crisis, social benefits in Germany were not cut (as happened in some other countries), but the structural problems in the social protection system remained unresolved. Minimum income protection and family benefits were raised during the crisis. In both cases, it has repeatedly been the Constitutional Court that has forced legislators to act. Both minimum income guarantee and child benefit have gained constitutional status through a number of court decisions. Yet even if the subsistence minimum (in particular for children) is highly protected thanks to the court, the level of this minimum is set below the relative poverty line, and therefore does not solve the problem of child poverty, though it certainly alleviates it (Nelson, 2010; Van Mechelen and Marchal, 2013).

Family policy in Germany focuses on median earners and even higher-income earners. Though the child benefit is universal and flat-rate (depending solely on the number of children) higher-income earners profit from higher tax allowances. The tax authorities calculate in each case which of the two alternative benefits—the universal child benefit or the child tax allowance—is higher and therefore applicable. In practice, families in the highest income decile usually benefit from the (higher) tax allowance, because of higher marginal tax rates. High-income earners also usually benefit more from the married couples' tax-splitting scheme. It is available to married couples and, since recently, also to registered partnerships with or without children. Even if family policy in Germany has moved in favour of dual-earner couples, mainly through the extension of childcare and the earnings-related parental benefit introduced in 2007, the married couples' tax-splitting scheme still highly privileges single-earner families. It also sets strong incentives for mothers of young children to temporarily withdraw from the labour market.

The level of universal child benefit does not cover all the child-related additional expenses of families. In case of need, the benefit works in combination with the child-related minimum income protection benefit. In practice, this means that the latter benefit is assessed against the former for needy families. The child benefit is fully regarded as 'income' in the means test for minimum income protection, and is therefore deducted in full from the minimum income benefit actually paid. Families that receive minimum income protection in fact do not profit from an increase in child benefits, because this is fully deducted from their minimum income benefit payment. This feature seems to be logical for a benefit of last resort, but it clearly disadvantages low-income earners and those who are most in need. A recent global evaluation of German family policy showed that many individual policies are not very effective at improving the balance between work and family, at preventing poverty, or at increasing fertility (Bonin et al., 2013). Though Germany is one of the highest spenders on family policy in Europe, the system is not effective. Moreover, it clearly disadvantages poorer families (Becker and Hauser, 2012).

Even in the years before the most recent crisis, family policies in Germany have gained ground, and not only in childcare (as described above; see Bäcker, 2016). In 2003 (effective from 1 January 2005) a new child benefit supplement for low-income earners was introduced, as a complement to the newly established system of minimum income protection that came into effect the same year. Both are described in more detail below. In 2006 (effective from 1 January 2007) a new earnings-related parental leave benefit was introduced, replacing the former flat-rate benefit. The new benefit replaces 67 per cent of net income if a parent interrupts employment in order to care for a newborn or adopted child. If working time is reduced, the benefit is granted as a proportion of the reduced time. The benefit is granted for twelve months, and an additional two months are available if the partner also interrupts or reduces employment. Both parents can share the caring time. Single parents receive the benefit for fourteen months. Non-working parents receive a flat-rate amount equal to the former (abolished) benefit of €300 per month. During the crisis, several family benefits were increased, but not in direct response to the crisis. In January 2010, child benefit was increased to €184 for the first and second child, €190 for the third, and €215 for each subsequent child. The benefit was increased in January 2015 and again in January 2016. Due to these changes, total spending on child benefits increased from around €30 billion in 2008 to around €35 billion in 2010 (Statistisches Bundesamt, 2015).

As in labour market and family policies, so in minimum income protection the decisive reforms took place a few years before the most recent crisis (Bäcker, 2016). As part of the structural labour market reforms enacted in 2003–5, the systems of unemployment insurance and minimum income protection were fundamentally reformed. Back in 2001 (effective from 1 January 2003), a new minimum income protection scheme was introduced for the elderly (65+) and for younger persons unable to work (*Grundsicherung im Alter und bei Erwerbsminderung*). This new scheme has provided better conditions for recipients than the existing universal system of the *Sozialhilfe*. In particular, the income of recipients' children is not taken into account in the means test if it does not exceed €100,000 per annum, which is well above the average income. In 2003 (effective from 1 January 2005), finally a new system of minimum income protection was introduced for persons aged 15–65 who are able to work for at least three hours per day (*Grundsicherung für Arbeitsuchende*). At the same time, unemployment insurance benefits (*Arbeitslosenversicherung*) were limited to twelve months (with rules of transition and some exceptions for older workers), and the former system of unemployment assistance (*Arbeitslosenhilfe*) was completely abolished. This system had been a hybrid of insurance and assistance: it had provided wage-related benefits to those who had formerly received insurance benefits, but on a means-tested basis. Those who did not qualify for insurance because of low or non-existent labour market attachment before unemployment could not receive the benefit. In this sense, the new system is more universal than the old one, but it establishes stricter rules and employs means-tested, flat-rate, minimum-subsistence benefits. This benefit, however, is also granted to low-income earners whose income is below the subsistence line defined by the scheme. In parallel, in 2003 (effective from 1 January 2005) a child benefit supplement was introduced for low-earning parents (see section 4.4.2). The maximum child benefit supplement is set at €140 per month per child.

During the crisis, the minimum income protection benefit formula for children was changed—not because of the crisis, but on account of a decision by the Federal Constitutional Court on 9 February 2010. It declared that the benefit rates for children did not cover all the items necessary for the constitutionally guaranteed minimum subsistence (Bundesverfassungsgericht, 2010). The court argued that the benefit rates for children should be more realistic. In particular they should take account of the fact that the basic necessities of life differ more between children's age groups than had been accounted for under the old benefit scheme. Thus since 2011, four age brackets have been distinguished, with different benefit levels: children below the age of 7; aged 7 to below 14; aged 14 to below 18; and aged 18 and above. The benefits for children between 7 and 14, especially, were increased substantially by this reform. Even if these changes were not a direct response to the crisis, they helped to mitigate the impact of the crisis on poor families.

Since the major reform of unemployment protection in 2005, the number of persons depending on minimum income benefits has been high. Before the crisis, in 2007, approximately 10 per cent of the German population—and more than 13 per cent of children below the age of 18—received minimum income protection benefits each year on average (Bahle et al., 2011).[15] These shares have since fallen, but even in 2014 around 8 per cent of the total population and 10 per cent of children depended on these benefits. Their level is, in most cases, below 50 per cent of median equivalent income, hence below the poverty line—and far below the at-risk-of-poverty line defined by the EU. According to the Panel on Labour Market and Social Security (*Panel Arbeitsmarkt und Soziale Sicherung*, PASS), which is based on representative data of the German population and administrative data on households receiving minimum income protection, in 2013 some 13.4 per cent of children below the age of 15 were receiving minimum income protection, and another 10.8 per cent were relatively poor (at the 60 per cent threshold), but did not receive these benefits (Tophoven et al., 2015: 10). Children receiving minimum income protection are (compared to other children) younger, live in larger families, and more often have a migrant background. In 39.7 per cent of cases, the educational qualifications of the parent(s) were low (compared to 12.6 per cent among children not in minimum income protection), in 51 per cent of cases the parent(s) were unemployed, and in 46.7 per cent of cases the children lived with a single parent (compared to 8.9 per cent of children not receiving benefits). Hence, children receiving minimum income protection benefits very often live with a single parent, with unemployed parent(s), or in a family in which the parents have low qualifications or a migrant background. These are the main groups at risk of (child) poverty.

The living conditions of these children are much worse than those of other children. Though the basic necessities of life (such as housing and nutrition) are guaranteed at a minimum standard, the financial situation of these families is usually very bad, and their participation in social life is severely hampered. Even the housing situation differs significantly from the average. For example, around 20 per cent of children who depend on minimum income protection have no room of their own (around 4 per cent among other children). Around 10 per cent (as against 1 per cent) have no adequate winter clothes, and 14 per cent (1 per cent) no access to the internet. Most severe are financial calamities

[15] This means that on an annual average, more than a tenth of children living in Germany depend on minimum income benefits.

and lack of social participation. More than 50 per cent of families that depend on minimum income protection are unable to meet unexpected expenses; 76.4 per cent cannot afford one week off for holidays; and 30 per cent cannot invite friends round for dinner once a month. Some 54.3 per cent cannot afford to go to the cinema and 60 per cent cannot afford to go to a restaurant once a month (Tophoven et al., 2015). It is thus clear that for children, living on minimum income protection means doing without many things that are regarded as part of ordinary social life in modern society.

4.4.4. Unequal Educational Opportunities

A highly debated issue related to child poverty in Germany has been the unequal educational opportunities for children who live in poor families. In the public discourse, perhaps paradoxically, it is not the reasons for child poverty that have dominated, but the negative impact of poverty on children, in particular with respect to social integration and educational opportunity. Child poverty has been regarded as a problem for the life chances of children, but there has been little acknowledgement that child poverty is ultimately rooted in the poverty of parents. Policies during the crisis have at least tried to compensate for some of the negative consequences for children, by promoting education for underprivileged children. An education package for poor children was introduced on 1 January 2011. Those entitled to the education package are children living in families that receive minimum income protection, the child benefit supplement, or housing benefits. Also entitled to the package are children whose parents have such low income that they cannot afford the necessities that it covers. The package consists of a number of different benefits covering education-related expenses in various activities, and these benefits can be combined. First, there is a subsidy for a hot meal at school or in a childcare facility (families have to contribute €1 per meal). Second, support for extracurricular education (*Nachhilfe*) is granted if there is no equivalent service provided by the school. Third, each child can receive up to €10 per month for cultural, sporting, and leisure activities—e.g. for fees for music education or sports clubs. Fourth, €100 is granted each year for each school-aged child to cover school equipment. Fifth, the costs of participation in class excursions are borne. Finally, transport costs are covered for children who have to take public transport to attend high school. The education package benefits have to be claimed at the Jobcentre or at the local social welfare department. In most cases, the authorities cooperate directly with non-profit agencies, which provide the services. Parents and children can receive vouchers, but in many cases the authorities pay the providers direct. These benefits certainly help many children in need, but they are not an adequate substitute for free services available to all children. They also certainly do not solve the problem of unequal educational opportunities. Many schools and sports clubs also have private support arrangements. Parents' initiatives, for example, often pay for the participation of poor children in extracurricular school activities. Sports clubs often have funds to help with the integration of poor children and to provide equipment for free.

Another highly debated policy was the home-care allowance, introduced by the current 'grand coalition' government on 1 August 2013 at the urgent request of the conservative Bavarian Christian Social Union (CSU), which is part of the coalition government. The home-care allowance is granted to parents who do not send their child to a childcare facility. The argument in favour of this policy was that parents who take care of a child themselves should be supported on the same terms as those who use a childcare service. Concerns were raised against this policy that it could cement the traditional role model, in particular among low-qualified parents. This then could lead to lack of social integration and education among the most disadvantaged children, because they would not gain from the socializing environment of a childcare facility. On 21 July 2015, the Constitutional Court declared the policy measure unconstitutional—not because of any anticipated bad consequences for children, but because the federal state is not allowed to intervene in the legal jurisdiction of the Länder. As a consequence, the federal law was abolished after this decision; but in three of the sixteen Länder (including Bavaria) similar measures are in force. For families who had already claimed the benefit, it is being continued, but no new applications are being accepted.

4.5. SUMMARY AND CONCLUSIONS

Child poverty rates in Germany increased markedly at the beginning of the new millennium up until 2005. This was related to an ongoing increase in market incomes for the entire population and to high unemployment, and was accompanied by further convergence between western and eastern Germany. After 2005, child poverty rates remained high, but hovered around the overall poverty rates for the entire German population. We have also seen that child poverty in Germany did not change much during the crisis. This relative stability is due to three main facts. First, the crisis as such did not have long-lasting consequences for employment and average incomes. By contrast, Germany soon regained a stable, modestly growing economy, and there were substantial increases in employment. Second, labour market policy, minimum income protection, and family policies had already been overhauled before the crisis, in response to the severe crisis on the German labour market in the early 2000s. These new policies may have added another buffer against the impact of the new crisis. In particular, employment conditions for parents have become better than before. Third—and this is the 'bad' part of the story—the long-lasting structural problems lying at the heart of child poverty have only been partially resolved by these reforms, since the fundamental features of the old German welfare system linger on. The strong employment-based character of social protection is still highly institutionalized in many parts of the system, and tends to exclude those with low employment chances, mainly those without qualifications and low-income earners. The male-breadwinner model is also still present in the main institutional features of the system, in particular in the tax system and social protection. These features tend to disadvantage in particular single-parent families. The continuing impact of these 'old' structural features is perhaps responsible for the fact that child poverty did not decline more after the quick recovery from the crisis. So far, the rise in employment and the decline in unemployment (and welfare dependency) after the crisis have not resulted in a proportionate decline in child poverty. It seems that the groups that are most at risk of child poverty have not yet gained enough from the overall improvements in the economy and on the labour market. Therefore, it is time to think about these remaining structural problems and about another reorientation in German social and family policies: the idea of introducing better-targeted instruments for those groups most in need. Targeting per se is certainly not a good instrument for risk groups, as the 'paradox of redistribution' (Korpi and Palme, 1998) argues; but if it is embedded in a universal family policy and an employment-related social policy tradition, it may indeed achieve better results.

REFERENCES

Achatz, Juliane, Andreas Hirseland, Torsten Lietzmann, and Cordula Zabel (2013). 'Alleinerziehende Mütter im Bereich des SGB II. Eine Synopse empirischer Befunde aus der IAB-Forschung'. *IAB-Forschungsbericht 8/2013* (Nürnberg: Institut für Arbeitsmarkt- und Berufsforschung).

Alkire, Sabina, Paola Ballon, James Foster, Jose Manuel Roche, Maria Emma Santos, and Suman Seth (2015). *Multidimensional Poverty Measurement and Analysis: A Counting Approach* (Oxford: Oxford University Press).

Alkire, Sabina and James Foster (2011a). 'Counting and Multidimensional Poverty Measurement'. *Journal of Public Economics* 95, no. 7–8: pp. 476–87.

Alkire, Sabina and James Foster (2011b). 'Understandings and Misunderstandings of Multidimensional Poverty Measurement'. *Journal of Economic Inequality* 9, no. 2: pp. 289–314.

Bäcker, Gerhard (2016). *Dauerbaustelle Sozialstaat: Chronologie gesetzlicher Neuregelungen in der Sozialpolitik, 1998–2015* (Duisburg: Universität Duisburg-Essen).

Bahle, Thomas (2008). 'Family Policy Patterns in the Enlarged EU'. In Jens Alber, Tony Fahey, and Chiara Saraceno (eds), *Handbook of Quality of Life in the Enlarged European Union* (London: Routledge).

Bahle, Thomas, Bernhard Ebbinghaus, and Claudia Göbel (2015). *Familien am Rande der Erwerbsgesellschaft: Erwerbsrisiken und soziale Sicherung familiärer Risikogruppen im europäischen Vergleich* (Baden-Baden: Nomos-Edition Sigma).

Bahle, Thomas, Vanessa Hubl, and Michaela Pfeifer (2011). *The Last Safety Net: A Handbook of Minimum Income Protection in Europe* (Bristol: Policy Press).

Bahle, Thomas, Michaela Pfeifer, and Claus Wendt (2010). 'Social Assistance'. In Francis Castles, Stephan Leibfried, Jane Lewis, Herbert Obinger, and Christopher Pierson (eds), *The Oxford Handbook of the Welfare State* (Oxford: Oxford University Press).

Becker, Irene and Richard Hauser (2012). 'Kindergrundsicherung, Kindergeld und Kinderzuschlag: Eine vergleichende Analyse aktueller Reformvorschläge'. *WSI-Diskussionspapier Nr. 180* (Düsseldorf: Wirtschafts- und Sozialwissenschaftliches Institut der Hans-Böckler-Stiftung).

Biewen, Martin and Andos Juhasz (2012). 'Understanding Rising Income Inequality in Germany, 1999/2000–2005/2006'. *Review of Income and Wealth 58*, no. 4: pp. 622–47.

Bonin, Holger, Anita Fichtl, Helmut Rainer, C. Katharina Spieß, Holger Stichnoth and Katharina Wrohlich (2013). 'Zentrale Resultate der Gesamtevaluation familienbezogener Leistungen'. *DIW Wochenbericht 40.*

Bosch, Gerhard (2011). 'The German Labour Market after the Financial Crisis: Miracle or Just a Good Policy Mix?'. In Daniel Vaughan-Whitehead (eds), *Work Inequalities in the Crisis? Evidence from Europe* (Cheltenham: Edward Elgar).

Bosch, Gerhard (2015). 'The German Welfare State: From an Inclusive to an Exclusive Bismarckian Model'. In Daniel Vaughan-Whitehead (eds), *The European Social Model in Crisis* (Cheltenham: Edward Elgar).

Brandl, Bernd (2013). 'Die Repräsentativität von Arbeitgeberverbänden in Europa: Eine Standortbestimmung des "deutschen Modells"'. *WSI-Mitteilungen 66*, no. 7: pp. 510–18.

Bundesagentur für Arbeit (2015). Kindergeldstatistik.

Bundesverfassungsgericht (2010). Pressemitteilung no. 5/2010, 9 February.

Cantillon, Bea, Natascha Van Mechelen, Olivier Pintelon, and Aaron Van den Heede (2014). 'Social Redistribution, Poverty, and the Adequacy of Social Protection'. In Bea Cantillon and Frank Vandenbroucke (eds), *Reconciling Work and Poverty Reduction: How Successful are European Welfare States?* (Oxford: Oxford University Press).

Chzhen, Yekaterina and Jonathan Bradshaw (2012). 'Lone Parents, Poverty and Policy in the European Union'. *Journal of European Social Policy 22*, no. 5: pp. 487–506.

Dingeldey, Irene (2011). *Der aktivierende Wohlfahrtsstaat: Governance der Arbeitsmarktpolitik in Dänemark, Großbritannien und Deutschland* (Frankfurt: Campus).

Ebbinghaus, Bernhard and Claudia Göbel (2014). 'Mitgliederrückgang und Organisationsstrategien deutscher Gewerkschaften'. In Wolfgang Schroeder (ed.), *Handbuch Gewerkschaften in Deutschland* (Wiesbaden: Springer Fachmedien).

Eichhorst, Werner and J. Timo Weishaupt (2013). 'Mit Neokorporatismus durch die Krise? Die Rolle des sozialen Dialogs in Deutschland, Österreich und der Schweiz'. *Zeitschrift für Sozialreform 59*, no. 3: pp. 313–35.

Foster, James, Joel Greer, and Erik Thorbecke (1984). 'A Class of Decomposable Poverty Measures'. *Econometrica 3*, no. 52: pp. 761–66.

Foster, James, Joel Greer, and Erik Thorbecke (2010). 'The Foster–Greer–Thorbecke (FGT) Poverty Measures: 25 Years Later'. *Journal of Economic Inequality 8*: pp. 491–524.

Geißler, Rainer (2014). 'Armut und Prekariat'. In Rainer Geißler (ed.), *Die Sozialstruktur Deutschlands* (Wiesbaden: Springer Fachmedien).

Goebel, Jan, Markus M. Grabka, and Carsten Schröder (2015). 'Einkommensungleichheit in Deutschland bleibt weiterhin hoch—junge Alleinlebende und Berufseinsteiger sind zunehmend von Armut bedroht'. *DIW Wochenbericht 25*: pp. 571–86.

Goebel, Jan and Peter Krause (2016). 'Einkommensentwicklung—Verteilung, Angleichung, Armut und Dynamik'. In *Datenreport 2016, Ein Sozialbericht für die Bundesrepublik Deutschland* (Bonn: Statistisches Bundesamt (Destatis)/Wissenschaftszentrum Berlin für Sozialforschung (WZB)).

Graaf-Zijl, Marloes de and Brian Nolan (2011). 'Household Joblessness and its Impact on Poverty and Deprivation in Europe'. *Journal of European Social Policy 21*, no. 5 (2011): 413–31.

Heidenreich, Martin and Peter Aurich-Beerheide (2014). 'European Worlds of Inclusive Activation: The Organisational Challenges of Coordinated Service Provision'. *International Journal of Social Welfare 23*, Supplement S1.

Holst, Hajo and Klaus Dörre (2013). 'Revival of the "German Model"? Destandardization and the New Labour Market Regime'. In Max Koch and Martin Fritz (eds), *Non-Standard Employment in Europe: Paradigms, Prevalence and Policy Responses*, (Basingstoke: Palgrave Macmillan).

Korpi, Walter and Joakim Palme (1998). 'The Paradox of Redistribution and Strategies of Equality: Welfare State Institutions, Inequality, and Poverty in the Western Countries'. *American Sociological Review 63*, no. 5: pp. 661–87.

Krause, Peter (2015). 'Einkommensungleichheit in Deutschland 1994 bis 2013'. *Wirtschaftsdienst, Zeitschrift für Wirtschaftspolitik 95*, no. 8: pp. 572–74.

Krause, Peter (2016). 'Quality of Life and Inequality'. In Luigino Bruni and Pier Luigi Porta (eds), *Handbook of Research Methods and Applications in Happiness and Quality of Life* (Cheltenham: Edward Elgar): pp. 111–52.

Kroll, Christian (2015). *Sustainable Development Goals: Are the Rich Countries Ready?* (Gütersloh: Bertelsmann Stiftung).

Lohmann, Henning (2009). 'Welfare States, Labour Market Institutions and the Working Poor: A Comparative Analysis of 20 European Countries'. *European Sociological Review 25*, no. 4: pp. 489–504.

Marx, Ive and Brian Nolan (2014). 'In-work Poverty'. In Bea Cantillon and Frank Vandenbroucke (eds), *Reconciling Work and Poverty Reduction: How Successful are European Welfare States?* (Oxford: Oxford University Press).

Müller, Kai-Uwe, C. Katharina Spieß, and Katharina Wrohlich (2014). 'Kindertagesbetreuung: Wie wird ihre Nutzung beeinflusst und was kann sie für die Entwicklung von Kindern bewirken?'. *Vierteljahreshefte zur Wirtschaftsforschung 83*, no. 1: pp. 49–67.

Nelson, Kenneth (2010). 'Social Assistance and Minimum Income Benefits in Old and New EU Democracies'. *International Journal of Social Welfare 19*, no. 4: pp. 367–78.

OECD (2015). *In It Together: Why Less Inequality Benefits All* (Paris: OECD Publishing). <http://dx.doi.org/10.1787/9789264235120-en>.

Pfau-Effinger, Birgit (2004). 'Socio-historical Paths of the Male-breadwinner Model—an Explanation of Cross-national Differences'. *British Journal of Sociology 55*, no. 3: pp. 377–99.

Prognos (2014). *Gesamtevaluation der ehe- und familienbezogenen Maßnahmen und Leistungen in Deutschland: Endbericht für das Bundesministerium der Finanzen und Bundesministerium für Familie, Senioren, Frauen und Jugend* (Berlin: Prognos).

Rippin, Nicole (2012). 'Distributional Justice and Efficiency: Integrating Inequality within and between Dimensions in Additive Poverty Indices'. *CRC-PEG Discussion Paper 128* (Göttingen: Universität Göttingen).

Rippin, Nicole (2014). 'Considerations of Efficiency and Distributive Justice in Multidimensional Poverty Measurement'. Doctoral thesis. Universität Göttingen. 2014. <http://hdl.handle.net/11858/00-1735-0000-0022-5E2E-B>.

Schelkle, Waltraud (2012). 'Policymaking in Hard Times: French and German Responses to the Eurozone Crisis'. In Nancy Bermeo and Jonas Pontusson (eds), *Coping With Crisis: Government Reactions to the Great Recession* (New York: Russell Sage Foundation).

Statistische Ämter des Bundes und der Länder (2014). *Kindertagesbetreuung regional* (Wiesbaden: Statistisches Bundesamt).

Statistisches Bundesamt (2011). *Bruttoinlandsprodukt 2010 für Deutschland. Begleitmaterial zur Pressekonferenz am 12. Januar 2011 in Wiesbaden* (Wiesbaden: Statistisches Bundesamt).

Statistisches Bundesamt (2015). Destatis database. <https://www.destatis.de/DE/ZahlenFakten/ZahlenFakten.html>.

Tophoven, Silke, Claudia Wenzig, and Torsten Lietzmann (2015). *Kinder- und Familienarmut: Lebensumstände von Kindern in der Grundsicherung* (Gütersloh: Bertelsmann Stiftung).

Trappe, Heike, Matthias Pollmann-Schult, and Christian Schmitt (2015). 'The Rise and Decline of the Male-breadwinner Model: Institutional Underpinnings and Future Expectations'. *European Sociological Review 31*, no. 2: pp. 230–42.

Van Mechelen, Natascha and Sarah Marchal (2013). 'Struggles for Life: Social Assistance Benefits, 1992–2009'. In Ive Marx and Kenneth Nelson (eds), *Minimum Income Protection in Flux* (Basingstoke: Palgrave Macmillan).

Visser, Jelle (2010). 'Variations and Trends in European Industrial Relations in the 21st Century's First Decade'. In *Industrial Relations in Europe 2010* (Brussels: European Commission).

Wagner, Gert G., Joachim R. Frick, and Jürgen Schupp (2007). 'The German Socio-economic Panel Study (SOEP): Scope, Evolution and Enhancements'. *Schmollers Jahrbuch127*, no. 1: pp. 139–69.

Wagner, Gert G., Jan Göbel, Peter Krause, Rainer Pischner, and Ingo Sieber (2008). 'Das Sozio-oekonomische Panel (SOEP): Multidisziplinäres Haushaltspanel und Kohortenstudie für Deutschland—Eine Einführung (für neue Datennutzer) mit einem Ausblick (für erfahrene Anwender)'. *AStA Wirtschafts- und Sozialstatistisches Archiv 2*, no. 4: pp. 301–28.

5

The Impact of the Great Recession on Child Poverty in Greece

Manos Matsaganis

5.1. INTRODUCTION

The Great Recession has been far more painful and protracted in Greece than in any other country in Europe and elsewhere. Its effects on children are likely to continue to be felt for many years to come. Poor children run a higher immediate risk of undernourishment, ill-health, poor performance at school, and low overall development, while low skills and other scarring effects make low pay and high unemployment more likely in the future. Inadequate income is not the only matter of concern: lack of access to services (such as childcare, healthcare, and education) may be just as important, if not more so.

While some of these effects will take years to unfold, others are already visible. In this chapter I discuss the impact of the crisis (and of policy responses) on children in Greece. The structure of the chapter is as follows. Section 5.2 recounts the story of the economic crisis that hit the country when the fiscal crisis of 2009 mutated into a sovereign debt crisis in 2010, leading to the deep recession of 2010–13, followed by a stagnation from which (at the time of writing, December 2016) Greece seemed unable to escape. Attention then turns to the transmission mechanisms from economy to society, focusing on the impact on children. That the economic crisis was allowed to become a social emergency in the first place was partly because policy responses failed to rise to the occasion: key policy initiatives to counter poverty are analysed and formally assessed from the viewpoint of families with children. The final section draws tentative conclusions, deriving broader insights from the predicament of Greece in 2010–15.

5.2. THE ECONOMIC CRISIS

Recent years have been harsh for families and children in Greece. In 2007–13, gross domestic product (GDP) contracted by 26.5 per cent in real terms. This was far greater than the equivalent contraction in other European economies affected by the crisis.[1] There is no precedent for such a deep and drawn-out recession in the peacetime economic history of most advanced economies, and it comes close to the US Great Depression (a 30 per cent drop in GDP in 1929–32).

5.2.1. The Boom Years

The country's current predicament is largely rooted in its unsustainable growth prior to the current crisis. In 2000–2007, the Greek economy grew twice as fast as the rest of Europe (+32.4 per cent in real terms, compared to +17.1 per cent in the EU-28 and +14.2 per cent in the Euro area of twelve countries). However, behind the facade of prosperity, fuelled by strong consumer demand and boosted by cheap credit, lay a largely uncompetitive economy, its many weaknesses shown up in the gradual deterioration in the balance of payments, with the current account deficit reaching 14.9 per cent of GDP in 2008. At the same time, fiscal chronic imbalances took the form of both large public deficits (culminating in 15.6 per cent of GDP in 2009) and steeply rising public debt (from 103.1 per cent of GDP in 2007 to 126.7 per cent in 2009).[2]

5.2.2. The Bailout

As Greece's imbalances came under scrutiny, its fiscal crisis rapidly turned into a sovereign debt crisis, with the cost of borrowing from late 2009 climbing to prohibitive levels. In April 2010, Greece effectively lost access to the international financial markets. In May 2010, the 'no-bailout' clause of the Maastricht Treaty was quietly set aside, clearing the way for a massive €110 billion loan from the European Commission, the European Central Bank (ECB), and the International Monetary Fund (IMF) (jointly termed the 'Troika'). In return for the bailout, the government signed a Memorandum of Economic and Financial Policies, which committed it to 'fiscal consolidation' (sweeping spending cuts and steep tax increases).

[1] Specifically, from peak to trough: Portugal −7.8 per cent (in 2008–13); Spain −8.6 per cent (in 2008–13); Italy −9.0 per cent (in 2007–14); Ireland −7.7 per cent (in 2007–9). All figures in this section are from the Eurostat online database, unless otherwise indicated.

[2] On the run-up to the Greek crisis, see also Katsimi and Moutos (2010); Featherstone (2011); Mitsopoulos and Pelagidis (2011); Galenianos (2015); and Christodoulakis (2015).

The specific provisions of the bailout loan and the austerity programme were revised several times over the following years, most importantly in March 2012, when a second economic adjustment programme was agreed. Under that programme, the Euro area Member States and the IMF pledged an additional €130 billion for the years 2012–14. Notably, the European side of it was financed by the European Financial Stability Facility (which became fully operational in August 2010), rather than through bilateral loans, as had been the case with the first programme.

At the same time, private sector involvement—or, more colloquially, a 'haircut'—was arranged in order to improve the sustainability of the country's debt: private investors were asked to agree to write off 53.5 per cent of the face value of any Greek government bonds they were holding. The operation proved a success: three-and-a-half years later, almost 96 per cent of the total value of all bonds eligible for the exchange offer (approximately €197 billion) had been exchanged.[3]

5.2.3. Record Fiscal Consolidation

Under close international supervision, public finances improved spectacularly. Using the appropriate definition ('abstracting from bank resolution costs and other programme adjustments'), the general government deficit was reduced to 3.2 per cent in 2013 (from 15.6 per cent of GDP in 2009), while the primary balance (i.e. net of interest payments on debt) went from a deficit equal to 10.3 per cent of GDP in 2009 to a *surplus* of 0.8 per cent of GDP in 2013 (European Commission, 2014: 10). As a result, in 2013 Greece had 'the highest cyclically-adjusted primary balance in the euro area' (IMF, 2014: 5). Observers admitted that this was 'a record fiscal consolidation' (OECD, 2013: 13).

The turnaround was also dramatic in terms of the balance of payments, which registered a surplus of 0.7 per cent of GDP in 2013 (from a deficit of 14.9 per cent of GDP in 2008). Crucially, the improvement was almost exclusively driven by a precipitous fall in imports. Greek exports grew by only 8 per cent in 2009–13. The export performance of firms in Portugal (+17 per cent) and Ireland (+19 per cent) was significantly better (Arkolakis et al., 2015).

5.2.4. A Low-performing Economy

The poor performance of exports, in the context of a deep recession, revealed the structural flaws of Greece's growth model. As domestic demand plummeted, most Greek firms were incapable of switching to international

[3] For an analysis, see Xafa (2014).

markets—whether because their products were of poor quality, or were sold at high prices, or both. 'Internal devaluation'—the Troika's solution for engineering an export-led recovery by lowering labour costs (including wages)[4]—failed to reverse the decline in the number of workers in employment, which in February 2016 remained 4 per cent lower than in February 2012, and 22 per cent lower than in February 2008 (near the pre-crisis peak). Given that exports failed to revive much either, it seems clear that fiscal consolidation was achieved in spite of a low-performing economy, rather than on the back of a new dynamism. Eliminating the twin deficits had been accomplished by simply moving the economy to a much lower equilibrium.

5.2.5. The Failures of Austerity

There is little doubt that the 'higher' equilibrium pre-crisis rested on shaky foundations, and hence was unsustainable. Even so, questions about the content and pace of externally imposed austerity lingered. The Greek bailout averted a messy default, and most probably even more misery for the Greek people. But the heavy rhetoric with which it was accompanied obscured the fact that what was being 'rescued' was not simply irresponsible Greek governments, but equally irresponsible commercial banks in France, Germany, and elsewhere. As Dyson (2014) pointed out, it is hardly possible to have 'feckless debtors' without 'reckless creditors'. As explained in the recent consensus narrative report published by a group of leading economists from across the spectrum of opinion:[5] 'By 2007 banks in Eurozone core nations were heavily invested in the debt of periphery nations. This inhibited some natural solutions, such as the writing down of Greek government debt in the early days of the Crisis' (Baldwin et al., 2015).

As it turned out, the damage inflicted by bailout packages that asked debtor countries to shoulder most of the costs of adjustment was enormous. What is more, the *size* of these costs (i.e. the depth of recession associated with austerity) had been seriously underestimated by the Troika. As a study by

[4] The strategy had two main features. On the one hand, in February 2012, the national minimum wage was cut by 22 per cent in nominal terms (from €745 to €586 per month, gross), while a sub-minimum wage for workers aged below 25 years was also introduced (at €511 per month, gross), resulting in a 32 per cent cut in their case. Furthermore, various allowances that topped up the minimum wage were abolished, with the exception of seniority allowance. Unemployment insurance benefit was also cut, from €454 to €360 a month (i.e. by 22 per cent), for all workers, irrespective of age. On the other hand, labour market institutions, from employment protection legislation and collective bargaining to working time regulations and non-wage costs, were subject to sweeping deregulation.

[5] The report was signed by Olivier Blanchard (Chief Economist at the IMF until October 2015), Daniel Gros (Director of the Centre for European Policy Studies), Christopher Pissarides (Nobel Laureate, London School of Economics professor), and others.

leading IMF economists (Blanchard and Leigh, 2013) conceded, while early forecasts had assumed a 'fiscal multiplier' of about 0.5 (i.e. that reducing the budget deficit by €10 would lead to a drop in GDP of €5), the actual effect was around 1.5 (i.e. a deficit reduction of €10 led to a self-defeating drop in output of €15) or more. Larger fiscal multipliers are now believed to be present in the early phases of a recession, and in countries where the size of fiscal consolidation is larger. This seems a fair description of the case of Greece in 2010–11, when the government's fiscal consolidation effort was most radical (8 per cent of GDP).

The above seems to indicate that austerity was both inevitable and catastrophic. On the one hand, given huge fiscal imbalances, spending cuts and tax increases were to a large extent inescapable, and would probably have taken place even if the country had never joined the monetary union.[6] On the other hand, it is now almost universally accepted that the policies pursued under the terms of the bailout agreement(s) made the recession deeper and longer.[7] So, short of a politically unlikely debt write-down in 2010, was there no alternative to Greece's Great Recession?

5.2.6. Elusive Alternatives

With hindsight, it may be worth reiterating that 'bailing in' commercial banks in France, Germany, and other creditor countries—i.e. forcing them to take some of the losses—would have been not just fairer, but also less costly for the European economy as a whole; it would also have permitted a less drastic fiscal consolidation in Greece.

Beyond that, the disappointing export performance of Greek firms (far inferior to that of Irish, Spanish, or Portuguese companies) hinted at a deeper malaise, resistant to the Keynesian-type reflation advocated by critics of austerity both at home and abroad: allowing public spending to grow, other things being equal, would merely have caused imports to rise again, setting in motion once again the vicious cycle that had led to the debt crisis in the first place. But the obsolescence of Greece's growth model meant that the conventional prescription of 'austerity plus structural reforms' administered by the

[6] Although, of course, in that case the Greek economy would not have grown so fast in 2000–7 either.

[7] In November 2015, a team of IMF economists (Decressin et al., 2015) explained why internal devaluation 'can only work well if supported by accommodative monetary policies. In the absence of such policies, wage moderation does not deliver much of a boost to output in the countries that are undertaking it, and also ends up lowering output in the Euro area as a whole'. Given that it was the IMF itself that, as part of the Troika, had urged internal devaluation upon Greece, the statement had the flavour of an explicit departure from, if not disavowal of, a previous position.

Troika was also flawed. Sustainable growth was unlikely to spring magically from the ruins of 'creative destruction', and nor was it simply a matter of lowering labour costs. Preparing the ground for it was demanding and expensive: it required reform of the product markets, not just the labour markets (and the latter needed to be made less segmented, not just more flexible); reform of the welfare state to protect the poor and unemployed, not just cuts to pension benefits; upgrading of public administration, not just a reduction in the number of civil servants; investment in education and training—and more. Perhaps as a result, it was never seriously pursued.

5.2.7. Political Instability

In the absence of a modernizing effort of the type sketched above, Greece seemed to be caught in a deadly spiral. The recession readily translated into a social crisis, which caused political unrest, and in turn made the recession deeper than it might have been.

The political crisis culminated in 2015. In January of that year, a new government came to office promising to renegotiate the bailout agreement and 'end austerity'. Protracted negotiations with the country's lenders were concluded in August 2015, when the Greek government signed a third Memorandum of Understanding that committed it to yet another economic adjustment programme, in return for further financial assistance to the tune of €86 billion over three years (2015–18). In the meantime, the fear of exit from the Euro area ('Grexit') had reached a climax in July 2015, as bank deposits were drained and capital controls were imposed on the eve of the bailout referendum.

5.2.8. Stagnation and Divergence

In that context, the timid recovery of 2014 (GDP up by 0.7 per cent) proved short lived: the economy plunged into recession again in 2015 (–0.2 per cent), and is currently forecast by Eurostat to shrink further (–0.7 per cent) in 2016. The growth curve of the last decade seemed to be L-shaped, not U-shaped. The unprecedented decline of 2007–13 was followed by stagnation, not recovery. Based on these figures, the size of the Greek economy at the end of 2016 will be a massive 27 per cent below its 2007 level. Compared to the rest of Western Europe, relative living standards in Greece first converged to 86 per cent of the average at the pre-crisis peak (in 2009), and then plummeted to 65 per cent in 2016.[8]

[8] Gross domestic product at current market prices, in purchasing power standards, per head of population, relative to the EU-15 average. Source: AMECO Eurostat.

5.3. THE SOCIAL CRISIS

The social effects of an economic crisis are not as straightforward as may appear at first sight. The impact on family incomes will vary substantially and will depend on the earnings and employment status both of the workers directly affected and of other members of the households in which they live, as well as on the capacity of the tax-benefit system to absorb macroeconomic shocks. Moreover, the distributional impact may vary, depending on the dimension considered: in a crisis, average living standards may decline, but inequality need not rise; and the estimated effect on poverty will be less pronounced when the poverty line is set as a proportion of average (or median) incomes than when it is held constant in purchasing power terms (Jenkins et al., 2013). In this section, we review labour market developments (job losses and falling earnings), effects on income distribution (inequality and poverty), and access to essential services (such as healthcare, education, and locally provided food aid).

5.3.1. Jobs

As a result of the recession and the austerity, labour market conditions deteriorated rapidly. The employment rate fell from 61.4 per cent in 2008 to 48.8 per cent in 2013, undoing in five years the progress of the previous two decades and more (it had stood at 53.7 per cent in 1992). The effect of the crisis was asymmetrical: more jobs were lost in private enterprises than in the public sector, in micro firms (employing 0–9 workers) than in larger ones, in construction and manufacture than in services. In other respects, job losses affected men proportionately more than women, foreign workers more than native ones, temporary workers more than permanent ones. Part-time employment grew (to 9.5 per cent of all jobs in 2014, from 5.7 per cent in 2008), but remained well below the EU average (20.4 per cent in 2014), and largely involuntary—that is, taken up not by choice, but because no full-time jobs were available (71.2 per cent of all part-time workers in 2014, vs 29.6 per cent in the EU-28).

Unemployment rose precipitously (from 7.8 per cent in 2010 to 26.5 per cent in 2014, having peaked at 28.7 per cent in November 2013). Given the length of the recession, the majority of jobless workers had been out of work for over a year: the long-term unemployment rate went from 3.7 per cent in 2008 to 19.5 per cent in 2014 (relative to an EU average of 5.1 per cent). New entrants to the labour market faced unfavourable prospects, often choosing to prolong full-time education. Thus the proportion of those aged 15–24 who were not in employment, education, or training increased less than might have been expected: from 11.4 per cent in 2008 to 19.1 per cent in 2014 (compared to 12.5 per cent in the EU-28).

Furthermore, until the onset of the crisis, labour market institutions and norms in Greece, whether formal or informal, protected 'male breadwinners', often at the expense of their wives and (grown-up) children. No doubt this pattern stifled mobility, forced many women to remain housewives, and prevented many young adults from leaving the parental home before an unusually late age. However, it had one advantage: by protecting 'primary earners', it ensured that unemployment did not directly translate into poverty. What is more, there seemed to be little overlap between the unemployed and the poor: the former comprised mostly wives of employed men and youth sharing the parental home, while the latter mainly concerned the elderly and others living in rural areas. This was to change dramatically under the impact of the crisis. In the second quarter of 2008, the unemployment rate for men aged 30+ was a mere 3.1 per cent; six years later it had reached 20.2 per cent. Often, joblessness (or low work intensity, with one adult unemployed and another in a part-time job) was the fate of entire households. Families with children were not spared: the proportion of the population aged less than 60 years that lived in households with dependent children, and that had low or very low work intensity, grew almost threefold—from 6.2 per cent in 2009 to 17.1 per cent in 2013 (10.4 per cent in the EU-28).

5.3.2. Earnings

For those still in employment, real earnings fell as a result both of the recession (because of lower demand for labour) and of 'internal devaluation' (through policy-driven compression of wages via labour market deregulation, including a drastic cut in the minimum wage). The relevant changes affected to a greater extent the overlapping categories of newly hired and young workers. Administrative data from IKA (the social insurance agency for private sector employees) indicate that the median reported earnings of newly hired workers declined by 34.2 per cent, and of workers aged below 30 by 34.8 per cent, in real terms in 2010–14. In contrast, the median earnings of those who kept their job with the same employer were cut by 9.6 per cent. On the whole, Bank of Greece estimates show that average gross earnings of all employees in 2014 were 25.4 per cent below their pre-crisis peak (in 2009), and as much as 8.4 per cent below their 2000 level. In the 'informal sector' (typically in construction, agriculture, tourism, and other services), where employers are often subject to no legal or other constraints, except those implicit in the free play of unregulated market forces, earnings fell even more. Because of the rising tax pressure, earnings losses were more pronounced in net terms.

5.3.3. Income Distribution

As median incomes tumbled (by 41 per cent in 2009–13, according to Eurostat figures),[9] the relative poverty rate went up by less than might have been expected (from 20.1 per cent in 2009 to 23.1 per cent in 2012, falling to 22.1 per cent in 2013). Still, the proportion of the population with 'equivalized' income below a lower poverty threshold (40 per cent, rather than 60 per cent of median income) rose steeply—from 7.3 per cent in 2009 to 11.1 per cent in 2012 (i.e. almost twice the 5.8 per cent average for the European Union as a whole—before falling back to 10.4 per cent in 2013 (vs 6.3 per cent in the EU-28). Moreover, the 'anchored' poverty rate (i.e. the proportion of the population with 'equivalized' income below 60 per cent of the 2008 median, adjusted for inflation) reached 48.0 per cent in 2013, compared to 18.9 per cent in the EU-28. Finally, the severe material deprivation rate almost doubled, from 11.0 per cent in 2009 to 21.5 per cent in 2014 (the EU-28 average was 9.0 per cent in 2014).

Both rich and poor ended up with far less income at the depth of the recession than they had pre-crisis, but income losses were higher than average at the bottom of the distribution. The poorest 20 per cent of the population lived on 6.4 per cent of total income in 2013 (down from 7.2 per cent in 2009), whereas the income share of the richest 20 per cent rose slightly, from 40.3 per cent to 41.0 per cent. As a result, inequality went up: in terms of the S80/S20 income quintile share ratio, from 5.6 in 2009 to 6.5 in 2013.

5.3.4. Child Poverty

Child poverty increased significantly. Defined with reference to a relative threshold (at 60 per cent of median income), it rose from 23.0 per cent in 2009 to 28.8 per cent in 2012, before sliding back about halfway (to 25.5 per cent in 2013). On the other hand, if measured with reference to a fixed threshold (60 per cent of the 2008 median), child poverty went up precipitously in 2009–12 (from 20.7 per cent to 51.8 per cent), and kept rising (to 52.3 per cent) in 2013. Moreover, the proportion of children below a lower relative poverty threshold (40 per cent of median) reached an alarming 16.5 per cent in 2012, falling back to 13.3 per cent in 2013. Turning to severe material deprivation, the proportion affected was 23.8 per cent of all children in 2014 (up from 10.4 per cent in 2008).

[9] Mean and median income by age and sex (source: EU-SILC), corrected for inflation (+8.8% per cent in 2009–13).

The above picture, based on Eurostat data, is further complemented by our recent microsimulation estimates (Matsaganis and Leventi, 2016), using the European tax-benefit model EUROMOD. In Table 5.1, we extend estimates to the year 2015 and compute the 'extreme poverty rate', defined as the proportion of persons living in families unable to purchase a basket of basic necessities, adequate to sustain a family just above destitution level, without dissaving or running into debt.[10] We find that the proportion of children below that threshold reached an alarming 18.0 per cent in 2015 (up from 12.0 per cent in 2011), having peaked at 21.0 per cent in 2013. According to an earlier estimate (Matsaganis and Leventi, 2013), in 2009 the extreme child poverty rate was a mere 4.1 per cent. Poverty risks were highest among children aged 12–17 (and older children still living in the parental home) and among smaller families (apart from among families with four or more children, which accounted for a mere 0.3 per cent of the population). Lastly, poverty rates were distressingly high for jobless households with children (an *extreme* poverty rate of over 90 per cent).

5.3.5. Access to Services

Income losses might have been less painful if the victims of the recession could at least rely on the public provision of healthcare and other vital social services (free of charge—or nearly so—at the point of use). In fact, given the extent of waste and inefficiency before the crisis, it would not have been impossible to cut costs, and at the same time maintain an adequate quantity and quality of service. As it turned out, the opposite happened: austerity cuts were often indiscriminate, reforms were disruptive and/or raised user costs, many suppliers reacted to payment arrears by withholding supplies, industrial action contributed to the general unreliability of public provision, and some public sector workers reacted to wage cuts by reducing effort (though most others were resigned to working more for less). As a result of all that, the cost of adjustment was often passed on to the users of public services.

[10] We also find that our extreme poverty threshold has converged to the relative poverty threshold, at 50 per cent of median income in 2013 (47 per cent in 2015). This is in spite of the fact that our basket of goods (whose cost, for a couple with two children living in Athens, in owner-occupied housing, we estimated at €640 per month in 2015) is very spartan indeed. By comparison, the 'social participation budget' *for food alone* ('healthy diet and kitchen equipment') was estimated under the EU reference budgets project (Goedemé et al., 2015) to be €915 per month (67 per cent of median) for a couple with two children living in Athens in 2015. Note that healthcare is explicitly not part of the basket of basic goods, on the assumption that health services are free at the point of use (at least for the poor). We know this is not true: Household Budget Survey figures show that in Greece the poor spent 8.3 per cent of their income on health (in 2012).

Table 5.1. Estimated poverty rates, Greece (2015)

	Population share (%)	Poverty rates (%) by threshold		
		relative	anchored	extreme
A. All households	100.0	23.3	45.3	15.2
Gender				
men	49.1	23.5	45.4	15.9
women	50.9	23.1	45.3	14.6
age				
0–5	*6.0*	20.7	43.9	15.3
6–11	*5.7*	23.8	45.0	18.8
12–17	*5.8*	28.6	50.3	20.1
0–17	17.5	24.3	46.3	18.0
18–29	13.5	34.7	58.6	24.6
30–44	23.0	23.1	42.8	16.6
45–64	26.5	25.6	46.3	16.7
65+	19.5	11.6	37.0	2.7
B. Households with children	40.1	25.4	46.5	18.9
Household head				
unemployed	3.5	91.0	97.6	85.3
employee (public)	8.2	1.7	10.5	0.7
employee (private)	15.5	15.9	47.5	10.3
liberal profession	2.0	9.4	16.1	6.3
own-account worker	6.9	33.9	53.9	25.4
farmer	3.5	43.5	71.8	21.9
inactive, student, other	63.8	86.0	52.8	63.8
Tenure				
rent	9.1	32.3	60.0	32.3
mortgage	8.5	14.8	27.6	14.7
outright owner	22.5	26.6	48.2	15.1
No. of children				
0	*57.3*	*21.4*	*43.4*	*12.5*
1	13.7	28.2	49.2	21.4
2	25.1	23.6	44.1	17.5
3	1.0	25.0	60.7	14.7
4+	0.3	53.6	81.3	40.6
Households with children by no. of earners and type of contract				
0	3.4	95.8	99.8	90.7
1 (part-time)	1.9	80.4	90.4	60.4
1 (full-time)	15.9	24.2	64.7	16.0
2 (part-time)	0.6	38.1	73.5	6.7
2 (1 part-time 1 full-time)	3.2	15.7	39.2	8.4
2 (full-time)	14.4	4.0	8.9	2.0

Notes: Poverty rates estimated using the tax-benefit model EUROMOD. Panel B includes households with children, with head aged 25–59, excluding pensioners. The relative poverty threshold is set at 60 per cent of median net equivalized household disposable income (€823 per month for a couple with two children in 2015). The anchored poverty threshold is set at 60 per cent of median net equivalized household disposable income in 2009, adjusted for inflation (€1,271 per month for a couple with two children in 2015). The extreme poverty threshold is equal to the cost of a basic basket of goods (€640 per month for a couple with two children living in Athens in owner-occupied accommodation in 2015). 'Public employees' include bank workers. 'Outright owners' include others living in rent-free accommodation.

Source: Matsaganis and Leventi (2016).

5.3.6. Healthcare

As a result of funding shortages and policy reforms that aimed at 'efficiency savings' (reviewed in Matsaganis, 2013), access to affordable healthcare has been compromised in recent years. The evidence is limited as yet, given that there is a considerable time lapse before current developments are captured in official statistics. In the meantime, the data that are already available (reporting on the early phase of the crisis) paint a worrying picture. For instance, according to EU Statistics on Income and Living Conditions (EU-SILC), whereas in 2009 only 4.0 per cent of the population reported having been unable to seek necessary medical care because it was 'too expensive', by 2013 this figure had risen to 7.8 per cent. Among respondents in the lowest income quintile (i.e. the poorest 20 per cent of the population), the proportion increased over the same period from 8.4 per cent to 13.9 per cent. These figures are now among the highest in the EU: only Latvia reports higher rates of unmet need of medical care (because it is 'too expensive'), with the rates in Bulgaria and Romania fluctuating around the Greek level.

5.3.7. Education

Even though education policy was not formally part of the 'structural reforms' under the terms of the bailout agreements, funding shortages adversely affected the quantity of public provision. As for quality, that had been frequently criticized for its many failings well before the current crisis (see e.g. OECD, 2011). A taste of those failings is given by the results of the Programme for International Student Assessment (PISA) survey (OECD, 2014). In Greece, the average performance of 15-year-olds across all three areas (reading, mathematics, science literacy) was significantly below the average score in all Organisation for Economic Co operation and Development (OECD) countries in 2009 (a shortfall of 2 per cent, 6 per cent, and 6 per cent, respectively). In 2012, average performance in Greece fell further, so that its distance from the OECD average grew (to 4 per cent in reading, 8 per cent in mathematics, and 7 per cent in science literacy). In 2012, the share of high achievers in mathematics had shrunk to 3.9 per cent (vs an OECD average of 12.6 per cent), while the proportion of low achievers was 35.7 per cent (vs 23.0 per cent).

Differences in socio-economic background mattered, sometimes more than elsewhere in the OECD area. For instance, students who had attended pre-primary education for more than a year performed much better than those who had not, the score differential being one of the largest among the participating countries. Moreover, students with a migrant background faced difficulties: the gap in maths performance between non-immigrant students who speak the language of assessment at home, and immigrant students who do not (accounting for differences in economic, social, and cultural status), was one of the highest in the OECD countries.

5.3.8. Food Aid

While public services run by central government faced considerable disruption, local services flourished in conditions of extreme adversity. Certain local governments managed the seemingly impossible feat of expanding services while cutting costs. One of the best examples of that is the provision of school meals in Athens. In response to mounting evidence of children turning up for school clearly undernourished, the Athens Municipal Nursery started to offer school meals on a daily basis. In 2012–13, the number of children receiving school meals amounted to over 8 per cent of all children attending the schools concerned, or approximately 2 per cent of the total school population in the City of Athens. Other local councils ran a similar (though less ambitious) service. Furthermore, emergency food aid is also provided in soup kitchens run by local councils, the Church, and voluntary organizations. In 2014, a survey of 500 persons attending soup kitchens in Athens found that 54 per cent received food for both themselves and their families, while 37 per cent reported having children.

5.4. POLICY RESPONSES

In principle, a well-designed system of social protection should be able to mitigate the social effects of an economic crisis:

> These are precisely the kinds of emergencies that welfare state programmes and institutions are designed to deal with, so that when a financial crisis turns up we have routine mechanisms... for coping with its consequences. Long lines of the unemployed caused by economic crises are the core business of the welfare state.
> (Castles, 2010: 96)

It is probably fair to say that the depth and duration of the Greek crisis, including mass joblessness, would have posed insurmountable challenges to any welfare state, even the most advanced. But the configuration of the Greek welfare state, in spite of rising social spending pre-crisis, rendered it particularly unfit for the challenge. When the crisis hit, there was little to prevent the hundreds of thousands of families suffering losses in terms of jobs and/or earnings from falling into poverty. The social protection system generally failed to support the living standards of vulnerable groups.

5.4.1. Greek Welfare prior to 2009

On the eve of the crisis, the Greek welfare state fitted perfectly the characterization of the Southern European model of welfare as a combination of 'unparalleled peaks of generosity reserved for the protected core of the labour market' and serious gaps in the social safety net (Ferrera, 1996: 21).

Peaks of generosity were evident in the pension rights of public sector employees (in the civil service and the utilities), liberal professionals (judges and lawyers, doctors and pharmacists, engineers and architects), and other groups. Elsewhere in the system, the heavy reliance on contributory social insurance disenfranchised non-standard workers and their families. The risks of dualism were fully exposed by the crisis: hundreds of thousands of workers, on losing their jobs, also lost access to social benefits for themselves and their dependants.

Coverage gaps abounded. Contributory unemployment insurance seemed reasonable in terms of benefit level (around 60 per cent of the minimum wage), but its duration was short (maximum 12 months), and its coverage less than complete. As a result of stringent eligibility conditions and low rates of take-up, the number of recipients of non-contributory unemployment assistance was extremely low. Child benefits were adequate for large families, as were family allowances for workers in the 'protected categories' (civil service, banks, and public utilities); in contrast, most families with one or two children received little or no support, even when in poverty. Public assistance with housing costs was limited. Social rented accommodation was practically unknown, while a means-tested rent subsidy was only available on a contributory basis, which was beyond the reach of most families in poverty. Disability benefits were extremely fragmented even by Greek standards, with no fewer than ten different categories with twenty-two sub-categories, often hiding absurd cases of differential treatment. Short-term benefits in case of sickness or maternity ranged from quite generous (for labour market insiders) to non-existent (for non-standard workers). Last but not least, Greece remained the only EU country where a broad social assistance scheme acting as a social safety net of last resort was unavailable even on a local or regional basis, as in Italy, Spain, and Hungary (Matsaganis, 2011).

The above suggests that, on the eve of the crisis, Greek welfare was singularly unfit for what was to follow. And when the crisis did arrive, the policy response initially merely involved a string of 'special support schemes', targeting existing benefit recipients, to whom a few hundred euros were paid as a lump sum. Then came the May 2010 bailout package, and social policy (like all public policy) came under strict international supervision.

5.4.2. Social Protection under Austerity (2010–14)

Under successive austerity programmes, the welfare state became subject to fiscal consolidation, just like any other policy area. The extent of waste and inefficiency in resource use, ineffectiveness in terms of social objectives, poor administration, outright fraud in some cases, overlaps or duplication between schemes, as well as coverage gaps, suggested that the scope for strengthening social protection while cutting social expenditure was considerable, although political and technical constraints limited what could realistically be achieved. As it turned out, welfare state 'recalibration' (Ferrera and Hemerijck, 2003) was not pursued at all until 2013. In the meantime, the supply of social protection was being reduced, just as the demand for it reached unprecedented heights.

In absolute terms (per inhabitant, at constant 2005 prices), expenditure on social benefits peaked in 2009, the last year pre-crisis. Thereafter, as the recession deepened, social spending started to decline (by 15.1 per cent in 2009–12, according to Eurostat). OECD estimates, using a different definition, but updated to 2014, indicate that social expenditure in 2009–14 fell by as much as 22.2 per cent (per head of population, in fixed prices). In relative terms, as a share of GDP, expenditure on social protection in 2008–12 grew according to Eurostat by 6.3 percentage points to 31.6 per cent, that is, well above the EU-28 average (28.6 per cent). In 2012–14, as the cuts in social protection under fiscal consolidation took effect, social spending fell faster than GDP (by 2.1 percentage points, according to OECD figures). Not all policy areas fared equally. Pensions expenditure, driven by the opposing forces of nominal benefit cuts and rising pensioner numbers, continued its upward trend, temporary setbacks notwithstanding, to reach 17.9 per cent of GDP in 2015 (from 14.6 per cent in 2009), according to government estimates. Predictably, the growth in pensions spending crowded out other components of Greek welfare, to an even greater extent than had hitherto been the case.

5.4.2.1. Unemployment Benefits

The diminished capacity of the welfare state to respond to the increased need for social protection can be seen most clearly in the area of income support for the unemployed (Matsaganis, 2016). In 2010–14, unemployment protection became subject to a flurry of legislative or administrative changes. On the one hand, the benefit rate of contributory unemployment insurance was cut (from €454 to €360 per month), and the duration of repeat spells over a period of four years was limited. On the other hand, access to means-tested unemployment assistance was relaxed (with the benefit rate left unchanged), while a benefit for formerly self-employed workers was also introduced.

Yet the combined result of these changes was *reduced* coverage. As unemployment soared and unemployment spells grew longer, the coverage of unemployment benefits declined. Between 2010 and 2014, as the number of jobless workers doubled (from 624,000 to 1.27 million), the number of recipients of any of the three unemployment benefits mentioned *fell* considerably (from 226,000 to 155,000). In view of that, the coverage rate over the same period decreased steeply, from 36.2 per cent to 12.7 per cent of all jobless workers. It is hard to reconcile this evidence with the claim of Blanchard et al. (2014: 20) that, under IMF advice, in Greece unemployment benefit coverage 'expanded'.

The low coverage of unemployment benefits (and the cut in the level of unemployment insurance benefit), together with the lack of a broad-based social assistance scheme of last resort, helps explain why child poverty is so high among families whose head is unemployed. Of course, persistently high child poverty figures also imply that other policy changes failed to make up for those protection gaps. Still, some improvements did take place in 2013–14. Three policies are worth mentioning here: the introduction of a non-categorical means-tested 'unified child benefit' in 2013; the payment of a lump sum 'social dividend' in 2014; and the launch of a guaranteed minimum income pilot in a number of local areas in 2014–15.

5.4.2.2. Child Benefit

Until recently, the structure of family allowances was fragmented and regressive. Benefit amounts were generous for two categories: large families (with four or more children, broadened to three or more from 2008), and employees of public utilities, banks, and the civil service. In contrast, the overwhelming majority of children lived in families that received little or no benefit, even when they were poor.

In 2013, contributory family allowances, benefits for large families, and tax relief for families with children were all replaced by a 'unified' (i.e. non-categorical) child benefit, payable on an income-tested basis. The benefit level varied according to family income and the number of children (from €13 to €40 per month per child), while the income threshold also varied with household size. For instance, a family with two children, with annual income of below €10,000, was eligible for €80 per month. Moreover, large families that passed the income test were eligible for an additional €500 per child *per year*. For example, a family with four children all below the age of 23, with annual income below €12,000, was eligible for €327 per month.

Several policy issues remain unaddressed. To start with, benefit amounts are low, and income conditions stringent. Clearly this can be attributed to tight fiscal constraints. However, it should also be seen as a reflection of the relatively low priority accorded to income support for poor families. Furthermore, the new structure preserves the disproportionate support for large families, over and above what might be expected, given the poverty risks; this can only be understood as a remnant of outdated notions of what constitutes family policy. Lastly, the requirement (introduced in 2011) that claimants must provide proof of legal residence for at least ten years excluded thousands of families of foreign migrants with children, even when they met all other conditions.

On a positive note, the 2013 policy change extended public assistance to hundreds of thousands of poor families that had been ineligible for income support under the previous system. Unlike most of the programmes it replaced, the new child benefit is available from the first child, and for a larger age group (up to 18, or up to 23 if in college, or irrespective of age if disabled). As a result, according to official figures, the number of families receiving child benefit in 2014 was approximately 756,000 (i.e. 53 per cent of all households with at least one resident child under 25 years), compared to 292,000 families receiving the corresponding benefits in 2009.

Spending on the scheme reached 0.33 per cent of GDP in 2014 in gross terms. In net terms (i.e. once the fiscal cost of the previously existing family allowances, including tax relief, that were abolished when the new child benefit came into force is taken into account), the scheme actually made a saving.

5.4.2.3. Social Dividend

In 2014, as the economy showed signs of stabilization, registering a positive growth rate (GDP up by 0.7 per cent) for the first time since 2007, the conservative–socialist coalition government decided to return part of the primary fiscal surplus achieved under austerity to vulnerable groups in the form of a one-off 'social dividend', paid as a lump sum. Families with an annual income of up to €7,050 for a single person—increased by a third (€2,350) for every additional adult or in the case of single parenthood, and by a sixth (€1,175) for every child or household member suffering from disability—were eligible, provided their housing wealth was below €125,000 (single person) or €200,000 (couple with or without children). The level of the social dividend was set at €500 for a single person, rising to €833 for a couple with two children (€647 per receiving household on average). According to official figures, more than 691,000 households were paid the social dividend, at a fiscal cost of 0.25 per cent of GDP (in 2014).

5.4.2.4. Minimum Income Pilot

The onset of the crisis revived interest in minimum income, especially on the part of external actors. In May 2010, the Memorandum of Understanding that committed the Greek government to austerity measures and policy reforms, in exchange for the bailout loan, listed the provision to 'review the scope for improvements in the targeting of social expenditures to enhance the social safety net for the most vulnerable' (IMF 2010: 88). In March 2012, the IMF strongly advocated a broad-based minimum income scheme as part of a strategy aimed at streamlining social assistance (and reducing its cost). In November 2012, the conservative–socialist coalition government was persuaded to enshrine in law (as part of the Medium-term Fiscal Strategy 2013–14) the pledge to launch in 2014 a guaranteed minimum income pilot in (originally) two local areas, setting aside the modest sum of €20 million.

The pilot was eventually launched in November 2014, under the name Guaranteed Social Income, in thirteen municipalities (i.e. one in each region). Technical assistance was provided by the World Bank, with the support of the European Commission's (Athens-based) Task Force for Greece. It essentially took the form of a cash transfer paid via the tax system to families with very low income, with no 'activation' measures attached. The annual income threshold for eligibility was set at €2,400 for a single person, rising by €1,200 for every additional adult, and by €600 for every child (and an extra €600 in the case of single parenthood). Households' assessed income was net of taxes and social contributions; income disregards applied to disability benefits and to 20 per cent of earnings from dependent employment. The asset test provided that housing wealth could not exceed €90,000 for a single person, rising by €15,000 for every additional adult, and by €10,000 for every child (subject to a ceiling of €200,000). The cash transfer paid under the scheme was set equal to the difference between the guaranteed minimum income and the receiving household's assessed income.

Implementation was rather haphazard to start with, and was further disrupted by the January 2015 general election and the resulting change in government. Overall, the pilot ran for a mere six months, with the last instalment of income support under the scheme paid to recipients seven months after its formal end (on 23 December 2015). Central government proved unwilling, as well as unable, to provide much logistical support (let alone leadership) to the pilot municipalities, which lacked the resources to tackle the task effectively at the local level. The total number of receiving households reached 18,690 (approximately 9 per cent of the population of the thirteen municipalities selected for the pilot). The average cash transfer was €220 per month per participating household.

On launching the 2014 pilot, the then government had announced its commitment to rolling the scheme out nationally in 2015 'if adequate funding is available'. For some time after the January 2015 general election and the resulting change in government, the future of minimum income in Greece looked bleak, as ministers complained of 'insufferable' EU/IMF pressure to extend the MI pilot nationwide and argued that the introduction of guaranteed minimum income in Africa on the advice of IMF has been 'disastrous'. Later on the government must have had a change of heart: at the time of writing (December 2016), a second pilot was underway in 30 municipalities under the name of Social Solidarity Income, with the view to a nationwide roll-out in 2017.

5.4.2.5. Retrenchment vs Expansion

The policies described above, though welcome, were far too limited to tackle effectively the social emergency: the vast majority of jobless households, including those in extreme poverty, remained without income protection. Moreover, because of the strict cash limits attached to the changes, the balance of 'retrenchment' vs 'expansion' remained overwhelmingly tilted towards the former. For each €100 saved as a result of cutbacks in social expenditure under the 2013–14 Spending Review, only about €7 was 'reinvested' in the four policies mentioned above.

5.4.3. Dealing with the 'Humanitarian Crisis' (2015–)

The anti-austerity coalition that won the January 2015 general election had amassed considerable political capital by denouncing the country's 'humanitarian crisis' (its preferred term for the social situation in Greece) when in opposition. Nevertheless, once in government, its much-awaited social programme proved something of an anticlimax.

Legislation on 'immediate measures to fight the humanitarian crisis' actually boiled down to three income- and asset-tested schemes: an electricity allowance (worth up to €40 per month) for poor families, some of which had had their homes disconnected because of unpaid bills; a rent benefit paid directly to home owners on behalf of their tenants (worth €160 per month for a couple with two children);[11] and a food subsidy in the form of a smart card accepted at supermarkets and other shops (also worth €160 per month for a couple with two children).

The sum of €200 million was set aside to pay for these three policies in 2015 (0.11 per cent of GDP), while the actual cost turned out to be below €130 million (0.07 per cent of GDP), including the projected cost of 2015 entitlements paid in 2016. The food card accounted for the lion's share (€114 million). The previous government's discretionary measures, rightly criticized as inadequate, had cost more: €654 million (0.36 per cent of GDP) in 2013 and €1,135 million (0.64 per cent of GDP) in 2014.

[11] A similar scheme, aimed at private sector workers who met contributory and income conditions, had existed prior to 2010.

5.4.4. Assessing the Poverty Impact

Recent research (Matsaganis and Leventi, 2016) on the impact on extreme child poverty of three key policies (child benefit, social dividend, and food card) shows that they made a limited contribution. The introduction of unified child benefit in 2013 had the greatest effect on child poverty, reducing the proportion of children below the extreme poverty threshold by 1.9 percentage points. In terms of poverty gap efficiency, the reduction of the extreme child poverty gap that can be attributed to unified child benefit was estimated at 17.5 per cent. The 2014 social dividend had a smaller effect on children both in terms of extreme poverty headcount rates (−1.7 percentage points) and in terms of poverty gap efficiency (−10.5 per cent). As for the 2015 food card (assessed as if it were a cash transfer), its contribution to reducing extreme child poverty was negligible in terms of headcount rates (−0.4 percentage points), but more substantial in terms of poverty gap efficiency (−13.5 per cent). All in all, the three flagship policies, launched with great pomp by the government of the day, are distinguishable only by the modesty of both the resources involved and their anti-poverty impact.

5.4.5. The Policy Discourse

It is difficult to comment on the discourse surrounding the protection of vulnerable families with children in the policy debate, while at the same time keeping a distance from politics. (Particularly in Greece, where political debates have always been very polarized—and in recent years downright toxic.) But it seems fair to say that the questions that have dominated the political discourse tended to be located at a higher level of abstraction: not so much 'what can we do to protect children (or other vulnerable groups)?', but rather 'how can it be that we are in crisis?', 'whose fault is it?', 'why do foreigners hate us?', etc. As a result, actual policy debates tended to be rare, unsophisticated, and usually initiated by the demands of the country's lenders, rather than by domestic policy actors.

This cavalier attitude to the bread-and-butter questions with which social policy is typically concerned is shared across the political spectrum. On the one hand, the anti-austerity bloc argued that policy details were irrelevant, so long as the 'big' questions of 'putting an end to austerity' and 'achieving debt relief' remained unresolved. On the other hand, all governments tended to react passively to the ensuing distributive fight, allocating scarce resources according to each group's political influence or power to deliver a veto. Given this, and the weakness of 'advocacy coalitions', it is hardly surprising that the poor, the unemployed, migrant groups, and others lost out—and so did their children.

5.5. CONCLUSIONS

As the preceding analysis illustrates, the social costs of the crisis for children and other vulnerable groups in Greece have been unnecessarily high. Prior to 2009, the welfare state was unusually unfit for the challenge, in spite of high and rising social expenditure. Under austerity, the social policies recommended by the EU–ECB–IMF Troika and pursued by national governments of all political hues failed to compensate for, and eventually reinforced, the adverse effects of the recession. While some changes did produce improvements, most cuts were indiscriminate, causing hardship and disrupting social provision. For all the rhetoric of political actors at home and abroad on the need to strengthen the social safety net, actual policies can only be described as misguided or inadequate. The new child benefit, the minimum income pilot, and the recently introduced food card can all be seen as welcome steps towards strengthening the social safety net. But as seen in the previous section, their impact on child poverty has been very limited, even when a low threshold of 'extreme poverty' is adopted. In view of that, in order to deal effectively with Greece's new social question, a far more concerted effort will be required than anything seen so far.

Was this inevitable? The severity and duration of the Greek crisis would quite probably have posed insurmountable challenges to any welfare state, even the most advanced. But experience from countries like Latvia and Ireland shows that, even under austerity, social policy can still make a difference. What is more, social rights in Greece have always been so unequally distributed between categories that the scope for improving social protection, while at the same time reducing budget deficits, remained enormous. Nevertheless, since the onset of the Greek crisis, policy makers have done little to expand coverage and mend holes in the social safety net. The rationing of resources (now scarcer than ever) by political power, rather than by need of social protection, has reaffirmed itself as the guiding principle behind the exercise of social policy in Greece.

As Pierson (2011) has argued, the main reason that social programmes have proved relatively 'resilient' in the 'era of permanent austerity' is that, by benefiting large sections of the electorate, they help create coalitions in favour of the status quo. This implies that alternative coalitions in favour of new social programmes, not yet in force, whose potential beneficiaries are politically weaker, will be far less powerful. There is evidence that this is exactly what has been happening in Greece. Defenders of the status quo, ranging from trade unions in public utilities to professional associations (judges, engineers, medics) with good connections to the political establishment, have been quite successful in resisting cuts. As a result, the burden of fiscal consolidation has fallen on less powerful categories (private sector employees, own-account workers), leaving little space for policies aimed at protecting the real victims of the recession (the unemployed, the poor).

Meanwhile, as the spotlights on the 2015 EU–Greek confrontation were turned off, another drama unfolded: last year over a million migrants and refugees crossed into Europe, as many as 85 per cent of them landing on Greece's shores, with some (including many children) losing their lives in the attempt. At the time of writing, an effective, coordinated response on the part of the EU to avert a genuine humanitarian crisis was not yet in sight, leaving Greece to cope with the bad luck of its geographical position. As thousands of refugees were trapped inside the country's northern borders, in makeshift camps already packed beyond capacity, the omens seemed anything but good.

REFERENCES

Arkolakis, Costas, Aristos Doxiadis, and Manolis Galenianos (2015). 'The Challenge of Trade Adjustment in Greece'. Social Science Research Network (12 November 2015). <http://dx.doi.org/10.2139/ssrn.2689545>.

Baldwin, Richard, Thorsten Beck, Agnès Bénassy-Quéré, Olivier Blanchard, Giancarlo Corsetti, Paul de Grauwe, Wouter den Haan, Francesco Giavazzi, Daniel Gros, Sebnem Kalemli-Ozcan, Stefano Micossi, Elias Papaioannou, Paolo Pesenti, Christopher Pissarides, Guido Tabellini, and Beatrice Weder di Mauro (2015). 'Rebooting the Eurozone: Step I—Agreeing a Crisis Narrative'. *CEPR Policy Insight 85* (London: Centre for Economic Policy Research.

Blanchard, Olivier and Daniel Leigh (2013). 'Growth Forecast Errors and Fiscal Multipliers'. *IMF Working Paper 13/1* (Washington, DC: International Monetary Fund).

Blanchard, Olivier, Florence Jaumotte, and Prakash Loungani (2014). 'Labor Market Policies and IMF Advice in Advanced Economies during the Great Recession'. *IZA Journal of Labor Policy 3*, no. 2: pp. 1–23.

Castles, Francis G. (2010). 'Black Swans and Elephants on the Move: The Impact of Emergencies on the Welfare State'. *Journal of European Social Policy 20*, no. 2: pp. 91–101.

Christodoulakis, Nicos (2015). *Greek Endgame: From Austerity to Growth or Grexit* (London: Rowman & Littlefield).

Decressin, Jörg, Raphael Espinoza, Ioannis Halikias, Daniel Leigh, Prakash Loungani, Paulo Medas, Susanna Mursula, Martin Schindler, Antonio Spilimbergo, and Teng Teng Xu (2015). 'Wage Moderation in Crises: Policy Considerations and Applications to the Euro Area'. *Staff Discussion Note 15/22* (Washington, DC: International Monetary Fund).

Dyson, Kenneth (2014). *States, Debt, and Power: 'Saints' and 'Sinners' in European History and Integration* (Oxford: Oxford University Press).

European Commission (2014). 'The Second Economic Adjustment Programme for Greece: Fourth Review—April 2014'. *European Economy Occasional Papers 192* (Brussels: Directorate-General for Economic and Financial Affairs).

Featherstone, Kevin (2011). 'The Greek Sovereign Debt Crisis and EMU: A Failing State in a Skewed Regime'. *Journal of Common Market Studies 49*, no. 2: pp. 193–217.

Ferrera, Maurizio (1996). 'The "Southern Model" of Welfare in Social Europe'. *Journal of European Social Policy* 6, no. 1: pp. 17–37.

Ferrera, Maurizio and Anton Hemerijck (2003). 'Recalibrating Europe's Welfare Regimes'. In Jonathan Zeitlin and David M. Trubek (eds), *Governing Work and Welfare in a New Economy: European and American Experiments* (Oxford: Oxford University Press).

Galenianos, Manolis (2015). 'The Greek Crisis: Origins and Implications'. *Crisis Observatory Research Paper 16/2015* (Athens: Hellenic Foundation for European and Foreign Policy).

Goedemé, Tim, Bérénice Storms, Tess Penne, and Karel Van den Bosch (2015). *The Development of a Methodology for Comparable Reference Budgets in Europe—Final Report of the Pilot Project* (Brussels: European Commission Directorate-General for Employment, Social Affairs and Inclusion).

International Monetary Fund (IMF) (2010). 'Greece: First review under the stand-by arrangement'. *Country Report No.10/286* (Washington, DC: International Monetary Fund).

International Monetary Fund (IMF) (2014). 'Greece: Fifth Review under the Extended Arrangement under the Extended Fund Facility, and Request for Waiver of Non-observance of Performance Criterion and Rephasing of Access; Staff Report; Press Release; and Statement by the Executive Director for Greece'. *Country Report No.14/151* (Washington, DC: International Monetary Fund).

Jenkins, Stephen P., Andrea Brandolini, John Micklewright, and Brian Nolan (2013). *The Great Recession and the Distribution of Household Income* (Oxford: Oxford University Press).

Katsimi, Margarita and Thomas Moutos (2010). 'EMU and the Greek Crisis: The Political-economy Perspective', *European Journal of Political Economy 26*, no. 44: pp. 568–76.

Matsaganis, Manos (2011). 'The Welfare State and the Crisis: The Case of Greece'. *Journal of European Social Policy 21*, no. 5: pp. 501–12.

Matsaganis, Manos (2013). *The Greek Crisis: Social Impact and Policy Responses* (Berlin: Friedrich-Ebert-Stiftung).

Matsaganis, Manos (2016). 'Austerity and the Welfare State in Greece: The Case of Labour Market Policies'. In Sotiria Theodoropoulou (ed.), *Welfare States and EU Austerity: The Case of Labour Market Policies* (Brussels: European Trade Union Institute).

Matsaganis, Manos and Chrysa Leventi (2013). 'Poverty in Greece: Trends in 2013'. *Policy Analysis Research Unit Newsletter 5/2013* (Athens: Athens University of Economics and Business).

Matsaganis, Manos and Chrysa Leventi (2016). 'The Impact of Social and Fiscal Policies: Addressing Extreme Poverty in Greece (2013–2015)'.

Mitsopoulos, Michael and Theodore Pelagidis (2011). *Understanding the Crisis in Greece: From Boom to Bust* (Basingstoke: Palgrave Macmillan).

Organization for Economic Co-operation and Development (OECD) (2011). *Education Policy Advice for Greece*. Strong Performers and Successful Reformers in Education (Paris: OECD Publishing).

Organization for Economic Co-operation and Development (OECD) (2013). *Economic Surveys: Greece* (Paris: OECD Publishing).

Organization for Economic Co-operation and Development (OECD) (2014). *PISA 2012 Results in Focus: What 15-year-olds Know and What They Can Do with What They Know* (Paris: OECD).

Pierson, Paul (2011). 'The Welfare State over the Very Long Run'. *ZeSArbeitspapier 02/2011* (Bremen: Zentrum für Sozialpolitik, Universität Bremen).

Xafa, Miranda (2014). 'Sovereign Debt Crisis Management: Lessons from the 2012 Greek Debt Restructuring'. *CIGI Papers no. 33* (Waterloo, ON: Centre for International Governance Innovation).

6

Recession, Recovery, and Regime Change: Effects on Child Poverty in Hungary

András Gábos and István György Tóth

6.1. INTRODUCTION

The well-being of children is a product of a number of factors (historical developments, demographic characteristics, redistributive institutions, etc.). It is difficult to identify what 'causes' what, and to add relative weights to the various factors. When describing why the Great Recession affected children in Hungary in a negative way, one can identify three major transmission channels between macro developments on the one hand and the relative positions of families with children on the other (UNICEF Office of Research, 2014). The first relates to the negative effect of the crisis on labour markets: the appearance of unemployment in the household and the fall in real incomes. The second channel relates to financial markets: in addition to a loss of private wealth due to a deterioration in access to, and the loss of, credit, we might mention here the volatility of the exchange rates for the national currency, given the direct exposure of Hungarian family expenditure to this. Finally, the volatility of public sector expenditure—creating a link between macro (national) and micro (household) balances—constitutes the third transmission channel. Since data are selectively available, the chapter focuses on the first and the third channel; but we also try to reflect on the effect of the financial markets.

The chapter starts with an introduction to the understanding of what the Great Recession meant in Hungary. In order to do that, we need to clarify what shape the country was in in 2007/8, having already experienced waves of austerity before other European countries started feeling the winds of bad times (sections 6.2.1 and 6.2.2). Following this, we discuss the policy context and policy developments (sections 6.2.3 and 6.2.4). Then, the bulk of the chapter is devoted to analysing the situation of children in the crisis (starting with a description of relevant structural changes (section 6.3.1) and continuing with a presentation of the incidence and trends of child poverty (the remainder of section 6.3). Section 6.4 briefly analyses the effects of the policies applied, and section 6.5 contains some conclusions.

6.2. HUNGARY'S ECONOMIC CRISIS

6.2.1. Introduction: A Short Account of How Hungary Faced the Outbreak of the Crisis

Probably the most difficult legacy of the structural adjustment in Hungary's economy after the post-1989–90 systemic change—a development that, in practical terms, continued until the outbreak of the Great Recession—was the large-scale shift in the employment equilibrium. The dramatic fall in employment between 1990 and 1993 resulted in sustained low activity rates in the country. The total average number of employed people fell from 4.9 million (4.5 million of active age) in 1990 to 3.7 million (3.6 million of active age) by 1995.[1] Part of the massive drop in employment was absorbed by early retirement schemes; but as many of those pushed out were active-age people (most of them low-educated), they ended up in inactivity (Köllő, 2009). Badly calibrated labour market policies at the time kept large masses on welfare, creating inactivity traps for most of them. For subsequent governments (which generally regarded these groups as 'cheap voters', easily swayed to get them re-elected), this high level of inactivity was a short-term problem only. However, a massive budget expansion in the early 2000s, initiated by the then socialist government, proved unsustainable, given the low tax base caused by inactivity. Mounting deficits accumulated into large piles of foreign debt, prompting austerity measures as early as 2006—and, from time to time, later on. This left very little room for manoeuvre when the real crisis arrived in Hungary in autumn 2008.

The first half of the 2000s was characterized by increasing real incomes, falling inequalities (Fábián et al., 2014) and reduced (child) poverty—and, at the same time, by increased indebtedness on the part of both the government and households. While government deficits may provide a buffer in times of expansionary fiscal policies, indebtedness presented a more immediate threat for households. As in many other parts of the world, the collateral required to obtain a mortgage had fallen in the previous decade. Also, the very high interest rates charged on mortgages taken out in the Hungarian national currency, the forint (HUF), incentivized banks to offer very cheap loans denominated in euros or Swiss francs, given that Hungary was not a member of the Eurozone. This became very serious for mortgage holders in 2008, when the Hungarian currency weakened significantly against the euro and the Swiss franc.[2]

[1] The active-age population is taken to be aged 15–64 years.

[2] In October 2008, the indebtedness of the general government and of households prompted the Hungarian government to turn to the IMF for a large loan package, which was then paid back a few years later (the full package being cleared by April 2016).

6.2.2. Economic Developments in the Period 2007–2014

Based on economic and policy development data (see Figures 6.1 to 6.3 and Table 6.1), we can distinguish three phases in the period 2007–14. First, between 2007 and 2009, the country experienced a rise in unemployment (from around 8 per cent to around 10 per cent), particularly youth unemployment (a rise from 20 per cent to 27 per cent). The same period witnessed a drastic fall in gross domestic product (GDP) and net real incomes (–5 per cent); meanwhile the collapse of the mortgage market (and of lending as a whole) made it very difficult to smooth consumption over time for those families most in need. Inflation, stagnating wages, and cuts in social spending (including pensions) led to falling real incomes in this period.

Second, between 2010 and 2012, the rise in unemployment continued (to around 11 per cent), while the net real income of households wobbled: it fell in 2010 (–2.9 per cent), started to increase in 2011 (+2.6 per cent), but then fell

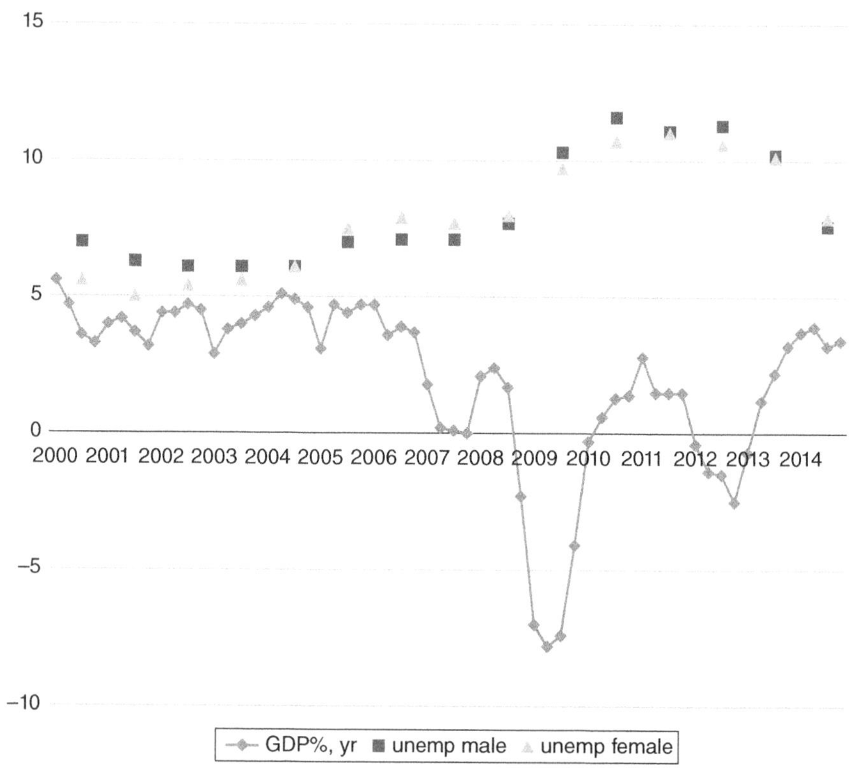

Figure 6.1. GDP growth and unemployment levels by gender, Hungary (2000–2014)

Notes: GDP: In per cent of the corresponding quarter of the previous year. Unemployment: yearly average.

Source: Kopint-Tárki macroeconomic database, Hungarian Central Statistical Office (HCSO).

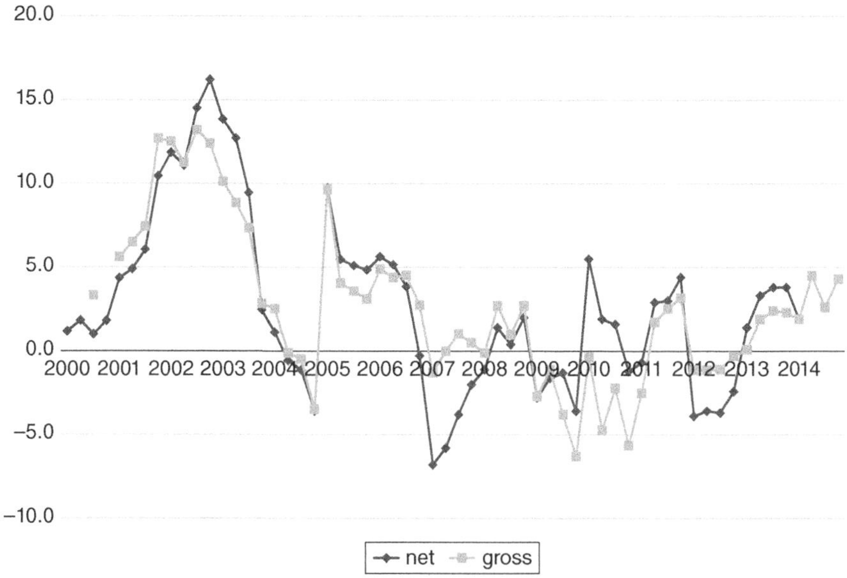

Figure 6.2. Development of net and gross real incomes in Hungary (2000–2014, quarterly, as a per cent of the previous year)

Source: Kopint-Tárki macroeconomic database, HCSO.

again in 2012. As a result of a multitude of causes (related to political dynamics, living standards, and the opening up of the Western European labour markets to migrants from the New Member States (NMS)), outward migration started to accelerate in these years.[3]

The third period (2013–14) saw a favourable macroeconomic context: GDP growth was accompanied by practically zero inflation, sharply reduced unemployment, and increasing employment (albeit initially achieved via large-scale public works programmes to encourage many inactive people to re-enter the labour market). Also, outward migration (counted as taking employment, but not within the country) tended to contribute, at least in statistical terms, to increased activity in this period. Some rise in employment on the internal primary labour market was also visible in this period. And the real income of households also started to increase.

In political terms, the second and third periods of economic development belong together: up until 2010, there was a socialist government (albeit only a caretaker administration between mid-2009 and the 2010 elections); but after

[3] Until very recently, the Hungarian population was among the least mobile of the countries of Central and Eastern Europe. However, since 2006 the country has witnessed increased outward migration, and by 2013 some 2–3 per cent of Hungarian households had someone working abroad either temporarily or permanently (Blaskó et al., 2014).

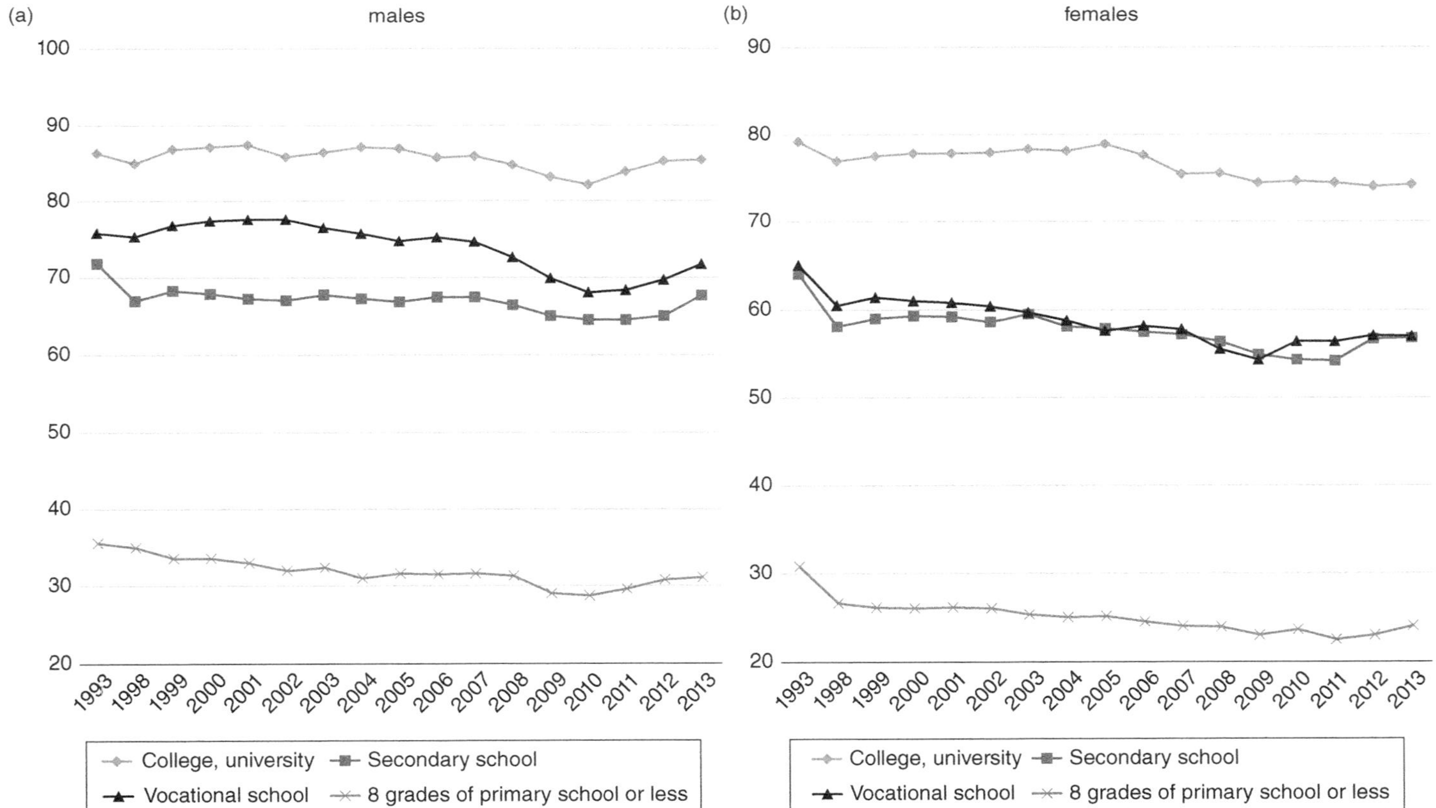

Figure 6.3. Employment rates by gender and education in Hungary (1993–2013) (per cent of population aged 15–64)

Note: Up to 2000 data are weighted on the basis of the 1990 population census.

Source: Fazekas and Neumann (*2014*). Data based on the Labour Force Survey of the HCSO.

Table 6.1. Sequence of policy measures through the crisis, 2007–2014, Hungary

2007–9 A period of austerity

Austerity in general social policy

- Public sector wage bill frozen (for two years)
- Thirteenth-month pension abolished, retirement age increase accelerated
- Increase in value added tax (VAT) from 20 per cent to 25 per cent
- Freeze of minimum pensions, cuts in sickness benefits

Austerity regarding family benefits

- Parental leave shortened to two years (from three)
- Maximum age of a child eligible for family allowance reduced (23 to 20 years)
- Almost total abolition of family tax credits (starting from 2006)
- Freeze on family allowance (after a significant increase in 2006) and on childcare allowance

Steps toward workfare and conditionality

- Cash social assistance switched from individual level to household level ('one benefit per household rule')
- Start of the expansion of public works schemes and the introduction of work-related conditions
- Introduction of conditional cash transfers for kindergarten enrolment

2010–14 The period of a sharp turn to workfare

General social policy

- Cutbacks in unemployment benefit (ninety days maximum)
- Further cuts in social assistance
- Expansion of public works schemes (for lower than the minimum wage), and a further expansion (2013–14)
- Flat-rate income tax, two brackets in 2011–12, withdrawal of tax credit for low wage earners
- Increase in minimum wage (HUF 73,500/month to HUF 93,000/month)
- Reduction in the age limit for compulsory public education
- Price regulation on utilities (*rezsicsökkentés*)

Extended conditionality and increasing ties to employment in family policy

- Reintroduction of, and subsequent substantial increase in, personal income tax deductions for families with children
- Parental leave restored to three years
- Conditionality elements introduced in family allowance (eligibility tied to school attendance)
- Child tax credit also deductible from social insurance contributions
- Childcare fee extended (GYED Extra): right to the benefit remains even if the parent goes back to work

a landslide victory in the 2010 general election, a right-wing conservative government came to power, heralding a major shift in the flagship family and social policies (as will be explained later in the chapter).

6.2.3. Institutional Legacy of Social and Family Policies

Political commitment to institutional family policies has deep roots and long traditions in Hungary.[4] Through a century-long history of institutional

[4] Family allowances were first introduced in 1912 for public servants (extended later). Also, relatively generous maternity and parental provisions (long paid break for mothers with

developments, a dual focus can be traced: to regulate the labour supply of mothers[5] on the one hand, and to increase fertility on the other. Vertical equity considerations (targeting help at poorer families) were not particularly emphasized.

The overall level of public spending on children has traditionally been high in Hungary: according to Eurostat, family- or child-related expenditure in 2009 was around 3 per cent of GDP, compared to 2.3 per cent in the EU-27 generally. And it has remained relatively high in more recent years (2.7 per cent vs. 2.2 per cent in 2012). This level is exceeded only by some Scandinavian (Denmark, Finland, Sweden) and Continental (Austria, Germany, Luxembourg) welfare states.

The forms of public intervention are biased towards cash benefits, while less emphasis is put on the provision of services (Gábos, 2013). Mothers have rather been encouraged to stay at home with their children for a long time (up to three years per child, but parents also frequently choose to time the arrival of their next child towards the end of the third year, so as to extend the period), while the availability of early childhood care institutions has varied over time (the widespread pre-transition availability of kindergartens and crèches collapsed soon after 1990, with employer-provided institutions closing down and local government provisions underfunded and reduced for almost two decades).

Though rather simplistic, a differentiation between the two policy regimes may be useful. Family allowances and universal parental benefits are representative of universalistic citizenship-based policies, while employment-related maternity and parental benefits and child-related tax benefits belong to insurance-based policy models.

6.2.4. Policy Changes: General Social Policy and Family Policy Measures

6.2.4.1. The Political Context

The Great Recession hit Hungary in the second term of an eight-year socialist administration (2002–10). In these years, economic and social policy was characterized by successive waves of budget expansion and austerity. Regarding family policy, the socialist government's second term in office brought two

children, with cash benefits and labour protection legislation) were introduced in the 1960s and have been extended several times since then (Sipos and Tóth, 1998; Blaskó, 2010; Gábos et al., 2009).

[5] Quite paradoxically, the introduction of long paid maternity and parental breaks at the end of the 1960s was partly motivated not only by worries of declining fertility, but also by fears of potential female unemployment arising as a result of the economic reforms of the time.

important structural changes. First, the amount of universal family allowance was doubled, at the cost of the almost total withdrawal of two complementary elements of the system: regular child protection allowance (a means-tested benefit) and family tax allowance. Second, a programme to overcome the shortage in institutional childcare supply was launched in 2008, focusing primarily on family day care centres.

The landslide victory of the conservatives in 2010 resulted in a sea change in the philosophy and practice of economic policies. It was considered possible to break the spiral of austerity (leading to increased foreign indebtedness) through various unorthodox economic policies (special sectoral taxes, instead of raising earnings-related taxes; direct cuts in expenditure; etc.). The conservative government's time in office has also seen a definite shift in social policies in general: a sharp turn to workfare, the cutting-back of rights-based policies, and the imposition of conditionalities on a number of provisions. For family policies and child support alike, the universalistic, social-democratic approach was set aside, and pro-natalist policies that supported the middle class came to the fore—most importantly, a shift in child-related support from family allowance[6] to family tax allowance, though entitlement to a childcare fee was also extended for those returning to the labour market (Szikra, 2014; Ferge and Darvas, 2014).

6.2.4.2. Shift in Policy Regimes in the Making: From Austerity to Workfare

After the shock of a potential default by the state budget in autumn 2008 (and an agreement to take International Monetary Fund (IMF) loans to help with the financing), austerity measures followed in 2009 (most of them at the time the caretaker government was inaugurated).[7]

Major steps affecting the public sector included a wage freeze for public sector employees, abolition of thirteenth month bonuses, and a cut in local government grants. In the pension system, the thirteenth-month pension (introduced as part a major expansionist move in 2003) was abolished, and the previously announced rise in the age of retirement was brought forward. More importantly for children, the thirteenth-month family allowance (in place since 2003) was also abolished, and the value of the family allowance was frozen for a two-year period, while the age of those eligible was reduced

[6] Family allowance (which accounted for about 60 per cent of all child-related benefits in Hungary by 2006; Gábos, 2008) was severely inflated (no change in nominal values since 2008) and later made conditional on compulsory school attendance (and on kindergarten attendance since September 2015).

[7] After the previous prime minister lost a vote of confidence.

from 23 to 20 years. The eligibility period for childcare allowance (a universal benefit) was shortened from three to two years. Though the basic trends were cuts in expenditure, even in this period (2007–9) certain elements of conditionality appeared in the social policy systems. Social assistance benefits were limited to one type of benefit per household. Also, back at this time, the socialist government introduced (on a relatively small scale) public works schemes—making certain social benefits conditional on work. Finally, a conditional cash transfer programme to encourage the parents of disadvantaged children to enrol them in kindergarten was introduced in 2009 (a summary of policy changes between 2007 and 2014 is provided in Table 6.1).

From 2010 onwards, the newly elected Orbán government also changed the rules in social policy. At the same time huge changes took place in virtually all spheres of public life: democratic institutions, economic policies, the tax system, the legal system, and central and local government (Szikra, 2014; Scharle and Szikra, 2015). Deep cuts were introduced in social assistance and the unemployment benefit system. The government recalibrated the relationship between the minimum wage and the available social assistance benefits (raising the minimum wage and limiting social assistance benefits at the same time). There followed a massive expansion of public works schemes, with eligibility for (a lower level of) social assistance made conditional on participation in public works.

In family policy, a definite shift could be observed from social-democratic values to conservative policies: attention moved away from the poor towards the middle classes. Together with the introduction of a flat, 16 per cent rate of personal income tax, a relatively large child tax allowance (relatively sizeable per child amounts, deductible from calculated tax) was introduced. Those who can claim it may not need to pay any tax at all, even if they earn around the average wage. Childcare allowance was restored to its former duration (it could be claimed up to the child's third birthday), while conditionality elements were introduced to family allowance (school absenteeism could be punished by withdrawal of family allowance). Means-tested cash benefits were increasingly converted (partly or fully) to in-kind benefits—for example, the amount of regular child protection benefit received in cash was significantly reduced, while several in-kind benefits, such as free school meals and free access to schoolbooks, were attached to it (Ferge and Darvas, 2014).

In the period between 2012 and 2014, there was no backward correction. Rather, the scale of public works was increased, and tax concessions for families were further extended (large families bringing in around the average wage could even be exempt from social insurance contributions). Also, maternity and parental benefits were extended in two ways. First, in a reversal of earlier practice, when a mother had to choose either to return to her job and receive a salary or else claim childcare allowance, eligibility for childcare allowance remained even if the mother went back to work (until the child's third birthday).[8] Second, unlike previously, when the various maternity and parental benefits were available for only one child, the new regulation made it possible to accumulate eligibility (i.e. claim maternity benefit concurrently for all children under the age of 3, regardless of their number).

6.3. CHILDREN IN HUNGARY'S CRISIS

The negative impacts of enduring and cyclical financial and economic crisis in Hungary were shared by the whole of society, but certain groups—such as families with children—were more affected than others. All the main indicators based on the EU Statistics on Income and Living Conditions (EU-SILC)—such as the at-risk-of-poverty (AROP) rate, anchored poverty, or severe material deprivation rate—point to an increased risk of poverty and social exclusion among these groups (see the overview chapter (Chapter 1) of this book). Research based on Tárki Household Monitor Survey (covering almost the whole period since the political system change), points out that the high pre-crisis vulnerability and poverty risk among children had persisted in Hungary since the early 1990s.[9]

6.3.1. Background and Underlying Structural Trends

The income of families with children was about the population average in 1990, in Hungary's first year under democratic rule (Gábos, 2000; Tóth 2005). Children with only one parent and (to a lesser extent) those in large families were already in a disadvantaged position, compared to their peers; but in terms of the number of children concerned, both between-group and within-group inequalities were relatively narrow (Tóth, 2005).

Since 1990, several changes have taken place in the Hungarian society, and we present these from the perspective of children. We choose to do this in order to show how developments in the current adult society translate into material

[8] From 2015, even eligibility for the employment-related childcare fee was kept when the mother returned to the labour market.

[9] Alongside the Hungarian survey of EU-SILC, Tárki Household Monitor Survey is another data source to analyse the material living conditions of Hungarian households. The survey is a follow-up to the Hungarian Household Panel survey, which ran from 1992 to 1997. While the sample size is only a fifth of the Hungarian SILC, the Tárki survey provides an opportunity to analyse long-term trends. Furthermore, the Tárki sample covers a larger range of the Hungarian income distribution, especially the top of the distribution (Havasi, 2011). Overall, Tárki data show larger income inequalities and higher risks of poverty (both in the overall population and among children) than does SILC.

Table 6.2. Composition of the total population, of children, and of poor children in 1992, 2007, and 2014, Hungary (column percentages by dimensions)

		Population			All children			Poor children		
		1992	2007	2014	1992	2007	2014	1992	2007	2014
Settlement type where the household lives	urban	60	66	77	59	63	67	46	50	60
	rural	40	34	23	41	37	33	54	50	40
Age of the household head	–35	23	18	17	34	25	24	36	20	35
	36–59	55	58	60	63	69	73	58	73	62
	60+	22	25	23	3	6	3	6	7	3
Number of children in the household	0	41	54	58	0	0	0	0	0	0
	1	21	19	22	24	30	41	14	21	24
	2	27	17	14	50	40	38	26	36	40
	3+	11	10	6	26	30	21	60	43	35
Education of the household head	primary or less	36	23	18	30	20	16	70	38	41
	vocational	32	38	37	36	37	34	21	47	40
	secondary	20	23	27	21	22	31	8	9	11
	tertiary	13	16	18	13	21	18	0	5	8

Source: 1992: Hungarian Household Panel (HHP); 2007 and 2014: Tárki Household Monitor survey, own calculations.

conditions for a future society that happens to be young now. To do this, we present changes in the composition of children (where they live, what material conditions they share with their siblings, etc.). This approach also enables us to highlight the way in which conditions in larger families are weighted when taking this 'futurospective' approach (looking at current things as if in retrospect from a future point in time).

The general decline in the rural population (a modern phenomenon) is also found in 'child society' (Table 6.2). The share of Hungarians living in villages declined from 40 per cent in 1992 to 23 per cent in 2014, while the share of children living in a rural environment also declined in the same period, from 41 per cent to 33 per cent. The composition of children in poor families has also changed a lot. Whereas in 1992 some 46 per cent of poor children lived in cities, by 2014 this share had increased to 60 per cent.[10] A large part of this shift seems to have occurred during the crisis, in the period 2007–14.

The change in the composition of children by the age of the household head (typically their parent, mostly their father) reflects one of the most important demographic changes in Hungary over the past twenty-five years: the rapid rise in maternal age when the first child is born. The age of mothers on the

[10] Due mostly to an increase in poverty in cities, while the situation in Budapest improved greatly.

birth of their first child has risen from around 23 in 1990 to over 28 in 2010—which means a quarter-year increase annually, a pace of change that hardly any other demographic indicator can beat.[11] Partly as a result, only 24 per cent of children in 2014 were living in a household whose head was below 35. However, it is precisely this group whose poverty rate increased greatly between 2007 and 2014. This is well illustrated by the fact that 35 per cent of poor children belong to this parental age group.

Another demography-driven development is that an increasing share of children tend to be born into families where there are no siblings. The share of children living in households with only one child went up from one in four in 1992 to two in five in 2014. The same period has brought an increase in the poverty risk of households with two children (see Table 6.3 for more detail).

Parents in general—again, a modern trend—have become better educated: children in households with well-educated heads accounted for some 13 per cent of all children in 1992, while the share had risen to around 20 per cent by the end of last decade. It should be mentioned that, in parallel with this, poverty has also appeared in the families of well-educated household heads.

Table 6.3. At-risk-of-poverty rate among children by main household characteristics in Hungary, 1992–2014 (per cent)

	1992	1996	2005	2007	2009	2012	2014
At-risk-of-poverty rate	12.3	19.8	15.8	16.5	20.6	26.0	21.9
Household type							
Single parent	20.8	25.3	31.9	23.9	31.3	29.6	33.3
Couple with 1 child	5.5	17.6	4.1	12.6	12.3	15.2	11.4
Couple with 2 children	5.3	11.4	9.6	14.1	16.0	14.6	12.3
Couple with 3+ children	26.3	32.7	24.3	24.1	19.3	40.9	51.5
Other households with children	12.3	19.0	17.7	12.6	27.2	30.2	22.0
Education of household head							
Primary	29.3	49.2	36.8	33.3	48.2	66.3	61.9
Vocational	7.5	14.9	15.3	21.5	19.0	21.5	25.4
Upper secondary	4.3	4.4	10.4	6.3	10.6	9.1	7.1
Tertiary	0.0	0.6	0.5	3.3	2.2	1.6	3.9
Settlement type							
Villages	18.0	29.1	24.7	24.4	28.8	34.1	28.4
Other cities	9.7	18.9	10.5	12.3	19.5	23.3	27.5
County seats	8.7	10.8	13.0	9.8	19.0	23.2	17.6
Budapest	5.7	6.3	5.0	13.3	3.2	10.3	1.6

Source: 1992–6: HHP; 2005–14: Tárki Household Monitor survey (own calculations).

[11] The process did not seem to have continued after 2010, though (Kapitány and Spéder, 2015).

6.3.2. Children in Crisis: Characteristics of Child Poverty and Trends over Time

According to Tárki data, the risk of poverty among Hungarian children started to increase slowly in the second half of the 2000s (2005–9), after a long preceding period of slight ups and downs (Fábián et al., 2014). This was followed by an acceleration of the process between 2009 and 2012 and a levelling thereafter (Gábos et al., 2015). The EU-SILC data show a somewhat different pattern between 2005 and 2010 (Figure 6.4): there is no indication of any change in the lower parts of the income distribution in this period (Fábián et al., 2014), but there is a significant increase (about 2.5 percentage points) between 2010 and 2013.

Children were among those hardest hit by the crisis: their relative income poverty risk (using a floating poverty threshold) increased against both the national average and the EU-27 child average. According to EU-SILC data, the at-risk-of-poverty rate among children increased by 5.8 percentage points between 2007 and 2014 (from 18.8 per cent to 24.6 per cent). While the risk of income poverty increased for all Hungarians in this period, the poverty dynamics among children was more than twice as strong as in the overall population (Figure 6.4). Furthermore, poverty deepened among children in this period: the relative median poverty gap increased from 19.5 per cent in

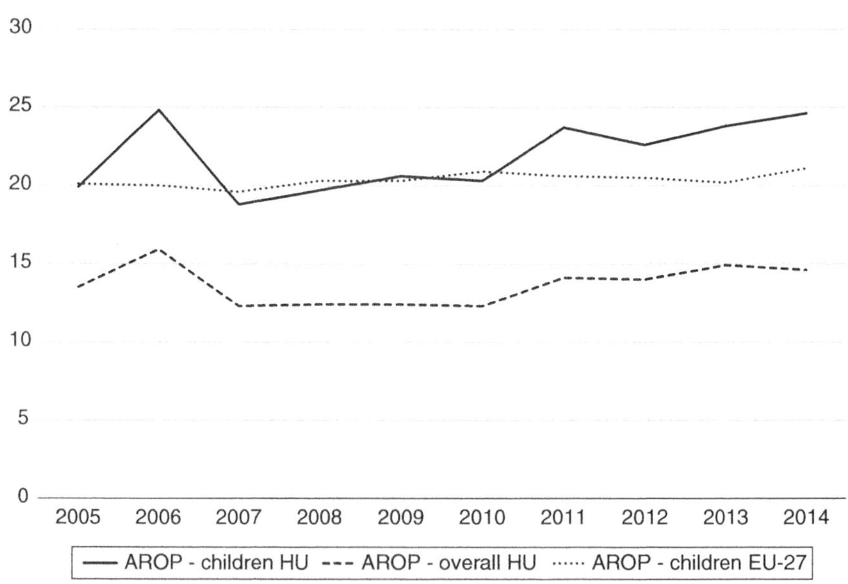

Figure 6.4. At-risk-of-poverty rate among children in Hungary and in the EU (2005–2014), per cent

Source: EU-SILC (Eurostat database).

2007 to 24 per cent in 2014 (being lowest in 2010, at 16.5 per cent). The figure is similar to the movement of the overall population average, and is lower than the EU-27 child average during the crisis period.

The figures describing overall child poverty trends in Hungary are robust and are confirmed by the Tárki Household Monitor Survey results, although this latter dataset indicates higher levels of poverty both for the overall population (12.6 per cent in 2007; 16.6 per cent in 2014) and for children (16.5 per cent; 26.0 per cent) (Gábos et al., 2015).

The relative position of Hungarian children also worsened compared to their European peers: while the at-risk-of-poverty rate among children in Hungary remained at the European average until 2010, the two trends started to diverge between 2010 and 2011. As a consequence, the Hungarian child poverty rates in 2014 were close to 4 percentage points higher than the EU-27 average.

The deterioration in the situation of children in terms of anchored poverty was even more accentuated during the Great Recession, following the decrease in real income between 2007 and 2010 (Figure 6.2), and to a lesser extent in 2012–13. Child poverty anchored in 2008 was boosted by 8.5 percentage points in two distinct phases (following the double peak of the crisis in Hungary): between 2008 and 2011, and between 2012 and 2014. However, while Hungarian child poverty was lower than the average of the twelve Member States that joined the EU in 2004 or later, the Hungarian figures deteriorated more severely at the time of the crisis (Figure 6.5).

The loss in real income and the weakened position of Hungarian families is also reflected in the severe material deprivation rates, with the value of this indicator rising by almost 11 percentage points—from 21.5 per cent in 2008 to 32.4 per cent in 2014 (peaking in 2013 at 35.6 per cent) (see Figure 6.6). Again, the divergence from the European children's benchmark is striking: from 2008 onwards, rapidly increasing severe material deprivation rates in Hungary contrasted with slightly decreasing risks in the New Member States. The considerable increase in material deprivation rates is attributable to certain items of the list included in the material deprivation index (as introduced in Chapter 1 of this book), first and foremost the inability to face unexpected financial expenses. According to Eurostat figures, the incidence of this among households with dependent children increased twice: between 2005 and 2007—before the outbreak of the crisis—and then between 2007 and 2009 (after which it levelled off at close to 80 per cent). This suggests that the financial stress for Hungarian households started increasing even before the crisis, during the 'good times' (of income growth). Inability to afford to go on a one-week holiday had been consistently very high over the previous ten years, while other items improved up until 2008/9, but then worsened until 2013.

EU-SILC data indicate that the relative position of Hungarian children was also among the worst in Europe when child-specific deprivation items are

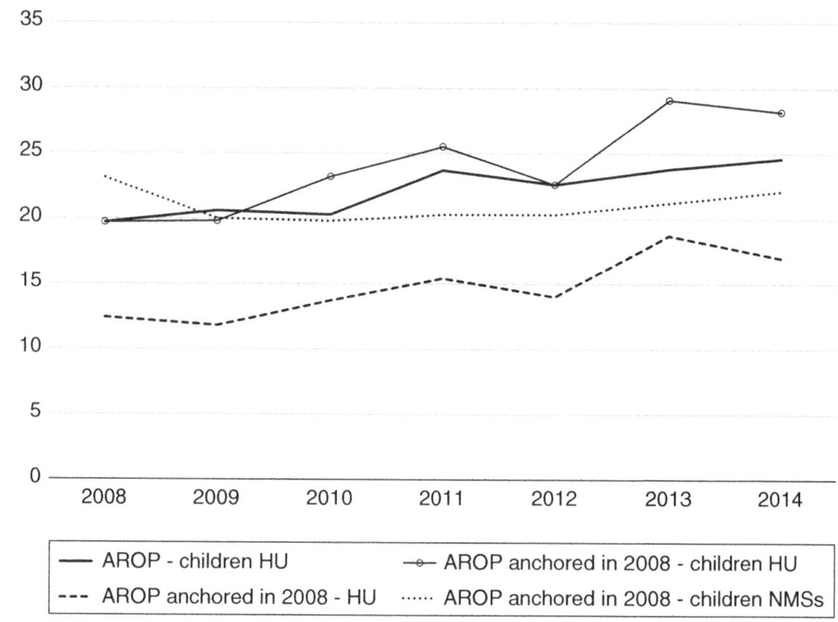

Figure 6.5. At-risk-of-poverty rate anchored in 2008 among children in Hungary and in the new EU Member States (2008–2014), per cent

Source: EU-SILC (Eurostat database).

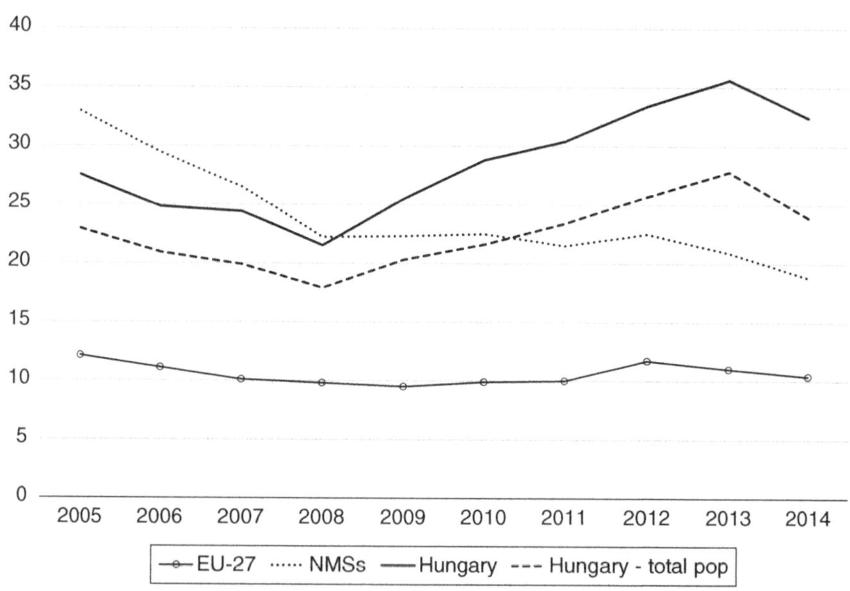

Figure 6.6. Severe material deprivation rate among children in Hungary and in the EU (2005–2014), per cent

Source: EU-SILC (Eurostat database).

considered.[12] According to the new child-specific measure of material deprivation proposed by Guio et al. (2012), in 2009 close to half of all Hungarian children lacked more than three items (on a list of eighteen), while a quarter of them lacked more than six items. In a cross-EU comparison, only children from Bulgaria and Romania (and Latvia, in the case of six or more items) had higher deprivation rates. Two-thirds of children in Hungary live in a family that cannot afford an annual one-week holiday—the highest figure in the EU. Also, some 30 per cent cannot afford to invite friends round, and a quarter cannot afford to participate in leisure activities. A fifth of Hungarian children cannot afford new clothes. Hungarian children score better than the EU-27 average only on the 'having a place to do homework' indicator.

In Hungary, the risk of poverty is strongly associated with a set of household-level characteristics, and these prove to be stable over time (Gábos et al., 2015). While living in a family with children is in itself associated with an increased risk of living in poverty, other characteristics (such as household type, education, labour market attachment, settlement type, and ethnic background) are strong and reinforcing factors that also differentiate among people in respect of their risk of poverty (Ferge and Darvas, 2014; Gábos and Szivós, 2006; Gábos et al., 2015; Tárki/Applica, 2010). The huge and enduring disparities that are present in Hungarian society overall, and specifically among families with children, show up when poverty rates are broken down by these characteristics. Table 6.3 summarizes our results for the period 1992–2014, based on the Tárki Household Monitor Survey. These results also indicate that children in groups with a high poverty risk (especially those in large families, living with a poorly educated household head, and in households with low or very low work intensity) were among those most affected by the crisis.

Large families and single-parent households are at highest risk when household type is considered. However, while the incidence of poverty was similar among children in these families at the outbreak of the crisis (every fourth child living in poverty in 2007 in both these groups), children in large families experienced a dramatic deterioration in their income situation relative not only to the average, but also to those in single-parent households. The increased poverty risk of children in large families is present in the EU-SILC data, too, but the magnitude of this increase is much smaller (28 per cent in 2007; 36 per cent in 2013).

Children with low-educated parents are at very high risk of poverty in Hungary—something that is strongly related to the high rate of inactivity in this social group. According to both Tárki and EU-SILC data, children with

[12] These data come from 2009, by which time: i) Hungarian society had already experienced a considerable setback in real income, compared to neighbouring countries; and ii) the crisis had already had an overall impact on European societies.

low-educated parents were among those most affected by the crisis: the incidence of poverty among them increased from one-third in 2007 to almost 70 per cent in 2012–13, though it decreased slightly afterwards (Table 6.3). Having a parent with upper secondary education, or especially with a diploma, is a very strong factor protecting against poverty in Hungary, although the crisis has highlighted the fragility of this protection in the face of external shocks.

The labour market attachment of the household is also an important correlate of child poverty in Hungary. The share of children in low and very low work-intensity households is high (also in a cross-European comparison; see Tárki/Applica, 2010; SPC, 2012). Also, the poverty risk of these children is high compared to their counterparts in medium or high work-intensity households. The role of household work intensity in shaping child poverty risk is discussed in more detail later in this section.

Geographical factors are strongly associated with the risk of poverty and child poverty in Hungary (Blaskó, 2010): settlement type and region are both important, although there is a strong compositional effect (in terms of education and employment). Poverty is mainly a rural issue in Hungary: there is a clear gradient of the risk of poverty and child poverty according to the type of settlement in which a household lives; this gradient has been stable over the past two decades. In addition, rural areas and some regions are characterized by poor-quality infrastructure and limited access to both transport facilities and a range of services (most importantly childcare and schooling) (Darvas and Tausz, 2007; Bass et al., 2008).

Roma children are of particular interest in poverty research and social policy practice in Hungary.[13] Although estimates are not totally reliable (due to the low share of the Roma in surveys), it is widely agreed that the poverty risk among the Roma is extremely high, not least because poverty risk factors (severe underemployment, low education, large families, and place of residence) are seriously concentrated in the Roma population (Blaskó, 2010). Estimates based on Tárki data show that 35 per cent of Roma children were living below the poverty line in 2005. These figures increased to about 80 per cent by 2012, improving slightly thereafter (Gábos et al., 2015). Other studies confirm that Roma at risk of poverty are more affected by extreme poverty than others (Bass et al., 2007; Ladányi, 2007). Living in a Roma family increases the risk of poverty considerably, even when additional factors are controlled for (Gábos and Szivós, 2008). Roma children are also at high risk of intergenerational transmission of poverty, which is strongly related to their

[13] The size of the Roma population is estimated to be around 6 per cent of the total population (Kemény et al., 2004). Their share is increasing: the proportion of 0–19-year-olds accounts for 45 per cent of the Roma population (Hablicsek, 2007) (compared to a figure of 23 per cent of 0–19-year-olds in the population generally).

weak opportunities in the educational system (Janky, 2004; Kertesi and Kézdi, 2008).

Using Tárki data, we fixed the poverty line in 2005. According to these results, the risk of poverty among children increased until 2012 in all types of household, with some important disparities. Children in single-parent families and those living with highly educated parents were somewhat less affected by the decline in the real income of the household in this period. Tárki data indicate a recovery between 2012 and 2014, with an estimated anchored child poverty rate in 2014 below the magnitude registered in 2009. This development did not affect all children: the poverty risk of those with a low-educated household head decreased, but was still higher than in 2009, while the anchored poverty rate among those in large families levelled between 2012 and 2014.

Overall, the role of labour market attachment of households is crucial for household income and poverty risk, while the effect of education is twofold: it has a very strong association with labour market participation (Figure 6.3), and, on the intensive margin, provides higher wage premiums for tertiary (and to some extent upper secondary) education (Kézdi, 2005; Strauss and de la Maisonneuve, 2009). Labour market attachment and education are strong correlates of poverty risk also when controlling for compositional effects (Gábos and Szivós, 2006; Gábos et al., 2015), while other factors (age of child, household type, settlement type, ethnic background) prove to be less significant.[14]

In the following, we aim to understand better how the effects of the crisis were mediated by the labour market and by public expenditure on households with children in Hungary. We present the results of a decomposition analysis (methodology proposed by Corluy and Vandebroucke, 2014) for two different periods: 2007–10 and 2010–13. We analyse how changes in the share of children belonging to households with different work-intensity levels and in the risk of poverty of these groups (see Figure 6.7) contributed to changes in overall child poverty rates; we also look at the extent to which the role of these two factors changed between the pre-crisis and the post-crisis periods.

The descriptive statistics of the indicators included in the decomposition exercise show three clear patterns:

(i) The share of children in very low and low work-intensity households increased, while the share of those in high and very high work-

[14] Regression-based decompositions of the overall income inequality by seven dimensions show between-group inequality to be around 46 per cent of total variance. Of this, employment and education are shown to be the dimensions with the highest weights in explaining between-group inequality (both around 15 per cent in 2014), followed by the number of children (7–8 per cent), settlement type, ethnicity of the household head, age, and gender of the household head (altogether around 8 per cent) (Tóth, 2015).

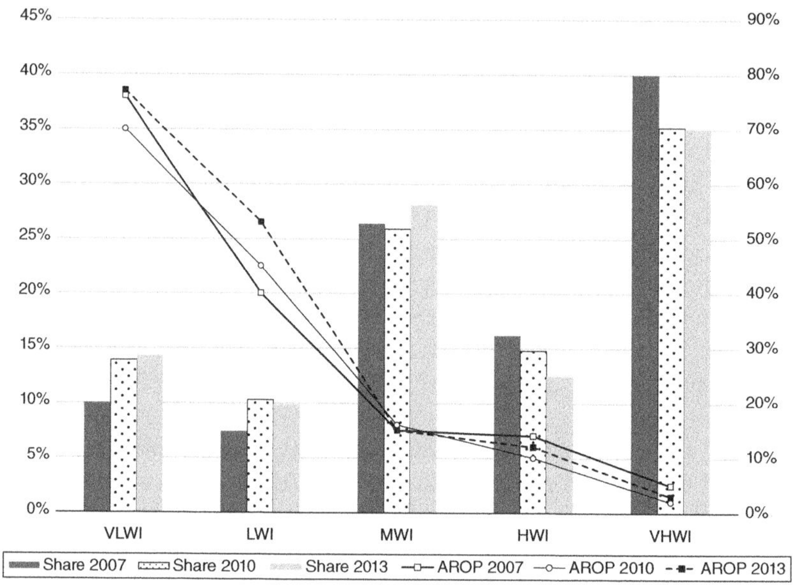

Figure 6.7. Share of children (left axis) and at-risk-of-poverty rate (right axis) among children by household work-intensity level in Hungary (2005–2014), per cent

Note: Work intensity is the ratio of the total number of months that all working-age (18–59, excl. students) household members have worked during the income reference year and the total number of months that the same household members could theoretically have worked in the same period.

VLWI=very low work intensity; LWI=low work intensity; MWI=medium work intensity; HWI=high work intensity; VHWI=very high work intensity.

Source: own calculations based on EU-SILC (Eurostat database)

intensity households decreased between 2007 and 2010, while all figures but the share of children in high work-intensity households (which further decreased between 2010 and 2013) remained unchanged thereafter.

(ii) The risk to children in very low work-intensity households (work intensity (WI)<0.2) decreased in the first period (from 76 per cent to 70 per cent), but returned to the 2007 level up until 2013 (77 per cent).

(iii) The risk of poverty of children in low work-intensity households ($0.2 \leq WI \leq 0.45$) increased in both periods, the second change being somewhat bigger (5 percentage points vs 8 percentage points, respectively).

The at-risk-of-poverty rate of children in Hungary increased by 1.5 percentage points from 2007 to 2010 (from 18.8 per cent to 20.3 per cent). According to

Table 6.4. Decomposition of changes in child poverty rates in Hungary between 2007–2010 and 2010–2013: analysis of households with different work-intensity levels (percentage points)

		2007–10	2010–13
Change in child AROP		1.5	2.8
Change in the share of children living in...	VLWI hhs	2.7	0.3
	LWI hhs	−1.0	−0.1
	MWI hhs	−0.1	0.3
	HWI hhs	−0.1	−0.2
Change in the AROP of children living in...	VLWI hhs	−0.7	1.0
	LWI hhs	0.4	0.9
	MWI hhs	0.1	−0.3
	HWI hhs	−0.7	0.3
	VHWI hhs	−1.3	0.5

Notes: Years are EU-SILC survey years.
VLWI=Very low work intensity; LWI=low work intensity; MWI=medium work intensity; HWI=high work intensity; VHWI=very high work intensity.

Source: Own calculations based on EU-SILC data.

the decomposition results[15] (Table 6.4), this increase is mostly due to the rising share of children in very low and low work-intensity households: this factor accounted for an increase of 3.7 percentage points in overall child poverty rates. This strong effect was counterbalanced to some extent by the decrease in the risk of poverty in certain households, mainly in those with very low, high, and especially very high work intensity. So, in the first place, it is the change in the distribution of children over households with different work intensity that is responsible for the increase in the at-risk-of-poverty rate of children between 2007 and 2010, as the share of children in lower work-intensity households was growing (similarly to what Gábos et al. 2015 found using the same method for the active-age population) and was not offset by the slight decrease in the at-risk-of-poverty rate in the groups of households with higher work intensity.

In the second period, from 2010 to 2013, the at-risk-of-poverty rate of children in Hungary increased further, by 2.8 percentage points (from 20.3 per cent to 23.2 per cent). Increasing poverty rates across households with low and very low work intensity contributed most (1.9 percentage points) to the change in overall child poverty rate, while there were no important changes in the share of children in various work-intensity groups.

15 See Corluy and Vandenbroucke (2014) for the description of the methodology.

6.4. AN ANALYSIS OF THE IMPACT OF POLICIES ON CHILDREN DURING THE CRISIS TIMES

Earlier, we distinguished between two (family) policy regimes that have been in the focus of policy debate and practice in Hungary since the systemic change: a universalistic, rights-based one; and one characterized by employment-related transfers, with a strong focus on demographic incentives. Both approaches target the well-being of children—hence proving that the advocates of both regimes are committed. However, the income-protection capacity of these measures (and their incidence) differs a lot (the first aims at a vertical redistribution, from the 'rich' to the 'poor', while the second focuses more on middle-class families and pays less attention to children of the marginalized). In what follows, we aim to understand better how changes in the tax-benefit system contributed to the increased poverty risk of children during the crisis.

6.4.1. The Poverty Reduction Effect of Cash Benefits

The Hungarian social benefit system, as presented earlier, provides relatively high expenditure in a regional comparison and is strongly cash focused. Overall, according to Eurostat, social protection expenditure (including pensions) accounts for more than a fifth of GDP (almost half goes on old-age-related benefits), which is lower than the EU-27 average, but higher than in any of the other Visegrad countries (Czech Republic, Poland, Slovakia). Family/child-related benefits represent close to 3 per cent of GDP, which is fairly high in a European comparison, following the Nordic countries, Germany, Austria, Luxembourg, and Ireland.

Turning to the outcome side, the child poverty reduction effect of Hungarian cash benefits is among the strongest in Europe (Tárki/Applica, 2010; SPC, 2012; Gábos, 2013). According to EU-SILC data (and reinforced by Tárki data), between 2005 and 2010 the at-risk-of-poverty rate among children would have been 2.2–2.4 times higher without cash social transfers (excluding pensions). This is equal to a 55–60 per cent poverty reduction index (PRI), which is considerably higher than the EU-27 average (about 40 per cent) and the NMS average (about 30 per cent), as is shown in Figure 6.8.[16] Microsimulation results indicate that structural changes in Hungarian social policy between 2001 and 2007 reduced disposable income and had a poverty-increasing effect in this period (Hills et al., 2014). This effect came from

[16] According to our estimates, based on Tárki data, family benefits accounted for about 80 per cent of the overall PRI among children in 2005 (Gábos and Szivós, 2006).

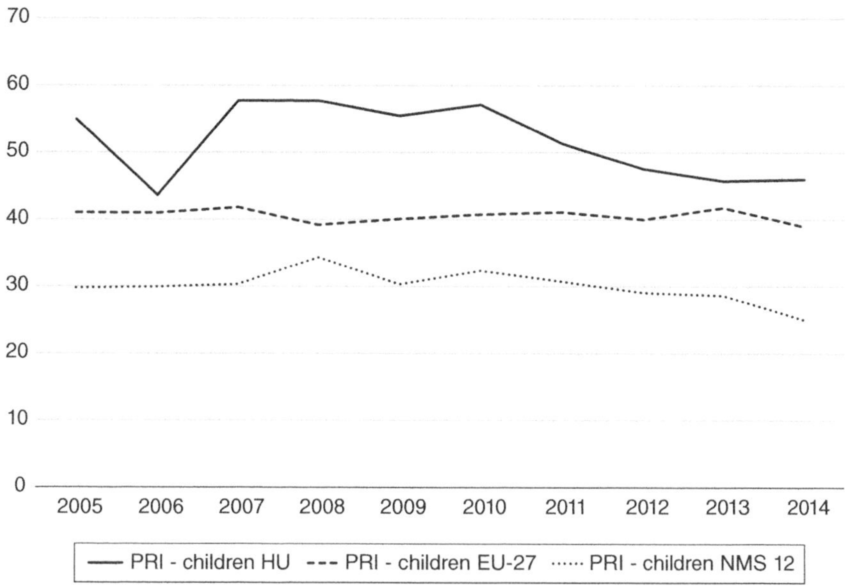

Figure 6.8. Poverty reduction index of social transfers (excluding pensions) among children, Hungary, EU-27, and NMS-12 (2005–2014), per cent

Note: The poverty reduction index (withdrawal rate) measures the distance in the at-risk-of-poverty rate before and after social transfers (excl. pensions), defined as PRI=(preAROP-AROP)/preAROP*100, where preAROP is the at-risk-of-poverty rate before social transfers (excl. pensions) of the active-age population.

Source: Own calculations, based on Eurostat data.

changes in means-tested benefits and social insurance contributions, and affected first and foremost the lowest income decile and large families.

The shift towards a lower poverty reduction capacity of the Hungarian social benefits system took place after 2010, and was strongly related to the policy regime change described earlier. While further waves of data are needed to gain a clear and robust picture, it would seem that the PRI levelled off at 45 per cent in a period that can be labelled both the post-crisis period and the consolidation period of the new policy regime. This 45 per cent is much closer now to the EU-27 average (though still higher). It is also well above the average capacity of the New Member States that joined the EU in 2004 or later (where an increase from 2007 to 2008 was followed by a steady, but less steep decline in the PRI).[17] The deterioration in the poverty reduction capacity of the Hungarian cash transfer system in this period went hand in hand with a considerable reduction in personal income tax, which increased disposable income throughout the whole income distribution. The increase in the

[17] For a Visegrad group comparison of child poverty and policy effectiveness, see Förster and Tóth (2001).

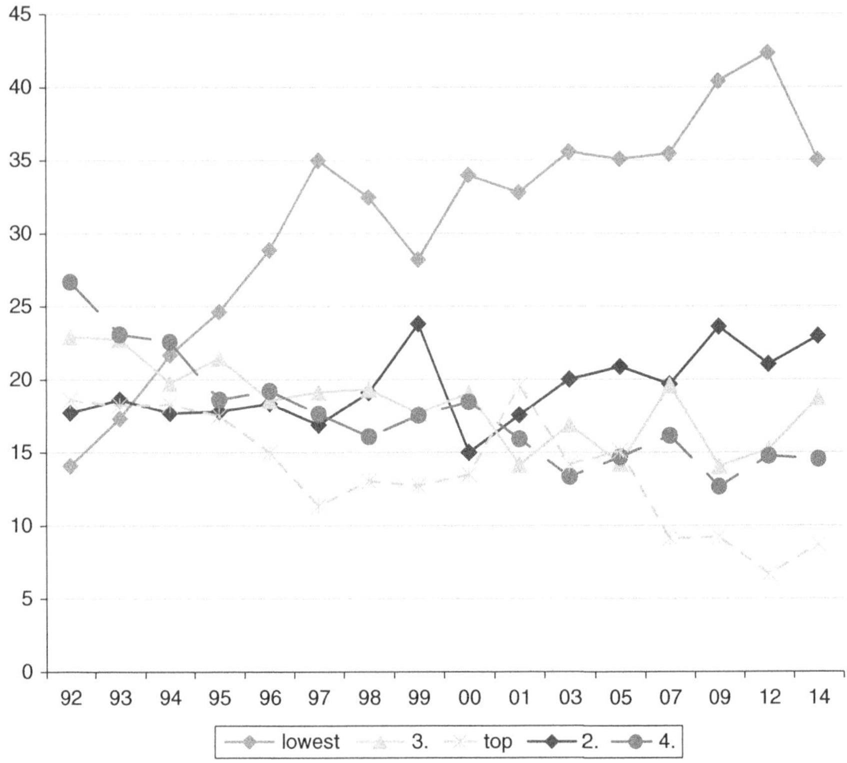

Figure 6.9. Change in incidence of family allowances over time in Hungary (1992–2014) (share of total family allowances received by the various quintiles, based on person equivalent household incomes), per cent

Note: Equivalent incomes calculated with e=0.73 coefficient.

Source: 1992–7: HHP; 1998–2014: Tárki Household Monitor survey.

disposable income of large families was offset to some extent by changes in non-means-tested benefits (Hills et al., 2014). These results are to some extent reflected in the fact that the pre-transfer at-risk-of-poverty (preAROP) rate among children decreased significantly (by 5 percentage points) from 2010 to 2011, and levelled off afterwards. The decreasing preAROP rate and the increasing AROP rate led to lower PRI values among children between 2011 and 2014.

PRI calculations indicate that higher levels of expenditure result in a higher return in terms of poverty reduction, and that the financial and economic crisis would have hit families with children even harder if the cash benefit system had not been in place. We cannot, however, ignore the potential behavioural responses to such incentives. The inactivity trap for parents is one such, highlighted also as a risk in the case of Hungary by the latest Social

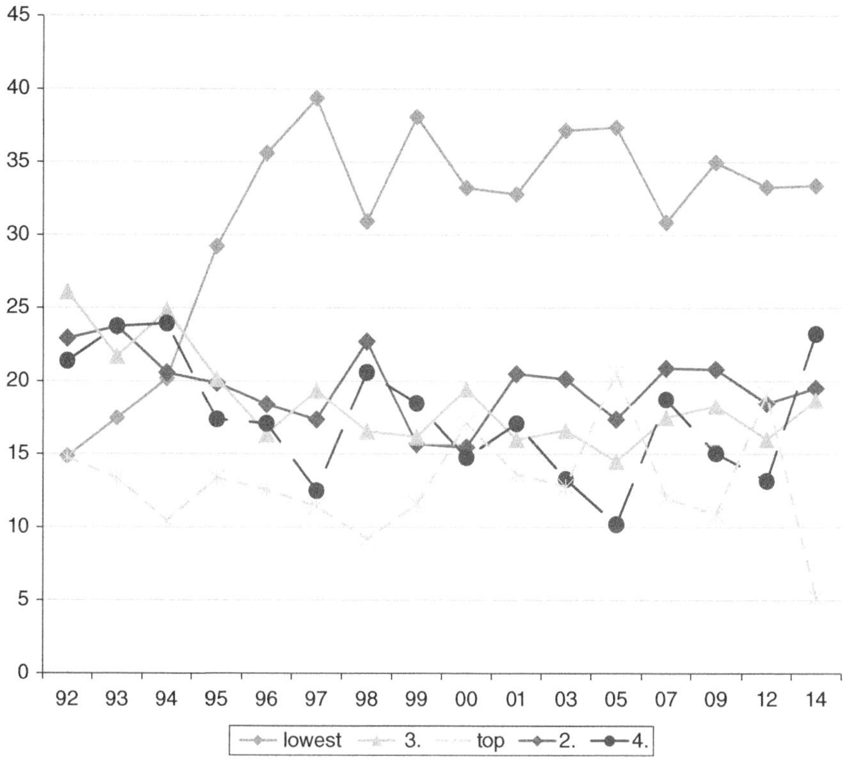

Figure 6.10. Change in incidence of maternity benefits over time in Hungary (1992–2014) (share of total family allowances received by the various quintiles based on person equivalent household incomes), per cent

Note: Equivalent incomes calculated with e=0.73 coefficient.

Source: 1992–7: HHP; 1998–2014: Tárki Household Monitor survey.

Protection Committee report on child poverty (SPC, 2012). The high share of children in jobless households and the low levels of maternal employment in Hungary seem to reflect the side-effects of high cash outflows.

6.4.2. Change of Incidence of Social Transfers over Time

A special presentation of the incidence of social transfers can be prepared if we observe the shares of total benefits that reach the various quintiles of the population. This is shown for the two major groups of family-related social transfers in Figures 6.9 and 6.10.

The basic trend over time for family allowances is increased targeting. Whereas in 1992 less than 15 per cent of all family allowances went to the bottom quintile (the same share as received by the top 20 per cent, while the middle quintiles received about 20–25 per cent each), by the end of the period the share going to the bottom 20 per cent had gradually increased to a level well above 35 per cent,[18] while the share going to the top quintile had decreased. The overall trend of an increasing share going to the bottom 20 per cent should be interpreted with care. On the one hand, it could mean an increased level of targeting (more resources allocated to the most needy). However, it could also result from a slide in the situation of families with children.

Very similar trends (though with different timing) can be traced for maternity benefits: the bottom quintile received some 15 per cent of all maternity benefits in 1992, a share that quickly increased to almost 40 per cent in 1997 and that has fluctuated around 35 per cent ever since.

6.5. CONCLUSIONS AND IMPLICATIONS

Despite high spending on family benefits by any international standards, and despite a traditionally wide portfolio of family support, and the high poverty reduction effectiveness of cash benefits in the country, the rates and risk of child poverty in Hungary have been higher than the EU average since the early 1990s. These outcomes are observed partly because the share of children in very low work-intensity households is relatively high. This suggests the existence of potential inactivity traps and disincentive effects.

The crisis period brought an even higher poverty risk for children: their at-risk-of-poverty rate increased more than the rate for the population overall and more than the at-risk-of-poverty rates among their peers in the European Union Member States. The deterioration in the situation of children is even more visible when either anchored poverty rates or severe material deprivation rates are examined. In addition, children in already high poverty risk groups (especially children living with low-educated parents, and living in low or very low work-intensity households) were among those most affected by the crisis in terms of income poverty, either the floating or the anchored poverty line is applied.

Within the period observed, the situation initially was characterized by spirals of macro imbalances–spending cuts–poverty increases. Moves towards workfare, conditionality, and activation policies (so important in a country that has suffered from very low economic activity rates since the beginning of the 1990s) started even prior to the massive political turn in 2010; but they were placed at the centre of social policy following the landslide victory of the conservative government: virtually all elements of the social system, including the traditionally large and complex family support system, moved in this direction.

[18] Data for 2014 need to be tested to see whether this is a trend or a measurement problem.

We found that the increase in child poverty in the first phase of the crisis (2007–10) was driven by labour market processes (an increasing share of children in low work-intensity households), while the (weakened, but still functioning) automatic stabilizers reduced the magnitude of these effects. By contrast, in the second phase (2010–13), labour market processes started to improve (although mainly through controversial policy tools, like public work and outward migration), though the shift towards a regressive social policy regime contributed to increased poverty rates via the reduced poverty reduction impacts of cash benefits. We also note that a decreased poverty reduction effect of social benefits was observed in the circumstances of declining pre-transfer poverty rates.

More recently, there seem to be signs of improvement in terms of poverty rates; but this very recent development needs to be understood more profoundly before any predictions can be made regarding its future sustainability.

REFERENCES

Bass, László, Ágnes Darvas, Ilona Dögei, Zsuzsa Ferge, and Katalin Tausz (2007). *A szegénység és kirekesztés változása 2001–2006* (Budapest: MTA KTI Gyerekprogram Iroda).

Bass, László, Ágnes Darvas, Zsombor Farkas, and Zsuzsa Ferge (2008). *A gyermekszegénység elleni küzdelem állása 2008-ig* (Budapest: MTA KTI Gyerekprogram Iroda).

Blaskó, Zsuzsa (2010). 'Policy Overview and Policy Impact Analysis. A Case Study: Hungary'. In *Child Poverty and Child Well-being in the European Union. Report prepared for the DG Employment, Social Affairs and Equal Opportunities (Unite E.2)* (Budapest and Brussels: Tárki/Applica).

Blaskó, Zsuzsa, Anna Sára Ligeti, and Endre Sik (2014). 'Magyarok külföldön: Mennyien? Kik? Hol?'. In Tamás Kolosi and István György Tóth (eds), *Társadalmi riport* (Budapest: Tárki).

Corluy, Vincent and Frank Vandenbroucke (2014). 'Individual Employment, Household Employment, and Risk of Poverty in the European Union: A Decomposition Analysis'. In Bea Cantillon and Frank Vandenbroucke (eds), *Reconciling Work and Poverty Reduction. How Successful are European Welfare States?* (Oxford: Oxford University Press).

Darvas, Ágnes and Katalin Tausz (2007). 'Tackling Child Poverty and Promoting the Social Inclusion of Children: A Study of National Policies—Hungary' (Brussels: European Commission).

Fábián, Zoltán, András Gábos, Marianna Kopasz, Márton Medgyesi, Péter Szivós, and István György Tóth (2014). 'Hungary: A Country Caught in its Own Trap'. In Brian Nolan, Wiemer Salverda, Daniele Checchi, Ive Marx, Abigail McKnight, István György Tóth, and Herman van de Werfhorst (eds), *Changing Inequalities and Societal Impacts in Rich Countries: Thirty Countries' Experiences* (Oxford: Oxford University Press).

Fazekas, Károly and László Neumann (eds) (2014). *The Hungarian Labour Market 2014* (Budapest: Research Centre for Economic and Regional Studies, Hungarian Academy of Sciences & National Employment Non-profit Public Company Ltd).

Ferge, Zsuzsa and Ágnes Darvas (eds) (2014). *Civil jelentés a Gyerekesélyekről, 2012–2013* (Budapest: Gyerekesély Közhasznú Egyesületet).

Förster, Michael F. and István György Tóth (2001). 'Child Poverty and Family Transfers in the Czech Republic, Hungary and Poland'. *Journal of European Social Policy 11*, no. 4: pp. 324–41.

Gábos, András (2000). 'Családok helyzete és családtámogatások a kilencvenes években'. In Tamás Kolosi, István György Tóth, and György Vukovich (eds), *Társadalmi riport 2000* (Budapest: Tárki).

Gábos, András (2008). 'Családtámogatási rendszer és a családok helyzete'. In Tamás Kolosi and István György Tóth (eds), *Társadalmi riport 2008* (Budapest: Tárki).

Gábos, András (2013). 'Successful Policy Mixes to Tackle Child Poverty: An EU-wide Comparison'. *GINI Discussion Paper 76* (Amsterdam: AIAS).

Gábos, András, Réka Branyiczki, Barbara Lange, and István György Tóth (2015). 'Employment and Poverty Dynamics before, during and after the Crisis'. *ImPRovE Discussion Paper 15/06* (Antwerp: Herman Deleeck Centre for Social Policy, University of Antwerp).

Gábos, András, Róbert I. Gál, and Gábor Kézdi (2009). 'The Effects of Child-related Benefits and Pensions on Fertility by Birth Order: A Test on Hungarian Data'. *Population Studies 63*, no. 3: pp. 215–31.

Gábos, András and Péter Szivós (2006). 'A gyermekszegénység és néhány jellemzője Magyarországon'. In Tamás Kolosi, István György Tóth, and György Vukovich (eds), *Társadalmi riport 2006* (Budapest: Tárki).

Gábos, András and Péter Szivós (2008). 'Lent és még lejjebb: jövedelmi szegénység'. In Péter Szivós and István György Tóth (eds), *Köz, teher, elosztás* (Budapest: Tárki).

Gábos, András, Péter Szivós, and Annamária Tátrai (2015). 'Jövedelmi szegénység és társadalmi kerekeszettség jellemzői Magyarországon'. In Péter Szivós and István György Tóth (eds), *Jól nézünk ki (...?!): Háztartások helyzete a válság után* (Budapest: Tárki).

Guio, Anne-Catherine, David Gordon, and Eric Marlier (2012). *Measuring Material Deprivation in the EU: Indicators for the Whole Population and Child-specific Indicators*, 2012 edn. Eurostat Methodologies and Working Papers (Luxembourg: Publications Office of the European Union).

Hablicsek, László (2007). 'Kísérleti számítások a roma lakosság területi jellemzőinek alakulására és 2021-ig történő előrebecslésére'. *Demográfia 50*, no. 1: pp. 7–54.

Havasi, Éva (2011). 'Jövedelem, életkörülmények, szegénység'. Manuscript in Hungarian.

Hills, John, Alari Paulus, Holly Sutherland, and Iva Tasseva (2014). 'A Lost Decade? Decomposing the Effect of 2001–11 Tax Benefit Policy Changes in the Income Distribution in EU Countries'. *ImPRovE Discussion Paper No. 14/03* (Antwerp: Herman Deleeck Centre for Social Policy, University of Antwerp).

Janky, Béla (2004). 'A cigány családok jövedelmi helyzete'. In Tamás Kolosi, István György Tóth, and György Vukovich (eds), *Társadalmi riport 2004* (Budapest: Tárki).

Kapitány, Balázs and Zsolt Spéder (2015). 'Gyermekvállalás'. In Judit Monostori, Péter Őri, and Zsolt Spéder (eds), *Demográfiai portré 2015: Jelentés a magyar népesség helyzetéről* (Budapest: KSH Népességtudományi Kutatóintézet).

Kemény, István, Béla Janky, and Gabriella Lengyel (2004). *A magyarországi cigányság 1971–2003* (Budapest: Gondolat).

Kertesi, Gábor and Gábor Kézdi (2008). 'A roma és a nem roma fiatalok középiskolai továbbtanulása. Első eredmények a TÁRKI Életpálya-felmérése alapján'. In Tamás Kolosi and István György Tóth (eds), *Társadalmi riport 2008* (Budapest: Tárki).

Kézdi, Gábor (2005). 'Education and Earnings'. In Károly Fazekas and Júlia Varga (eds), *The Hungarian Labour Market: Review and Analysis 2005* (Budapest: Institute of Economics).

Köllő, János (2009). *A pálya szélén: Iskolázatlan munkanélküliek a posztszocialista gazdaságban* (Budapest: Osiris).

Ladányi, János (2007). 'Az antiszegregációs programok szükségességéről és lehetőségeiről'. *Kritika* (October 2007).

Scharle, Ágota and Dorottya Szikra (2015). 'Recent Changes Moving Hungary Away from the European Social Model'. In Daniel Vaughan-Whitehead (ed.), *The European Social Model in Crisis: Is Europe Losing Its Soul?* (Cheltenham: Edward Elgar).

Sipos, Sándor and István György Tóth (1998). 'Poverty Alleviation: Social Assistance and Family Benefits'. In Lajos Bokros and Jean-Jacques Dethier (eds), *Public Finance Reform during the Transition: The Experience of Hungary* (Washington, DC: World Bank).

Social Protection Committee (SPC) (2012). 'Tackling and Preventing Child Poverty, Promoting Child Well-being'. SPC Advisory Report to the European Commission (Brussels: SPC).

Strauss, Hubert and Christine de la Maisonneuve (2009). 'The Wage Premium on Tertiary Education: New Estimates for 21 OECD Countries'. *OECD Journal: Economic Studies 2009*, no. 1: pp. 183–210.

Szikra, Dorottya (2014). 'Democracy and Welfare in Hard Times: The Social Policy of the Orbán Government in Hungary between 2010 and 2014'. *Journal of European Social Policy*, no. 11: pp. 1–15.

Tárki/Applica (2010). *Child Poverty and Child Well-being in the European Union. Report prepared for the DG Employment, Social Affairs and Equal Opportunities (Unite E.2)* (Budapest and Brussels: Tárki/Applica).

Tóth, István György (2005). *Jövedelemeloszlás. A gazdasági rendszerváltástól az uniós csatlakozásig* (Budapest: Andorka Rudolf Társadalomtudományi Társaság/Századvég Kiadó).

Tóth, István György (2015). 'Jövedelem-eloszlás 2009–2014 között'. In Péter Szivós and István György Tóth (eds), *Jól nézünk ki (...?!): Háztartások helyzete a válság után* (Budapest: Tárki).

UNICEF Office of Research (2014). 'Children of the Recession: The Impact of the Economic Crisis on Child Well-being in Rich Countries'. *Innocenti Report Card No. 12* (Florence: UNICEF Office of Research—Innocenti).

7

Children of the Celtic Tiger during the Economic Crisis: Ireland

Brian Nolan and Bertrand Maître

7.1. INTRODUCTION

Ireland had the most precipitous decline in national output of any country in the Organisation for Economic Co-operation and Development (OECD) following the onset of the Great Recession. This was accompanied by a banking crisis of unprecedented scale, soaring national debt, a dramatic increase in unemployment, declining real incomes, and substantial increases in taxation and cuts in public spending. What impact did this have on children? How well were they protected from the worst effects of recession? And what lessons can be drawn with respect to the institutional settings and policy choices most conducive to protecting children in the future? These are the questions on which this chapter focuses.

We begin by briefly describing the nature of Ireland's economic crisis, to bring out its distinctive features, and in particular its impact on the labour market—the most direct channel by which household incomes and living standards were affected. We then turn to how children fared in terms of the evolution of the disposable income of the households in which they live. This is assessed vis-à-vis both conventional relative income poverty thresholds and also 'anchored' thresholds that move over time in line with prices, rather than median incomes; this is particularly relevant in situations where the median falls significantly in real terms, as it did in Ireland's crisis. To help understand the patterns observed, we then look at the evolution of poverty risk and incidence over the recession by a range of characteristics and circumstances, for both relative and 'anchored' thresholds. We also go beyond income to incorporate indicators of deprivation, which have for many years been included in the way poverty is measured for the purposes of Ireland's official national poverty target—including specific targets for children—and more recently have also been included in the way the EU's 2020 target for the reduction of poverty and social exclusion is framed. The role of policy, in particular with respect to social transfers and direct taxes, over the period of recession and 'austerity' is then examined, to draw out how children may have been affected. Finally, the conclusions are brought together and their implications brought out.

7.2. IRELAND'S ECONOMIC CRISIS

In understanding the nature of Ireland's economic crisis and its impacts, it is essential to place it in the context of what went immediately before: as a consequence of the so-called 'Celtic Tiger' boom from the mid-1990s, Ireland's gross national product (GNP) per capita had risen to be one of the highest in the European Union (EU) by the mid-2000s. This was a very different Ireland from that of a mere decade before, most dramatically in the number of people in work (which had increased from 1.2 million to almost 2.2 million). However, the latter part of the Celtic Tiger period was accompanied by an unbridled property boom and a very rapid increase in levels of household debt, fuelled by low interest rates. This came as Ireland, like other 'periphery' members of the Eurozone, saw substantial inflows of capital from the Eurozone centre. The tax base became highly dependent on taxes on property development and sales, and the construction sector grew to 14 per cent of total employment. This left the economy and the public finances in a particularly vulnerable state.

The global financial crisis and the bursting of the domestic property bubble then led to an unprecedented contraction in national output and income from 2008–9. The economic crisis had a more negative immediate impact on national output in Ireland than in any other OECD country: by 2010 GNP per head in nominal terms had fallen by close to a fifth, compared with 2007, and in real terms was back to levels seen a decade earlier. This went together with a bursting of the property bubble, a collapse in asset values, a banking crisis of unprecedented proportions, and a ballooning fiscal deficit. The general government balance went from surplus to a deficit of 14 per cent of national income in 2009, and support for the banking system drove that deficit to over 30 per cent in 2010. Government debt, having fallen to 25 per cent of national income by 2007, soared to 90 per cent by 2010, and 120 per cent by 2012, with support for the banks accounting for about a third of that total. By 2010, despite substantial increases in taxation and expenditure cuts (discussed in more detail below), the Irish government was no longer able to borrow on international financial markets at acceptable rates, and had to avail itself of a 'bailout' by the European Union and the International Monetary Fund (IMF) and implement a fiscal adjustment programme. This involved both very substantial reductions in current and capital expenditure and increases in taxation, with cuts in expenditure accounting for about two-thirds of the total; this was one of the largest budgetary adjustments seen in the OECD in recent years. The effects of this domestic 'austerity', combined with weak external demand, meant that the economy 'flat-lined', with no increase in GNP until 2012.

The economic crisis had an immediate and deep impact on the labour market, with the unemployment rate rising very rapidly to 15 per cent. The decline in employment was very heavily concentrated among young men: unemployment rates for those aged 20–24 rose from 8 per cent to 32 per cent, and for those aged 25–34 it increased from 5 per cent to almost 20 per cent. Net emigration also returned. The proportion of working-age individuals in 'jobless' households became one of the highest in the EU (Watson et al., 2012). The number in (involuntary) part-time employment rose, and other forms of precarious employment such as zero-hours contracts became much more prevalent. Earnings fell sharply in the hardest-hit sectors, such as construction, while cuts in public sector wage levels (as well as in numbers) were imposed. There was no collective negotiation to minimize lay-offs in return for wage and/or working-time concessions, as in some other countries, as centralized wage bargaining/social partnership processes disintegrated. The minimum wage was initially cut at the onset of the crisis, but was subsequently restored to its previous level after a change of government in 2010.

The beginnings of an economic recovery were seen by 2013, and economic growth then picked up more strongly, driven by strong export growth as competitiveness improved. By 2015, Ireland once again had one of the fastest rates of economic growth in the EU. The unemployment rate fell at an accelerating pace to below 9 per cent by end-2015. Average weekly earnings began to recover, the minimum wage was increased, and with the fiscal deficit on target vis-à-vis EU Stability and Growth Pact limits, some reduction in direct taxes and reversal of the cuts in public sector pay began to be implemented. Even with sustained growth in output, employment, and earnings, though, dealing with the effects of the recession will be a central challenge for policy for years to come.

7.3. CHILDREN IN IRELAND'S CRISIS

To set the context for what happened to children and their households, we look first at the overall effects of the crisis on incomes, income inequality, and poverty across all households. The initial impact of the recession on household income was less than that on national output (as also found elsewhere—see, for example, Jenkins et al., 2013), as automatic stabilizers in the form of increasing social transfers and declining tax revenues buffered disposable income. Self-employment incomes fell immediately, however, while direct taxes were increased successively and social transfers for those of working age were cut in order to address the fiscal deficit, as discussed in detail in section 7.4 below. By 2012, median household disposable income had fallen by about 12 per cent from its 2008 peak, at which point it stabilized. The distribution of disposable income among households was relatively stable. The top 10 per cent and the bottom two deciles saw some decline in their income shares from 2008 to 2012, while the Gini coefficient (the most widely used summary indicator of income inequality) briefly fell at the immediate onset of the crisis[1] before returning to about the level seen at the outset. Average income in real terms fell sharply for all deciles, with the largest decline in proportionate terms being at the bottom. If we focus on the most widely used measure of relative income poverty, we see that the percentage of persons in households below 60 per cent of the median income in the year in question did not rise—at 15.7 per cent in 2012, it was about the same as in 2008, and lower than in 2007. This has to be seen in the context of the sharp fall in the level of the median in real terms (as highlighted earlier), which meant that the relative poverty threshold linked to it was also about 12 per cent lower by 2012.

How did children fare? In 2008, before the effects of the recession were felt, the relative income poverty rate for children (aged under 18) in Ireland was 18 per cent. This placed the country towards the middle of the distribution among EU countries in terms of this child poverty measure, but higher than in most EU-15 countries (though not as much higher as before the economic boom). As Figure 7.1 illustrates, the relative poverty rate for children then fluctuated somewhat from year to year throughout the crisis, but was back to 18 per cent in 2012. The rate for adults of working age followed a similar path to that for children. The distinctive feature is the rate for older persons (aged 65 or over), which fell sharply in the first few years of the crisis. This reflects the fact that the incomes of pensioners were relatively well protected (as discussed in more detail below) and did not fall to the same extent as in other households on average, leaving them much less likely to be below the 60 per cent relative income threshold than they had been.

The fact that—most unusually—median income fell markedly through the crisis means that it is very important also to look at how poverty evolved when measured against a fixed, rather than a declining, adequacy standard. A more 'absolute' income poverty standard can be derived by taking 60 per cent of the pre-crisis median and holding that fixed in purchasing power terms, with the standard for subsequent years adjusted in line with consumer prices (which increased modestly over the crisis period). Assessed against such an 'anchored' income poverty threshold, the percentage in poverty overall had risen very substantially by 2012, as shown in Figure 7.2. The increase was greatest for

[1] This short-term dip in the Gini coefficient reflects the fact that incomes towards the top from profits/self-employment income were particularly hit at the onset of the crisis, while social transfers benefiting those towards the bottom were temporarily increased, as discussed in section 7.4.

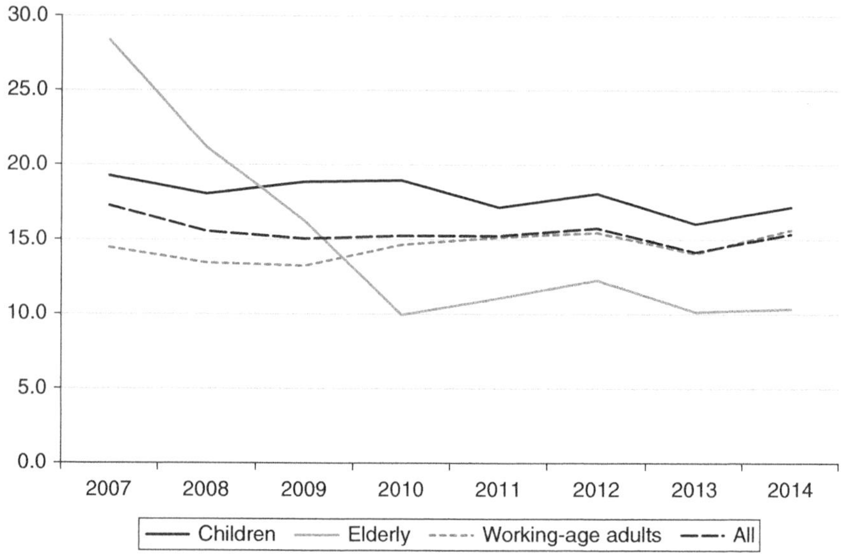

Figure 7.1. Percentage of persons below 60 per cent of median disposable income, by age, Ireland (2007–2014)

Note: The Eurostat definition of total gross income did not include private pensions until 2011 and therefore the poverty figures from Eurostat prior to 2011 differ greatly from the published figures by the Irish Central Statistics Office.

Source: Eurostat EU-SILC, last update 18 December 2015.

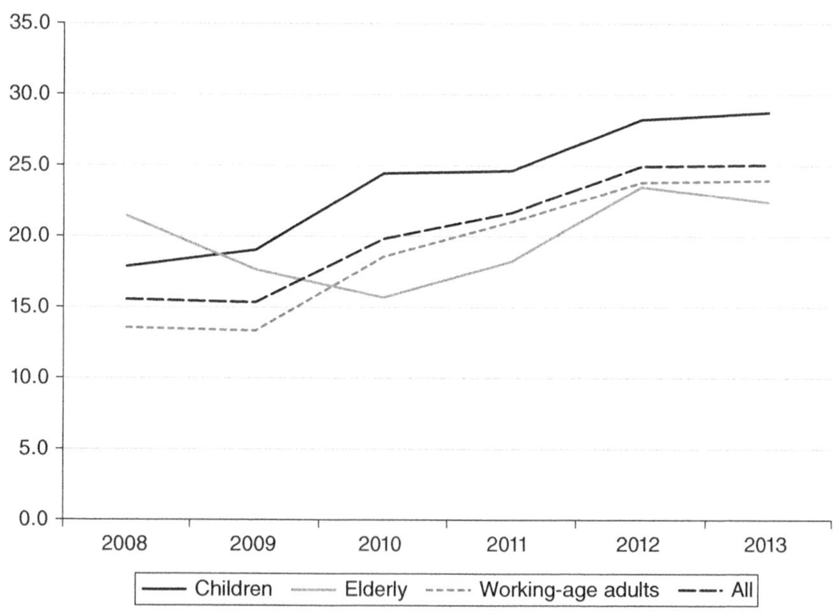

Figure 7.2. Percentage of persons below 'anchored' threshold (60 per cent of 2008 median disposable income, adjusted for changes in consumer prices), by age, Ireland (2008–2013)

Source: Central Statistics Office, SILC. Authors' calculations.

children and for adults of working age, though even those aged 65 or over saw an increase in the income poverty rate constructed in this fashion; for children, it rose from 18 per cent to 28 per cent. (It is worth noting that anchored child poverty has been falling since 2012, when economic growth resumed, and was down 2 percentage points by 2014, as unemployment fell and real incomes began to rise.)

To understand the patterns shown by these income-based poverty indicators over the crisis and to bring out the underlying driving forces, it helps to look at the way in which the likelihood of being below the income threshold changed for different children and households, and how the composition of those below the threshold evolved as a consequence. We start in Table 7.1 with the poverty risk facing different children—in terms of their own and their household's characteristics—in 2008 and 2012, using the relative income poverty threshold of 60 per cent of median income. We see that at the outset in 2008, the poverty rate was highest for older children (aged 12–17) and lowest for pre-school children (aged under 5). This is related to family size, where school-age children are more likely to have younger brothers and sisters than pre-school children, and so a higher income is needed to keep the family above the poverty threshold. A more striking feature of the pre-crisis situation—a long-standing feature in Ireland—is the very high poverty rate for children in households with only one adult. This reflects the relatively high rate of labour market inactivity and welfare dependency for that group in the Irish case, even during the boom years.

With the overall rate for children stable over this period, the patterning of poverty risk was also generally quite similar in 2012, at the depth of the crisis, to the time before its effects came to be felt in 2008. The poverty risk for older children was slightly higher by 2012, with an offsetting decline for younger children, while there was a more marked increase for those in households where the youngest child was a teenager. In a similar (though more pronounced) vein, there was a marked increase in the poverty risk for children living in households with three or more adults of working age, while the rate for those with only one such adult declined. The poverty rate for children in households containing pensioners fell, reflecting the extent to which those in receipt of pensions were more protected, though these account for only a small proportion of all children. The poverty rate for children living in 'jobless' households, captured via the EU's low work-intensity measure, was rather stable over the crisis, while the corresponding rate for those in households that had significant work actually declined.

There were, however, important changes in the make-up of the underlying population in terms of some central risk factors, as shown in the first part of Table 7.2. We see that, of all children in the population, the proportion in families of three or more children, or in households with three or more adults, was lower in 2012 than in 2008. The proportion of all children who were aged 5

Table 7.1. Risk of relative income poverty for children, Ireland, 2008 and 2012 (per cent)

	2008	2012
Children	17.9	18.0
Children in single-parent household	44.1	33.2
Children in large family (3+ children)	23.3	23.2
Age of the child		
Under 5	14.2	12.6
6–11	18.6	17.7
12–17	20.9	23.1
Age of the youngest child in the household		
Under 5	16.8	15.0
6–11	20.4	19.7
12–17	16.7	23.6
Number of working-age adults		
1	43.6	32.2
2	12.5	14.2
3+	15.1	21.7
Number of pensioners		
1	28.4	4.2
2+	43.2	0.0
Dependency ratio (DR)		
Children living in household with DR lower or equal to 0.5	8.7	11.4
Children living in household with DR greater than 0.5	9.6	8.3
Location		
Urban, population >=1000	15.4	16.2
Rural, population < 1000	21.7	20.8
No foreign born in the household	17.6	17.5
Foreign born in the household	19.7	19.9
Not living in a jobless household	10.7	6.8
Living in a jobless household	56.4	54.9

Source: Central Statistics Office, SILC. Authors' calculations.

or under was somewhat higher in 2012 than in 2008, while the proportion in their teenage years was lower. The proportion living in households that included a foreign-born member was substantially higher in 2012. By far the most striking change, though, was in the proportion of children living in a household where the working-age adults were effectively 'jobless'—as reflected in the 'low work-intensity' measure included in the EU's suite of social inclusion indicators. While 15 per cent of Irish children lived in such a household in 2008 (still a rather high figure for an economy where unemployment was then so low), by 2012 this had risen to 23 per cent, among the highest in the EU.

Table 7.2. Composition of relative income poverty for children, Ireland, 2008 and 2012 (per cent)

	Overall composition		Composition of poor	
	2008	2012	2008	2012
Household type				
2 adults, 1 child	12.0	15.0	7.6	8.5
2 adults, 2 children	27.5	29.9	15.5	22.3
2 adults, 3 children	18.5	17.0	14.8	14.5
2 adults, 4+ children	7.4	8.4	8.8	10.3
1 adult with children	14.7	14.4	36.2	26.5
3 or more adults with children	20.0	15.4	17.0	17.9
Percentage of children in large family (3+ children)	35.5	32.0	46.4	41.4
Age of the child				
Under 5	31.2	36.4	24.8	25.5
6–11	30.7	30.7	31.9	30.1
12–17	38.1	33.0	43.3	44.4
Age of the youngest child in the household				
Under 5	45.1	52.6	42.5	43.8
6–11	30.3	27.4	34.6	30.0
12–17	24.6	20.0	22.9	26.3
Number of working-age adults				
1	15.5	14.8	38.0	26.5
2	65.1	70.4	45.6	55.6
3+	19.3	14.9	16.4	17.9
Number of pensioners				
0	98.05	98.58	96.8	99.7
1	1.81	1.29	2.9	0.3
Dependency ratio (DR)				
In household with DR lower or equal to 0.5	60.8	63.9	42.9	53.2
In household with DR greater than 0.5	39.2	36.1	57.1	46.8
Location				
Urban, population >=1000	60.2	60.8	51.7	54.8
Rural, population < 1000	39.8	39.2	48.3	45.2
No foreign born in the household	87.7	78.2	86.4	75.9
Foreign born in the household	12.3	21.8	13.6	24.1
Not in a jobless household	84.9	77.1	51.7	29.3
In a jobless household	15.1	22.9	48.3	70.7

Source: Central Statistics Office, SILC. Authors' calculations.

Together with the changes in poverty risk in Table 7.1, these changes in the household circumstances in which children live meant that the profile of children below the poverty threshold evolved in the way shown in the final two columns of Table 7.2. The proportion of poor children who were in large families declined, there was little change in their age profile, there was a substantial increase in the proportion living with two adults rather than just one, and there was also an increase in the proportion living in households with a dependency ratio under 0.5 (reflecting the lower proportion living in families with three or more children and in households that included a pensioner). There was also a substantial increase in the percentage of poor children in households with a foreign-born member, from 14 per cent to 24 per cent. However, the most striking change was the increase in the proportion living in a jobless household, which went up from 48 per cent to over 70 per cent.

Turning to the changes in risk and composition vis-à-vis the threshold 'anchored' in real terms at 60 per cent of the median in 2008, Table 7.3 shows that the poverty rate constructed on this basis went up substantially for all the

Table 7.3. Risk of anchored income poverty for children, Ireland, 2008 and 2012 (per cent)

	2008	2012
Children	17.9	28.2
Children in single-parent household	44.1	50.4
Children in large family (3+ children)	23.3	33.0
Age of the child		
Under 5	14.2	21.3
6–11	18.6	27.7
12–17	20.9	35.3
Age of the youngest child in the household		
Under 5	16.8	24.3
6–11	20.4	29.2
12–17	16.7	37.1
Number of working age adults		
1	43.6	49.2
2	12.5	23.1
3+	15.1	31.4
Number of pensioners		
1	28.4	11.6
2+	43.2	28.5
Dependency ratio (DR)		
In household with DR lower or equal to 0.5	10.1	22.4
In household with DR greater than 0.5	14.1	17.4
Location		
Urban, population >=1000	15.4	26.6
Rural, population < 1000	21.7	30.6
No foreign born in the household	17.6	27.1
Foreign born in the household	19.7	32.1
Not living in a jobless household	10.7	14.1
Living in a jobless household	56.4	74.9

Source: Central Statistics Office, SILC. Authors' calculations.

categories of children and types of household distinguished there. The increase was, however, particularly pronounced for children in large families, for older rather than younger children, for children living with two or more adults rather than only one, and (strikingly) for children in a household with a foreign-born member and children in a jobless household. Even children in households with significant work saw their poverty rate rise, but for those with little or no work the increase was from 56 per cent to 75 per cent.

Combined with the changes in the profile of children and their households already described from Table 7.2, these changes in poverty risk meant that the composition of poor children and their households measured in this way changed from 2008 to 2012, as shown in Table 7.4. The changes in composition are similar to what we saw with the relative income threshold: the proportion of poor children living in larger families declined, the proportion living with two rather than one adult rose considerably, the percentage living in a household where someone was foreign born rose (from 14 per cent to 25 per cent), and the percentage living in a jobless household rose sharply, from 48 per cent to over 60 per cent.

The changes in the composition of poor children with respect to the type of household in which they live—where households with two rather than with only one adult become more important—reflect the fact that the poverty risk for children in lone-parent families was already high, as noted earlier. Most households with two working-age adults had at least one person in work during those years, but many were hit hard by the crisis, losing one or even both jobs, or seeing their income from work decline. The centrality of the loss of employment in driving up the overall 'anchored' poverty rate for children is highlighted by the fact that over four-fifths of the increase in that rate is accounted for by the rise in the proportion of children living in 'jobless' households, combined with the increased likelihood that such children would be below the threshold; of these two factors, the shift of households into the 'jobless' category was the more important. Although, as we shall see, the increase in the poverty rate for jobless households partly reflected reductions in the rate of income support provided, the increase in the numbers of children in such households was a direct result of the severity of the crisis and its impact in the labour market.

The centrality of job loss in the Irish 'story' is also seen when one looks at the labour force status of the household reference person for poor children in the crisis. By 2012, at the depth of the crisis, only a quarter of the children below 60 per cent of median income had their household reference person in work, and three-quarters were in households that depended on social transfers for at least 75 per cent of their total disposable income. This went together with a change in the educational profile of the adults in poor households: a higher proportion had post-school education in 2012, as younger, better-educated cohorts were hard hit by unemployment and had very limited labour

Table 7.4. Composition of anchored income poverty by characteristics, Ireland, 2008 and 2012 (per cent)

	2008	2012
Household type		
2 adults, 1 child	7.6	9.5
2 adults, 2 children	15.5	25.1
2 adults, 3 children	14.8	12.5
2 adults, 4+ children	8.8	10.5
1 adult with children	36.2	25.7
3 or more adults with children	17.0	16.8
Percentage of poor children living in large family (3+ children)	46.4	37.5
Age of the child		
Under 5	24.8	27.4
6–11	31.9	30.1
12–17	43.3	42.5
Age of the youngest child in the household		
Under 5	42.5	45.3
6–11	34.6	28.3
12–17	22.9	26.4
Number of working age adults		
1	38.0	25.8
2	45.6	57.7
3+	16.5	16.5
Number of pensioners		
0	96.8	99.3
1	2.9	.5
Dependency ratio (DR)		
Children living in household with DR lower or equal to 0.5	42.9	57.4
Children living in household with DR greater than 0.5	57.1	42.6
Location		
Urban, population >=1000	51.7	57.4
Rural, population < 1000	48.3	42.6
No foreign born in the household	86.4	75.1
Foreign born in the household	13.6	24.9
Not living in a jobless household	51.7	38.8
Living in a jobless household	48.3	61.2

Source: Central Statistics Office, SILC. Authors' calculations.

market opportunities. An upsurge in emigration was one result, particularly for the better educated, including not only young single adults, but also some families with children, which saw very limited employment prospects in Ireland.

The changing composition of the households with children below the poverty threshold reflects the re-ranking produced by movements up and down the income distribution. In the absence of comprehensive longitudinal data,[2] this mobility is difficult to track at the household level, but households directly affected by soaring unemployment and collapsing business/self-employment income in the bust will have displayed particularly high levels of mobility, while the relative position of those that relied primarily on social pensions will have improved vis-à-vis those that depended on other social transfers and some of those that still relied on income from work and whose earnings fell. Savage et al.'s (2015) analysis of the limited year-to-year panel data in the EU Statistics on Income and Living Conditions (EU-SILC) concludes that declines in the income of those in the bottom decile at the onset of recession were central to the relatively marked decline in average income and income share for that decile, and that most of those households came from the bottom third rather than from the middle or upper parts of the income distribution.

Income is a key determinant of household living standards, but is by no means the only one. It may thus not always be a reliable indicator of how living standards are changing in absolute or relative terms: income in earlier periods, accumulated assets and debts, and support networks also play an important role. It is now common in assessing poverty and social exclusion to complement income with other information, such as levels of deprivation and self-assessed financial stress. This is reflected in the multidimensional nature of the Laeken social inclusion indicators adopted by the EU in 2001 (see Atkinson et al., 2002), and more recently in the framing of the EU's poverty reduction target for 2020 in terms of a measure that includes income, deprivation, and household 'joblessness'.

Figure 7.3 shows the evolution of one indicator of material deprivation included in the EU's social inclusion suite. It represents the percentage of households reporting the enforced absence of at least three out of nine items/activities. We see that the rate of deprivation (as captured by this indicator) increased very substantially over the crisis, but also that the level of deprivation has been much higher for children than for working-age adults throughout, and very much higher than for older persons. By 2012, 32 per cent of children versus 25 per cent of working-age adults and 10 per cent of older persons were in households that reported such deprivation.

Similar patterns are to be seen with the more restrictive EU indicator of 'severe material deprivation', which represents the enforced absence of at least four out of the nine-item set: the percentage of children in households reporting such deprivation went up from about 7 per cent before the crisis to about 13 per cent by 2012–13. For older persons, by contrast, the corresponding rate went up from about 1 per cent pre-crisis to 3 per cent at its height.

[2] EU-SILC includes only a relatively small rotating panel component, in which the small numbers make it hard to track the impact of the recession on particular individuals and households.

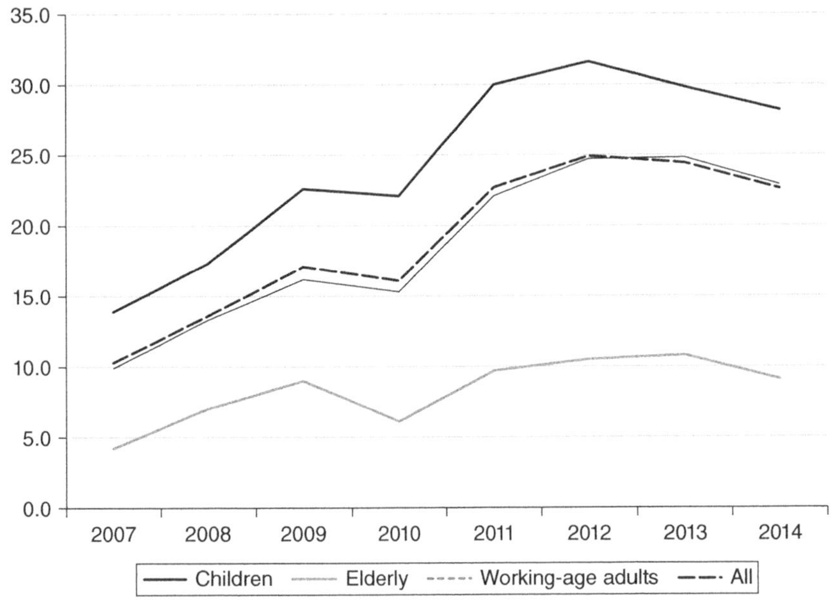

Figure 7.3. Percentage of persons reporting material deprivation, by age, Ireland (2007–2014)

Source: Eurostat EU-SILC, last update 26 January 2016.

Ireland was among the first EU Member States to adopt a formal poverty target, in the mid-1990s, and from the outset this has been framed in terms of the numbers both falling below relative income poverty thresholds and manifesting material deprivation—a measure that came to be termed 'consistent poverty' (see, for example, Callan et al., 1993; Nolan and Whelan, 1996). This measure has also been using in monitoring and targeting child poverty (along with a range of other indicators) at the national level. While the precise calibration of the measure employed for this purpose has changed over time, substantial reductions were achieved as deprivation levels fell during the boom years; but this was reversed during the crisis. The indicator currently in use takes as 'consistently poor' those living in households below 60 per cent of median income and also reporting deprivation of two or more out of a set of eleven 'basic deprivation' items or activities. The consistent poverty rate for children before the crisis struck was 6.3 per cent; despite a sharp fall during the boom, this was higher than the corresponding rate for all working-age adults (4.2 per cent), and much higher than for those aged 65 or over, which was below 2 per cent. The recession then saw this poverty measure for children rise to 9.9 per cent by 2012 and almost 12 per cent by 2013. This represented a continuation of the substantial excess over the corresponding rate for working-age adults, which was 8 per cent by 2013, and particularly over the rate for those aged 65 or over, which was still below 2 per cent. The rate of consistent poverty was higher for individuals living in households with children than for those living in households without children; it was lower for children aged under 5 and was highest for children in the 12–17 age group both before and throughout the crisis. The link between non-employment and consistent poverty was striking throughout: by 2012, the consistent poverty rate for households where the reference person was in work remained as low as 2 per cent, whereas for those households in which that person was unemployed, it reached 25 per cent.

The fact that the income component of the consistent poverty measure continued to be framed in relative terms through the crisis to some extent masks the impact of the crisis (except to the extent that falls in income are reflected directly in increased levels of deprivation). Ireland's official overall target for poverty reduction in the *National Action Plan for Social Inclusion 2007–2016* (Government of Ireland, 2007) had been to reduce the rate of consistent poverty to 2–4 per cent by 2012, and to eliminate it by 2016. However, this was re-framed following the substantial negative impact of the recession. There was also a need to align the plan with the Europe 2020 strategy's poverty target of lifting at least 20 million people in the EU out of the risk of poverty or exclusion by 2020, using 2010 as the baseline year. Ireland's 'National Social Target for Poverty Reduction' is now to reduce consistent poverty to 4 per cent by 2016 (interim target) and to 2 per cent or less by 2020, from a baseline rate of 6.3 per cent in 2010. (This would also allow Ireland to make its contribution to the EU poverty target by lifting a minimum of 200,000 people out of the risk of poverty or exclusion by 2020.)[3] There are two national sub-targets, one of which relates to reducing poverty among children (and the other to jobless households). The sub-target for the reduction of child poverty is to narrow the differential in consistent poverty between children and adults from the baseline year of 2010, when the rate for children was 8.2 per cent, compared to 5.5 per cent for adults—a differential of 50 per cent. No commitment is given as to the size of the reduction in the differential, and it had not narrowed by 2013.

So far, in discussing levels and trends in material deprivation for children, we have focused on indicators relating to the household in which children live,

[3] The official review of Ireland's poverty target in 2012 (Department of Social Protection, 2013) envisaged that the consistent poverty target by 2020 would be met by reducing both the at-risk-of-poverty and the basic-deprivation components in a way that would lead to an overall reduction in the population at risk of poverty or exclusion, as measured in the EU target, of 200,000; this would contribute 1 per cent to the overall EU poverty target. The sub-target for children was to reduce the extent of children in consistent poverty by narrowing the differential between children and adults. Subsequently, in 2014, the child-specific target was changed to lifting over 70,000 children out of consistent poverty by 2020, a reduction of at least two-thirds on the 2011 level (Department of Social Protection, 2014).

rather than to indicators designed to capture the circumstances of children themselves. This reflects the very limited availability of child-specific deprivation indicators in the representative household surveys by which poverty and living standards are monitored. However, while we cannot look 'before and after' to assess the impact of the recession, the 2009 EU-SILC contained a special module on child-specific deprivation that provides a unique window into the extent of deprivation that affected Irish children as the crisis had its initial impact. This has been analysed by Watson et al. (2012), who constructed an index of child-specific deprivation that is based on thirteen questions answered by the householder regarding goods, services, and activities that the child does not have or cannot do because the household cannot afford them. These include adequate food and clothing, books, toys and games, leisure equipment, school trips, and doctor/dentist visits. (The childhood deprivation measures were recorded for children aged 2–15.) The researchers found that 13 per cent of these children—or just over one in eight—lacked one or more of these items. Unsurprisingly, this was strongly related to income level: 30 per cent of children in the lowest (equivalized) income quintile lacked one or more of the child-specific items, compared to only 2 per cent of children in the highest quintile. The characteristics that were found to be significantly associated with a higher risk of child-specific deprivation, controlling for other factors, included the mother having only very low educational qualifications, lone-parent households, and households where the household reference person had never worked.

Another longitudinal perspective on what happened to Irish children through the recession is provided by the analysis of data from the Growing Up in Ireland study, a national longitudinal survey of children following two nationally representative cohorts of children born in 1998 and 2008. The families of children born in 2008 were interviewed when the child was aged 9 months in the first wave and 3 years in the second wave; children born in 1998 were surveyed in 2007–8, when they were aged 9, and in 2011–12, when they were 13. The families of each cohort were thus surveyed both before and during the Great Recession. Watson et al. (2015) have used these data to analyse the impact of the recession on both sets of children. Rather than relying on a single indicator of poverty, they use a multidimensional measure of economic vulnerability that combines indicators of relative income poverty, economic stress, and household joblessness. They find that economic vulnerability increased for both cohorts, reaching 25 per cent of children in each by the second wave. The factors behind economic vulnerability were similar for both cohorts, and were particularly strong for those vulnerable in both waves of the survey: that was significantly associated with lone parenthood, parents with lower levels of education and, to a lesser extent, parents who were younger when the child was born, the number of children in the family, and whether a parent left or died between the waves.

Similar factors were associated with 'transient' vulnerability (being vulnerable in wave 1 only), but the effects were weaker, particularly in relation to lone parenthood and the level of education of the parents. These factors were substantially weaker again in relation to children who became economically vulnerable between waves 1 and 2. Those who were economically vulnerable in the second wave were not only a larger, but also a more diverse group than those historically at risk of disadvantage and poverty: there were more couple families (for example, for the 1998 cohort, 11 per cent of economically vulnerable children in wave 1 lived in a two-parent and two-children type of household, while the figure was 22 per cent in wave 2) and more with higher levels of education. This is consistent with the changing composition of poor children by family type and parental education from the EU-SILC survey through the crisis, as noted earlier.

7.4. POLICY AND THE IMPACT OF THE CRISIS ON CHILDREN

While the immediate effect of Ireland's economic crisis was on employment and incomes from the market, the need to close the yawning fiscal deficit meant that a series of 'austerity' measures was implemented. These also had a major impact, in a manner which varied across the income distribution and by family/household type and that had serious implications for children. The effects are most obvious and direct in the case of the changes to taxes and social transfers, which constituted one of the main planks in the Irish government's response to the fiscal challenge. With the numbers relying on social welfare payments rising rapidly—the total number of beneficiaries (including dependants) of weekly social welfare payments rose very rapidly from about 1.6 million (out of a total population of 4.2 million) to 2.2 million—social protection support rates became even more important.

It is worth looking in some detail at how the policy choices with respect to transfers and direct taxes played out as the crisis unfolded, with key changes in structures and parameters listed in Table 7.5. The Budget for 2009 introduced a new income levy to be applied at a rate of 1 per cent to gross income up to €100,100 per annum, and 2 per cent to income in excess of that amount, with none of the allowances or reliefs that apply in the standard income tax system (though social welfare payments were not liable). Social welfare rates, surprisingly, were increased by a little over 3 per cent, in a context where price inflation was falling away. As the scale of the collapse in government revenue became apparent, a special 'emergency' Budget in April 2009 doubled the rates of the new income levy and of the long-standing health levy on gross income; a

Table 7.5. Key tax and social transfer budgetary measures, 2009–2012, Ireland

Budget 2009
Income levy introduced
3% rise in welfare payment rates
Supplementary Budget April 2009
Income levy and health levy rates doubled
Pay-related social insurance (PRSI) ceiling raised
Social welfare Christmas bonus abolished
Early Childcare Supplement halved
Social welfare payment rates for unemployed under 21 cut
Budget 2010
Cuts in social welfare for working age of 4%
Larger cuts for 21–25-year-olds
Child benefit cut by 10%, with compensation for welfare recipients
Budget 2011
Cuts in welfare for working age of 4%
Child benefit cut by 10%, with no compensation for welfare recipients
Universal Social Charge—combining income and health levies
Increases in income tax via reduced credits
Cuts in public service pensions
Restriction of tax reliefs on employee pension contributions
Budget 2012
€100 household charge
Cuts in child benefit for 3+ children
Cut in Fuel Allowance
Reduction in earnings 'disregard' for lone parents
Reduction in back-to-school payments

new pension-related levy on public sector workers was also introduced. Savings in social welfare spending were sought by abolishing the customary double payment at Christmas, and by halving the universal Early Childcare Supplement payment for children under the age of 6 from 1 May, and then abolishing it from the end of 2009. (As a replacement, a new scheme was subsequently introduced to provide some free pre-school hours.)

The 2010 Budget introduced significant reductions in the nominal rates of social welfare support. The cuts of about 4 per cent in weekly social welfare rates were confined to recipients of working age, while pensioners were unaffected. Unemployment payments for those aged under 25 were also sharply reduced. In addition, the rates of universal child benefit paid every month were cut by 10 per cent, although families with children who were dependent on social welfare received a compensatory increase in their weekly payment. There were also substantial cuts in the nominal rates of pay for workers in the public sector (unprecedented in the Irish experience since the 1930s).

A fundamental restructuring of direct taxation was implemented in 2011, whereby the income and health levies were brought together and restructured as a new Universal Social Charge (USC). Income tax revenue was also raised by further restricting allowances and reliefs, and public sector pensions were reduced. Child benefit was cut by a further 10 per cent, this time with no compensation for families dependent on social transfers.

In the 2012 Budget, a new (and much-resented) 'household charge' of €100 was introduced, child benefit was cut once more for the third (and any subsequent) child in a family, and some other elements of social transfers (such as the allowance for heating costs and back-to-school expenses) were also reduced.

Analysis of the impact of these discretionary changes in the transfer and direct tax systems from 2008 to 2012, using a tax-benefit simulation model, suggests that their combined effects were quite progressive, in the sense that the consequent reductions in income in proportionate terms rose as one moved up the income distribution.[4] As illustrated in Figure 7.4, compared with a benchmark of the change in average wages (which itself fell over the period), the tax and transfer changes will have reduced the income of the bottom 20 per cent of the distribution by about 2 per cent; this figure rises in steps to reach over 10 per cent for the top 20 per cent. The impact on different

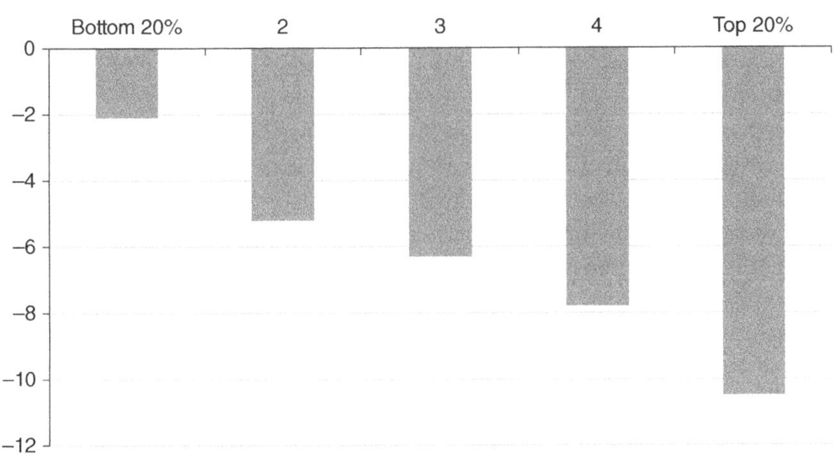

Figure 7.4. Impact of direct tax increases and social welfare reductions on household disposable income, by quintile, Ireland (2008–2012), per cent

[4] Tax-benefit simulation analyses of the distributional effects of a range of policies over different periods through the Crisis are reported in Callan, Nolan, and Walsh (2011), Nolan, Callan, and Maitre (2013), Callan, Keane, Savage, Walsh, and Colgan (2014), Callan, Nolan, Keane, Savage, and Walsh (2014), Keane et al. (2014).

family types is also of central interest when we focus on children. It has also been analysed with the tax/transfer simulation model at the level of the 'tax unit', i.e. an individual or couple, together with dependent children (if any), rather than the broader household unit. The average decline for families with children is generally greater than for other working-age family types, reflecting the impact of the cuts in child benefit and the Early Childcare Supplement in particular. (It is important to note in this context that such universal payments for children had increased substantially during the years of the economic boom, to the point where child-related social transfers were among the most generous in the OECD.) Young, single, unemployed individuals were hit particularly hard by the cuts to their benefits; pensioners were much less affected than those of working age.

The overall redistributive impact of the direct tax and transfer system increased markedly over the period from 2008 to 2012, as reflected in the percentage reduction in the Gini coefficient (often used as a summary indicator of redistribution) when one moves from market to disposable income, which went up from 20 per cent to 27 per cent. This reflected the combination of the discretionary changes in parameters and structures just described, together with the increased levels of expenditure on transfers as the numbers depending on them rose, and the increased level of revenue raised by taxes and levies/charges. About three-quarters of the total reduction in inequality came from transfers and one-quarter from direct taxes in each year. Indeed, the Irish fiscal adjustment achieved over this period was seen as quite distinctive not only for its success in bringing down the fiscal deficit, but also for the distributionally progressive way in which this was achieved. The effectiveness of the social safety net in protecting those towards the bottom, in particular, also featured strongly in, for example, commentaries by the OECD.

For the most part, the Irish social transfer system's combination of insurance-based and means-tested schemes designed to deal with different contingencies, together with a means-tested safety-net for those who fail to qualify for any of those schemes, appears to have been effective in providing an income floor. One exception is that the self-employed, who saw their income from work fall away but who remained 'in work', may have faced particular problems in accessing income support: they certainly came to comprise a larger proportion of households seen at the bottom of the income distribution. The cuts in weekly income support rates for those of working age will have reduced the level of the floor provided to those relying on social transfers, while the reductions in monthly universal payments for children during the crisis will have impacted both on that floor and on family incomes across the distribution. The increases in direct taxes and charges will have had less impact on families towards the bottom of the distribution than on those in its middle and upper parts, but some of the charges (as well as increases in indirect taxes) will have had a negative effect.

The reduction in public sector employee pay rates and numbers was another core component of the government's efforts to address the fiscal deficit in the crisis. A levy of 5–10 per cent on pay was first introduced to help fund public sector pensions, and salaries were then cut by 5 per cent on the first €30,000, 7.5 per cent on the next €40,000, and 10 per cent on the next €55,000. The distributional impact of these cuts has also been simulated: their direct impact on those below the 60 per cent of median threshold will have been very slight (Callan et al., 2011)—indeed, the impact was mostly on the top 60 per cent and was progressive, even within that part of the distribution, reflecting both where public sector workers were located in the distribution and the fact that the cuts were structured to have greater impact on higher earners. These pay cuts were combined with substantial reductions in public sector numbers, brought about by a recruitment embargo and the incentive of early retirement.

The reduction in the numbers working in the public sector and the broader cuts in expenditure on public services entailed by 'fiscal correction' will have impacted on the quality of services provided across the healthcare and education systems in particular, which account for much of the expenditure, as well as social services. These will undoubtedly have impacted on children, but in ways that are very difficult to capture empirically and assess. The increasing waiting lists for hospital treatment and the falling numbers of special needs teachers in schools give some indication of the most immediate effects, but it is difficult adequately to capture the impact on disadvantaged and vulnerable children in particular. The embargo on new recruitment into public employment will also have had an impact, particularly on young people coming onto the labour market during these years.

Another important aspect of Ireland's crisis that is not discussed in any detail here, but that will certainly have had implications for some children, relates to housing and household debt. The explosion in borrowing during the latter part of the boom left some households highly vulnerable; the onset of the crisis and the resultant collapsing property values were particularly damaging (Lydon and McCarthy, 2013; McCarthy, 2014; Lawless et al., 2015). Those who bought their first house at the peak of the boom—mostly younger households—were hardest hit, and substantial numbers struggled to keep up their repayments (with larger numbers suffering 'negative equity'). Mortgage arrears soared, and by the depth of the recession about 13 per cent of mortgage holders were in arrears for 90 days or more on their principal dwelling, as were a further 20 per cent of buy-to-let mortgage holders; one mortgage holder in four faced some form of difficulty in meeting their repayments. A majority of those in such debt-repayment difficulties were still in employment and would not, for the most part, have been in poverty as conventionally measured; but the position of those who had lost their jobs was particularly serious. While only small numbers of families had their houses repossessed by the lender, far more significant numbers had difficulties with their lender on resolving their mortgage debt. Significant numbers in rented accommodation also struggled to pay their rent, and the limited supply of social housing available meant that more low-income families were pushed into the private rented sector, where rent levels increased as economic recovery set in, leading to a marked increase in homelessness, including for families with children.

While we have concentrated here for the most part on the 2008–12 period—in effect covering the peak to the trough of the recession and the associated fiscal austerity measures—it is worth noting that subsequent discretionary changes to the tax and transfer system have been less progressive overall. Over the entire period from 2009 through to the budgetary changes announced in late 2015 for implementation in 2016, the impact on income has been to reduce average income by 8–11 per cent across most of the income distribution, with an above-average effect on the bottom decile, but with the greatest reduction at the top (Keane et al., 2014). The impact on different family types did not differ markedly between working-age families with and without children: most family types have seen losses of 8–13 per cent, though single unemployed people without children once again suffered by far the largest losses (of more than 22 per cent). The smallest losses (5–6 per cent) have been for single retired tax units and retired couples, reflecting the protection afforded to pension payments throughout crisis budgets.

As far as discourse is concerned, the importance of 'protecting the vulnerable' featured strongly in the way policy was presented and debated domestically over the 'austerity' period from 2008 to 2012, with considerable attention being paid in that context to the impact on children, and on child poverty in particular. The reductions in universal child benefit rates and in support rates for working-age households relying on cash transfers featured strongly in this context, as did the impact of unemployment, of increased direct and indirect taxes, and of expenditure constraints on the education system and health services. Certain specific increases in taxes and charges, such as the introduction of a tax on residential property and charges for water supply, have proved particularly contentious; at the same time, the extent of homelessness is coming to be seen as one of the most serious socio-economic problems facing the country, with the plight of the children affected being highlighted. The central question in assessing the policy choices made, of course, is whether there was a feasible, implementable alternative that would have protected children and their families more effectively, while recognizing the scale of the challenge posed by the fiscal crisis and responding to it. With economic growth now under way, and with unemployment declining substantially, choices will be made about the appropriate balance between reducing taxes and reinforcing public spending, with important consequences for Irish children and for poor and vulnerable children in particular.

7.5. CONCLUSIONS AND IMPLICATIONS

Ireland's exceptionally deep economic and fiscal crisis had an immediate and profound impact on employment and on household incomes, with median disposable income falling by 12 per cent from 2008 to 2012. Over that period, the relative income poverty rate for children, measured vis-à-vis a threshold of 60 per cent of median household income, fluctuated somewhat from year to year through the crisis, but was no higher in 2012 than it had been in 2008. Using an 'anchored' income poverty threshold that does not decline in line with that median, though, the percentage of children below that 2008 threshold indexed to prices rose from 18 per cent to 28 per cent. A similar increase was seen for working-age adults, while those aged 65 or over saw a much more modest increase. The percentage of children in households experiencing material deprivation also increased very substantially over the crisis, so that by 2012, 32 per cent of children, versus 25 per cent of working-age adults and 10 per cent of older persons, were in households reporting such deprivation (as captured by the indicator employed by the EU's social inclusion process).

The impact of the recession on the incomes of households with children was significantly buffered by a social security system that effectively provided a floor for those who lost their jobs (though specific groups, such as the self-employed, may have faced particular problems). The distributional implications of the austerity measures required to address the yawning fiscal deficit, including their impact on children, have been a matter of some contention, in Ireland as elsewhere. The redistributive impact of the direct tax and transfer system increased markedly, as taxes were raised and expenditure levels responded to increased levels of welfare dependency. Cuts implemented in the rates of social transfers and increases in taxes and charges will have reduced the level of the floor provided to those relying on social transfers and had an impact on family incomes across the distribution. In assessing the policy choices made, judgements differ as to whether there was a feasible, implementable alternative that would have protected children and their families more effectively, while recognizing the scale of the challenge posed by the fiscal crisis and responding adequately to it. As far as structures are concerned, though, for the most part the Irish social protection system has demonstrated its capacity to cope with dramatic macroeconomic fluctuations and an unprecedented economic crisis, in terms of providing an income safety net for those most seriously affected; the fact that the income support provided is at a flat rate, rather than related to earnings, does mean however that loss of employment can bring with it a pronounced fall in income. More broadly, the Irish welfare state has proved reasonably robust, bringing about a relatively rapid fiscal adjustment and seeing growth resume, albeit at considerable cost in terms of living standards and deprivation, and with a level of debt that will severely constrain the capacity to address the socio-economic legacies of the crisis.

While the Irish experience highlights the centrality of the tax-transfer system in protecting children in recession, it also brings out the multidimensional nature of living standards and the multifaceted nature of the policies required to underpin them. The impact of reductions in public expenditure on the availability and quality of public services is an important aspect of the impact of recession and 'fiscal correction' on the welfare of children that is not captured by conventional indicators of poverty and social exclusion. Awareness of the importance of housing as a core aspect of living standards has also been reinforced by recent Irish experience and the failure of current policies to generate adequate affordable housing. The impact of the crisis on the relatively small numbers of children who are in specific circumstances that leave them highly vulnerable and reliant on, for example, effective intervention by social services is also difficult to measure and assess. For most children, though, while the income and other financial resources available to their families do not tell the whole story, it is a central component, and recent Irish experience offers important lessons about the design of tax and transfer systems and about the choices made in that respect.

REFERENCES

Atkinson, Tony, Bea Cantillon, Eric Marlier, and Brian Nolan (2002). *Social Indicators: The EU and Social Inclusion* (Oxford: Oxford University Press).

Callan, Tim, Claire Keane, Michael Savage, John R. Walsh, and Brian Colgan (2014). 'Ireland's Economic Adjustment: From Crisis to Recovery'. *Intereconomics 49*, no. 6: pp. 318–22.

Callan, Tim, Brian Nolan, Claire Keane, Michael Savage, and John R. Walsh (2014). 'Crisis, Response and Distributional Impact: the Case of Ireland'. *IZA Journal of European Labor Studies 3*, no. 9: pp. 1–17.

Callan, Tim, Brian Nolan, and John Walsh (2011). 'The Economic Crisis, Public Sector Pay, and the Income Distribution'. In Herwig Immervoll, Andreas Peichl, and Konstantinos Tatsiramos (eds), *Who Loses in the Downturn? Economic Crisis, Employment and Income Distribution*. Research in Labor Economics 32 (Bingley: Emerald): pp. 207–25.

Callan, Tim, Brian Nolan, and Christopher T. Whelan (1993). 'Resources, Deprivation and the Measurement of Poverty'. *Journal of Social Policy 22*, no. 2: pp. 141–72.

Department of Social Protection (2013). *Social Inclusion Monitor 2011* (Dublin: Department of Social Protection).

Department of Social Protection (2014). *Social Inclusion Monitor 2012* (Dublin: Department of Social Protection).

Government of Ireland (2007). *National Action Plan for Social Inclusion 2007–2016* (Dublin: Stationery Office).

Jenkins, Stephen P., Andrea Brandolini, John Micklewright, and Brian Nolan (eds) (2013). *The Great Recession and the Distribution of Household Income* (Oxford: Oxford University Press).

Keane, Claire, Tim Callan, Michael Savage, John R. Walsh, and Brian Colgan (2014). 'Distributional Impact of Tax, Welfare and Public Service Pay Policies: Budget 2015 and Budgets 2009–2015'. *Quarterly Economic Commentary*, Special Article, Winter 2014.

Lawless, Martina, Reamonn Lydon, and Tara McIndoe-Calder (2015). 'The Financial Position of Irish Households'. *Central Bank of Ireland Quarterly Bulletin 01*, January 2015: pp. 66–89.

Lydon, Reamonn and Yvonne McCarthy (2013). 'What Lies Beneath? Understanding Recent Trends in Irish Mortgage Arrears'. *Economic and Social Review 44*, no. 1: pp. 117–50.

McCarthy, Yvonne (2014). 'Dis-entangling the Mortgage Arrears Crisis: The Role of the Labour Market, Income Volatility and Negative Equity'. 2013–14 Barrington Lecture. *Journal of the Statistical and Social Inquiry Society of Ireland 43*: pp. 71–90.

Nolan, Brian, Tim Callan, and Bertrand Maître (2013). 'Country Case Study—Ireland', in Stephen P. Jenkins, Andrea Brandolini, John Micklewright, and Brian Nolan (eds), *The Great Recession and the Distribution of Household Income* (Oxford: Oxford University Press).

Nolan, Brian and Christopher T. Whelan (1996). *Resources, Deprivation and Poverty* (Oxford: Oxford University Press).

Savage, Michael, Tim Callan, Brian Nolan, and Brian Colgan (2015). 'The Great Recession, Austerity and Inequality: Evidence from Ireland'. *ESRI Working Paper 499* (Dublin: Economic and Social Research Institute).

Watson, Dorothy, Bertrand Maître, and Christopher T. Whelan (2012). *Work and Poverty in Ireland: An Analysis of the CSO Survey on Income and Living Conditions 2004–2010* (Dublin: Department of Social Protection and ESRI).

Watson, D., C. T. Whelan, B. Maître, and J. Williams (2015). 'Family Economic Vulnerability and the Great Recession: An Analysis of the First Two Waves of the Growing Up in Ireland Study'. *Longitudinal and Life Course Studies 6*, no. 3: pp. 230–44.

8

The Impact of the Great Recession on Child Poverty: The Case of Italy

Luisa Natali and Chiara Saraceno

8.1. INTRODUCTION

The duration and depth of the crisis in Italy, as well as its impact both in general and specifically on child poverty, were largely a consequence of long-term structural features of the Italian economy and its social safety net. Government choices in reaction to the crisis (and under pressure from the EU) further influenced what happened.

Even long before the global downturn, within a persistent North–South divide, the national economy was struggling, with protracted sluggish growth: average real gross domestic product (GDP) increased by less than 1.5 per cent per year in the decade preceding the onset of the crisis (see Figari and Fiorio, 2015). Italian firms were relatively uncompetitive internationally, relying largely on low salaries rather than on investment in human capital and research and innovation (OECD, 2012a). The traditional duality of the labour market, with its ample informal and grey economy, had developed into a duality within the formal sector, too, with the introduction since the 1990s of new, more flexible and precarious labour contracts. These were (and largely still are) concentrated among the young, whose entry to, and stabilization in, the labour market had become increasingly delayed and precarious. Finally, the relatively low labour force participation of women in the years preceding the crisis had been increasing at a much slower pace than in other European countries. The employment rate of working-age women in Italy was more than 10 percentage points lower than the EU average: 50.6 per cent vs 62.8 per cent in 2008 (Eurostat). This in turn accounts for the high incidence of single-earner households, particularly in the south, among the lower educated, and in larger households, which is one reason for the comparatively high incidence of poverty in these households and among children.

Also the *policy framework* was ill-prepared for the crisis and its long duration—and even less for its impact on children, who, ever since the 1990s, had been emerging as the most vulnerable group, particularly those living in single-earner households, with more than one sibling, and in the south of the country. The combination of low support for mothers' employment, regional differentiation in both labour demand and welfare state provisions, high de facto reliance on intergenerational family solidarity as the main social protection means, inadequate and fragmented child-linked income transfers, and lack of a national minimum income provision for the poor proved particularly risky in the face of the crisis—especially given its long duration.

8.2. THE NATURE OF THE CRISIS: ORIGINS AND TRANSMISSION CHANNELS

In Italy, the crisis was experienced as a double-dip recession. Following the collapse of Lehman Brothers in September 2008 a sharp drop in foreign demand quickly spread to the rest of the economy, not only because of the intense subcontracting relations that characterize the production system in the country but also because the conditions required to obtain a loan were tightened (Bugamelli et al., 2010). The sharpest drop was experienced between the first quarter of 2008 and the first quarter of 2009, when GDP fell by 7.3 per cent in just twelve months (International Monetary Fund statistics; Brandolini, 2014), one of the largest drops in a European country. The onset of the sovereign debt crisis in the second quarter of 2011 interrupted the weak recovery begun in 2010, giving way to a second recession that lasted well into 2014, with a real GDP drop of 5.6 per cent (between the second quarter of 2011 and the last quarter of 2014).[1]

Labour market conditions, which had already started to worsen, deteriorated further in the second phase of the crisis. Between 2008 and 2013, employment diminished by almost a million units (of which almost half were recorded in 2013 alone) and the employment rate slipped from 58.7 per cent to 55.6 per cent. As the crisis hit the manufacturing and construction industries most severely, it was almost exclusively male employment that suffered. The drop was most marked in the South of Italy, where most job losses were concentrated (Istat, 2014a; 2015), therefore widening the territorial gap even further. In parallel, the unemployment rate increased sharply (from

[1] Figures were elaborated by the authors, based on Istat Quarterly National Accounts (update 1 December 2015), Table: GDP and expenditure components: chained volume measures (millions of euro: reference year 2010).

6.7 per cent in 2008 to 12.2 per cent in 2013), with the youth particularly vulnerable; the same was true of the inactivity rate (rising from 15.6 per cent in 2008 to 21.7 per cent in 2013) (Istat, 2014a). Though there was some improvement from 2014, the unemployment rate in 2015 remained high (11.9 per cent, down from 12.7 per cent in 2014); the inactivity rate remained largely stable (35.9 per cent), with the rate diminishing for men but increasing for women (having fallen in previous years) (Istat, 2016).

The crisis also entailed a reduction in the per capita real disposable income of Italian households (14 per cent between 2007 and the first half of 2013, according to Brandolini, 2014). Not only did household income diminish, but the cost of living also increased and purchasing power fell, particularly for the poorest (Saraceno, 2014; 2015).

Given the fragmented nature of the social protection system, family solidarity (which had offered a relatively efficient buffer against the loss of jobs and income in the first period of the crisis) proved no longer strong enough to cope with the protracted crisis.

8.3. CHILDREN IN CRISIS: CHARACTERISTICS OF CHILD POVERTY AND TRENDS OVER TIME

8.3.1. Child Poverty in Italy before the Crisis

In Italy, child poverty had started its upward trend in the mid-1990s, long before the crisis hit (Saraceno, 2015). In 2008, across the country some 24.7 per cent of children—one child in four—was at risk of poverty; this was higher than the 20.3 per cent EU-27 average (Eurostat).[2] Children were at greater risk of poverty than the population as a whole (18.7 per cent) and than the elderly (20.9 per cent), typically another socially disadvantaged group.[3]

Some groups of children faced a greater poverty risk than others: those living in the South experienced a much higher risk than those living in the Centre and North. This territorial skewness of children's poverty risks dates back to Italian unification in the late nineteenth century, and did not substantially change over the decades of democracy and development (Amendola et al., 2011; Saraceno, 2015). In 2008, the at-risk-of-poverty rate for children in

[2] All poverty estimates in this section, unless otherwise specified, are based on computations from EU-SILC microdata (version of 01.01.2016) and refer to the at-risk-of-poverty rate, a relative poverty measure commonly used in the EU. The year reported (2008) represents the survey year of EU-SILC, whereas the year of reference for income is 2007.

[3] According to the Commission for the Study of Poverty and Social Exclusion (2002), as far back as the mid-1990s the incidence of poverty among children had overtaken elderly poverty.

the South was 41.7 per cent, compared to 12.4 per cent in the North, and 16.9 per cent in the Centre. This territorial gap may be explained by a combination of lower employment rates (and higher unemployment rates) among men, lower female labour participation rates, and a relatively large household size in the South, compared to other regions.

The at-risk-of-poverty rate for children was also extremely high among large families: the larger the family (and particularly the more children there were), the higher the risk of poverty. Having an extra child (sibling) increased the risk of poverty: poverty rates were 19 per cent, 24.7 per cent, and 38.1 per cent for children living in households with one, two, and three or more children, respectively. In particular, even though only 15.1 per cent of children lived in households with more than two children in 2008, they were over-represented among the poor.

Children living in households with low work intensity were particularly exposed to poverty: 78.3 per cent of children living in households with very low work intensity and 57.3 per cent of children living in low work-intensity households were at risk of poverty in 2008. The at-risk-of-poverty rate for children was higher than the overall risk (36.1 per cent vs 24.7 per cent) even in households with medium work intensity (typically single-earner households), which highlights the very high level of in-work poverty that afflicted the country as far back as 2008. These included lone-parent (and particularly lone-mother) households: in 2008, four children in ten (39.3 per cent) raised in a single-parent household were threatened with poverty, compared to two children in ten (23.4 per cent) living in a household where two adults were present.

The majority of children living in single-earner households at risk of poverty, however, belonged to a two-parent family, where the heavy burden of domestic and care responsibilities (due to family size and the scarcity of social services) often deterred mothers from participating in the labour market; this was particularly the case in the South, and particularly among the lower educated. The interaction between parental education, parental wages, and mother's employment also explains why children with low-educated parents (ISCED 0–2)[4] were more at risk of poverty (over 40 per cent) than children living in households where parents had obtained higher levels of education (ISCED 5–6) (7 per cent risk).

Immigration, a relatively recent phenomenon in Italy, has increased very rapidly in the past fifteen years. Since migrants settling in Italy tend to have lower skills and education levels than those settling in other countries, they are particularly exposed to the risk of poverty. Even when in work, in fact, migrants are located at the bottom of the social and occupational stratification

[4] The International Standard Classification of Education (ISCED) has a total of ten levels (0–9); ISCED 0, for example, corresponds to 'Early childhood education'.

(Fullin and Reyneri, 2011; Cingano et al., 2013; Saraceno et al., 2013). Migrant households are also larger on average than Italian ones. Consequently, children in migrant households suffer a higher risk of poverty than native Italians (31.8 per cent vs. 23.4 per cent).

To sum up, at the onset of the crisis, children living in large families, in the South, in low or medium work-intensity households, with low-educated parents, and in migrant households all faced a greater risk of poverty than either children in other situations or adults. The different conditions of vulnerability often overlapped.

8.3.2. Trends and Drivers of Child Poverty since the Onset of the Crisis

Not surprisingly, the long-term upwards structural trend in child poverty was further worsened by the crisis, strengthening the specific features of child poverty risks summed up above.

To better assess changes, in this section we focus on child 'anchored' poverty estimates from the EU Statistics on Income and Living Conditions (EU-SILC),[5] basically fixing the poverty line with reference to 2008 and only uprating it for inflation. We integrate these data with indicators concerning material deprivation and absolute poverty.

Over the years after the onset of the crisis, the at-risk-of-poverty rate for children increased moderately, whereas child anchored poverty worsened considerably, particularly after 2010 (see Figure 8.1). It sky-rocketed between 2010 and 2011, and kept rising in the following two years to peak in 2013 (32.6 per cent, up from 24.7 per cent in 2008), when one child in three was living below the anchored poverty line. The worst affected were children who possessed characteristics that rendered them vulnerable even previously (see Table 8.1). In 2014, for the first time, there was no increase in child anchored poverty, and even some small sign of improvement (31.6 per cent).

Also the duration, or persistence, of poverty among children—captured by the persistent at-risk-of-poverty rate—worsened, peaking at 19.7 per cent in 2013 and reversing the downward trend (from 20.9 per cent to 14.9 per cent) observed between 2007 and 2010 (not shown in the table). The 2014 data again show some slight improvement: 17.4 per cent (Eurostat).

[5] Child anchored poverty estimates up to 2014 were computed based on EU-SILC microdata (version of 01.01.2016); the same applies to all other indicators used in this section (severe material deprivation, work intensity, and child-specific deprivation), apart from relative and absolute child poverty (provided by Istat) and persistence of poverty (obtained from Eurostat).

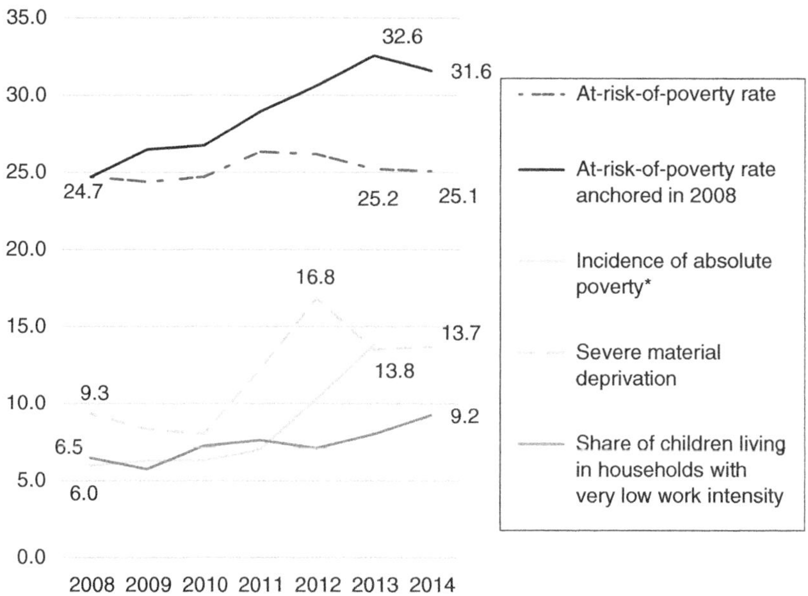

Figure 8.1. Trends in child (0–17) poverty by different measures 2008–2013/2014

Note: Estimates for the at-risk-of-poverty rate, the at-risk-of-poverty rate anchored in 2008, severe material deprivation, and the share living in households with very low work intensity are based on the authors' elaborations of EU-SILC microdata for the 2008–14 time series.

* The incidence of absolute poverty was directly provided by Istat (and is based on the old methodology).

Table 8.1. Trends in child anchored poverty, Italy, by sub-groups, 2008–2014

		2008	2009	2010	2011	2012	2013	2014
Child anchored poverty		*24.7*	*26.5*	*26.8*	*29.0*	*30.6*	*32.6*	*31.6*
Region	North	12.4	13.7	15.5	15.2	19.5	19.7	19.6
	Centre	16.9	19.4	19.6	20.2	21.2	25.8	24.4
	South	41.7	44.4	43.4	49.6	48.9	52.1	50.4
Number of children	1	19.0	20.3	21.4	24.6	24.9	24.3	26.2
	2	24.7	27.1	26.2	28.4	28.9	31.8	31.0
	3+	38.1	39.6	44.1	42.4	48.2	52.6	45.8
Household type	Single parent with children	39.3	37.7	42.0	40.8	44.8	48.2	47.6
	Two adults with children	23.4	25.1	24.6	27.0	29.2	30.7	29.0
Work intensity	very low	78.3	75.0	80.4	84.0	80.3	82.6	84.6
	low	57.3	61.1	61.6	66.0	71.0	73.0	69.0
	medium	36.1	39.4	36.5	39.2	41.4	45.9	41.3
	high	10.7	15.2	13.5	15.9	16.7	15.5	18.4
	very high	5.5	7.0	5.0	6.7	9.2	8.8	7.2
Migrant	Migrant household	31.8	37.3	38.8	37.2	41.6	42.7	43.0
	Native household	23.4	24.1	24.7	26.8	27.6	30.0	28.5

Note: Estimates for the at-risk-of-poverty rate anchored in 2008 are based on the authors' elaborations of EU-SILC microdata.

The increase in child poverty was accompanied by an increase in the proportion of children living in severe material deprivation or, according to the Eurostat definition, living in a household that could not afford at least four of nine items considered necessary for a decent life. As highlighted in Figure 8.1, around 9.3 per cent of children lived in severely materially deprived households in 2008, a slightly lower percentage than the EU average. After remaining relatively stable in the following two years, it increased to 12.2 per cent in 2011 and sky-rocketed to 16.8 per cent in 2012, the highest peak since the onset of the crisis. The increase has been larger than in other EU countries, and in 2012 was 5.1 percentage points greater than the EU average. In 2013, this indicator improved to 13.5 per cent, and the difference from the EU average was almost halved. With 13.7 per cent in 2014, it remains at a much higher level than in 2008. Some of the deprivations that recorded worse evolution are particularly crucial for children's well-being, such as the inability to eat meat or proteins regularly (this almost doubled for children between 2008 and 2014, from 7.8 per cent to 13.8 per cent, with a peak of 18.2 per cent in 2014), to keep the home adequately warm (from 11.5 per cent in 2008 to 18.4 per cent in 2014), and to go on holiday (51.5 per cent of children lived in households that could not afford to go for a week away from home in 2012, compared to 40.3 per cent in 2008).

In 2009, EU-SILC included an ad-hoc module with some child-specific items to measure child deprivation. The Italian National Statistical Office (Istat) repeated this in its 2013 and 2014 surveys, so that the trend in deprivations that are relevant to children as such can be monitored, as well as those experienced at the household level. Each of the thirteen listed child deprivations that were analysed, and that were comparable over time, experienced a worsening between 2009 and 2013–14 (see Table 8.2). In particular, the proportion of children that do not have new (not second-hand) clothes because the household cannot afford them almost doubled, from 6.2 per cent in 2009 to 11.7 per cent in 2013.[6] As in the case of non-child-specific deprivation, 2014 showed a slight improvement, although the figures were not yet back to their 2008 levels.

The share of children living in jobless or very low work-intensity households has also increased over the years of the crisis, although by less than the other indicators: from 6.5 per cent in 2008 to 9.2 per cent in 2014.

The drastic worsening of children's conditions is evidenced most clearly by what happened to absolute poverty. This measure is provided by Istat. The threshold represents the monetary value of a basket of goods and services considered necessary for households of different compositions and living in

[6] The share of deprived adults with regard to the same four indicators is higher than that of children, suggesting that parents/adults try to shelter their children from these kinds of deprivation.

Table 8.2. Child-specific deprivations, Italy, 2009–2014

	BASIC NEEDS FOR ALL HOUSEHOLD CHILDREN				EDUCATIONAL OR LEISURE NEEDS FOR ALL HOUSEHOLD CHILDREN								
	Some new clothes	Two pairs of properly fitting shoes	Fresh fruit and vegetables once a day	One meal with meat, chicken or fish (or vegetarian equivalent) at least once a day	Books at home	Outdoor leisure equipment	Indoor games	Regular leisure activity	Celebrations on special occasions	Invite friends round	Participate in school trips/events that cost money	Suitable place to study	Go on holiday away from home
2009	6.2	2.7	2.4	4.5	6.5	4.1	4.6	12.8	6.0	7.2	7.1	11.8	30.3
2013	11.7	4.6	2.9	5.9	9.4	6.9	6.8	16.3	9.4	9.0	9.8	14.9	30.5
2014	8.5	2.8	2.6	5.6	7.6	6.0	5.6	13.6	7.1	7.4	10.1	13.3	29.3
Absolute change (2009–13)	5.5	1.9	0.4	1.3	2.9	2.8	2.2	3.5	3.4	1.7	2.6	3.1	0.2
Relative change (2009–13)	88.5	70.8	18.2	29.6	43.8	67.4	48.5	27.3	56.0	23.9	37.0	26.1	0.8
Absolute change (2009–14)	2.3	0.1	0.1	1.0	1.1	1.9	1.0	0.8	1.1	0.2	2.9	1.6	−1.0
Relative change (2009–14)	36.9	4.0	4.7	23.1	17.0	45.4	22.7	6.3	17.8	2.7	40.9	13.3	−3.2

Note: Questions are asked at the household level and refer to children aged under 16. If at least one child does not have the item or does not participate in the activity, the whole group of children in the household is assumed to be deprived of that item/activity different areas. This measure, which is not sensitive to the economic conjuncture, captures the most severe poverty. It also offers a methodologically stronger measure than the 'severe deprivation' one developed by Eurostat (Sabbadini, 2014).

Even though this measure is not directly comparable to the EU-SILC ones discussed above,[7] a similar pattern emerges. Whereas in 2008, 6.0 per cent of children were living in absolute poverty, this percentage had more than doubled by 2013 to reach 13.8 per cent, i.e. 1,434,000 children (see Figure 8.1). The increase in child absolute poverty was much greater than for the population as a whole. For the latter, in fact, absolute poverty reached 9.9 per cent in 2013, up from 4.9 per cent in 2008.[8]

Among those children most severely hit by the crisis (Figure 8.2), we find children living in households where neither parent is employed or where neither parent has any schooling beyond primary education (around a 20 percentage point increase in absolute poverty), and children living in single-earner households (a 10 percentage point increase). Also the situation of children living in the South worsened considerably, with an increase in absolute poverty from 9.4 per cent in 2008 to 19.1 per cent in 2013. A similar increase concerned children in large families (with three or more children), for whom absolute poverty doubled from 11.1 per cent to 22.9 per cent. Furthermore, for the first time even children with only one sibling recorded a consistent increase in absolute poverty, since their rate more than doubled, jumping from 5.8 per cent in 2008 to 13.4 per cent in 2013.

The presence of a similar pattern in all the above-mentioned indicators shows that the crisis most affected those groups that were already disadvantaged to start with. In particular, the drivers behind the increase in child poverty are basically the same (though at a higher level) as those that characterized child poverty in Italy before the onset of the crisis. The increase in unemployment reduced the already comparatively low number of workers per household, and also often weakened the position of the main earner. Although absolute poverty did also increase in the Centre and North, because job losses

[7] One indicator is based on consumption and the other on income; moreover different equivalence scales are used.

[8] Data were provided directly by Istat, for which we express our thanks; we express our gratitude in particular to Nicoletta Pannuzi and Alessandra Masi for their help. Between 2013 and 2014, the Household Budget Survey was renewed. In order to make data comparable, as the methodology changed, Istat reconstructed the time series of the main poverty indicators at the aggregate level. At the time of writing, however, the new, full, disaggregated series were not available. For this reason, we decided to use estimates based on the old methodology, as they allowed us to disaggregate by group, even though they are available only up until 2013; 2014 Istat estimates are based on a new methodology and are therefore not directly comparable with the ones discussed here. The trend, however, indicates that child and total absolute poverty remained relatively stable between 2013 and 2014.

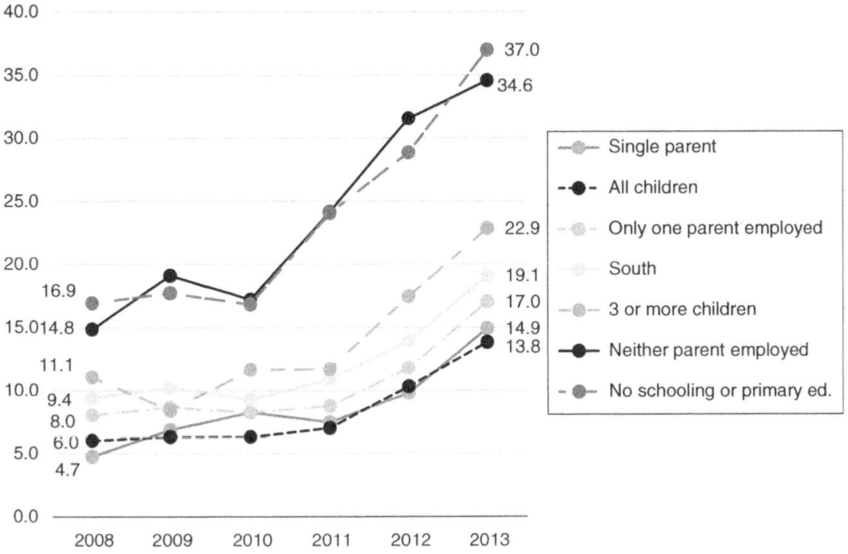

Figure 8.2. Trends in child (0–17) absolute poverty by group (2008–2013)

Note: Estimates of the incidence of absolute poverty across groups were directly provided by Istat (and are based on the old methodology).

mainly affected the South, households living in southern regions saw their traditionally higher vulnerability to poverty increase.

It should be added that poor children often encounter conditions that are less favourable than those that affect non-poor children—in terms of the provision of services, schools, and so forth. This is particularly true of those living in the South; thus, on average, their deprivation is more general and intense (Save the Children Italia, 2014). In particular, educational poverty is another dimension that is worth exploring when discussing children's well-being and life chances. This refers not only to educational outcomes (school performance, cognitive skills), but also to access to and quality of education, both through the school and through access to culturally enriching activities (Save the Children Italia, 2014). According to international tests (Programme for International Student Assessment—PISA), almost one child in four aged 15 in Italy failed to reach the minimum level of competency (level 2) in maths, and one child in five in reading (OECD, 2012b). The figures increase to 36 per cent and 29 per cent respectively for children from low-income families. Children with migrant parents, as well as children living in southern Italy, are more disadvantaged, compared to the children of Italian parents and children living in the North. These gaps overlap with important disparities in the supply of educational services and extracurricular opportunities (Save the Children Italia, 2014; 2016).

Child monetary and educational poverty are clearly related. Most importantly, not only do they affect children in the present but they can have long-term effects

Table 8.3. Indicators of vulnerability among the young, Italy, 2008–2014

		2008	2009	2010	2011	2012	2013	2014
Not in employment, education or training (NEET) (%)	EU-28	10.9	12.4	12.8	12.9	13.2	13	12.5
	Italy	*16.6*	*17.6*	*19*	*19.7*	*21*	*22.2*	*22.1*
Youth unemployment rate (%)	EU-28	15.6	19.9	21	21.7	23.2	23.6	22.2
	Italy	*21.2*	*25.3*	*27.9*	*29.2*	*35.3*	*40*	*42.7*
Youth long-term unemployment rate (12 months or longer) (%)	EU-28	3.5	4.6	5.9	6.5	7.5	8.0	7.8
	Italy	*8.0*	*10.1*	*12.3*	*13.7*	*17.3*	*21.0*	*25.1*

Note: Eurostat data.

that last long into adult life and that threaten future generations. It is too early to grasp the long-term effects, such as 'scarring'; however, the PISA (and similar) data, as well as trends in the incidence of young people not in employment, education, or training (NEET), and in youth and long-term youth unemployment rates (Table 8.3) provide a far from reassuring picture of what might be expected.

8.4. POLICIES: STRUCTURAL FEATURES OF THE POLICY FRAMEWORK AND RESPONSES DURING THE CRISIS

8.4.1. The Social Safety Net before the Onset of the Crisis

Overall, at the onset of the crisis, social expenditure (as a percentage of GDP) was at the EU average. It showed, however, an unbalanced spending pattern, as more than half of social protection was absorbed by old-age pensions (59.1 per cent in Italy vs 43.7 per cent in the EU-15 between 2000 and 2008). Only a minor share of resources for social protection was devoted to other functions, including to families: 4.2 per cent in Italy vs 7.8 per cent in the EU-15 over the period 2000–8 (Ferrera et al., 2013; Madama et al., 2013; Pavolini, 2013). The main traditional features of the Italian social protection system, even before the crisis, included its skewness towards old-age pensions; its mainly categorical approach, which left many either unprotected or inadequately protected; the underdevelopment of family policy; and the lack of a minimum income scheme. Moreover in this highly fragmented context, *territorial inequality* existed in terms of coverage and quality of benefits and services (Madama et al., 2013; Simonazzi, 2015; Crepaldi et al., 2014).

The so-called recalibration process (Ferrera et al., 2000) initiated in the 1990s mainly targeted pension reform, leaving other features of the Italian welfare state substantially untouched: a fragmentation and inefficiency of child-related income transfers, a scarcity of work–family reconciliation measures, and a lack of a minimum income provision at the national level, in particular.

There was (and is) neither a universal child benefit nor a child benefit based on a purely income criterion (Pavolini, 2013; Saraceno, 2015). The main income support for families—family allowance (*Assegno al nucleo familiare*)—is a household means-tested transfer to the families of low-income employees.[9] It is therefore doubly selective, with regard to both the level of income and the category of income. Being basically conceived as a wage supplement for wage workers with dependent members, it excludes poor families (and children) without income from dependent work in the formal economy (Saraceno, 2007; 2014; 2015; Madama et al., 2013). For these reasons, its redistributive impact is limited (Di Biase, 2009; Baldini and Toso, 2011; 2012), as is its targeting efficiency (IRS/CAPP, 2011).

Another categorical measure in place since 1998 is the benefit for low-income households with three or more underage children (*Assegno per il terzo figlio*). It was introduced by the first Prodi government after a report by the Commission for the Study of Poverty and Social Exclusion had pointed out that children's poverty was increasing, particularly among large families. In 2007, it paid up to €122.80 a month for thirteen months to households with at least three minor children and a yearly income of less than €22,105 for a family of five. The allowance is lost once one of the children turns 18, irrespective of the income level of the family or the needs of the other children in the family. Both the allowance and the income threshold are indexed.

Two other measures that target poor households and that may indirectly benefit children were introduced in 1998: a five-month maternity allowance for insured mothers (with children below 1 year of age) with a low household income; and the fund to support low-income tenants, which aimed at reducing the burden on disposable income of rental costs (Madama et al., 2013).

It should be noted that some of the financial measures that target families with children, such as non-refundable tax credits for dependent children (*Detrazioni fiscali per i figli a carico*), are not available to households without a taxable income; this therefore includes the poorest households and children, since there is no reverse tax credit (Saraceno, 2014; 2015).

Policies that target families with children represent a negligible area of intervention, not only in terms of monetary transfers but also in terms of childcare services for children under the age of 3. The provision of such services is scarce and is distributed unequally across the country (Naldini and Solera, 2012; Crepaldi et al., 2014). This contributes to the weakness and uneven availability of work–family reconciliation policies that might facilitate

[9] Including unemployed on unemployment benefits and former-employee pensioners (Madama et al., 2013).

the labour market participation of mothers (Naldini and Saraceno, 2012). On the contrary, the provision for children aged from 3 years to school age is almost universal and free of charge, although (once again) coverage, daily time schedule, and quality are better in the Centre and North than in the South.

Finally, although the topic has been debated for years, ever since the end of 1980s, and although a scheme was even piloted in 1997 in a number of municipalities, Italy until June 2016 remains one of the few countries in the EU that lacks a statutory minimum income scheme for the poor (Madama et al., 2013; Caritas Italiana, 2014; Saraceno, 2015). Only with the 2016 Budget law have funds for such a scheme been allocated, although at a very minimal level. At the time of writing, the necessary law establishing criteria and rules for its implementation has been approved only by the Chamber of representatives and is waiting for approval by the Senate.

At the national level, social assistance transfers exist for only two specific categories: the elderly poor (over 65) and the (18–65) disabled who are totally unable to work. Children are not considered part of the 'unable to work' category—not even when they are of compulsory school age, since they are defined as dependent on their parents (Saraceno, 2014; 2015). Next to these national measures, there are also several local, regional, and municipal measures that vary widely across the country in terms of the criteria used, the level of generosity, and the approach (universal vs categorical)—and therefore are not necessarily implemented where they are most needed (Saraceno, 2014; 2015). They are often uncertain and they change (or are discontinued) with any change in local government (Granaglia and Bolzoni, 2010; Arlotti, 2013; Gambardella et al., 2013; Fargion and Gualmini, 2013; Madama et al., 2013).

To sum up, the social safety net before the crisis was highly categorical, and therefore conditional on specific characteristics; it was territorially unequal, with regard both to monetary transfers and to the provision of services; it tended to favour those who worked (the insiders), due to the bias towards work-based eligibilities; and it relied mostly on individual rather than household income measures. Finally, it was characterized by many temporary, or experimental, measures. Given the features of the social protection system, family solidarity in Italy, as in other Southern European countries, has often played a major role in providing care and income support for household members (Naldini, 2002; Saraceno, 2003).

8.4.2. Policy Responses throughout the Crisis at the General Level

In the early stages of the crisis (2008–10), the Italian government implemented some countercyclical measures. Existing instruments (earning integration, unemployment benefits) were strengthened, without any reform of the existing fragmented social assistance policies. In line with the categorical features that had traditionally distinguished the Italian social protection system, new elements and waivers were added to the existing measures.[10] Although these interventions were limited and provided comparatively little support to families (Borghi, 2012; Jenkins et al., 2013; Brandolini et al., 2013; Brandolini, 2014; Vandenbroucke and Diris, 2014; Verbist and Matsaganis, 2014; Baldini and Toso, 2013; Villa, 2015), together with the strength of family solidarity and recourse to savings (Brandolini, 2014; Saraceno 2014) they did play a shock-absorber role with respect to the impact of the crisis on households.

The persistent categorical and fragmented approach, however, helped to maintain inequalities and lack of protection for the young and for a large portion of atypical workers (Mocetti et al., 2011; Saraceno, 2014; 2015). Furthermore, funding for education (and research) started to be reduced, together with national funds for social policies allocated to local governments (for care services, income support, and the like). Thus, the already meagre safety net, which was more important for the most vulnerable families, started to be eroded.

In the second phase of the crisis, under pressure after the loss of international trust and the dictates of the 'Troika', the various Italian governments[11] put in place a series of fiscal austerity measures,[12] while also initiating a process of de-categorization and universalization of social protection instruments.

The main measure, taken by the Monti government in 2011, was a strong acceleration of pension reform (the so-called Fornero reform) in order to complete the transition to a contributory system, while raising the retirement age for both men and women (Crepaldi et al., 2014).

Two other major measures, which may indirectly affect households with children, concerned the regulation of labour contracts. In particular, notwithstanding fierce opposition from trade unions, entitlement to get back one's own job in the event of unfair dismissal was limited to a very few cases, and financial compensation became the rule (reform of article 18 of the Workers' Statute). At the same time, there have been attempts to reduce precariousness. In particular, the Renzi government approved a labour reform (Jobs Act) at the core of which was a new contract type (*contratto a tutele crescenti*). It stipulates that all new contracts (not only for first jobs, but also in case of job change) should in principle be open-ended ones, with (financial) protection

[10] Such as *Cassa Integrazione in deroga* or a waiver to the Wage Guarantee Fund.

[11] Since the onset of the recession, there have been four different executives: Silvio Berlusconi and his centre-right government (May 2008–November 2011); Mario Monti's technocratic Cabinet (November 2011–April 2013); the 'broad coalition' government led by Enrico Letta (April 2013–February 2014); and the centre-left executive led by Matteo Renzi (since February 2014).

[12] Martorano (2014) discusses how, in most European countries, government reactions differed in the two phases of the crisis.

against dismissal increasing with duration. In 2015, firms hiring with this new contract received substantial financial support in the form of a reduction in labour taxes/social contributions for three years. The size of this support was substantially lowered in 2016. The debate surrounding the trade-off between loss of the highest protection through reform of article 18 and the improved possibility of being hired with a formally indefinite contract is ongoing (see Fana et al., 2015 for a discussion of this measure).

Important changes towards greater universalism have occurred in unemployment protection. The Monti government (and then more radically the Renzi one) have replaced the unemployment indemnity scheme with the Social Insurance for Employment (now NASPI). The new scheme is more universal (expanding both eligibility and coverage) (Crepaldi et al., 2014) and in 2015 was accompanied by unemployment indemnity for workers under coordinated collaboration contract (DIS-COL).

In May 2014, the Renzi government also introduced a structural, non-refundable monthly tax allowance (a tax bonus of €80 a month) for low-income employees. Presented as an anti-poverty measure, it is better understood as a categorical measure to support the working poor on an individual, rather than a household, basis. But it does not support all the poor, and not even all the poorest: excluded, in fact, are the low-income self-employed, as well as those who earn too little to have to fill in a tax return. Only 9.5 per cent of the total spending on this measure has reached families in the poorest quintile; only 12.3 per cent of the poorest quintile are beneficiaries, compared to 39 per cent of individuals in families from the third and the fourth quintile. Moreover, since more than one worker per family may receive the tax bonus, it is mainly families with adult children that benefit, rather than households with underage children (Istat, 2014b). See Baldini and Toso (2015) for further discussion.

Furthermore, severe cuts both in the social funds and financial transfers made available to local authorities and in the school sector—cuts that were initiated in earlier years—have reduced the overall resources available to children and to families with children. Between 2008 and 2012, the Fund for Social Policies was reduced from €923 million to €70 million; the Fund for Family Policies and the Fund for Youth Policies were also severely cut (from €346.5 million in 2008 to €19.8 million in 2013; and from €137.4 million to €6.2 million, respectively). Finally, the national fund aimed at helping low-income households with their rental costs was cancelled (Misiani, 2012; 2014).

8.4.3. Specific Policy Innovations Concerning Children's Poverty

While all the measures concerning the labour market and pensions have been structural, those concerning the poor and children have not only been marginal but mostly occasional and/or experimental—largely because poverty as such, at least until the 2016 Budget Law, has never entered the policy agenda. Poverty, in fact, has never been to the fore in policy discourse in Italy, either on the left or among conservatives. Different reasons may be mentioned, including, the strong employment orientation of the left, the state–Church competition in the 'social sphere', and the North–South divide (Saraceno, 2015).

In recent years, however, mostly due to the empirical evidence of increasing poverty, the need for anti-poverty policies (and specifically for a minimum income provision) has become an important theme for many advocacy groups. Various proposals to this end have been presented, by both advocacy groups and political parties. A large coalition of civil society associations, trade unions, and the Catholic Caritas organization has formed a very vocal alliance against poverty, and has come up with a proposal for a law. During the Letta government, in the second half of 2013, a commission was instituted by the then minister of labour, with the aim of designing a universal minimum income provision. The minister, however, did not have the power to push the ensuing proposal through Cabinet, due to the prevalence of other political priorities in a context of budget constraints.

Following these developments in the public debate, and under pressure resulting from its dramatic and visible increase, child poverty slowly entered the policy agenda. In 2008, just after the onset of the crisis, a Social Card (*Carta Acquisti*) was introduced as an emergency (and therefore temporary) measure. This was a means-tested, flat-rate, pre-paid card to the value of €40 a month, intended to pay for food or household bills. It initially targeted low-income elderly people (over 65), but was then expanded to cover families with children under the age of 3 years. Because the target population was wrongly identified, particularly in the case of children (where it is not the age but the number of children that is the main cause of poverty), the funds allocated have not been fully spent. Furthermore, the amount of the benefit was too low and was inadequate to tackle the increasing impoverishment of families. Only 22 per cent of households receiving the Social Card were families with children under 3 years (Madama et al., 2013; Caritas Italiana, 2014; Simonazzi, 2015; Del Boca, 2010; Baldini and Toso, 2013).

Following the defeat of the then minister of labour's attempt to introduce a minimum income provision, a pilot scheme (New Social Card) was introduced in the 2014 Budget by the Letta government for twelve months in twelve major municipalities. Devised as a minimum income scheme and comprising both financial support and activation measures, it was reserved for very low-income households (€3,000 household equivalent income per year) with at least one underage child, and where at least one household member had a contribution history. Since the funding was limited, not all theoretically eligible households could actually receive it. Thus each municipality introduced further criteria. The level of the new benefit was more generous than the original Social Card (which was kept in place) and varied according to family size: from €231 to a maximum of €404 per month. The pilot was slow in being implemented (so that the experiment had to be prolonged to the end of 2015), and the targeting has proved so narrow that not all twelve cities have been able to use the whole of the budget allocated. The pilot was supposed to be extended to other municipalities in the South (first) and then in North and Central Italy, but this did not happen, not least because of the change of government.

As pointed out above, the 2016 Budget Law seems to mark a partial shift towards greater attention being paid to children's poverty and a more systematic approach. It institutes a National Fund against Poverty, with €600 million for 2016, to be increased to €1 billion in 2017 and subsequent years, and tasks the government with reforming the whole system of income support. While maintaining both the old Social Card and the Social Assistance Unemployment Cheque, in the interim period before the reform and the introduction of a national minimum income scheme, the budget law extends the New Social Card across the country. The focus is (only) on households with underage children in absolute poverty. Given the amount of the funds allocated,[13] the Ministry of Labour estimates that at most only half of those children living in absolute poverty will receive any support. It should provide €80 per household member, up to a maximum of €400, with no equivalence scale; no account is taken of the degree of difference between the household's income and the defined threshold. Beneficiaries are expected to participate in training activities and to accept any job offer. The Budget Law also allocates €100 million, in the form of tax allowances for foundations, to pilot initiatives aimed at combating educational poverty.

No reform of child-linked transfers has been initiated, however much that is needed to overcome the existing categorical nature of the system and its fragmentation—even though various studies have shown that replacing the various transfers with a universal child allowance on a sliding scale would greatly reduce in-work poverty and would lift a substantial number of households with children out of poverty (IRS/CAPP, 2011, IRS 2016). The 2015 Budget law instead introduced yet another experimental and categorical measure: the Baby Bonus, a monthly allowance of €80, paid for three years to low-income families with new-born or newly adopted children (born/adopted between 2015 and 2018).

[13] Conservative estimates agree that, in order to reach all the absolute poor—irrespective of their being or living with children—at least €7 billion a year is necessary solely for the income transfer, plus whatever is necessary to implement the activation measures (even if the collaboration of non-profit and private actors is envisaged and necessary).

8.5. CONCLUDING REMARKS

The emergence of poverty, and particularly child poverty, as an issue that can no longer be ignored is demonstrated by the—albeit fragmented and inadequate—measures introduced in the last few years, and discussed above. Looking at these, and particularly at the measure introduced in the 2016 Budget Law, we can see that, alongside the persistent, strong, bipartisan resistance to the introduction of a minimum income provision for all the poor, irrespective of their family situation or work history, the idea that children may be a deserving category is gaining ground. Yet, in seeking to protect children against poverty—and against its short-term and long-term consequences for their well-being and capabilities—the introduction of a minimum income provision for the poorest is not enough. The specific features that render children vulnerable to poverty in Italy should be tackled in a systematic way. In our view, in addition to the issue of territorial differentiation and the North–South divide in economic performance, there are two main features: the redistributive inefficiency of child-related income transfers (allowances and tax deductions); and the low labour market participation of mothers, particularly in large households and among the lower educated. Any plan to reduce poverty among children should address these two issues. On the one hand, there should be a reform of the existing system of child-linked income transfers, to render it less fragmented and more efficient. On the other hand, work–family reconciliation policies should be developed, with particular attention to the crucial role they play for low-income households and women with a high family workload. At the same time, the pilot experiments that seek to address the educational deprivation of children should, following serious evaluation, be developed into full-fledged, structural policies that involve both the school system and the local communities.

REFERENCES

Amendola, Nicola, Fernando Salsano, and Giovanni Vecchi (2011). 'Povertà'. In Giovanni Vecchi (ed.), *In ricchezza e povertà: Il benessere degli italiani dall'Unità ad oggi*, edited by G. Vecchi (Bologna: Il Mulino).

Arlotti, Marco (2013). 'Regionalizzazione senza risorse: debolezza e differenziazione della spesa sociale nelle regioni italiane'. In Yuri Kazepov and Eduardo Barberis (eds), *Il welfare frammentato: Le articolazioni regionali delle politiche sociali italiane* (Rome: Carocci).

Baldini, Massimo and Stefano Toso (2011). 'Ammortizzatori sociali e spesa per l'assistenza: l'impatto della crisi e le risposte di policy'. In Maria Cecilia Guerra and Alberto Zanardi (eds), *La finanza pubblica italiana: Rapporto 2011* (Bologna: Il Mulino).

Baldini, Massimo and Stefano Toso (2012). 'Ammortizzatori sociali e spesa per assistenza: la via impervia delle riforme'. In Alberto Zanardi (ed.), *La finanza pubblica italiana: Rapporto 2012* (Bologna: Il Mulino).

Baldini, Massimo and Stefano Toso (2013). 'Sostegno del reddito e lotta alla povertà in Italia: le politiche pubbliche in tempo di crisi'. *Center for the Analysis of Public Policies, CAPPaper 104* (Modena: Università di Modena e Reggio Emilia, Dipartimento di Economia Marco Biagi).

Baldini, Massimo and Stefano Toso (2015). 'Crisi economica, distribuzione del reddito e politiche sociali', *Center for the Analysis of Public Policies, CAPPaper 118* (Modena: Università di Modena e Reggio Emilia, Dipartimento di Economia Marco Biagi).

Borghi, Elisa (2012). *The Impact of Anti-crisis Measures, and the Social and Employment Situation: Italy* (Brussels: European Economic and Social Committee Workers' Group).

Brandolini, Andrea (2014). 'Il grande freddo: I bilanci delle famiglie italiane dopo la grande recessione'. In Carlo Fusaro and Amie Kreppel (eds), *Politica in Italia: I fatti dell'anno e le interpretazioni, Edizione 2014* (Bologna: Il Mulino).

Brandolini, Andrea, Francesco D'Amuri, and Ivan Faiella (2013). 'Country Case Study—Italy'. In Stephen P. Jenkins, Andrea Brandolini, John Micklewright, and Brian Nolan (eds), *The Great Recession and the Distribution of Household Income* (Oxford: Oxford University Press).

Bugamelli, Matteo, Riccardo Cristadoro, and Giordano Zevi (2010). 'International Crisis and the Italian Productive System: An Analysis of Firm-level Data'. *Giornale degli Economisti e Annali di Economia* 69, no. 2: pp. 155–88.

Caritas Italiana (2014). *Il bilancio della crisi: Le politiche contro la povertà in Italia, Rapporto 2014* (Rome: Caritas).

Cingano, Federico, Federico Giorgi, and Alfonso Rosolia (2013). 'Lavoro, retribuzioni e vulnerabilità'. In Chiara Saraceno, Nicola Sartor, and Giuseppe Sciortino (eds), *Stranieri e disuguali: Le disuguaglianze nei diritti e nelle condizioni di vita degli immigrati* (Bologna: Il Mulino).

Crepaldi, Chiara, Flavia Pesce, and Manuela Samek Lodovici (2014). 'The Social and Employment Situation in Italy: Note for the EMPL Committee'. European Parliament Directorate-General for Internal Policies. (Luxembourg: Publications Office of the European Union).

Del Boca, Daniela (2010). 'Child Poverty and Child Well-being in Italy'. *Working Paper 1/2010* (Turin: Dipartimento di Economia 'S. Cognetti de Martiis', Università di Torino).

Di Biase, Rita (2009). 'Aliquote di imposta sul lavoro dipendente: analisi per figure tipo e dati campionari'. *Rivista di Diritto Finanziario e Scienza della Finanza 4.*

Fana, Marta, Dario Guarascio, and Valeria Cirillo (2015). 'Labour Market Reforms in Italy: Evaluating the Effects of the Jobs Act'. *ISIGrowth Working Paper 5/2015.*

Fargion, Valeria and Elisabetta Gualmini (eds) (2013). *Tra l'incudine e il martello: Regioni e nuovi rischi sociali in tempo di crisi* (Bologna: Il Mulino).

Ferrera, Maurizio, Anton Hemerijck, and Martin Rhodes (2000). 'Recasting European Welfare States for the 21st Century'. *European Review* 8, no. 3: pp. 427–46.

Ferrera, Maurizio, Matteo Jessoula, and Valeria Fargion (2013). 'At the Roots of the Italian Unbalanced Welfare State: The Grip of Cognitive Frames and "Red-White"

Political Competition'. Paper prepared for the seminar organized by Banca d'Italia Area, Rome, 18 March 2013. <https://www.bancaditalia.it/pubblicazioni/altri-atti-seminari/2013/paper-Ferrera.pdf>.

Figari, Francesco and Carlo V. Fiorio (2015). 'Fiscal Consolidation Policies in the Context of Italy's Two Recessions'. *Fiscal Studies 36*, no. 4: pp. 499–526.

Fullin, Giovanna and Emilio Reyneri (2011). 'Low Unemployment and Bad Jobs for New Immigrants in Italy'. *International Migration 49*, no. 1: pp. 118–47.

Gambardella, Dora, Enrica Morlicchio, and Marco Accoranti (2013). 'L'illusione riformista delle politiche di assistenza in Italia'. In Yuri Kazepov and Eduardo Barberis (eds), *Il welfare frammentato: Le articolazioni regionali delle politiche sociali italiane* (Roma: Carocci).

Granaglia, Elena and Magda Bolzoni (2010). 'Il reddito minimo di inserimento. Analisi e valutazioni di alcune esperienze locali', *Quaderno CIES 3* (Lisbon, CIES).

IRS/CAPP (2011). *Disegniamo il welfare di domani* (Milan: Istituto per la Ricerca Sociale).

IRS (2016). Costruiamo il welfare dei diritti, *Prospettive Sociali e Sanitarie*, 2 (Special issue).

Istat (2014a). *Rapporto Annuale 2014: La situazione del paese* (Rome: Istituto Nazionale di Statistica), ch. 3.

Istat (2014b). *Documento di Economia e Finanza 2014* (Rome: Istituto Nazionale di Statistica).

Istat (2015). *Rapporto Annuale 2015: La situazione del paese* (Rome: Istituto Nazionale di Statistica).

Istat (2016). 'Il mercato del lavoro. Statistiche flash'. 10 March (Rome: Istituto Nazionale di Statistica).

Jenkins, Stephen P., Andrea Brandolini, John Micklewright, and Brian Nolan (2013). 'The Great Recession and Its Consequences for Household Incomes in 21 Countries'. In Stephen P. Jenkins, Andrea Brandolini, John Micklewright, and Brian Nolan (eds), *The Great Recession and the Distribution of Household Income* (Oxford: Oxford University Press).

Madama, Ilaria, Marcello Natili, and Matteo Jessoula (2013). *National Report: Italy* (Oldenburg: Combating Poverty in Europe (COPE)).

Martorano, Bruno (2014). 'The Consequences of the Recent Economic Crisis and Government Reactions for Children'. *Innocenti Working Paper No. 2014–05* (Florence: UNICEF Office of Research—Innocenti).

Misiani, Antonio (2012). 'Fondi statali per le politiche sociali: nuovi tagli con la Legge di stabilità 2012'. <http://www.nens.it/_public-file/Fondi%20politiche%20sociali%202012.pdf>.

Misiani, Antonio (2014). 'Fondi statali per le politiche sociali: alcuni passi in avanti'. <http://www.nens.it/_public-file/MISIANI.%2010.1.14.pdf>.

Mocetti, Sauro, Elizabetta Olivieri, and Eliana Viviano (2011). 'Le famiglie italiane e il lavoro: caratteristiche strutturali e effetti della crisi'. *Stato e mercato*, no. 2: pp. 223–43.

Naldini, Manuela (2003). *The Family in the Mediterranean Welfare States* (London: Frank Cass).

Naldini, Manuela and Chiara Saraceno (2012). *Conciliare famiglia e lavoro: Vecchi e nuovi patti tra sessi e generazioni* (Bologna: Il Mulino).

Naldini, Manuela and Cristina Solera (2012). 'Quali politiche a sostegno della genitorialità?'. In Laura Gaiotti and Monica Terzago (eds), *Lavorare con il conflitto: Dare continuità ai legami famigliari* (Turin: Provincia di Torino).

OECD (2012a). *Italy: Reviving Growth and Productivity* (Paris: OECD).

OECD (2012b). 'Programme for International Student Assessment (PISA), Results from PISA 2012: Italy'. Country note (Paris: OECD).

Pavolini, Emmanuele (ed.) (2013). *L'Italia e le politiche per le famiglie fra immobilismo nazionale e dinamismo locale* (Modena: Fondazione Germanno Gorrieri).

Sabbadini, Linda Laura (2014). 'The Italian Approach to the Measurement of Absolute Poverty'. Paper presented at Social Protection Committee, Rome, 16 September 2014.

Saraceno, Chiara (2003). *Mutamenti della famiglia e politiche sociali in Italia* (Bologna: Il Mulino).

Saraceno, Chiara (2007). *Le politiche di sostegno alle famiglie con figli: Il contesto e le proposte* (Modena: Fondazione Gorrieri).

Saraceno, Chiara (2014). 'I paradossi delle politiche di contrasto alla povertà negli anni della crisi in Italia'. *Politiche sociali 1*, no. 1: pp. 27–40.

Saraceno, Chiara (2015). *Il Lavoro non basta: La povertà in Europa negli anni della crisi* (Milan: Feltrinelli).

Saraceno, Chiara, Nicola Sartor, and Giuseppe Sciortino (2013). *Stranieri e disuguali: Le disuguaglianze nei diritti e nelle condizioni di vita degli immigrati* (Bologna: Il Mulino).

Save the Children Italia (2014). *La lampada di Aladino: L'indice di Save the Children per misurare le povertà educative e illuminare il futuro dei bambini in Italia* (Rome: Save the Children Italia).

Save the Children Italia (2014). *Liberare i bambini dalla povertà educativa: A che punto siamo?Un'analisi regionale* (Rome: Save the Children Italia).

Simonazzi, Annamaria (2015). 'Italy: Continuity and Change in Welfare State Retrenchment'. In Daniel Vaughan-Whitehead (ed.), *The European Social Model in Crisis: Is Europe Losing its Soul?* (Cheltenham: Edward Elgar/ILO).

Vandenbroucke, Frank and Ron Diris (2014). 'Mapping At-risk-of-poverty Rates, Household Employment, and Social Spending'. In Bea Cantillon and Frank Vandenbroucke (eds), *Reconciling Work and Poverty Reduction: How Successful Are European Welfare States?* (Oxford: Oxford University Press).

Verbist, Gerlinde and Manos Matsaganis (2014). 'The Redistributive Capacity of Services in the European Union'. In Bea Cantillon and Frank Vandenbroucke (eds), *Reconciling Work and Poverty Reduction: How Successful Are European Welfare States?* (Oxford: Oxford University Press).

Villa, Paola (2015). 'Women and Austerity in Italy'. *Travail, genre et sociétés 1/2015*, no. 33: pp. 157–64.

9

The Recession and the Policy Response for Child Poverty in Japan

Aya K. Abe

9.1. INTRODUCTION

Japan provides a unique case study, compared to the other case studies presented in this book—at a very early stage of the economic crisis, Japan underwent a drastic political change, in which the conservative party was ejected from government for the first time in fifty years. To appreciate the significance of this change, it is important to understand Japan's social policy before the crisis. Japan used to be regarded as one of the most egalitarian societies of the developed countries (Burniaux et al., 1998). The belief that Japan is an equal society was widely shared not only by foreign scholars but also by the Japanese public, the bureaucrats, and politicians. The rapid economic development of the 1960s and 1970s was believed to have eradicated poverty and financial hardship for households, with an almost 100 per cent employment rate and life-long employment security provided by most corporations. On the other side of the coin, there was little provision by the public sector of measures to alleviate poverty (Abe, 2003). The government prioritized economic development over expanding welfare provision. This model was dubbed the *corporate welfare state* (Esping-Andersen, 1997) or *productivist welfare capitalism* (Holiday, 2000).

Such a model appeared to work well during the 1960s and 1970s. Unemployment was low and visible poverty, which had been rampant after the Second World War, disappeared. Thus, the government stopped collecting any data on poverty in the mid-1960s, and from then on Japanese public social security systems developed on the assumption that every citizen could (and should) share the burden of social security systems equally, and that there was little need for anti-poverty programmes and social safety nets. Thus, through the 1970s and up to the mid-2000s, just before the economic crisis, cash transfers and services to low-income households were very small, especially to those with children (because the heads of households with children are mostly of working age). In particular, there was no consideration for near-poor households with children, in terms of taxes and social insurance premiums. Thus, the tax burden was heavy and child benefit and other positive transfers remained small, making the net transfer to near-poor households with children negative. The logical conclusion of such a policy was that, up until the mid-2000s, the child poverty rate after tax and transfers was *higher* than the poverty rate before tax and transfers (see Appendix, Figure 9.A1) (Abe, 2008).

The purpose of this chapter is to shed light on how the economic crisis in the late 2000s affected children. To do this, we will examine the change in child poverty indices and policy development from 2006 to 2012. The chapter starts by describing the change in the Japanese labour market that has been going on for two decades, and then looks at how the crisis affected the country's macroeconomic status. Next, the chapter uses poverty statistics to show how children fared during and after the economic crisis, as compared to before its onset. In particular, it examines the possible causes of any increase or decrease in child poverty during the period, by looking at changes in the poverty rate for various household types with different labour market attachment. It will describe the change of government in 2009, when the liberal opposition party overthrew the conservative party (which had been in power for over fifty years) and then itself fell from power in 2012. It will also look at the policies introduced by the short-lived liberal government, especially the new income-transfer mechanisms, such as universal child benefit (at a generous level, compared to the previous child benefit), and the changes to the tax regime. The chapter concludes with an analysis of the transmission mechanisms by which the crisis affected child poverty, and with remarks about Japan's experience, as a warning to other countries.

9.2. THE ECONOMIC CRISIS

9.2.1. Japan's Changing Labour Market before the Crisis

Even before the economic crisis of 2008, Japan had been suffering from economic stagnation for nearly two decades. Growth in gross domestic product (GDP) had fallen to less than 1 per cent in 1992, and ever since has mostly remained at below 2 per cent (Figure 9.1). The decade after 1992 was termed the 'lost decade', but now that has turned into the 'lost two decades'. In reaction to the long period of low growth, firms have shifted away from the costly life-long employment, and toward a more flexible and cheaper labour force. Thus, the Japanese labour market is characterized by a 'dualism' (OECD, 2015), in which two distinct labour forces exist: those workers who are promised

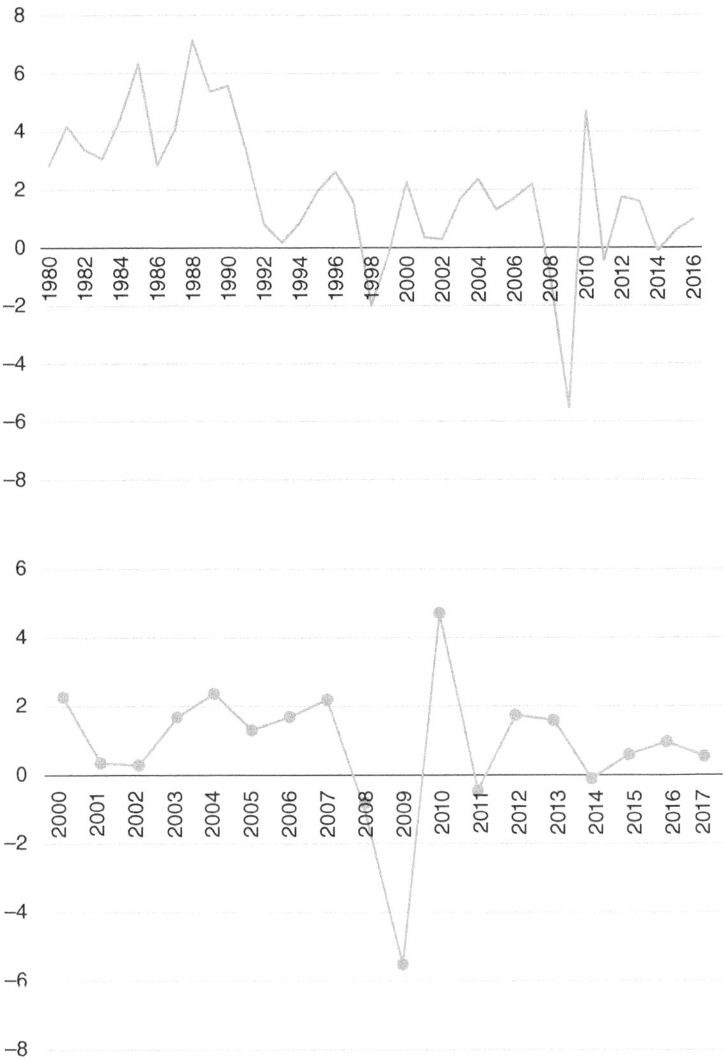

Figure 9.1. GDP growth, Japan (1980–2016), per cent
Source: OECD (2016).

life-long employment, with a rising salary as they get older, and who are also covered by social insurance (pension, health, and unemployment) (the so-called *Seiki* or 'regular' workers); and those workers who are used only temporarily for fluctuating labour needs of firms and who receive much lower wages, as well as minimal social insurance (so-called *Hiseiki* (non-regular) workers). *Hiseiki* workers have limited employment contracts and no social insurance, and they earn about 60 per cent of *Seiki* workers (MHLW, 2016).

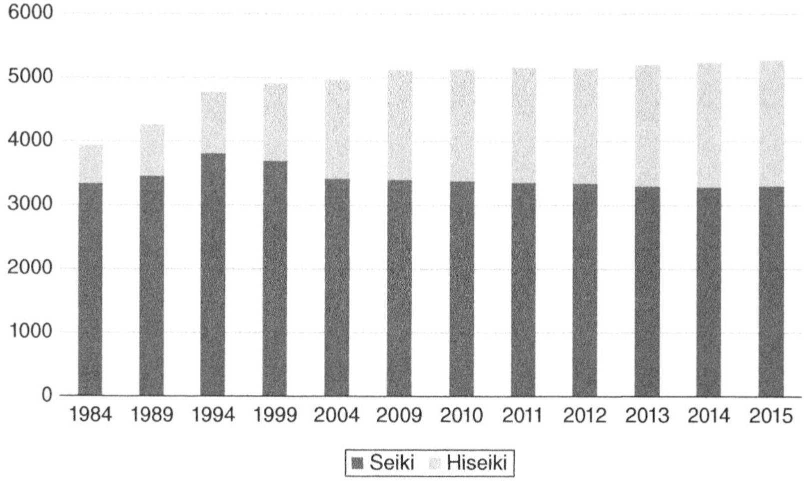

Figure 9.2. Number of workers by type of employment (*Seiki/Hiseiki*) (1985–2014) (100,000 persons)

Source: Statistics Bureau, *Rodoryoku Chosa* [Labour Force Survey], 'Historical data 10: Employees by age group and type of employment—Whole Japan'.

From the latter half of the 1980s, the share of *Hiseiki* workers in the total labour force has been increasing rapidly. While the total number of workers remains the same and the unemployment rate fairly stable, the share of *Hiseiki* workers has risen from 15.3 per cent in 1984 to 37.4 per cent in 2014 (Figure 9.2). Among female workers, the share of *Hiseiki* workers is more than 50 per cent (Statistics Bureau, 2016). Even though the highest incidence of these *Hiseiki* workers is among the elderly and the young (15–24), the share of *Hiseiki* workers in the child-rearing generation (25–55) is increasing rapidly.[1] Since it is extremely hard to transit to a *Seiki* job if the first job is *Hiseiki* (Kondo, 2007) and since the first *Hiseiki* job is known to have other negative outcomes, such as lower mental health status (Oshio and Inagaki, 2014), the increase of *Hiseiki* among the young generation is especially worrisome.

The result is a decline in living standards for most households, but the decline was especially severe for those whose household head is of working age, including those with children. The average income of households generally has been falling since 1994 and that of households with children since 1996. At its peak in 1996, the average income of households with children under the age of 20 was 7.81 million yen; by 2013, it had fallen to 6.96 million yen (in nominal terms) (MHLW, 2015).

[1] By age group, among men, the highest rate of *Hiseiki* workers can be found among men aged over 65, followed by men aged 15–24, men aged 55–64, and men aged 25–34. Among women, the share of *Hiseiki* workers among all workers is high in all age groups, but especially among those over 45 and between 15 and 24.

Another problem caused by the long recession is the fiscal deficit. Japan has one of the highest government deficits of all Organization for Economic Co-operation and Development (OECD) countries and the highest government debt. Government revenue has been declining, due to the drop in the income of individuals, but the government has also been plagued by ever-increasing social security spending, because of an increasing share of the elderly in the population. Total central government debt reached 166.8 per cent of GDP in 2009 and nearly 200 per cent in 2012 (World Bank 2016). Because of the tight fiscal conditions, it has been extremely difficult to expand the (minimal) social spending on the poor.

9.2.2. The Double Crisis of 2008 and 2011

Thus, the global economic crisis of the late 2000s was yet another downturn in the economic conditions faced by people in Japan. It started with the bankruptcy of a major insurance company, Daiwa, in 2008, and was followed by the Lehman Brothers shock of September 2008. GDP growth fell to −5.5 per cent in 2009 (Figure 9.1), and the unemployment rate, which until then had been fairly low, rose to 5.3 per cent for those of working age (15–64). The unemployment rate was especially high for young people aged 15–24, and it is this group that saw the sharpest rise—1.9 percentage points—from 2008 to 2009 (see Figure 9.3).

By 2010, the economic outlook had started to improve, as GDP growth rose above 4 per cent and as the unemployment rate started to fall for the core age group of 25–34, as well as for the 35–44 group. However, Japan was again rocked by an immense shock: this time the Great East Japan Earthquake in March 2011. The earthquake, which killed nearly 19,000 people, was followed by meltdown at nuclear power plants in Fukushima. The huge loss of life and property caused by the earthquake and the subsequent tsunami, and the massive evacuation of over 40,000 people (sometimes whole towns) from Fukushima and the Tohoku region, were disasters on an unprecedented scale. GDP growth was again negative in 2011. However, the unemployment rate was unaffected by this second shock and continued to decrease throughout 2011.[2] Meantime, the share of *Hiseiki* jobs increased throughout these two shocks, but the increase was gradual and simply continued the trend that had

[2] Even though Japan's unemployment rate has been low, compared to other countries (even during the two crises), among the unemployed, the share of long-term unemployment is rather high and increased from 2000 to 2014. This is another characteristic of the Japanese labour market, which lacks dynamism.

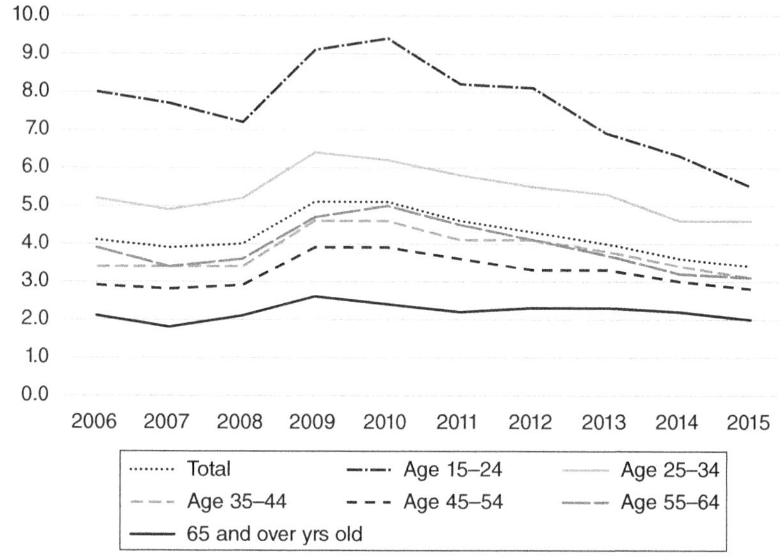

Figure 9.3. Unemployment rate, Japan, by age (2006–2015), per cent

Source: Statistics Bureau, *Rodoryoku Chosa* [Labour Force Survey], 'Historical data 3(9): Unemployed persons and unemployment rate by age group—Whole Japan'.

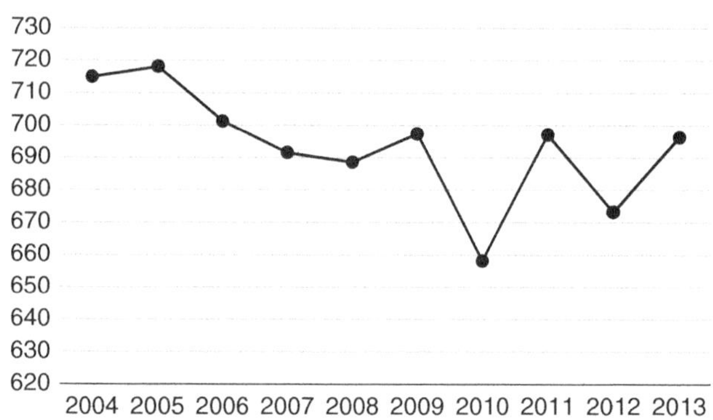

Figure 9.4. Average income of households with children (nominal, in 10,000 yen), Japan (2004–2013)

Source: Ministry of Health, Labour, and Welfare (MHLW), Kokumin Seikatsu Kiso Chosa (Comprehensive Survey of Living Conditions), multiple years.

already been in evidence. The effect of the two shocks is seen more clearly in income. As noted above, the average income of households with children had been decreasing since 1996, but there was a sharp drop in 2010 and a further, less severe drop in 2012 (Figure 9.4; MHLW, 2015). It bounced back in 2013, but it is still much lower than in 1994.

9.3. HOW CHILDREN FARED

9.3.1. Change in the Relative and Anchored Poverty Rates and Material Deprivation

We now turn to child poverty statistics[3] and see how children fared during and after the economic crisis. First, let us look at the relative and anchored poverty rates from 2006 to 2012 (income years)[4] (Figure 9.5). The effect of the economic crisis that began in 2008 can clearly be seen in the relative and anchored poverty rates for children.[5] The highest rate was observed in 2008, when there was a jump of more than 4 percentage points over 2007 in the anchored poverty rate, and of more than 2 percentage points in the relative poverty rate. The rise in the relative poverty rate is less severe than the rise in the anchored poverty rate because from 2007 to 2008 the relative poverty line dropped. In this same period, the anchored poverty rate for the overall population did not rise as much (+2.1 percentage points), and the relative poverty rate did not rise at all (−0.4 percentage points);[6] thus it can be said that children were more severely affected than the overall population.

After 2008 both relative and anchored rates decreased, returning to near the 2007 level in 2009 and 2010. The year 2011 saw the lowest poverty rate in the six-year period from 2007 to 2012 in both anchored and relative poverty rates. However, both rates again increased from 2011 to 2012. We will examine these changes more closely in later sections. Since the relative and anchored rates show more or less the same pattern from that point, only the anchored poverty rates will be shown.

[3] To calculate the anchored and relative poverty rates, the paper uses the data from the MHLW's Comprehensive Survey of Living Conditions, years 2008 to 2013 (income years 2007 to 2012). These are the data that the Japanese government uses in calculating its official poverty statistics. However, it should be noted that for survey years 2007, 2010, and 2012 (income years 2006, 2009, and 2012) the data cover more than 10,000 children, but for other years only about 3,000 children. Because of the small sample size, the Japanese government does not publish poverty rates for small sample years. Also, data for the income years 2010 and 2011 should be treated with caution, because the Fukushima Prefecture (about 1.5 per cent of the population, according to Statistics Japan Population Estimates at <http://www.stat.go.jp/data/jinsui/index.htm>) and some parts of Iwate and Miyagi Prefectures were not surveyed, due to administrative difficulties after the Great East Japan Earthquake of 2011.

[4] All the poverty and deprivation figures are in income years in this chapter.

[5] The relative poverty rate is calculated using 60 per cent of the median as the poverty line for each year represented. The anchored poverty rate is calculated using 60 per cent of the median in 2007 (income year) as the poverty line.

[6] The anchored poverty rate for the whole population rose from 22.1 per cent to 24.2 per cent, and the relative poverty rate fell from 22.1 per cent to 21.7 per cent. This is due to the fairly stable and improving economic status of the elderly, even during the time of economic crisis. The poverty rate for the elderly has been declining for the past thirty years, as the public old-age pension matured.

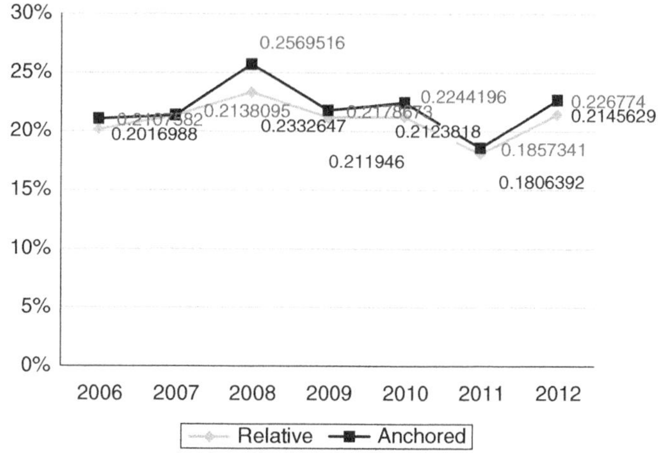

Figure 9.5. Percentage of children below 60 per cent of median disposable income, Japan (2006–2012): relative and anchored rates at 2007 poverty lines

Source: Author's calculations using the MHLW's Comprehensive Survey of Living Conditions, 2008–13.

Looking at the change in anchored child poverty rates (Figure 9.6), we see the same pattern as in Figure 9.5, but the fluctuation in the rates is much more pronounced in one-parent families (two generations, i.e. single parents living with only their children).[7] One-parent families, whose poverty rates were very high to begin with, saw a large increase from 2006 to 2008. However, the rate fell drastically for one-parent families from 2008 to 2011, with a drop of nearly 20 percentage points. It again rose from 2011 to 2012, leaving the anchored poverty rate in 2012 at the same level as in 2006. Two-parent families showed the same pattern, but the fluctuation was much less. Still, the rise from 2006 to 2008 was 3 percentage points, and the drop from 2008 to 2011, nearly 5 percentage points. These changes show that the economic crisis affected children drastically from 2006 to 2012.

9.3.2. Material Deprivation

Many scholars have pointed out that measures of income alone do not completely capture poverty, and suggest using non-income measures, such

[7] Two-generation families are those in which only parent(s) and child(ren) are present. Even though the share is decreasing, many households in Japan still contain three generations, in which grandparent(s), parent(s), and children live together. Three-generation families are fairly common among single-parent households. About a third of single parents cohabit with their parent(s). In Figure 9.6, only two-generation households are shown in the comparison of one-parent and two-parent households.

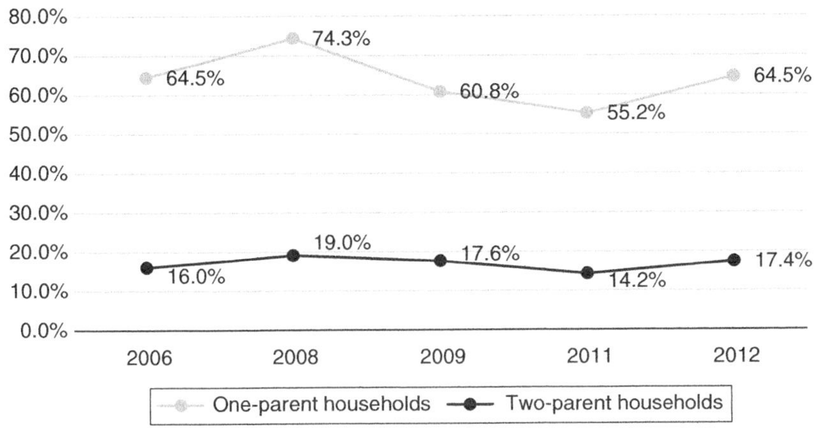

Figure 9.6. Anchored child poverty rates, by family type, Japan (2006–2012)
Source: Author's calculations using the MHLW's Comprehensive Survey of Living Conditions, 2008–13.

as material deprivation (Nolan and Whelan, 1996). Unfortunately, the Japanese government does not collect data on material deprivation, and there are only sporadic surveys on the material deprivation of children. One such survey was conducted by the National Institute of Population and Social Security Research in 2007 and 2012; in this some questions on material deprivation were included. Table 9.1 shows the percentage of households with children (under the age of 20) with material deprivation (unable to buy food, clothes, or to pay the electricity, gas, telephone, and rent). On most items, and for all family types, the percentage of households that experienced material deprivation fell between the two years. The largest drop was for one-parent, two-generation households, albeit from a higher deprivation rate to start with. At the outset, they faced the severest poverty; thus it comes as some relief to find a marked improvement in material deprivation for this family type.

Thus, the trend in material deprivation confirms the trend in the income poverty rate (Figures 9.5 and 9.6), and it can be said that from 2007 to 2012 the living conditions of households with children seem to have improved.

9.4. MECHANISMS EXPLAINING THE POVERTY TRENDS

In order to assess the effect of the economic crisis, and specifically how it affected children and households with children, we now examine the movement of poverty rates by household characteristics and the working status of parents. The question in mind is 'what is the transmission mechanism?', that

Table 9.1. Material deprivation of children, 2007 and 2012

	2007	2012	Difference
Food deficiency *1)			
All households with children	3.1	1.7	−1.4
Two-parent (three generations)	2.2	0.7	−1.5
Two-parent (two generations)	2.6	1.5	−1.1
One-parent (three generations)	4.2	3.5	−0.7
One-parent (two generations)	8.3	3.8	−4.5
Clothes deficiency *2)			
All households with children	4.3	3.3	−1.0
Two-parent (three generations)	2.4	1.7	−0.7
Two-parent (two generations)	3.9	2.9	−1
One-parent (three generations)	5.3	4.2	−1.1
One-parent (two generations)	11.6	9.4	−2.2
Unable to pay electricity bill *3)			
All households with children	6.2	6.1	−0.1
Two-parent (three generations)	4.4	4	−0.4
Two-parent (two generations)	5.4	5.3	−0.1
One-parent (three generations)	8.4	11.3	2.9
One-parent (two generations)	16.2	14.1	−2.1
Unable to pay gas bill *4)			
All households with children	6.0	6.3	0.4
Two-parent (three generations)	3.2	4	0.8
Two-parent (two generations)	5.3	5.4	0.1
One-parent (three generations)	8.4	10.7	2.3
One-parent (two generations)	17.1	16.2	−0.9
Unable to pay telephone bill *5)			
All households with children	6.7	6.6	−0.1
Two-parent (three generations)	4	5.5	1.5
Two-parent (two generations)	5.7	5.5	−0.2
One-parent (three generations)	11.6	10.9	−0.7
One-parent (two generations)	18.5	15.3	−3.2
Unable to pay housing rent bill *6)			
All households with children	6.9	5.9	−1.0
Two-parent (three generations)	4.2	0	−4.2
Two-parent (two generations)	6	6.4	0.4
One-parent (three generations)	12.5	3.7	−8.8
One-parent (two generations)	18.4	13.4	−5

Source: National Institute of Population and Social Security Research (2009, 2013).

is, what factors contributed to the rise or fall of child poverty rates. Several possible causes are examined: 1) the change in the composition of family characteristics, such as the increased share of single-parent households; 2) the increase or decrease in worklessness; 3) the increase or decrease in in-work poverty; 4) the increase or decrease in poverty among jobless or job-poor households; and 5) the change in social benefits. We divide the period of analysis into three phases: the initial phase is when the child poverty rate increased from before the crisis to the peak of the crisis (2006–2008); the second phase is when child poverty decreased from the peak to the trough (2008–2011); and the last phase is the period of the increase in child poverty (2011–2012).

The main index used in the analysis is the anchored poverty rate, as described in footnote 6.[8] To capture the three causes mentioned above, the composition and poverty rates of children by their household structure, work intensity, and *Seiki/Hiseiki* category are shown. Work intensity (WI) is an EU-devised concept, and is defined as is the ratio of the total number of months that all working-age household members have worked during the income reference year and the total number of months the same household members theoretically could have worked in the same period'(Eurostat, 2014). Since the dataset used for the analysis does not contain information on the number of months worked within the survey year, it was not possible to calculate the WI, as defined by the EU. Instead, we use a variable, which is the answer to the question: 'What is your main activity during a day?' If the answer is 'mainly work', it is assumed that the person is working full time throughout the year, and a value of 1 is assigned. If the answer is 'work and studying' or 'work and household duties' or 'work and other activities', it is assumed that the person is working part time, and a value of 0.5 is assigned. If the answer is 'household duties', 'studying', or 'other activities', it is assumed that the person is not employed and a value of 0 is assigned. The WI rate is then calculated as the sum of the values of all household members between the age of 18 and 59 (excluding dependants aged 19–24), divided by the value that would be obtained if all members worked full time. For this analysis, households with WI of less than 0.5 are considered 'low-WI' households.

The household's work status is determined by the *Seiki* or *Hiseiki* status of parents' work. The household is categorized as *Seiki* if at least one of the parents has *Seiki* work status, and as *Hiseiki* if both parents (or the only parent, if it is a single-parent household) have *Hiseiki* work status or are not working.

9.4.1. Household and Child Characteristics

First, let us examine the change in household structure and age of children (Table 9.2).

In Japan, about 90 per cent of all children live in two-parent households. The figures for children living in single-mother and single-father households are about 9 per cent and 1 per cent, respectively. Even though single-mother households are on the rise, that increase is fairly slow (1.3 percentage points over the period 2007 to 2013). The percentage of single-father households continues to be very low. Three-generation households, in which grandparent(s), parent(s),

[8] The relative poverty rate is not shown in this section, since it has the same trend as the anchored rate.

Table 9.2. Composition of children, by household type and child age

Survey year	2007	2008 (peak)	2009	2010	2011 (trough)	2012	2013
Single-mother households							
All	7.6	8.1	7.9	8.0	8.7	8.1	8.9
Two generations	5.4	5.7	5.6	5.5	6.3	5.5	6.2
Three generations	2.2	2.4	2.4	2.5	2.4	2.6	2.7
Single-father households							
All	1.4	1.4	1.4	1.3	1.3	1.2	1.3
Two generations	0.7	0.7	0.7	0.6	0.8	0.6	0.6
Three generations	0.8	0.6	0.7	0.7	0.5	0.6	0.6
Two-parent households							
All	90.9	90.5	90.7	90.6	90.0	90.7	89.8
Two generations	70.2	72.2	73.1	71.6	75.0	75.4	72.0
Three generations	20.8	18.4	17.6	19.0	15.1	15.3	17.8
Large households (three or more children under 18)	25.6	27.1	26.8	25.1		23.2	26.6
Small households (one or two children under 18)	74.4	72.9	73.2	74.9		76.8	73.4
Region urban	44.6		57.9	49.0		52.3	52.4
Rural	55.4		42.1	51.0		47.7	47.6
Age of the child (under 5)	24.4	24.7	23.7	23.3	25.1	24.7	24.4
Age of the child (6–11)	39.7	40.7	40.0	39.9	39.2	39.7	38.5
Age of the child (12–17)	35.9	34.6	36.4	36.8	35.7	35.6	37.0

Note: For large/small family composition, the data for 2011 were not available. The 'peak' and 'trough' are labelled for years which show the highest poverty rate and the lowest poverty rate during the analysis period.

Source: Author's calculations using Ministry of Health, Labour, and Welfare Comprehensive Survey of Living Conditions, 2008–2013.

and child(ren) live together, are fairly common in both single-parent and two-parent households. About a third of single-mother households, half of single-father families, and a fifth of two-parent families consist of three generations.

From 2007 to 2013, the composition of the household structure of children did not change significantly, though there was a continuation of the underlying trend caused by the demographic change that has been happening in Japan for some time. Due to a continuously declining fertility rate, the share of older children has kept increasing, and the share of households with more than three children has kept declining. However, these changes are not apparent from this particular dataset.

One trend that can be observed is the shift away from three-generation households to two-generation households. In two-parent households, the share of three-generation households dropped by 3 percentage points (of the total), while the share of two-generation households increased by 2 percentage points.

Another trend is the shift from rural to urban dwelling. In 2007, 44.6 per cent of children lived in an urban setting, but by 2013, the share had increased to 52.4 per cent.

9.4.2. Child Poverty Rate by Household Structure

Table 9.3 shows the relative and anchored poverty rates of children by their household structure and age.

Overall, it can be said that in the first period of economic crisis (2006–2008) the child poverty rate rose; it then fell during the second period (2008–2011); and finally it increased again in the third period (2011–2012). This goes for all household types and for all ages of children. We will call this trend the base trend of 'up-down-up'. However, the size of the increase and decrease are different, depending on the household characteristics. One-parent families, especially two-generation one-parent families, were affected quite badly in the first period, seeing a sharp rise in the already high poverty rate. During the second period, the child poverty rate dropped significantly (in fact, by more than the rise in the first period) for all one-parent families. The rise and fall in the poverty rate during the first and second periods are also observed among two-parent families (including three-generation families). However, for single-parent families, the drop in the second period was large enough for the poverty rate in 2012 to be lower than in 2006, even after the rise in the last period; but this was not the case for two-parent families.

Comparing large (those families with three or more children under 18) and small families (those with 1–2 children under 18), the overall movement of poverty rates (up-down-up) is the same for both. However, the fluctuation is much bigger for large families than for small families.

Looking at the age of children, the general movement is the same, but the drop in the poverty rate in the second period is definitely larger for younger children. For children under 5, the drop in this period is more than 10 percentage points for the anchored poverty rate, while for children aged 6–11 it is 8.5 percentage points; for children aged 12–17 the fall is only 3.2 percentage points.

There is no apparent difference in the movement of the child poverty rate by the degree of urbanization of residence.

9.4.3. Work Intensity

Next, we turn to work intensity (WI). Since work intensity is significantly affected by the number of adults in the household, let us examine the movement in the low WI rate (percentage of children living in households with WI of less than 0.5) separately for single-parent and two-parent households (Figure 9.7).

Single-parent households show a much higher rate of low WI than two-parent households: 18.9 per cent, as against 8.2 per cent in 2007, a significant

Table 9.3. Relative and anchored child poverty rate, by household type and child age

Survey year	2007	2009	2010	2012	2013				
income year	2006	2008 (peak)	2009	2011 (trough)	2012	change 2006–2008	Change 2008–2011	change 2011–2012	change 2006–2012
Relative poverty rate (60% median)	20.2	23.3	21.2	18.1	21.5	3.2	−5.3	3.4	1.3
Anchored poverty rate (60% median 2007)	21.1	25.7	21.8	18.6	22.7	4.6	−7.1	4.1	1.6
One-parent households (incl. three-generation households)									
Relative poverty rate	56.4	58.6	52.2	44.6	54.1	2.2	−14.0	9.5	−2.3
Anchored poverty rate	58.9	63.2	53.2	44.6	56.9	4.3	−18.6	12.3	−2.0
One-parent households (two-generation households)									
Relative poverty rate	64.4	71.7	59.3	55.2	61.9	7.3	−16.5	6.7	−2.5
Anchored poverty rate	64.5	74.3	60.8	55.2	64.5	9.9	−19.1	9.3	0.0
Two-parent households (incl. three-generation households)									
Relative poverty rate	16.4	18.8	18.2	15.2	17.4	2.4	−3.7	2.3	1.0
Anchored poverty rate	17.1	20.9	18.8	15.7	18.4	3.8	−5.2	2.7	1.3
Two-parent households (two-generation households)									
Relative poverty rate	15.2	17.1	17.2	13.7	16.4	1.9	−3.3	2.6	1.2
Anchored poverty rate	16.0	19.0	17.6	14.2	17.4	3.1	−4.8	3.2	1.4

Large households (three or more children under 18)									
Relative poverty rate	27.0	35.9	28.4	22.3	29.3	8.9	−13.6	7.1	2.4
Anchored poverty rate	28.1	39.0	28.9	22.3	30.7	10.8	−16.7	8.4	2.6
Small households (one or two children under 18)									
Relative poverty rate	18.0	18.8	19.1	16.8	19.0	0.8	−2.0	2.2	1.0
Anchored poverty rate	18.8	20.9	19.7	17.5	20.2	2.1	−3.4	2.7	1.4
Age of the child (0–5)									
Relative poverty rate	19.5	23.5	19.6	15.8	20.0	4.0	−7.7	4.1	0.4
Anchored poverty rate	20.2	26.6	20.3	16.0	21.2	6.4	−10.6	5.2	1.0
Age of the child (6–11)									
Relative poverty rate	18.7	22.4	20.4	15.6	19.5	3.6	−6.8	4.0	0.8
Anchored poverty rate	19.7	24.8	21.0	16.3	20.9	5.1	−8.5	4.6	1.1
Age of the child (12–17)									
Relative poverty rate	22.2	24.3	23.1	22.4	24.4	2.1	−1.9	2.1	2.2
Anchored poverty rate	23.2	26.1	23.7	22.9	25.5	2.9	−3.2	2.6	2.3
Degree of urbanization (urban)									
Relative poverty rate	17.4	20.4	18.1	15.1	19.6	3.0	−5.3	4.5	2.2
Anchored poverty rate	17.8	22.6	18.8	15.8	20.9	4.8	−6.8	5.0	3.0
Degree of urbanization (rural)									
Relative poverty rate	22.7	27.1	24.6	21.1	23.8	4.4	−6.1	2.7	1.1
Anchored poverty rate	24.1	29.8	25.1	21.4	24.9	5.7	−8.4	3.5	0.8

Source: Author's calculations using Ministry of Health, Labour, and Welfare Comprehensive Survey of Living Conditions, 2008–13.

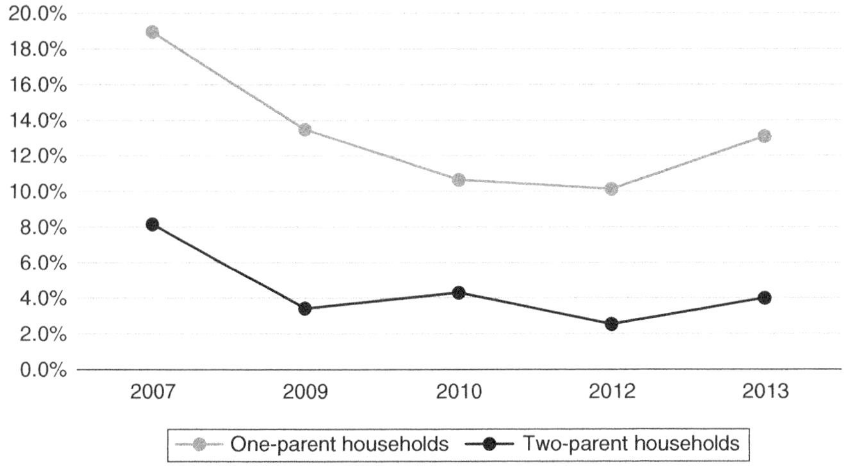

Figure 9.7. Percentage of children living in low-work-intensity households, by household type, Japan (2007–2013)

Source: Author's calculations using the MHLW's Comprehensive Survey of Living Conditions, 2007, 2009, 2010, 2012, and 2013.

difference. However, the rate for both household types drops significantly in 2009, and still further in 2012. Thus, during the first two stages of the economic crisis, the proportion of households with children whose WI was low decreased. This is in contrast to the general trend of unemployment, which showed an increase from 2008 to 2009, and then decreased until 2012. We cannot say for sure, but there is speculation that at the onset of the economic crisis, households with children responded by increasing the labour participation of those who were previously not in the labour force (in particular, housewives), thus increasing the work intensity within a household. These erstwhile 'housewives' had not been looking for a job prior to the economic crisis, and thus had not been included in unemployment figures before the crisis.

Turning now to the poverty rate for two-parent households (Figure 9.8, upper graph), the child poverty rate for those with low WI increased sharply. There is very little social benefit for poor two-parent households in Japan. Aside from Public Assistance, which is a means-tested social benefit for the poor, and child benefit, there is no social benefit to support the income of the working-age poor in Japan. Public Assistance imposes a harsh means test, and less than 2 per cent of the population receives the benefit; more than half of recipients are elderly people whose pension is not enough to support them. Thus, those who could not increase their work intensity suffered a high rate of poverty due to a decrease in earnings. This is in stark contrast to the movement of the poverty rate for high-WI, two-parent households, which described the same up-down-up general trend, but remained fairly stable, at a low level throughout the period of analysis.

For single-parent households (Figure 9.8, lower graph), it is those with high WI that experienced a sharp drop in the poverty rate in the second phase, while households with low WI also had the same general trend, but with much smaller fluctuation, even though the starting poverty rate in 2006 was very similar.

During the third phase (2012 to 2013), the share of low-WI households increased again for both types of household, but the poverty rate also increased, especially for high-WI households.

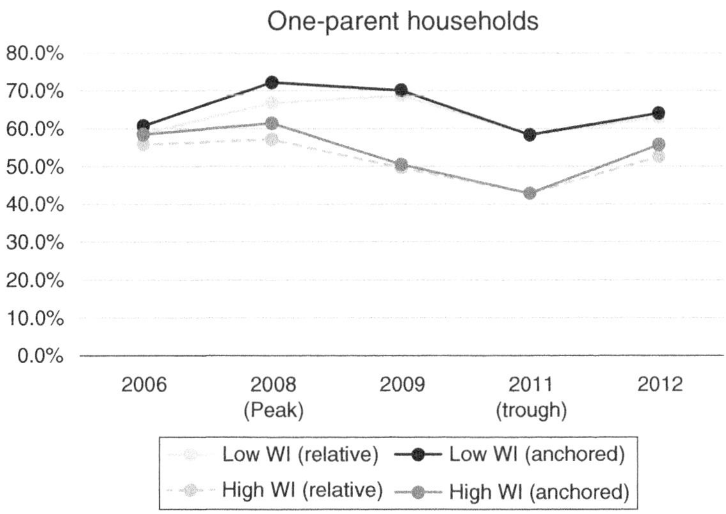

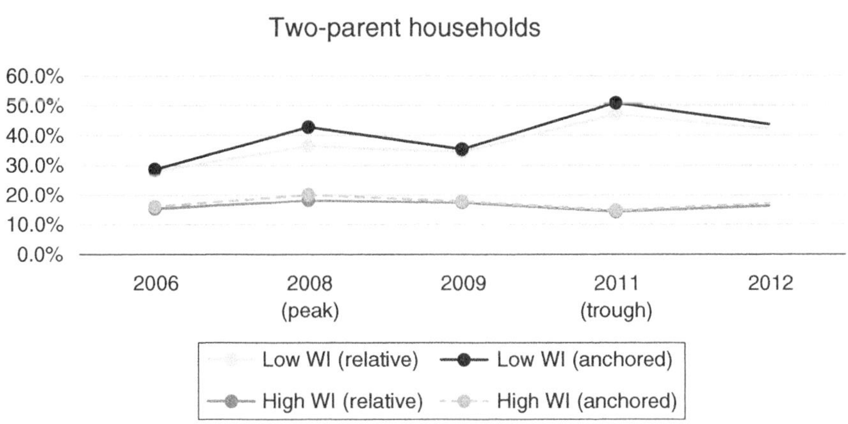

Figure 9.8. Child poverty rate by work intensity: two- and one-parent households, Japan (2006–2012)

Source: Author's calculations using the MHLW's Comprehensive Survey of Living Conditions.

9.4.4. Work Status (*Seiki/Hiseiki*)

Lastly, let us look at the child poverty rate by the household's *Seiki/Hiseiki* status. Contrary to our hypothesis, the percentage of children living in a *Hiseiki* household (*Hiseiki* rate) dropped in the period from before to after the economic crisis (Figure 9.9). For single-parent households, there was a significant drop at the beginning of the economic crisis (from 2007 to 2009), and then the rate remained more or less the same throughout the analysis period. For two-parent households, the *Hiseiki* rate decreased at the onset of the crisis (from 2007 to 2009), and then increased again in 2010, before dropping again in 2011 to remain about the same throughout 2013. Again, compared to before the economic crisis, the *Hiseiki* rate is lower during and after the crisis.

Figure 9.10 shows child poverty rates by *Seiki/Hiseiki* category. For two-parent households (Figure 9.10, upper graph), the trend is apparent. For *Seiki* households where at least one parent has *Seiki* work status, the poverty rate fluctuates in accordance with the general trend of 'up-down-up', but the fluctuations are relatively small. However, for *Hiseiki* households, the increase from 2006 to 2008 is quite large; the decrease in the middle phase is significant; and then the further increase in the last phase of the crisis is again sharp. In the end, the poverty rate after the crisis in 2012 is significantly higher than before the crisis in 2006. Thus, it can be said that the economic crisis affected *Hiseiki* households much more severely than *Seiki* households, and it also left a negative lasting impact on them.

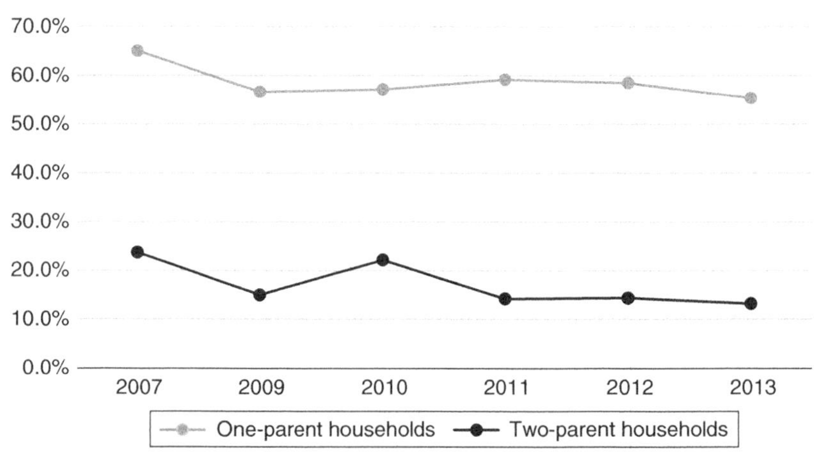

Figure 9.9. Percentage of children Living in *Hiseiki* households, by household type, Japan (2007–2013)

Source: Author's calculations using the MHLW's Comprehensive Survey of Living Conditions.

For single-parent households (Figure 9.10, lower graph), the fluctuations are larger for *Seiki* households. Especially the decrease in the child poverty rate during the second phase of the crisis is significant, as is the rise in the last phase. For *Hiseiki* households, the base trend is the same, but the impact of the crisis is much smaller, and the poverty rate remains high before, during, and after the crisis. This is because, for *Hiseiki* single-parent households, the poverty rate was already very high even before the crisis, and the economic crisis did not make much difference.

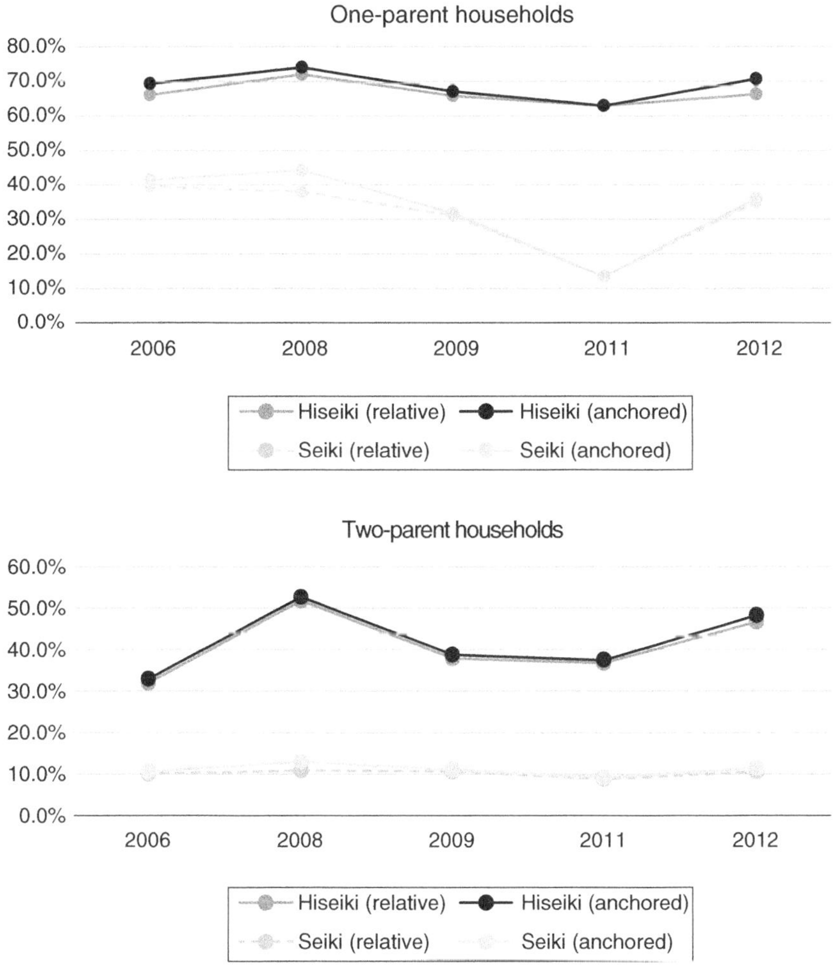

Figure 9.10. Child poverty rate, by household work status, for two- and one-parent households, Japan (2006–2012)

Source: Author's calculations using the MHLW's Comprehensive Survey of Living Conditions.

9.5. POLICY RESPONSE

The analysis in section 9.4 leaves one big question: what is the cause of the decrease in the poverty rate during the second phase (2008 to 2011)? There was an underlying declining trend in the overall unemployment rate, and a slight decrease in low WI and the *Hiseiki* rate among households with children, but the child poverty rate fell in almost all family types (Table 9.3), as did material deprivation (Table 9.1). The fall was especially large for one-parent households with high WI and *Seiki* jobs (Figures 9.8 and 9.10).

It is speculated that the policy response—and in particular the increase in social benefit for households with children—is the cause of the decrease. Let us explain.

9.5.1. The Change of Government in 2009

The Lehman shock in 2008 created a general atmosphere of fear and anxiety. The media also played a big part in encouraging such an atmosphere.[9] In early 2009, the news of children not being covered by public health insurance hit the media.[10] The notion that there could exist a child who did not have health insurance (and thus no access to healthcare) came as a big shock to the public. For the first time in decades, child poverty became a political issue, and the problem of health insurance was quickly addressed by amending the National Health Insurance Law to cover children under the age of 15, even if their parents were unable to pay the insurance premiums. The conservative government also tried to implement some anti-poverty measures for unemployed people, by setting up an emergency fund to finance programmes for the newly unemployed. For example, a cash benefit to cover part of their housing costs was introduced for newly unemployed people; this was the first housing benefit in Japan, aside from Public Assistance (which is notoriously difficult to access).

[9] The biggest blow to the public psyche was the 'Toshikoshi Hakenmura' (translated literally as the 'New Year's Contract Workers' Village'). The Hakenmura saw a non-profit organization put up a tent village right in front of the Ministry of Health, Labour, and Welfare building in the centre of Tokyo, just before New Year's Eve 2008. A stream of contract workers whose contracts were terminated before the long holidays lost their homes, as well as their work, since their employment was generally tied to a dormitory. They were forced out of their accommodation when their jobs were terminated. Hundreds of labourers turned up, and the event was covered continuously by the news media. In the end, the ministry was forced to open its auditorium to shelter these people.

[10] In Japan, every family is entitled to coverage by national health insurance, but in order to receive actual health services, households must pay social insurance premiums. The structure of social insurance premiums is highly regressive, since some portions of it are based on family size, regardless of family income. Thus, if a family fails to pay the premiums, it can no longer receive the benefits of insurance and has to pay 100 per cent of the service cost.

However, the public was not satisfied. In the general election of August 2009, the long reign of the conservative coalition of the Liberal Democratic Party (*Jimin-To*; LDP) and the largely Buddhist Komei Party (*Komei To*) came to an end, when the Democratic Party of Japan (*Minshu-to*; DPJ) won a landslide victory. The alleviation of poverty was at the top of the DPJ's political agenda, and the most important item in its manifesto was the introduction of the first truly universal child benefit, worth 26,000 yen per month, for every child below the age of 16 (DPJ, 2009).

After the handover of power in September 2009, the first thing that the DPJ government did was to announce the relative poverty rate for the whole population and for children under 18: these were 15.7 per cent and 14.2 per cent, respectively (poverty line set at 50 per cent of the median, equivalence scale is the square root of the family size). In April 2010, universal child benefit was introduced, as promised in the DPJ's manifesto. The new government was keen to push its liberal social policy, and it launched a number of policies to help the poor. Aside from the *Kodomo Teate* (Universal Child Allowance), another major policy initiative was the universal provision of high-school tuition, making public high-school tuition virtually free of charge.[11] The DPJ also had a manifesto commitment to create a scholarship for all university and professional school students,[12] and to increase the provision of public day-care centres in order to eliminate waiting lists.[13]

9.5.2. Reform of Child Benefit

This section describes the policy reform that took place during the political turmoil of the economic crisis. To understand the impact on the child income-poverty rate, we focus on the reform of the income-transfer mechanisms implemented during the DPJ government's tenure. Other policy mechanisms (such as benefits in kind) are not discussed here, as they do not directly affect the child poverty rate based on income data.

[11] In Japan, compulsory education lasts nine years (from the age of 6 to 15, i.e. primary school and junior high school). For ages 16–18, most children go to public or private high schools. Public high schools have smaller tuition fees than private ones, but the number of places is limited and enrolment can be quite competitive.

[12] Japan had (and still has) public student loan programmes with no or low interest rates, but no public scholarship programmes on a grant basis.

[13] Japan has fairly extensive public day-care programmes for 0–5 (pre-school) children, but they are awarded on the basis of need, and in certain urban centres the number of places is often smaller than the number of applicants.

9.5.2.1. *Child Benefit*

Table 9.4 summarizes the reforms of child benefit from 2000 to 2012. Prior to the DPJ government, child benefit was expanded to include more and more children, by raising the age of eligibility for the benefit, but the amount of benefit was set at 5,000 yen (about €40 at the current rate) per child per month. When the DPJ came to power in 2009, it increased this amount to 13,000 yen (about €105), with effect from April 2010. The amount remained the same until October 2010, when it was reduced to 10,000 yen (about €81). In April 2012, the universality was rescinded and an income threshold introduced; however, those in the lower half of the income distribution were largely unaffected. So in terms of the annual amount of the benefit there was a big increase from 2009 to 2010, and the benefit remained at this level throughout the period of analysis. The trend can be confirmed against social spending: there was a big leap in family-related social spending from 2009 to 2010, when child benefit was expanded (from 4.3 per cent of total social expenditure in 2009 to 5.6 per cent in 2010). Almost the whole increase was due to the child benefit increase (Figure 9.11).

It should be noted that the impact of the reform was quite different, depending on the age of the child. Whereas for children aged 12–14, the 2010 reform meant an entirely new benefit (because prior to the reform they were not eligible), for children aged under 3 the previous benefit was anyway 10,000 yen, and so the increase was only marginal. For children aged 3–11, the reform more than doubled their benefit amount.

9.5.2.2. *Tax Increase for Households with Children*

On the other side of the coin, the DPJ government decided to cut the income deduction for dependants allowed under the income tax regime, in order to finance some of the budget required for child benefit (see Table 9.5). Starting in 2011, the deduction for dependants aged 15–19 was cut to finance the high-school tuition waiver, and the deduction for dependants under 15 was totally abolished. In 2012, the local tax regime was also amended to implement the same reform.

The income deduction under the tax regime should not affect those at the very bottom of the income distribution (who are mostly under the minimum tax floor), but it might affect those near the poverty threshold. Suppose a household was in the lowest income bracket and was subject to income and local taxes. We can calculate the impact of the reform on such a household. In 2010, the combination of child benefit and the increase in income and local tax resulted in a fairly large increase (over 2008) in the net transfer for children aged 0–15, and especially to those aged 13–15, who received no child benefit in 2008.[14] The

[14] Assuming that the household is in the 10 per cent income tax and 10 per cent local tax bracket, the increase per year for a household with one child aged 0–2 was 45,000 yen in 2010

Table 9.4. Reforms of child benefit in Japan, 2000–2012

Year/ Month	Target children (age and number of siblings)	Income threshold	Monthly amount
2000	Children under 6	Gradually increased	5,000
2004	Children under 9		5,000
2006	Children under 12		5,000
2007			5,000 (10,000*)
2010 April	Universal Child Benefit introduced		
	Children under 15	None	13,000
2010 Oct	Children under 15	None	10,000 (15,000*)
2012 April	Universal Child Benefit rescinded	Yes (but quite high)	10,000 (15,000*)
	Children under 15		5,000**

* For children aged 0–2; ** Special benefit for those above the income threshold.
Note: In 2012 the 10,000 yen per month benefits totalled 120,000 yen per year, while the poverty threshold was 1,220,000 yen a year of equivalent household income. For a four-person family with two children receiving child benefit, that child benefit in 2012 amounted to about 10 per cent of the poverty threshold.

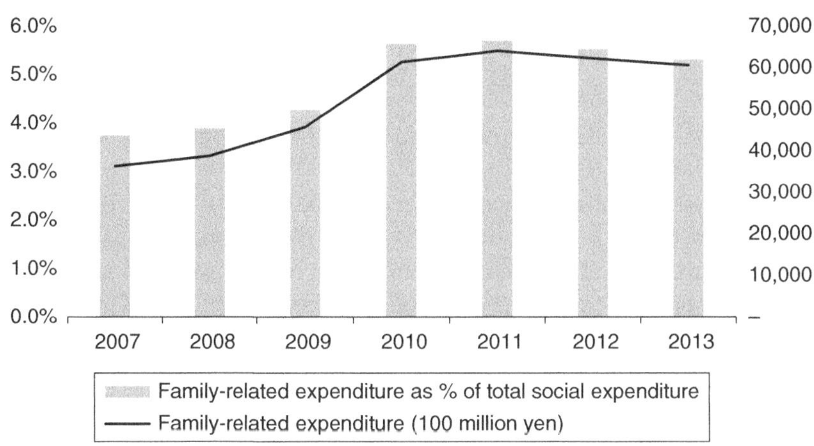

Figure 9.11. Family-related expenditure, total amount and as a percentage of total social expenditure, Japan (2007–2013)

Source: National Institute of Population and Social Security Research (2015). Table 1. Social Expenditure by social policy area, FY 1980–2013 '*Shakai Hosho Kyufuhi FY2013* [The Financial Statistics of Social Security in Japan FY 2013]', (Tokyo: National Institute of Population and Social Security Research, 2015).

and 22,000 yen in 2011; for a household with one child aged 3–12 the figures were 63,000 yen (2010) and 22,000 yen (2011); for a household with one child aged 13–15 the figures were 108,000 yen (2010) and 82,000 yen (2011).

Table 9.5. Amount of income deduction for dependants in income tax calculations

Year/Month	Age of dependants	Deduction amount
Up to 2010	General dependants	380,000 yen
	Ages 15 to 23	630,000 yen
After 2011	Under 16	0 yen
	Ages 16 to 18	380,000 yen
	Ages 19 to 22	630,000 yen
After 2012	Local tax was also amended to follow the income tax	

increase was much smaller in 2011, because the cut in deductions in the local tax regime also took effect. However, for children aged 16–18, there was a net reduction in 2010, and a much larger reduction in 2011.[15] However, after 2012, except for children aged 13–15, the net transfer resulting from the combined reform was actually smaller than before the 2009 reform for all ages of children.

It is not possible to evaluate the actual impact of the reforms on the net transfers to households with children without conducting microsimulations; however, it is noteworthy that the entire reform may have worsened the economic standing of households at the lower end of the tax-paying spectrum, and there is a possibility that the reform may have pushed them over the poverty threshold.

9.5.3. Failure of the DPJ Government

The DPJ government's attempt to pursue a liberal social policy did not last long. The party, a first-time novice at running the nation, quickly lost popularity and credibility. Laws, budgets, and other policies were left stranded in mid-stream because the DPJ did not possess the political skill to manoeuvre the policies, and the LDP, which still had a majority in the upper house, tried its best to discredit the DPJ government. To make matters worse, Japan was hit by the Great East Japan Earthquake in March 2011, and the government was severely criticized for its mishandling of the situation.

The universal child benefit also became a bone of political contention. Even though the public bought into the idea of a universal benefit at the time of the election, it soon realized that its implementation would require a big budget; at that point, all the justifications for it started to seem inadequate. The DPJ tried to argue that a child should be raised by 'the entire society' (DPJ, 2009), that generous child benefit might increase the fertility rate, that child benefit would boost the economy by raising the consumption of households with children,

[15] Assuming the same as footnote 14, the net reduction per year for a household with one child aged 16–18 was 25,000 yen (2010) and 50,000 yen (2011).

etc. But though at one time a political issue, child poverty became a non-issue after the disaster of the earthquake.

Public enthusiasm for the universal child benefit started to wane even before it was introduced. Influenced by a massive negative campaign by the (now) opposition LDP and by media, public opinion turned against it completely. Thus, the universality was rescinded and the benefit reduced in April 2012, only two years after its introduction. Soon after, in December 2012, the DPJ lost the elections to the LDP, and government was once again in the hands of the conservative coalition.

9.6. CONCLUSION

To summarize (see also Table 9.6), it can be said that during the first phase of the economic crisis (2006–2008), households with children responded by increasing the work intensity within the household. Thus, the number of households with low WI actually decreased, in spite of economic recession. At the same time, the poverty rate of households with low WI rose sharply, especially among two-parent households. There was also a slight movement from *Hiseiki* to *Seiki* work, and thus the percentage of children in households where no one had a *Seiki* job decreased. There was also a sharp rise in the poverty rate, especially among two-parent households. Thus, the increase in the poverty

Table 9.6. Summary of transmission mechanisms for the three phases of the economic crisis

Phase	Poverty rate	Change in household structure	Worklessness	*Hiseiki* rate	In-work poverty	Income transfer
I 2006–2008	Increase	Slightly	Decrease	Decrease	Increase for low- WI	Minimal
II 2008–2011	Decrease	Slightly	Decrease	Flat	Decrease for high-WI, *Seiki* single-parent, *Hiseiki* two-parent	Increase especially for 0–2-year-olds, but also significantly for 3–15-year-olds
III 2011–2012	Increase	Slightly	Increase	Flat	Increase for single parents (*Seiki* and high WI). Increase for *Hiseiki* two-parent households	Slight decrease but still positive, but negative for near-poor tax-paying households

rate during the initial stage was not due to an increase in worklessness or to low WI, but rather to a deterioration in income among those who had poor-quality jobs and who were only marginally integrated into the labour market. At this stage, there was still no policy response in terms of income-transfer mechanisms for poor households with children.

The second phase (from 2008 to 2011) was marked by a drop in the poverty rate for all household types and child demographics. During this phase, low-WI households slowly continued to decrease, while the *Hiseiki* rate remained about the same. However, the poverty rate decreased for almost all. In terms of the age of children, those aged 0–5 saw the largest decrease in the poverty rate; they were followed by children aged 6–11; and finally children aged 12–17. Also, the rate decreased significantly for single-parent households with high WI and with *Seiki* jobs, and for two-parent households with *Hiseiki* jobs. Large households, with more than two children, also witnessed a big drop in the rate. While all these households already had a high poverty rate, and experienced a rise in the rate during the first phase, this drop was quite large. However, at the same time there was a downward trend in work intensity. Since it is hard to imagine that the market income of these household groups improved so much during this short period, the speculation is that the policies had some impact, and the fact that households with many children also fared better seems to confirm this. The universal child benefit introduced by the newly elected DPJ government was fairly large compared to previous child benefits, and there was an increase in net benefit in 2010 and 2011.

During the last phase, when the poverty rate again started to rise, we see for the first time an increase in low-WI households. The poverty rate also increased significantly for single-parent households, especially in *Seiki* jobs and with high WI. Among two-parent households, there was an increase in low-WI households, but the poverty rate for low-WI two-parent households actually fell. However, the poverty rate for those with *Hiseiki* jobs rose sharply. It is hard to evaluate what the main mechanisms were for the increase in the child poverty rate during this phase; but the change in child benefit and the tax regime resulted in a reduction in the net benefit for near-poor households in all age groups of children, and thus it is suspected that policy had some impact in raising the child poverty rate.

Japan's experience during the economic crisis might seem a very peculiar case. The crisis actually forced a very radical change in government and the implementation of progressive reform. However, after examining the evidence presented in this chapter, we must conclude that the Japanese government failed to respond to the root cause of the child poverty that had been plaguing Japan since long before the crisis—the deterioration in income for those who are in work but on the fringes of the labour market (that is, those who have *Hiseiki* jobs, and single parents (both *Seiki* and *Hiseiki*)). These seem to be the main drivers of child poverty; although the progressive policies implemented by the DPJ government did make a dent and reverse the trend of rising poverty, the policies were too expensive and could not be sustained, either politically or fiscally. Japan's experience serves as a warning that, with the spread of in-work poverty globally, it is politically and economically extremely difficult to mitigate its impact through income-transfer schemes alone.

APPENDIX

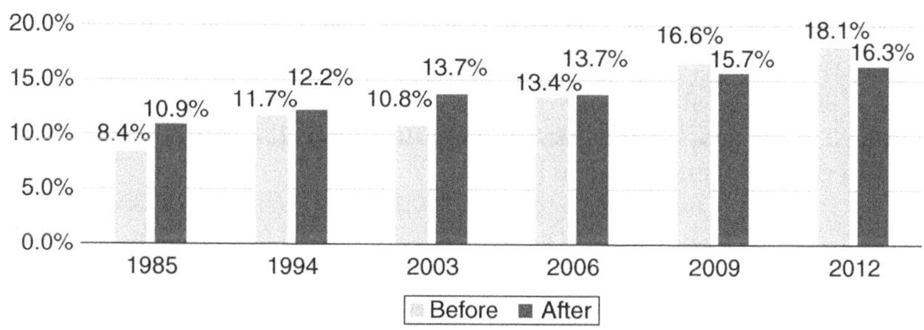

Figure 9.A1. Child poverty rate (50 per cent of median) before and after redistribution: 1985, 1994, 2003, 2006, 2009, 2012

Note: The poverty threshold is at 50 per cent of median equivalized income, with the equivalence scale equal to the square root of household size. Children are defined as those below the age of 18.

Source: Abe (2016).

REFERENCES

Abe, Aya K. (2003). 'Low Income People in Social Security Systems in Japan'. *Japanese Journal of Social Security Policy 2*, no. 2: pp. 59–70.

Abe, Aya K. (2008). *Kodomo no Hinkon* [Child Poverty] (Tokyo: Iwanami).

Abe, Aya K (2016). 'Hinkon-ritsu no Chokiteki Doko' [Long-term Trend of Poverty Rates from 1985–2012]. In: *Heisei 26 Nen Kosei Rodo Kakenhi Jigyo Kodomo no Hinkon no Jittai to Shihyo no Kochiku ni kansuru Kenkyu* [Ministry of Health, Labour and Welfare Scientific Research Grant Project Research on Child Poverty and Construction of Poverty Indices, Report FY 2015]. <http://mhlw-grants.niph.go.jp/niph/search/NIST00.do>.

Burniaux, Jean-Marc, Thai-Thanh Dang, Douglas Fore, Michael Förster, Marco Mira d'Ercole, and Howard Oxley (1998). 'Income Distribution and Poverty in Selected OECD Countries'. *OECD Economics Department Working Papers No. 189* (Paris: OECD Publishing, 1998).

Democratic Party of Japan (DPJ) (2009). *Minshuto no Seiken Seisaku Manifesuto 2009* [Manifesto of Democratic Party of Japan 2009] (Tokyo: DPJ). <http://www.dpj.or.jp/policies/manifesto2009>.

Esping-Andersen, Gøsta (1997). 'Hybrid or Unique?: The Japanese Welfare State between Europe and America'. *Journal of European Social Policy 7*, no. 3: pp. 179–89.

Eurostat (2014). 'Glossary:Persons living in households with low work intensity'. <http://ec.europa.eu/eurostat/statistics-explained/index.php/Glossary:Work_intensity>.

Holiday, Ian (2000). 'Productivist Welfare Capitalism: Social Policy in East Asia'. *Political Studies 48*, no. 4: pp. 706–23.

Kondo, Ayako (2007). 'Does the First Job Really Matter? State Dependency in Employment Status in Japan'. *Journal of the Japanese and International Economies 21*, no. 3: pp. 379–402.

Ministry of Health, Labour, and Welfare (MHLW) (2015). 'Heisei 26 Nen Kokumin Seikatsu Kiso Chosa no Gaikyo' [Overview of Results for 2014 Comprehensive Survey of Living Conditions]. <http://www.mhlw.go.jp/toukei/saikin/hw/k-tyosa/k-tyosa14>.

Ministry of Health, Labour, and Welfare (MHLW) (2016). '2015 Nen Chingin Kozo Kihon Tokei Chosa' [Basic Survey on Wage Structure 2015]. <http://www.mhlw.go.jp/toukei/list/chinginkouzou.html>.

National Institute of Population and Social Security Research (2009). 'Shakai Hosho Jittai Chosa Kekka no Gaiyo' [Overview of Results from 2007 National Survey on Social Security and People's Lives].

National Institute of Population and Social Security Research (2013). 'Seikatsu to Sasaeai Chosa Kekka no Gaiyo' [Overview of Results from 2012 National Survey on Social Security and People's Lives]. <http://www.ipss.go.jp/ss-seikatsu/j/2012/seikatsu2012.asp>.

National Institute of Population and Social Security Research (2015). 'Shakai Hosho Kyufuhi FY2013' [The Financial Statistics of Social Security in Japan FY 2013], (Tokyo: National Institute of Population and Social Security Research). <http://www.ipss.go.jp/ss-cost/j/fsss-h25/fsss_h25.asp>.

Nolan, Brian and Christopher T. Whelan (1996). *Resources, Deprivation and Poverty* (Oxford: Clarendon Press).

Organisation for Economic Co-operation and Development (OECD) (2016). Real GDP forecast (indicator). doi: 10.1787/1f84150b-en.

Organisation for Economic Co-operation and Development (OECD) (2015). *OECD Economic Surveys Japan 2015* (Paris: OECD).

Oshio, Takashi and Seiichi Inagaki (2014). 'Does Initial Job Status Affect Midlife Outcomes and Mental Health? Evidence from a Survey in Japan'. *RIETI Discussion Paper Series 14-E-025* (Tokyo: Research Institute of Economy, Trade and Industry).

Statistics Bureau (2016). 'Roudouryoku Chosa 2016' [Labour Force Survey 2016]. <http://www.stat.go.jp/data/roudou/longtime/03roudou.htm>.

Statistics Bureau, 'Rodoryoku Chosa [Labour Force Survey]', Historical data 10 Employee by age group and type of employment—Whole Japan.<http://www.stat.go.jp/data/roudou/longtime/03roudou.htm>.

World Bank (2016). *World Development Indicators*. <http://data.worldbank.org/data-catalog/world-development-indicators>.

10

Growing up in Poverty: Children and the Great Recession in Spain

Sara Ayllón

10.1. INTRODUCTION

The economic downturn in Spain started in 2008, after a huge housing bubble burst. The overall economy came to a jarring halt and entered a period of economic recession that has been particularly protracted and that has had particularly profound social consequences. This chapter provides a diagnosis of the economic ill-fare of Spanish children during this period, in order to assess the impact that the Great Recession has had on them. Now, almost nine years after the start of the crisis, when the economy is beginning to show some signs of recovery, is a good moment to look back and learn what could have been done differently and what can be done in future to protect the most vulnerable—those that can do nothing to change their situation.

This chapter contains four sections. In section 10.2, I describe the nature of the crisis in Spain by placing special emphasis on the changes that took place in the labour market, since they have had direct consequences on the economic well-being of children. I then turn in section 10.3 to a diagnosis of child poverty, while describing relative and anchored poverty trends. I complement this analysis by looking at the low work-intensity status of households and material deprivation indicators, including child-specific items. Next, and in order to understand the different trends observed, I use household and individual characteristics to identify those children at greatest risk of poverty. Section 10.4 contains a description of the policy choices made during the period and an analysis of how effectively social transfers have protected Spanish children. Finally, the conclusions summarize my findings and discuss possible implications for the future of children in Spain.

10.2. NATURE OF THE CRISIS

Until the Great Recession broke, Spain had experienced the longest period of continuous economic growth in the democratic era. As Figure 10.1 shows, from 1996 up to the beginning of 2008, Spanish gross domestic product (GDP) grew annually by between 2 per cent and 5 per cent. This high level of economic growth evolved in tandem with a major housing boom that was partly fuelled by low interest rates and easy access to credit, and partly also by a strong preference for housing ownership (favoured by fiscal policy), high rents, and a small stock of public housing. As a result, real estate prices more than doubled between the late 1990s and 2008; and family indebtedness likewise grew. Economic growth was also sustained by large public infrastructure projects and high consumer demand. Jobs were being created, but mostly in labour-intensive sectors and often on the basis of temporary contracts. Attracted by the opportunities that a booming economy had to offer, Spain received large numbers of immigrants: in 2008, they represented 11.4 per cent of the population, whereas just a decade earlier the figure had been 1.6 per cent. Aided by the boom, Spanish gross public debt remained at a relatively low level (39.4 per cent of GDP in 2008) and public finances showed a surplus in several years, according to data from the Organization for Economic Co-operation and Development (OECD).

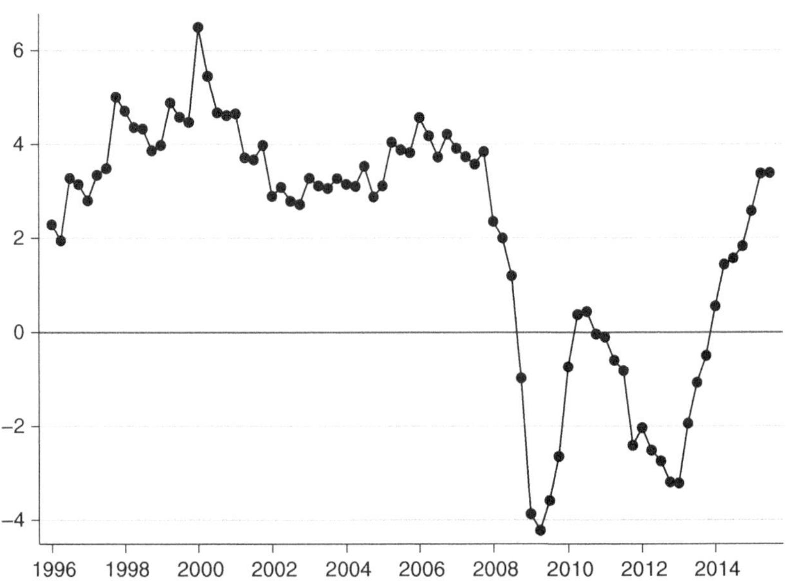

Figure 10.1. Percentage rate of inter-annual variation in real gross domestic product (quarterly data), Spain (1996–2015)

Source: National Accounts (quarterly data), Spanish National Statistics Institute.

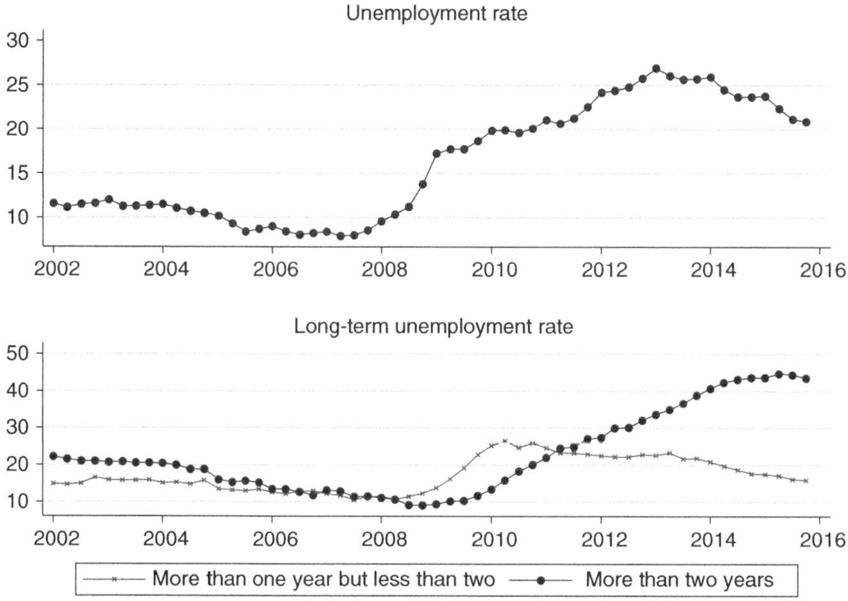

Figure 10.2. (a) Unemployment rate (quarterly data) and (b) long-term unemployment rate, Spain (2002–2015), per cent

Source: Labour Force Survey, Spanish National Statistics Institute.

After the start of the international financial crisis, the housing market bubble burst, and in 2008 the economy came to a sudden halt. This translated into an abrupt deceleration of activity and rapidly growing unemployment rates, especially in the construction sector. As early as in the first quarter of 2009, the unemployment rate reached 17.2 per cent, whereas just a year earlier it had stood at 9.6 per cent (Figure 10.2a). The socialist government at the time reacted by launching expansionary measures in 2008 and 2009—mainly cuts in income and corporate tax and increased public investment programmes (see section 10.4). However, while a certain effect can be observed in the GDP for 2010, these measures had no effect on unemployment, which continued to grow.

The overall slowdown in the economy rapidly reduced tax revenue and reversed the situation in relation to public finances and debt.[1] The Spanish public deficit reached 11 per cent in 2009. The situation was worsened by the sovereign debt crisis in the peripheral Eurozone countries, which also affected Spain. This meant that the Spanish government had to pay higher interest

[1] The Spanish government had collected revenue from the housing market on a large scale: from taxes on the purchase and sale of dwellings, corporate taxes from builders and banks, and VAT.

rates for the money it was borrowing. Spain came under intense pressure from the 'troika' and was forced to give up on its previous efforts to reactivate the economy. Instead it embarked on austerity measures and structural changes, such as labour market and pension reforms. A first package of cuts in social spending, a reduction in public sector wages, and tax increases was announced in spring 2010. Further spending cuts and tax increases were introduced in 2012 by the newly elected conservative People's Party government. These measures were followed by a further round of reforms in the labour market and the pension system that (among many other things) relaxed the rules of contract termination, reduced the cost of dismissals, extended the probationary period for new workers, gave firms the chance to opt out of collective agreement, and increased the retirement age from 65 to 67.

At this stage of the crisis, and given the government's difficulties in accessing the credit market, there were fears in Europe that there was a need for a full-scale bailout. These fears never materialized. But the Spanish banking sector entered an acute crisis, as important capital shortfalls were identified in a number of banks. In 2012, the Eurogroup granted Spain €100 billion for the Fund for Orderly Bank Restructuring (FOBR) to save the banking system. In total, by January 2014, when the European Stability Mechanism (ESM) financial assistance programme expired, some €41.3 billion had been disbursed for the recapitalization of the banking sector.

Throughout 2012 and 2013, the economy continued in recession. The number of unemployed peaked at the beginning of 2013, with 27 per cent of the active labour force without a job. This figure has remained very high (21 per cent in the last quarter of 2015), though there has been a trend toward job creation since mid-2013. High unemployment has affected especially young people (16–24), with unemployment rates well above 50 per cent since 2011. To the problem of mass unemployment, we need to add the fact that many individuals lack the protection of unemployment insurance. It is estimated that in 2012 only 64 per cent of the registered unemployed received unemployment benefits. The number of unemployed covered has continued to fall—to just 55 per cent in December 2015, according to data from the Ministry of Employment and Social Security. This is partly due to very high long-term unemployment rates (Figure 10.2b), but it is also partly because of the cuts and reforms that have imposed smaller benefits and less coverage. The economic problems associated with lack of work become really severe in those households where all the active members are unemployed: in the first quarter of 2013, the number of households with at least one active member and no one employed reached 15.0 per cent. And matters are even worse if no adult receives any income (either from the labour market or from the pension or the unemployment insurance systems): in the first quarter of 2015, this figure peaked at 4.2 per cent of all Spanish households. So, clearly there are two channels that stand out as the main transmission mechanisms of the crisis for children in Spain. On the one hand, the lack of attachment to the labour market of the adult persons with whom children live and, on the other hand, the lack of sufficient income protection—in particular, assistance directly targeted at children in need.

Although the country resumed its economic growth in the first quarter of 2014, the social aspects of the crisis persist. The patterns of job destruction during the recession and the exceptionally high unemployment figures distinguish Spain from comparable European countries. Post-recession working conditions are worse than before, with lower salaries and fewer employment protection guarantees. New job creation has been based mainly on temporary contracts, which in the last quarter of 2015 accounted for 26 per cent of all waged workers. And this is the economic context in which households with children have had to function throughout the recession—and even today. For many, this has been a hard task, as we will see in the following pages.

10.3. SPANISH CHILDREN DURING THE CRISIS

This section provides an overview of how children in Spain fared during the Great Recession. The data come from the Spanish component of the European Union Statistics on Income and Living Conditions (EU-SILC), called the Living Conditions Survey (in Spanish, *Encuesta de Condiciones de Vida*). It is important to note that in 2013 there was a change in the method for calculating household income: now a mixed methodology is used, combining information provided by the Tax Administration Agency and the Ministry of Employment and Social Security with survey data. This new data series is available from 2008 to 2014 and is the one mainly used in this chapter, labelled EU-SILC (base 2013). Given the methodological change, the results are not directly comparable to the previous data series, from 2004 to 2012.[2]

10.3.1. Relative and Anchored Child Poverty Trends

Figure 10.3 shows the relative and the anchored poverty rate trends by age group in Spain, from 2008 to 2014.[3] It can readily be observed that, if we take a relative approach to poverty measurement, the poverty rate in the total

[2] See Ayllón (2015) for an in-depth analysis of child poverty trends in Spain, using data from the first series (2004 to 2012) now known as EU-SILC (base 2004).

[3] All the results refer to the number of individuals, and not the number of households in which they live. Bootstrapped confidence intervals were computed, but they do not exceed 1 percentage point (+/−) per age group and year, and are therefore not included on the graph.

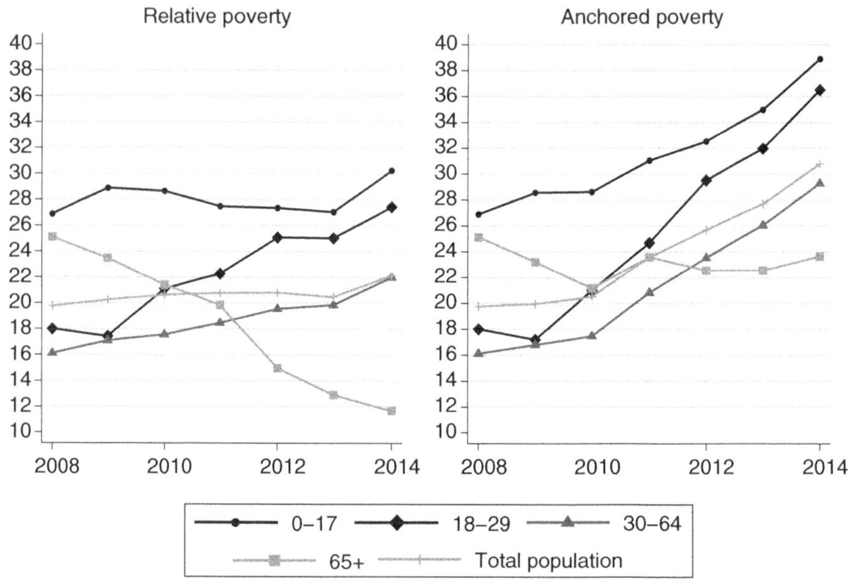

Figure 10.3. Relative and anchored poverty rate trends, by age group in Spain (2008–2014), per cent

Source: Author's computation using the Spanish component of the EU-SILC, Living Conditions Survey (base 2013) from 2008 to 2014.

population did not increase much (if at all), apart from between 2013 and 2014 (from 20.4 per cent to 22.1 per cent). Such an evolution may seem surprising, if we consider the context of the economic crisis described above; but it is important to bear in mind the *threshold effect*: the relative poverty line kept decreasing throughout the period, so the percentage of poor individuals remained stable at first and then increased, even if we consider that the monetary need of households fell.

Moreover, Figure 10.3 also shows that the different age groups in the population fare very differently over time: children make up the age group that suffers the highest risk of relative poverty throughout the period. While the child poverty rate remained stable between 2008 and 2013, it increased between 2013 and 2014, reaching 30.8 per cent. One child in three in Spain lived below the relative poverty line. We must also note the deterioration in the situation of young people (18–29), whose economic well-being worsened most during the crisis. At the opposite end of the scale, the 13 percentage point decline in the relative poverty rate of individuals aged 65 and over is worthy of note. As a matter of fact, taking a longer time perspective, elderly people have moved from being the age group most at risk of poverty during the period of economic growth, to being the group with the lowest risk—as low as 11.7 per cent in 2014. This should not be regarded as a great improvement in the real economic well-being of the elderly; rather it demonstrates the *threshold effect* mentioned earlier: as the poverty line drops due to the general decline in household income, those individuals who manage to maintain their level of income are no longer considered poor. This is precisely what has happened with those aged 65 and over in Spain.

Results that refer to anchored poverty paint a more worrying picture of the economic ill-fare of Spanish households during this period of crisis—and in particular of children. It is important to remember at this point that anchored poverty measurement may reflect better the impoverishment of a society during an economic crisis, because such analysis assumes that the resources that are required for someone to avoid being considered poor do not change over time. That is, the standard of living for a specific year (in this case 2008) is taken as a basis, and the poverty threshold only varies if prices do, too. In Spain, prices increased modestly over the period; and therefore so does the anchored poverty line.

As can be observed from Figure 10.3, the anchored poverty rate reveals a very serious deterioration in the situation of children in Spain. We are looking at an increase of 45 per cent in the poverty rate—moving from 26.9 per cent to 38.9 per cent—in just seven years. This means that nearly four children in ten in Spain lived below the anchored poverty line in 2014. The situation worsened for the whole population, but the overall levels of economic hardship were nothing like those faced by children and young people. These are the two age groups that in terms of economic well-being clearly have suffered the worst consequences of the economic crisis.

A sensitivity analysis using different definitions of the relative poverty threshold (30 per cent, 40 per cent, 50 per cent, 60 per cent, and 70 per cent of median equivalent income) reveals an even more worrying trend in the case of children than that described above. Here I refer to severe poverty. Individuals who live in a household with less than 30 per cent of the median are said to be in severe poverty (Ayala et al., 2006). And this is the case for many children in Spain. In 2014, one boy or girl in ten below the age of 18 lived in severe poverty. This means that in single-parent homes with one child, they had to make do with less than €5,192 a year (€431 a month)—or €8,387 a year (€699 a month) for a couple with two children. This is the result of a 56 per cent increase in the severe poverty rate since 2008 (from 6.4 per cent to 10.0 per cent).[4] Results reveal that the differences between the beginning and the end of the period under analysis are not so large if we consider a higher poverty line, which tells us that the economic crisis mainly translated into a large increase in the number of children in the most vulnerable situation—those at the very bottom of the income distribution.[5]

[4] This difference over time is statistically significant at 99 per cent confidence level. All the tests contained in the chapter are *t*-statistics for a linear combination of coefficients.

[5] Results relative to severe anchored poverty (not shown for reasons of space) depict an even worse trend, with a severe poverty rate for children that more than doubles over the period and reaches 13.2 per cent of children in 2014.

10.3.2. Low Work Intensity and Poverty among Children

A complementary way of assessing the economic well-being of children during this period is to analyse the number of children who live in a household with low work-intensity status: that is, children who live in households that worked for less than 20 per cent of their potential and that therefore receive little or no income from the labour market.

Table 10.1 shows the percentages of the whole population, of children, and of adults who lived in a low work-intensity household: 7 per cent of adults and 4 per cent of children in 2008. These figures are the lowest observed and are similar to those found during the period of economic growth. It can also be argued that they are relatively low compared to other European countries (Ayllón and Gábos, 2017). However, from 2009, the attachment of household members to the labour market changed completely for many families, and the risk of living in a low work-intensity household increased markedly, peaking in 2014. The problem among children is particularly worrisome, as that is the group that saw the biggest rate increase—from 4 per cent to 14 per cent.

Moreover, the second and third panels of Table 10.1 show that the relationship between household members' attachment to the labour market and poverty has become even stronger. As Table 10.1 indicates, between seven and nine children out of ten who lived in a low work-intensity household were poor. These figures are much lower in the case of adults, which points to the fact that lack of work and poverty are much more closely related among children than they are among adults. Importantly, it should be noted that this result is not specific to the period of economic crisis: back in 2008, 72 per cent of children in low work-intensity households were poor, which indicates that even when the economy was growing, children were unprotected if they happened to cohabit with workless adults. Indeed, further results (not shown for reasons of space) indicate that poor children are twice as likely to live in a low work-intensity household as are children overall, and the probability of this being the case has more than doubled during the period. As we will see at the end of the chapter, this is readily explained by the fact that in Spain the social insurance system that protects children when their parents are out of the labour market is neither sufficiently generous nor adequately comprehensive.[6]

[6] It is also true that over time it is the rate of poverty for adults in low work-intensity households that has increased most—possibly pointing to the fact that the duration of the economic crisis meant that unemployment insurance payments received by adults ceased to offer much protection.

Table 10.1. Percentage of the whole population, children and adults, living in a low work-intensity (LWI) household in Spain, 2008–2014

	2008	2009	2010	2011	2012	2013	2014	*test*
	Percentage in a LWI household							
All	6.6	7.6	10.8	13.4	14.3	15.7	17.1	***
Children	4.2	6.1	9.3	11.4	11.9	13.6	14.3	***
Adults (18–59)	7.2	8.0	11.3	13.9	15.0	16.3	17.9	***
	Relative poverty rate if in a LWI household							
All	51.3	55.0	58.2	57.8	61.3	61.3	63.1	***
Children	71.7	75.4	78.2	76.6	81.3	77.7	78.1	***
Adults (18–59)	48.1	50.8	53.6	53.7	56.8	57.4	59.7	***
	Anchored poverty rate if in a LWI household							
All	51.3	54.5	58.1	62.4	66.8	69.7	72.2	***
Children	71.7	75.4	78.2	80.5	86.0	85.7	85.5	***
Adults (18–59)	48.1	50.1	53.5	58.3	52.5	65.9	69.1	***

Note: *Test* indicates whether differences are statistically significant between the beginning and the end of the period at a given confidence level (*** 99 per cent, ** 95 per cent, and * 90 per cent).

Source: Author's computation using the Spanish component of the EU-SILC, Living Conditions Survey (base 2013) from 2008 to 2014.

10.3.3. Material Deprivation Trends among Children

The results for monetary poverty trends can be complemented by observing the evolution of indicators for material deprivation. Thus, from a unidimensional approach based solely on income, we move to a multidimensional one that, for example, takes account of the unaffordability of certain basic goods or a decent home. Table 10.2 shows the percentage of children in Spain who live in a household that suffers each indicator during three time periods: from 2004 to 2007 (i.e. the period of economic growth), from 2008 to 2010 (i.e. the time when the economic crisis started), and the current period from 2011 to 2014.[7]

In terms of consumption or access to services, it can be observed that around 3 per cent of children in Spain live in a household that cannot afford to eat proteins every second day. Also, nearly one child in ten lives in a household that cannot afford to heat the home adequately in winter, and between 15 per cent and 20 per cent of children live in a home with some structural problem. Out of the different indicators considered, possibly those most closely related to the poverty trends observed in the previous section are those associated with financial difficulties. In this sense, the percentage of

[7] In the case of material deprivation indicators, there is no data break in the time series, as is the case for income, and so results are comparable when using the EU-SILC base 2004 (2004–2012) and base 2013 (2008–2014).

Table 10.2. Percentage of children (<18) affected by material deprivation indicators, Spain, 2004–2014

	2004–2007	2008–2010	2011–2014	*Test*
Consumption, access to services				
The household cannot afford a meal with meat, chicken, or fish (or the vegetarian equivalent) every second day	2.6	2.6	3.3	***
At least one adult in the household had the need to see a dentist or receive dental treatment and did not do so because she or he could not afford it	8.0	8.5	11.9	***
The household cannot afford to go away for a week's annual holiday	42.2	43.1	47.4	***
Housing				
The household cannot afford to maintain the house at an adequate temperature in winter	8.9	7.3	9.0	NS
The house has problems with leaks, damp in the walls, floors, ceilings or rot in the floors, windows, or door frames	19.6	19.8	16.4	***
Financial difficulties				
The household has been in arrears with mortgage or rent payments in the last twelve months	5.7	9.9	9.3	***
The household has been in arrears with utility bills (heating, electricity, gas, water, etc.) in the last twelve months	9.3	9.9	10.6	***
It is difficult for the household to make it to the end of the month	14.1	19.4	18.8	***
The household cannot afford to pay unexpected expenses that arise	36.2	38.9	45.1	***
Housing costs are a heavy burden for the household	51.9	58.8	61.3	***
Environment				
The house does not have enough natural light	11.8	6.4	5.5	***
The house suffers too much noise from neighbours or from outside (traffic, factories, etc.)	26.0	20.2	15.9	***
The house is in an area with pollution, grime, or other types of environmental problems caused by industry or traffic	16.7	12.5	9.4	***
There is crime or vandalism in the area	18.3	14.5	11.1	***

Note: *Test* indicates whether differences are statistically significant between the beginning and the end of the period at a given confidence level (*** 99 per cent, ** 95 per cent and * 90 per cent); NS = not significant.

Source: Author's computation using the Spanish component of the EU-SILC, Living Conditions Survey (base 2004) from 2004 to 2012 and Living Conditions Survey (base 2013) from 2008 to 2014.

children who live in a household that has been in arrears with mortgage or rent payments in the previous twelve months rose from 5.7 per cent to 9.3 per cent between 2004–2007 and 2011–2014. In a similar vein, the percentage of those living in a household that cannot afford unexpected expenses rose from 36.2 per cent to 45.1 per cent during the same years; and the figure for those who consider housing costs to be a heavy burden climbed from 51.9 per cent to 61.3 per cent. Results indicate that while the Great Recession may not have translated into a large increase in deprivation in terms of certain goods or services—mostly because the number of children suffering the problem was already very high prior to the economic crisis—it has seriously damaged the situation of households in terms of financial difficulties. The last panel of Table 10.2 shows the percentage of children who live in households that suffer from other problems in the home or the neighbourhood (lack of natural light, noise, pollution, vandalism, etc.). Interestingly, the prevalence of these indicators fell throughout the period, which may indicate that households attach less importance to such problems in a context of economic difficulties.[8]

Finally, Table 10.3 contains a selection of indicators (collected in 2009 and in 2014) that refer to material deprivation situations as they affect children directly—that is, child-specific items. The first three columns show the percentage of all children who live in households that cannot afford certain items, while the last three columns give the same information for poor children. For simplicity's sake, results are for relative poverty only. Moreover, the table details indicators that show a significant change over time; the rest are simply commented on in the text.

In terms of basic consumption, there are only two indicators that show a significant increase. They refer to the impossibility for the household: 1) to afford some new (not second-hand) clothes for children aged 1–16; and 2) to provide them with a meal with meat, chicken, or fish (or vegetarian equivalent) at least once a day. As indicated, 7.3 per cent and 2.7 per cent, respectively, of children in Spain suffered these problems in 2014. Moreover, the high (and growing) percentage of poor children who live with such deprivation is worthy of note: the risk they face is more than double that faced by the child population generally. For instance, one poor child in five cannot have new clothes—a figure that has increased by more than 6 percentage points over the

[8] It is also true that Spain performs very well on some other indicators, with hardly any children living in a household that lacks certain durable goods (telephone, TV, washing machine) or that does not have running water or a bath/shower in the home. Partly for this reason, Spain ranks among the better-off countries when the 'severe material deprivation' indicator of the EU2020 poverty and social exclusion target is used. In 2008, 5.5 per cent of children were affected by the problem; only the Nordic countries, Luxembourg, and the Netherlands have a lower figure. That said, it should be noted that the percentage has increased considerably, with 9.5 per cent of Spanish children affected in 2014.

Table 10.3. Percentage of children (<18) affected by material deprivation indicators in child-specific items, Spain, 2009 and 2014

	Child population			Children in poverty (relative)		
	2009	2014	*Test*	2009	2014	*Test*
Basic consumption						
The household cannot afford some new (not second-hand) clothes for children aged 1–16	4.8	7.3	***	13.5	19.6	***
The household cannot afford to provide their children with a meal with meat, chicken, or fish (or vegetarian equivalent) at least once a day	1.0	2.7	***	3.3	7.7	***
Educational or leisure needs						
The household cannot afford to pay for regular leisure activities for the children (swimming, music lessons, etc.)	6.5	12.3	***	15.5	30.1	***
The household cannot afford celebrations on special occasions (birthdays, name days, etc.)	6.9	10.8	***	16.6	27.1	***
The household cannot afford to have the children invite friends round to play and eat from time to time	5.4	12.1	***	13.3	30.7	***
The household cannot afford to have the children participate in school trips and school events that cost money	6.4	10.3	***	14.8	25.6	***

Note: *Test* indicates whether differences are statistically significant between 2009 and 2014 at a given confidence level (*** 99 per cent, ** 95 per cent, and * 90 per cent).

Source: Author's computation using the Spanish component of the EU-SILC, Living Conditions Survey (base 2013) for 2009 and 2014.

period.[9] In terms of educational or leisure needs, there are four indicators whose prevalence clearly increased between 2009 and 2014, and all have to do with the affordability of (often paid-for) activities. The percentage of children who live in households that cannot afford to pay for after-school activities such as swimming or music lessons and the percentage of those who cannot invite friends both doubled in just five years. The number of children affected is also important in the case of inability to afford celebrations for special occasions and inability to afford to have children participate in school trips. In the case of poor children, the percentages for some of these indicators doubled. So from these results it can be concluded that, while Spanish families do their best to cover children's most basic needs, many are left out of activities that are

[9] Two other indicators collected in both 2009 and 2014 do not show any change over time: the impossibility for households 1) to afford two pairs of properly fitting shoes for children (including a pair of all-weather shoes) (2.7 per cent); and 2) to afford fresh fruit and vegetables once a day (1.6 per cent).

known to be important for their development (Lipscomb, 2007; Pfeifer and Cornelissen, 2010).[10,11]

10.3.4. Children at Most Risk during the Great Recession

So, who are the children most affected by economic hardship in Spain? Table 10.4 shows the at-risk-of-poverty rate when considering individual and household characteristics and using both a relative and an anchored approach to poverty measurement. As in the other tables, the number of asterisks indicates whether differences between the beginning and the end of the period are statistically significant. The last five columns complement the analysis by showing the composition of the child population and the population of poor children. That way we can determine which groups are under-represented or over-represented within the poor population.

Given the context of the economic crisis, it is important to look first at the parental attachment to the labour market. The first five rows of Table 10.4 show the at-risk-of-poverty rate for children depending on whether they live with one or two parents, and whether those parents are working or not. Unsurprisingly, the highest risk is faced by children with workless parents, and the situation of children who cohabit with both parents is particularly difficult. In this case, the relative poverty rate for 2014 is as high as 74 per cent.[12] Moreover, while the relative poverty rates show no difference between the beginning and the end of the period under study, anchored poverty indicates that the situation clearly worsened.

Naturally, the most protected children are those who live with two working parents: less than one child in ten was below the poverty line in 2014. However, it should be noted that one salary is no longer any guarantee of economic well-being, since more than three children in ten live below the poverty line, even if one of the parents works. According to the results for anchored poverty, the biggest deterioration has been in the situation of children who live with both parents, only one of whom works. The Great

[10] Interestingly, Spanish children rank consistently highly across most aspects of life when they are asked about their satisfaction with life, their families and friends, or their material situation. But they also report high levels of worries about family money (Rees et al., 2016).

[11] There are four items that do not show significant changes over time, but that a considerable proportion of children lack: 1) books suited to the child's age (2.2 per cent in 2014); 2) outdoor leisure equipment, such as a bicycle (5.7 per cent); 3) indoor games (3.3 per cent); and 4) a suitable place to study (5.0 per cent).

[12] Results drawn from the EU-SILC (base 2004) for the period between 2004 and 2012 indicate that the most important increase in the risk of poverty for children living with two jobless parents occurred between 2004 and 2008, despite this being a period of economic growth.

Table 10.4. Percentage of children living in poverty, by individual and household characteristics and composition of the child population and the poor children group, Spain, 2008 and 2014

	At-risk-of-poverty rate			Child population		Poor children composition		
	2008	2014	2014 anch.	2008	2014	2008	2014	2014 anch.
Number of parents and their attachment to the labour market								
Single parent, not working	59.7	60.4	67.3	3.0	6.3	6.6	12.7	11.0
Single parent, working	31.9	33.2	39.4 *	8.0	9.2	9.5	10.2	9.4
Couple, neither working	73.7	74.0	83.8 ***	6.4	10.6	17.6	26.3	23.1
Couple, one working	35.5	35.3	48.6 ***	35.1	33.5	46.6	39.5	42.1
Couple, both working	11.1	8.4 **	13.8 **	47.5	40.4	19.7	11.4	14.5
Children cohabiting with unemployed youth (18–24)								
At least one unemployed sibling	51.7	62.1	70.1 ***	2.4	3.5	4.6	7.1	6.2
Number of parents in the household and number of children								
Single parent								
1 child	26.9	40.1 ***	48.5 ***	5.0	8.2	5.0	11.1	10.3
2 children	41.9	41.3	48.1	3.8	5.5	5.9	7.6	6.9
3+ children	63.0	68.9	69.1	2.2	1.8	5.2	4.1	3.2
Two parents								
1 child	17.0	21.0 **	30.4 ***	29.9	28.3	19.0	19.8	22.2
2 children	21.7	26.9 ***	36.8 ***	44.2	43.1	35.9	38.7	41.1
3+ children	51.7	42.3 ***	47.9	15.0	13.2	29.0	18.7	16.4
Children's age								
0–2	27.0	25.9	33.9 **	15.3	13.5	15.4	11.5	11.8
3–7	26.3	27.6	34.5 ***	29.2	30.6	28.6	27.9	27.2
8–13	27.0	30.6 *	40.7 ***	32.9	33.8	33.0	34.3	35.4
14–17	27.4	36.0 ***	45.2 ***	22.5	22.1	22.9	26.3	25.7
Parents' immigrant origin								
Family of Spanish or European origin	21.0	24.1 ***	33.1 ***	80.7	83.6	63.2	66.9	71.3
Family of non-European origin	51.1	60.6 ***	67.8 ***	19.3	16.4	36.8	33.1	28.7

Note: Asterisks indicate whether differences are statistically significant between the beginning and the end of the period at a given confidence level (*** 99 per cent, ** 95 per cent, and * 90 per cent).

Source: Author's computation using the Spanish component of the EU-SILC, Living Conditions Survey (base 2013) from 2008 to 2014.

Recession has meant an important reduction in levels of pay, and so often one salary is not enough to keep families out of economic hardship.

If we look at population composition, it may be seen that only children living with both parents are under-represented within the poor population, while all other groups are over-represented. Especially striking is the increase in the number of children whose parents do not work (adding up both family types): they represented 9.4 per cent of the total child population in 2008, and 16.9 per cent in 2014. Among the poor, the figure rose from 24.2 per cent to

39.0 per cent. This means that four in ten poor children in Spain currently live with parents who do not receive income from the labour market.

Moreover, the economic well-being of children may not only be affected by the inability of parents to obtain a salary from the labour market; it may also be the result of lack of work among other household members. In this sense, it is interesting to look at the situation of children who cohabit with young unemployed people (18–24), mainly their own siblings. The youth unemployment rate peaked at the end of the period under study: 75 per cent for those aged 16–19 (in 2013) and 53 per cent for those aged 20–24 (in 2014). The results indicate that while the number of children living with at least one unemployed young person is not large, their economic situation has worsened, with an anchored poverty rate in 2014 that reached 70.1 per cent.

The second group of children particularly at risk is made up of those who live in large families—especially if those large families are in single-parent households. According to the results, children who live with at least two other children had an at-risk-of-poverty rate of 63 per cent in 2008 if they were in single-parent households and 52 per cent in two-parent households. Over time, however, we do not observe any differences that are statistically significant; but it should be noted that the poverty risk for children in large families was already extremely high at the start of the period being analysed. This explains why children in single-parent households and in large families are over-represented among the poor. Note also how the percentage of children in large families has decreased in Spain, while the percentage of children living with only one of their parents has increased.

Furthermore, it is important to highlight the increase in the poverty risk of children who live in the most common family types in Spain: single-child families in the case of single-parent households, and two-child families in the case of couples. Thus the Great Recession seems to have caused particular difficulties for children living in the *standard* family. Moreover, the results presented may suggest a change of profile, with more poor children living in households with fewer children.

The age of the children is another relevant characteristic to take into account when studying child poverty in Spain, and particularly its recent evolution. The results show that, at the start of the period under review, the risk of poverty was quite similar for different age groups within the child population.[13] However, the risk has evolved quite differently: those in age groups 8–13 and (particularly) 14–17 suffer the worst economic consequences of the Great Recession. As for the latter, the relative poverty rate rose from 27 per cent to 36 per cent—and to 45 per cent in the case of anchored poverty. These are increases of 9 and 18 percentage points, respectively. Consistent

[13] In the case of children aged 0–2, the risk of poverty was particularly low in the period of economic growth (Ayllón, 2015).

with these results, we find that children aged 0–7 are under-represented among the poor, while those aged 8–17 are over-represented. There may be several reasons for this, but one is particularly telling: children in the age group 14–17 are twice as likely to be living in a single-parent household as, for example, those in the age group 0–2; and the likelihood of this happening increased during the crisis (from 15 per cent to 23 per cent).[14]

Being of immigrant origin puts children at greater risk of poverty in Spain (as elsewhere, as other chapters in this book highlight). According to the results obtained, one child in two from a family of non-European immigrant origin was poor in 2008. While the situation worsened for all children, it deteriorated most for immigrant children, with an at-risk-of-poverty rate that increased from 51 per cent to 61 per cent in the case of relative poverty, and to 68 per cent for anchored poverty. If we pay attention to the child population percentages, we can see that at the start of the crisis period, two children in ten were of non-European immigrant origin. This figure has fallen to 16.4 per cent as a result of many families of immigrant origin deciding to return to their home countries. Nevertheless, it should be noted that the percentage of immigrant children in the poor population is double the figure for the total child population. Undoubtedly, these results have important consequences for the integration of the immigrant population into Spanish society and, in general, for social cohesion and equality of opportunity.

10.4. POLICY CHANGES DURING THE ECONOMIC DOWNTURN AND THE EFFECTIVENESS OF THE MONETARY TRANSFER SYSTEM

This section reviews the most important policy choices made during the period of economic crisis (mostly in terms of tax and transfers) that have had an impact on the economic well-being of children. In this respect, it is important to understand first the social policy framework in which all these changes have taken place. It has traditionally been a feature of Spain that it lacks a comprehensive and generous social transfer system aimed at protecting children from economic hardship.[15] Unlike many other countries in Europe,

[14] Last available data for Spain indicates that divorce occurs on average 15 years after marriage, according to the Spanish National Statistics Institute: <http://www.ine.es/prensa/np927.pdf>.

[15] While it is true that Spain devotes more than the OECD average to social spending, only a very small part of these resources goes to family policy (1.4 per cent of GDP in 2013, compared to the OECD average of 2.2 per cent). In 2007, before the Great Recession struck, 6 per cent of social spending went on the 'Family, children' function, compared to 31 per cent for 'Old age', or 12 per cent for 'Unemployment'. Moreover, resources dedicated to family policy kept decreasing over the period of economic downturn, after peaking in 2008.

Spain does not have a universal child benefit, and family transfers mostly consist of contribution-based paid maternity and paternity leave and a non-contributory means-tested child benefit (in Spanish, *prestación por hijo a cargo*) that is received by a fairly significant number of families, but that is very modest. Rather it is the fiscal system that is of greatest assistance to families with children, through personal income tax deductions for each child (Cantó et al., 2014). Nonetheless, it must be emphasized that such fiscal measures often do not benefit families on very low income, as they are exempt from this tax (Cantó et al., 2014; Cantó, 2014). Moreover, it is important to take into account the fact that in Spain the minimum income transfer system is very fragmented and that different policies can be found in different regions.

Before the Great Recession hit, possibly encouraged by still growing tax revenues, the socialist government made some attempts to increase the generosity of family policy in Spain. In 2008, the amount of means-tested child benefit for children under the age of 3 was nearly doubled (from €291 to €500 annually) and the income threshold for entitlement to the benefit was raised, so that more families were covered (Cantó and Ayala, 2014). Moreover, a one-off universal child benefit of €2,500, payable at birth, was introduced in 2007. There was a change to the maternity leave rules, so that mothers who had not contributed enough to the social security system could still be covered during their absence from the labour market; and paid paternity leave was increased from two to thirteen days. During this period, some regional governments also introduced their own family policy measures, mostly in relation to birth, adoption, or the reconciliation of family and working life.

In 2008 and 2009, and as part of the expansionary measures to try to reactivate the economy, a personal tax credit of €400 was introduced. Also a new benefit for the unemployed was created under the name PRODI (*Programa temporal por Desempleo e Inserción*): under certain circumstances, long-term unemployed people whose period of benefits entitlement had expired could claim a means-tested benefit of slightly above €400 a month for a period of six months (if they had less than 75 per cent of the minimum salary from other possible income sources). Other new measures included an extension for mortgage payments among the unemployed and a tax credit for rent for those at the bottom of the income distribution.

In 2010, with the sovereign debt crisis and shrinking tax revenue, and under pressure from the 'troika', austerity measures were imposed in order to control the budget deficit (which had seen the second-biggest increase in the Eurozone, after Ireland). Changes were introduced in personal income tax (particularly affecting higher incomes), and capital and savings taxes were increased. The government also approved the withdrawal of the personal income tax credit of €400, which was reserved for those at the bottom of the income distribution. Moreover, the wages of all public sector workers were cut by 5 per cent,[16] the inflation adjustment for pensions was suspended, the indicator used to determine certain social assistance benefits was frozen (IPREM, *Indicador Público de Renta de Efectos Múlitples*), and the amounts received for the means-tested child benefit were halved for children under the age of 3. Nonetheless, a new unemployment insurance was established for self-employed people (with enough contributions to the social security system) who had ceased their activity for economic reasons.

In 2011, the austerity measures continued: the universal child benefit of €2,500 payable at birth was eliminated; and the new benefit for the unemployed (PRODI) was replaced with a new programme called PREPARA, which had stricter requirements and slightly smaller payments. Moreover, VAT increased from 16 per cent to 18 per cent (general rate) and from 7 per cent to 8 per cent (reduced rate).

In 2012, the new centre-right government implemented further austerity measures. Unemployment benefits were modified: the amount received from the seventh month of unemployment was reduced; a special unemployment subsidy for those over 45 was eliminated; and the entitlement age for non-contributory unemployment benefit was raised from 52 to 55 in the case of individuals with no dependants (Cantó and Ayala, 2014). VAT was again increased—from 18 per cent to 21 per cent (general rate) and from 8 per cent to 10 per cent (reduced rate)—and a supplementary levy on personal and capital income was introduced. The number of tax brackets in the personal income tax was raised and the rates were increased. At the same time, many regional governments eliminated or reformed benefits that had been introduced in the period of economic growth.[17] It was also in 2012 that the most drastic cuts in education took place (more than €4 billion in just one year). These cuts translated, for example, into increased class sizes in primary and secondary school (from twenty-seven to thirty students and from thirty-three to thirty-six, respectively),[18] more teaching hours per teacher, no replacement of teachers in the first two weeks of sick leave, and, in practice, the elimination of the 'Compensatory Education Programme' targeted at children from particularly difficult socio-economic backgrounds who need special support. Moreover, social spending on healthcare was cut by 12 percentage points between 2009 and 2013 (involving a total of nearly €8 billion); but again it was between 2012 and 2013 that the most regressive measures were implemented (Bandrés and González, 2015). Key changes featured the exclusion of undocumented immigrants from access to free healthcare services, increased co-payment for certain drugs, fewer

[16] Several extensions of this measure were later approved.

[17] See all the detail in the Euromod Country Reports at <https://www.euromod.ac.uk/using-euromod/country-reports>.

[18] In the academic year 2015/16, class sizes returned to the level seen prior to the economic recession.

surgical procedures, increased waiting time to visit a specialist, and cutbacks in emergency services, among many others (see Legido-Quigley et al., 2013).

In 2013, after several extensions of the PREPARA programme, the Spanish government approved a decree-law that automatically extended this unemployment benefit programme until the unemployment rate falls below 20 per cent, according to the Labour Force Survey. Also, in January of that year, a pension reform came into force, by which the normal pensionable age will be gradually (until 2027) raised from 65 to 67, unless by the age of 65 a worker has 38.5 years' worth of contributions. In 2014, one more programme for the unemployed was initiated (*Programa de Activación para el Empleo*), granting the long-term unemployed a new means-tested benefit for six months if they have exhausted the other possible benefits and have still not found a job.[19] Also in 2014, a new tax reform for personal income received in 2015 and 2016 was approved, which will introduce a larger tax deduction per child. The reform implies a more progressive personal income tax, but according to López Laborda et al. (2015), it will also reduce revenue, which may make the system less redistributive in the future.

All in all, and while it is impossible to assess how each of these policy choices has impacted on children's economic well-being in Spain, they help us to understand the poverty and material deprivation trends observed in the previous section. What we can do with the data to hand is to analyse the impact of the transfer system on child poverty over the period, with the information broken down according to the benefits received. With this objective, I have calculated the difference in the poverty rate that results when we consider a) the distribution of *total* available income, and b) another distribution that does not take account of one or another household or individual benefit. This way, and while keeping the poverty threshold constant, we can determine the capacity of the monetary transfers to reduce poverty.[20] Results refer to children in the upper part of the table; to adults in the lower.[21]

Given the slender resources devoted to assistance and family transfers, it is not surprising that the capacity of the system to reduce child poverty should be very small; this is not because of the recent changes, but was the case even

[19] A new condition was established, by which if the unemployed person finds a job, the benefit can be used as a bonus by the employer.

[20] Results are, of course, an approximation of the real situation, since with the data to hand we cannot control for possible changes in behaviour that families could make if they do not receive a certain benefit. Results are an inexact measure of the real effect, but can be regarded as an informative approximation.

[21] This analysis necessarily ignores the redistributive power of such public services as childcare, which is also very important for the well-being of children (Cantó, 2014). As a matter of fact, Förster and Verbist (2014) show that particularly in Spain, in-kind benefits, mainly nursery services, have a stronger impact on poverty reduction than do monetary transfers.

Table 10.5. Effect of monetary transfers on the relative child poverty and adult poverty rate in Spain, 2008–2014

	Household benefits				Individual benefits					
	1	2	3	4	5	6	7	8	9	10
	Child population									
2008	−0.4	−0.2	−0.2	−0.1	−3.2	−1.6	−0.4	−0.8	−1.0	−0.3
2009	−0.8	−0.2	−0.3	−0.1	−4.2	−1.3	−0.4	−0.5	−1.1	−0.2
2010	−0.7	−0.1	−0.1	−0.0	−5.8	−1.9	−0.5	−0.4	−1.2	−0.2
2011	−0.7	−0.4	−0.2	−0.1	−6.5	−1.6	−0.9	−0.3	−1.2	−0.2
2012	−0.4	−0.2	−0.2	−0.2	−6.5	−1.1	−0.8	−0.3	−1.2	−0.3
2013	−0.7	−0.6	−0.2	−0.5	−8.1	−1.4	−1.0	−0.4	−1.3	−0.1
2014	−0.3	−0.2	0.0	−0.1	−6.3	−1.5	−0.7	−0.5	−1.7	−0.2
	Adult population									
2008	−0.2	−0.2	−0.1	−0.0	−2.6	−13.3	−0.7	−0.5	−2.2	−0.2
2009	−0.2	−0.2	−0.1	−0.0	−3.0	−14.0	−0.7	−0.5	−2.2	−0.2
2010	−0.3	−0.2	−0.1	−0.0	−4.8	−15.0	−0.9	−0.3	−1.9	−0.2
2011	−0.3	−0.3	−0.2	−0.1	−5.6	−13.2	−3.5	−0.4	−2.3	−0.2
2012	−0.2	−0.3	−0.1	−0.0	−4.8	−13.4	−4.3	−0.2	−2.2	−0.2
2013	−0.3	−0.7	−0.1	−0.1	−5.5	−14.8	−4.4	−0.4	−2.3	−0.2
2014	−0.2	−0.4	−0.1	−0.0	−5.3	−15.7	−4.4	−0.4	−2.5	−0.3

Notes: (1) Family/children allowances, (2) Social exclusion, (3) Housing allowances, (4) Net income on behalf of children aged under 16, (5) Unemployment benefits, (6) Retirement pensions, (7) Survivors' benefits, (8) Illness, (9) Disability, and (10) Education-related allowances.

Source: Author's computation using the Spanish component of the EU-SILC, Living Conditions Survey (base 2013) from 2008 to 2014.

prior to the Great Recession. This is precisely what the first four columns of Table 10.5 show in relation to household benefits. Clearly, the capacity of transfers to reduce child poverty is very small—and even smaller in the case of adult poverty. 'Family/children related allowances' is possibly the most effective household transfer, but its capacity never exceeds 1 percentage point. Note in particular column 4, which contains net income received on behalf of children under the age of 16: the number of families that benefit and the amounts received are both so small that hardly any impact is observed on the relative poverty rate.

Columns 5–10 show the poverty-reduction capacity of monetary transfers received by household members at the individual level. Unemployment benefits have the greatest capacity to combat child poverty; as an automatic stabilizer, such capacity increased over time as the crisis dragged on.[22] However, unemployment benefits received by households with children have not been

[22] This also means that families with children have become more dependent on monetary transfers and therefore more vulnerable to political decisions on the resources to devote and in what form.

enough to tackle the increasing child poverty associated with unemployment. Also, it is noticeable that between 2013 and 2014, when child poverty increased most, the capacity of unemployment insurance to reduce child poverty declined markedly. This is related to the fact that individuals are losing their entitlement and are not finding new employment.[23]

In comparison, note the strong capacity of pensions to reduce adult poverty in Spain, and how such capacity has been maintained—or has even increased—at the same time as there has been a big reduction in the risk of relative poverty among older individuals. As we can see, there is no transfer with similar capacity in the case of children. Nor do very many children benefit from the pension system, as three-generation households have become rarer. In the European context, Spain is one of those countries that not only spend little in the fight against child poverty, but do so ineffectively (compared to the situation pertaining to adult poverty).

10.5. CONCLUSIONS

Previous sections have shown Spanish children's great economic vulnerability to changes in the business cycle. The Great Recession has had an important impact on the economic well-being of many children—not only because of the sky-high unemployment rates of the adults that look after them, but also because of the lack of a generous and comprehensive social protection system that can be relied upon when the economy slows down. For example, the new means-tested unemployment benefit programmes implemented by the government as the crisis dragged on have proved inadequate to compensate for the lack of work in many families with children.

However, it is important not to forget that child poverty was a major social problem in Spain before this economic downturn: Spain had some of the highest child poverty rates in Europe prior to the period of time analysed in this chapter. The Great Recession has simply worsened the situation. At the same time, it has made the predicament more visible, as now it receives more attention in the media and social networks and in the political discourse.

So the ultimate cause of child poverty in Spain can probably be traced to certain characteristics of Spanish society, both structural and institutional. Spain is one of the few countries in Europe without a universal child benefit, even though it has been shown clearly that generous social benefits are closely linked to low child poverty rates (Gornick and Jäntti, 2012). Worse still, it seems

[23] Even when the monetary transfers received may not be sufficient to raise households above the poverty line, they certainly reduce the severity of economic hardship.

that the little progress made in terms of family policy during the period of economic growth has already been lost in the wake of the austerity measures.

Changes are necessary; and some of them are urgent. Perhaps the implementation of a universal child benefit can be regarded as unfeasible at the time of writing, when the economy is only showing weak signs of recovery; but it certainly has to be on the political agenda as one of the country's priorities. In the meantime, changes should be introduced in the means-tested child benefit to increase its quantity and coverage.

If nothing is done, too many children will have spent part or all of their childhood in poverty, with the serious consequences this has in all life domains. The lesson must be learned. The economic well-being of children can no longer be left to the mercy of the business cycle. Spain's political leaders and society as a whole must reflect on the kind of future they want for children in Spain. The country's youngsters deserve nothing less.

REFERENCES

Ayala Cañón, Luis, Rosa Martínez López, and Mercedes Sastre García (2006). *Familia, infancia y privación social* (Madrid: Fundación FOESSA and Cáritas).

Ayllón, Sara (2015). *Childhood, Poverty and the Economic Crisis*, Social Studies Collection No. 40 (Barcelona: 'La Caixa' Foundation).

Ayllón, Sara and András Gábos (forthcoming 2017). 'The Interrelationships between the Europe 2020 Poverty and Social Exclusion Indicators'. *Social Indicators Research*. doi: 10.1007/s11205-015-1212-2.

Bandrés, Eduardo and Rosa González (2015). 'La reducción del gasto sanitario en España durante la crisis'. *Cuadernos de Información Económica*, no. 248.

Cantó, Olga (2014). 'El papel de las políticas públicas en la lucha contra la pobreza infantil'. *Panorama Social*, no. 20: pp. 89–103.

Cantó Sánchez, Olga and Luis Ayala Cañón (2014). *Políticas públicas para reducir la pobreza infantil en España: análisis de impacto* (Madrid: UNICEF Comité Español).

Cantó, Olga, Luis Ayala, Marta Adiego, Horacio Levy, and Milagros Paniagua (2014). 'Going Regional: The Effectiveness of Different Tax-benefit Policies in Combating Child Poverty in Spain'. In Gijs Dekkers, Marcia Keegan, and Cathal O'Donoghue (eds), *New Pathways in Microsimulation* (Farnham: Ashgate).

Förster, Michael and Gerlinde Verbist (2014). 'Prestaciones familiares, distribución de la renta y la pobreza: el impacto de las transferencias para niños pequeños en 23 países europeos'. *Panorama Social*, no. 20: pp. 105–19.

Gornick, Janet C. and Markus Jäntti (2012). 'Child Poverty in Cross-national Perspective: Lessons from the Luxembourg Income Study'. *Children and Youth Services Review 34*, no. 3: pp. 558–68.

Legido-Quigley, Helena, Laura Otero, Daniel la Parra, Carlos Alvarez-Dardet, Jose M. Martin-Moreno, and Martin McKee (2013). 'Will Austerity Cuts Dismantle the Spanish Healthcare System?' *British Medical Journal*, no. 346: f2363.

Lipscomb, Stephen (2007). 'Secondary School Extracurricular Involvement and Academic Achievement: A Fixed Effects Approach'. *Economics of Education Review 26*, no. 4: pp. 463–72.

López Laborda, Julio, Carmen Marín González, and Jorge Onrubia Fernández (2015). 'Evaluación de la Reforma del IRPF 2015–2016: Impacto Recaudatorio y Redistributivo'. Fedea Policy Papers, no. 2015/05.

Pfeifer, Christian and Thomas Cornelißen (2010). 'The Impact of Participation in Sports on Educational Attainment: New Evidence from Germany'. *Economics of Education Review 29*, no. 1: pp. 94–103.

Rees, Gwyther, Sabine Andresen, and Jonathan Bradshaw (2016). *Children's Views on Their Lives and Well-being in 16 Countries: A Report of the Children's Worlds Survey of Children Aged Eight Years Old, 2013–15* (York: Children's Worlds Project).

11

Sweden: Child Poverty during Two Recessions

Jan O. Jonsson and Carina Mood

11.1. INTRODUCTION

In 2008–2009, while some Western countries were plunged into one of the deepest recessions in living memory, Sweden hardly noticed. A temporary drop in gross domestic product (GDP) left almost no trace in the economy, in welfare policy, in overall poverty, or in income inequality (e.g. Fritzell et al., 2014; Björklund and Jäntti, 2012; Jonsson et al., 2016). As we will show in more detail in this chapter, child poverty—a crucial indicator of a society's reaction to economic crisis—remained at a historically low level. If anything, there were signs of improvement in children's conditions in the period 2008–2013.

The story of child poverty in Sweden over a slightly longer time perspective is, however, more dramatic. This is because Sweden experienced a depression in 1991–1993 that, both in scope and character, bore great similarities to the 'Great Recession' in the US and several other countries. Unemployment surged, and both poverty and social assistance benefits soared (Gustafsson et al., 2007; Jonsson et al., 2010; 2016). A closer look at child poverty during the 1990s crisis in Sweden is relevant for at least three reasons. First, it is a necessary backdrop to the more recent period, as the restructuring of the Swedish economy following the depression was one reason for the swift recuperation in 2009 (Hassler, 2010; OECD, 2011). Second, it illustrates what the long-term impact on child poverty of macroeconomic crises may look like, and therefore may hint at where child poverty is heading in countries that were badly affected in the 2008–2010 crisis (although other countries, of course, may follow different post-recession paths). Third, and perhaps most pertinent in relation to the theme of this book, the case of Sweden contributes to a general understanding of the poverty consequences of deep recessions, in conjunction with other case studies.

As an important complement to the favourable development of breadline poverty after the post-1990s crisis in Sweden, families with children experienced a long, relatively steady, but rather slow trend towards increasing relative child poverty, following a similarly long-standing increase in income inequality (Björklund and Jäntti, 2012; Jonsson et al., 2016). This is echoed in several comparable countries (Atkinson, 2013). This trend did not coincide with a macroeconomic downturn, however, and is more likely to have been a function of national economic policies of a structural kind, endorsed by different governments.

In this chapter, we study child poverty across both these recessions in Sweden, comparing their amplitudes and characteristics. We do this partly in the conventional way, by using family income as a source for calculating child poverty rates, and by using indicators of material deprivation. For the period from 2000 onward, we transcend these 'indirect' methods by studying trends in children's own economic resources and vulnerability, using child-reported indicators from surveys (Mood and Jonsson, 2015). This is crucial for our understanding of child poverty, because how children fare is dependent not only on the household economy but also on the distribution of resources within households, and on the economic activity of children themselves. In addition, reforms that are implemented in order to improve children's living conditions directly may benefit children—not least those of poor parents—without having any effect on household income or material resources. This means that changes in child poverty may remain undetected when measurements are constrained to the household level.

11.2. THE NATURE OF THE CRISES

The depression in the early 1990s in Sweden, following an economic boom of vast proportions, was probably a consequence of domestic economic-structural problems, such as high inflation and increasing real interest rates in an overheated economy, an underfinanced (but on the whole necessary) tax reform, a deregulation of the financial market, and some bad timing (see, for example, Swedish Government Bill 1997/98:1, App. 6 and references). Beginning in 1991, the economy crashed spectacularly, with a rise in unemployment from less than 2 per cent to more than 10 per cent in only around a year, following acute problems in the financial sector, rapidly falling real estate values, a spiral of declining demand and lay-offs, and a fruitless defence of the Swedish krona (SEK). Unemployment was partly a 'normal' recession response, and partly structural in the sense that many jobs were just abolished and never replaced. The increase in unemployment was followed by a period of various austerity measures, such as decreasing benefits, increased taxes, and a reduction in coverage of different insurances (Palme et al., 2002; Fritzell et al., 2014).

The result was a strong upsurge in poverty (Jonsson et al., 2010; 2016), which, however, lagged a few years behind unemployment, probably because people could live off their savings, and because unemployment benefits and other benefits and insurances worked as 'automatic stabilizers' that managed to keep those affected above the poverty line for some time. The adoption of austerity measures probably also contributed to the increase in poverty, as this was driven predominantly by increasing poverty among the non-employed (Jonsson et al., 2016). The lag meant that poverty peaked in 1996. Then followed a recovery of the Swedish economy, strongly aided by the boom at the beginning of the 2000s, with growing real incomes across the income distribution.

The most recent recession—which had such severe consequences in other countries—should be seen in light of the earlier one (OECD, 2011). The crash in 1991 was followed by a restructuring of the labour market, including the destruction of (mostly low-skilled) jobs, and a restructuring of economic policy, including strong non-inflationary financial goals supported by a stronger Swedish National Bank, as well as a generally liberalized economy with increasing emphasis on privatization and marketization of the public sector. The financial sector was also restructured, following a large-scale bailout by the state of unprofitable institutions. The post-recession period was characterized by financial stability and growing real incomes—but also by a lingering high unemployment rate of around 5–6 per cent, in a country that had been used to full employment for most of the post-war era.

When the 2008–9 recession hit the USA and several other countries, it had a momentaneous effect on the Swedish economy. There was a quite dramatic fall in GDP, mostly because of declining international demand (Björklund and Jäntti, 2012), followed by an almost immediate recovery. Non-employment rose temporarily, but did not contribute to increasing poverty overall. However, a limited and brief increase in poverty resulted from the growing vulnerability of the non-employed (Jonsson et al., 2016)—something that most likely stemmed from declining coverage of the unemployment and social benefit system.

11.3. CHILD POVERTY ACROSS THE CRISES

So, how did children fare during this period? As we have shown in previous publications (Jonsson et al., 2010; Mood and Jonsson, 2015), we are well advised to use multiple indicators of child poverty when studying change over time. The three most commonly used—material deprivation, relative poverty, and absolute income poverty—often show different trends. This is not unreasonable, because they capture somewhat different dimensions of poverty, although each can be considered theoretically sound. In addition, using indicators of family economy rather than direct measures of children's economic situation, can also give a different answer to questions of trends (Mood and Jonsson, 2015).

11.3.1. Trends in Poverty among Families with Children

Taking a multi-indicator approach, we start by showing different kinds of poverty indicators for the period 1980–2013/2014 (the last year for which we have comparable data). This period covers both of the recessions we focus on here, and also gives some perspective by including years of 'normal' economic growth as well as years of a booming economy. For some indicators, we can only use parts of this period, and some of the trends are a bit patchy—but overall, they tell a fairly consistent story about the development of child poverty during the last thirty-five years. (All data sources are further described in Appendix B.)

Figure 11.1, using Statistics Sweden's annual ULF survey (see Appendix B), reports the proportion of children who are in families: 1) that lack cash margin, i.e. are unable to meet larger unexpected expenses; 2) that worry about their economic situation; and 3) that have, during the preceding year, on some occasion been unable to meet the cost of rent, bills, or food. The picture is quite clear, in that child poverty, measured with these indicators, follows the economic recessions quite well, increasing dramatically in the early 1990s, peaking in 1996–1997, and decreasing for a relatively long period afterwards. The change during and after the 2008–2009 recession is slight, and at all events inconsistent (although Statistics Sweden discontinued some of the time series covering these years; in particular, poverty levels after 2008 cannot be compared to those before). Trends in child poverty by age are shown in Appendix A.

When we turn to family incomes—recalculated to show the proportion of children in poverty—we find much the same trend for absolute ('breadline') income poverty as for the material deprivation in Figure 11.1 (we use a standard Swedish definition of poverty: see Appendix C). Figure 11.2, which has to be restricted to the period beginning 1991 (and with no comparable data for 1992), reveals an increase in the early 1990s—becoming more rapid a couple of years after the crisis started (1994–1995 and 1995–1996)—and a peak in 1996. The trend in the receipt of social assistance—a good indicator of poverty in Sweden (Halleröd and Larsson, 2008)—is very similar, although more muted.

Figure 11.2 also shows relative income poverty (using both 50 per cent of the median and 60 per cent as cut-off points for defining poverty), and here we find very different trends. Child poverty, according to this measure, increased from the mid-1990s all the way up to 2012 (with some bumps).

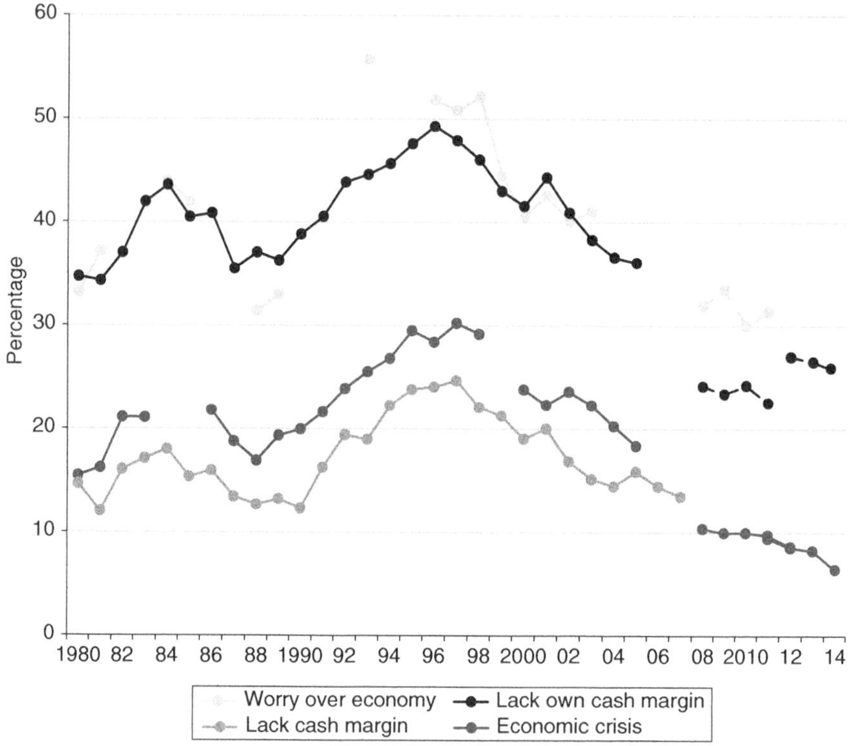

Figure 11.1. Percentage of children in poor families, defined as a) lacking cash margin entirely, b) lacking own cash margin, but can raise the money through loans, c) economic precariousness (inability to pay rent, etc.), and d) worried about the family economy, Sweden (1980–2014)

Source: ULF surveys, Statistics Sweden.

More detailed study demonstrates that this is because real income growth, which started at the beginning of the new millennium, was more pronounced for those on median incomes than for those with lower incomes (Jonsson et al., 2016). Because relative income poverty measures income inequality in the bottom half of the distribution, such a growing gap between the median and the lower income deciles inevitably leads to increasing relative poverty rates. It is important to relate this development to that of absolute poverty in Figure 11.2, which showed falling poverty rates during most of the post-2000 period—families with children experienced growing real incomes, resulting in decreasing absolute levels of poverty; but at the same time, more of them fell further behind the median income families. This may, at least in a longer time perspective, lead to increased relative deprivation among children from low-income backgrounds. Nevertheless, this development may be more

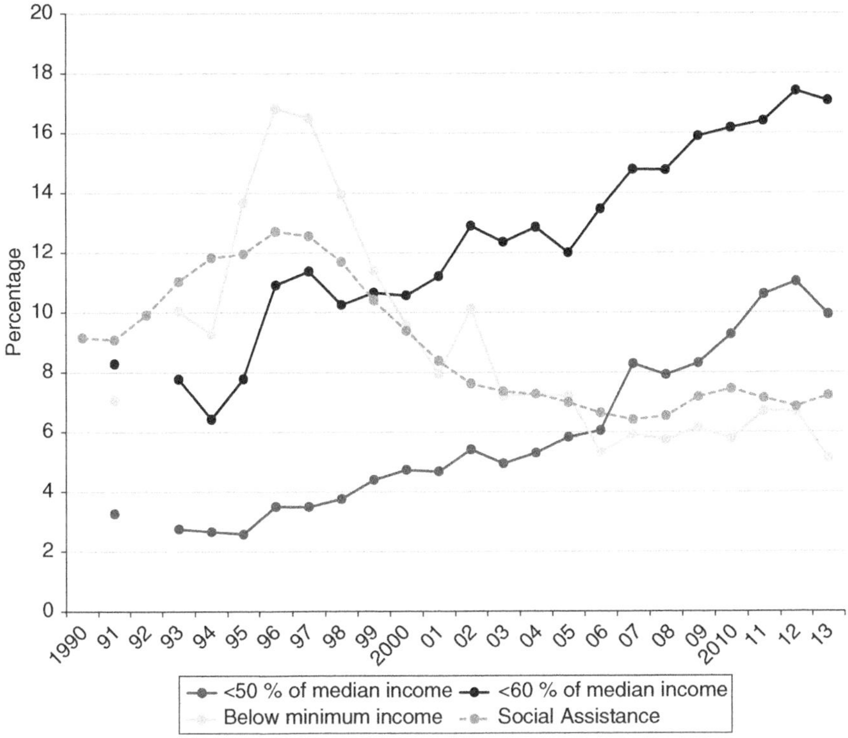

Figure 11.2. Percentage of children who are poor, measured as relative and absolute income poverty, and social assistance, respectively, Sweden (1990–2013)

Note: Data on income poverty cover children aged 0–19 who are living in parents' household; Data on social assistance cover children aged 0–17.

Source: HEK surveys, Statistics Sweden; Socialstyrelsen, based on population figures.

advantageous for children than one in which relative poverty decreased, but absolute poverty increased.

If we concentrate on the changes in the period following the 2008–2009 recession, it is clear that very little happened, as compared to the longer time perspective. The proportion of children below the absolute poverty line did not change at all, but there was an increase in social assistance, which subsequently receded between 2010 and 2012. These changes, it has to be said, were quite small, and the levels in the 'top year' of 2010 (7.4 per cent) were no different from those in the relatively good years of 2003–2004. Using a relative poverty line anchored in 2009, Försäkringskassan (2015) finds a small increase in poverty from 2009 to 2013.

Contrary to the other indicators, relative (non-anchored) income poverty increased slightly in 2009. However, it is difficult to believe that this was directly related to the recession, as these years fit in very well in the longer time trend evident from Figure 11.2 (and, in fact, several other year-on-year changes were more impressive than those that coincided with the recession).

Continuing with the searchlight on the 2008–2009 recession, we explore (in Figure 11.3) the EU Statistics on Income and Living Conditions (EU-SILC) data on economic deprivation for the period 2005–2014. Of the five indicators employed, only one shows an increase during this period: namely the proportion who say that they are unable to meet unexpected financial expenses (and this increase is due to an especially low value in 2010, which does not fit in with a recession narrative). The ability to pay for a week's annual holiday actually improved across the recession years (although this indicator is also dependent on exchange rates), and all other indicators remained stable. All in all, we can conclude that the changes in household-measured child poverty following the 2008–2009 recession in Sweden are scarcely visible, and in any case inconsistent.

The fact that we see no impact on deprivation arising from the most recent recession may have to do with its brevity: deprivation is more likely to be felt over longer spells of poverty. Long-term poverty increased markedly during the 1990s recession, but hardly at all during the 2008–2009 recession (Jonsson et al., 2016).

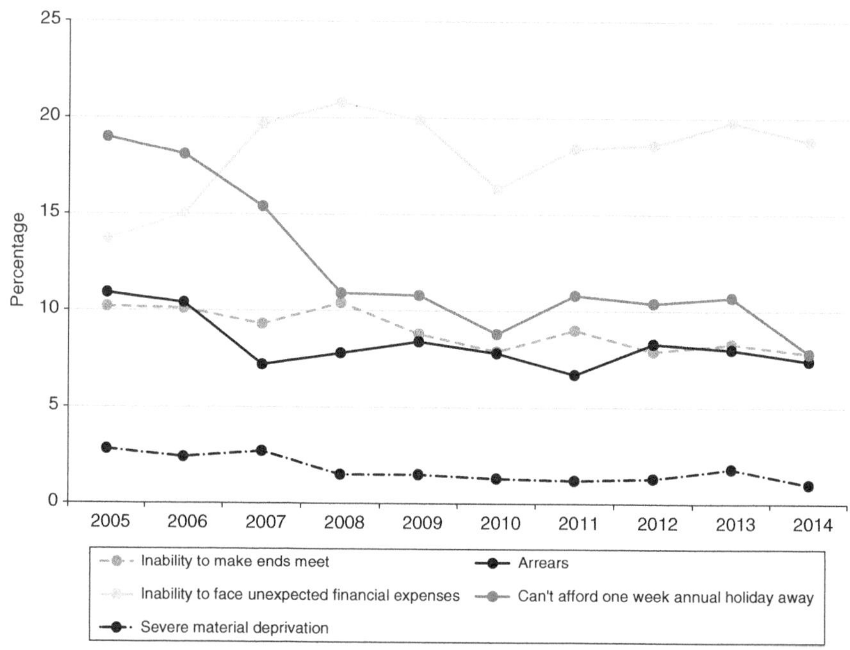

Figure 11.3. Percentage of households with dependent children that are economically deprived, Sweden (2005–2014)

Source: EU-SILC.

11.3.2. Trends in Child Poverty in Vulnerable Groups

It is common (seen in many countries) for child poverty to be high in certain vulnerable groups, such as lone parents and immigrants (Gornick and Jäntti, 2011; Smeeding et al., 2009; Eurostat, 2015). In Sweden, the main reason for this is that these groups are more likely to have a thin relation to the labour market, while few are 'working poor' (Mood and Jonsson, 2015). A large proportion of immigrants to Sweden come for humanitarian reasons (including family reunification), and therefore unemployment rates in this group are high, leading to a high risk of poverty, including persistent poverty (Mood, 2011; Gustafsson, 2013).

While it is rather unsurprising to find child poverty to be high in single-parent and immigrant families, an interesting question is whether these groups are also differently affected by economic downturns than more advantaged groups. A consistent and comprehensive vulnerability would suggest that poverty strikes faster and persists longer in these groups. Figures 11.4 and 11.5 test this by studying trends in absolute and relative income poverty among single and cohabiting (including married) parents with different immigrant statuses ('mixed' is a category with one native-born and one foreign-born parent).

Although the curves for foreign-born parents are shaky because of the small numbers, the trends we can discern mirror those we have seen above. For absolute poverty (Figure 11.4), there is a hump at the 1990s recession, when child poverty rates for both family types of foreign-born parents reached extreme levels—in 1996, half of all children of foreign-born parents, irrespective

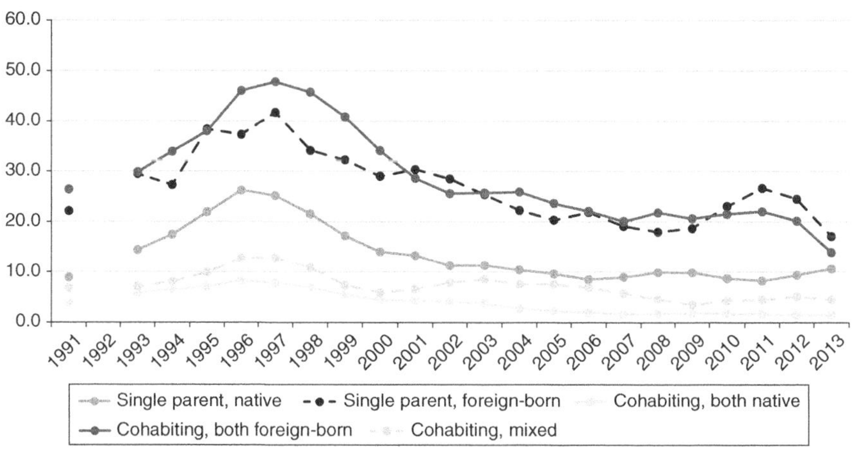

Figure 11.4. Percentage of children in absolute income poverty, Sweden (1991–2013), by immigrant status and family type

Note: Three-year moving averages.

Source: HEK.

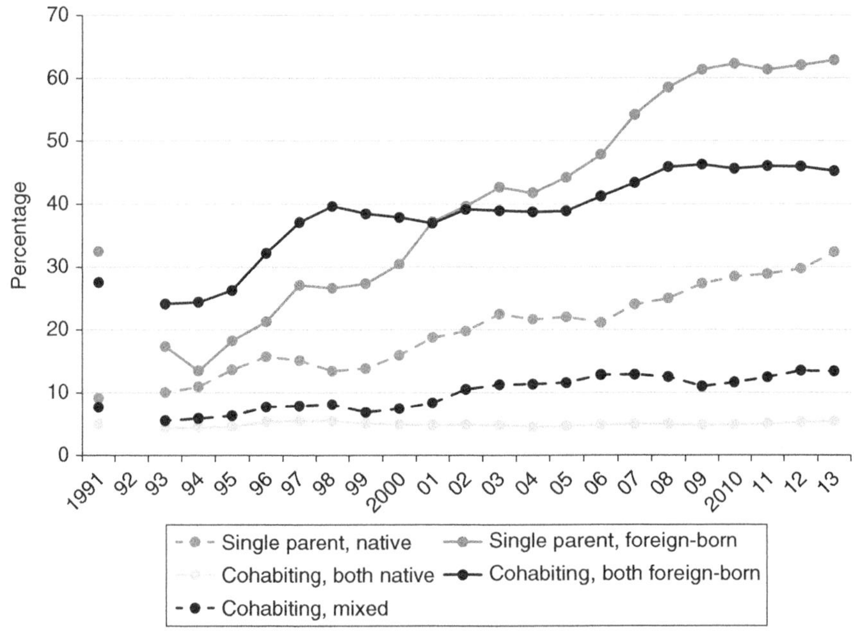

Figure 11.5. Percentage of children in relative income poverty, Sweden (1991–2013), by immigrant status and family type

Note: Three-year moving averages.

Source: HEK.

of family status, fell below the absolute poverty line. To some extent this is certainly to do with the big influx of refugees from Former Yugoslavia in 1993–1994, following the civil war, which coincided with the economic depression in Sweden. Also the children of native-born single parents reached high levels of poverty (around 30 per cent), and did not return to pre-recession levels for another five years. The increase among children of two native-born parents was subdued, but the 1996 level was still twice the level for 1991 or 2000.

The trends for the 2008–2009 recession do not reveal any general disadvantage for the children of lone or immigrant parents, although the children of lone immigrant parents saw small increases in poverty in 2010–2012. The small sample size for this group does, however, make this trend somewhat uncertain.

The trends for relative income poverty (Figure 11.5) show that the increase over much of the period we cover (and which was evident from Figure 11.2) falls on children of immigrant origin and—to a lesser extent—of single native-born parents. These trends reflect the fact that the increases in real incomes are driven by higher real earnings, and for immigrant and/or single parents earnings make up a smaller share of total incomes than among other groups. Increasing poverty among the children of immigrant origin is also expected, as the continuous high migrant inflow means that recent immigrants make up a larger fraction of this group. Most of these are refugees or humanitarian migrants (and their family members) who arrive with no knowledge of Swedish and who have low employment rates.

At the same time as the trends in absolute child poverty are overall quite favourable in Sweden, even for the most vulnerable groups, there is an emerging divide in the child population. At the advantaged end, the children of two native-born parents have experienced decreasing absolute poverty rates that are exceptionally low (since 2006 below 2 per cent), and they have persistently low relative poverty rates (around 5 per cent). At the other end, almost one child in five of foreign-born parents is below the absolute poverty line, and half are below the relative poverty line—and if they live with a single parent, the situation is even worse. How much of this divide in the child population trickles down to children themselves and becomes a source of everyday inequality? We will return to this important question with some surprising answers.

11.3.3. The Importance of Labour Market Attachment

As mentioned before, in Sweden there are few working poor, and it is also the case that part-time work has largely been replaced by full-time work, even among single parents; this is made possible by, among other things, a comprehensive and heavily subsidized day-care system. The importance of parental joblessness is illustrated in Figure 11.6 (absolute income poverty) and Figure 11.7 (relative income poverty), where we plot child poverty trends separately for employed and non-employed parents in different family types.

The difference between the groups is huge. Children whose parents are both non-employed (around 3 per cent of all children who live with two parents in 2013) have absolute poverty rates typically above 40 per cent, and the children of single parents with no job (around 25 per cent of all children who live with single parents in 2013) have rates that are normally 10 percentage points lower, while children whose parents are both employed (around 83 per cent of all children who live with two parents in 2013) almost never fall below the poverty line—since 2005, the figures have hovered between 0.5 per cent and 0.9 per cent. The trend has been downward for those with jobs, while for those without, poverty levels are sensitive to macroeconomic swings—the rise in the most recent recession illustrates that the (limited) poverty growth we registered then was due to increased poverty among the non-employed, rather than growing non-employment (Jonsson et al., 2016).

For relative income poverty, Figure 11.7 demonstrates that the long-term trend towards increasing income differences also in the bottom half of the income distribution has affected the children of non-employed parents particularly severely. Towards the end of the period, around nine children in ten

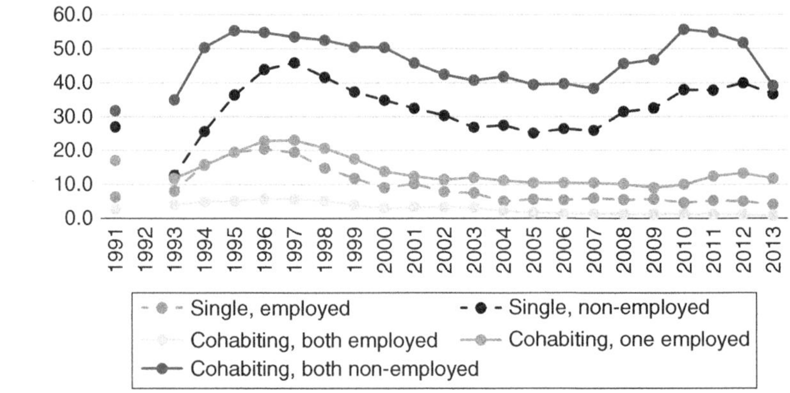

Figure 11.6. Percentage of children in absolute income poverty, Sweden (1991–2013), by employment status and family type

Note: Three-year moving averages.

Source: HEK.

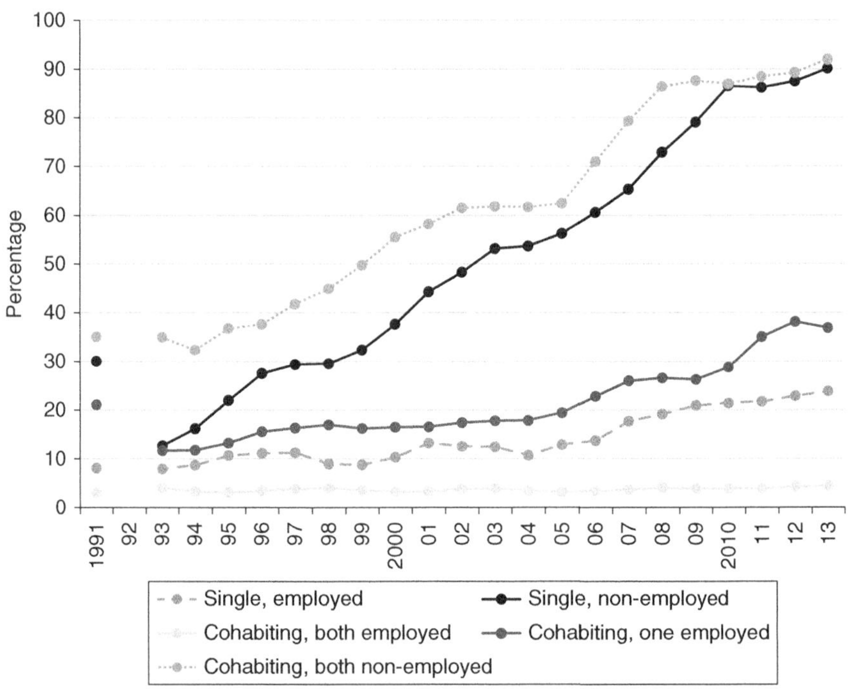

Figure 11.7. Percentage of children in relative income poverty, Sweden (1991–2013), by employment status and family type

Note: Three-year moving averages.

Source: HEK.

in this group (much the same whether the children have a single parent or two parents) fall below the relative poverty threshold. Non-employment cannot account for the entire upward trend, however, as the children of single parents who have jobs have also seen poverty rates increase—from around 10 per cent in 2004 to 20 per cent since around 2008. Earned income tax credits, introduced between 2007 and 2011, are likely to be one factor behind this trend, in combination with the declining real value of different benefits on which single parents rely more often (on average, 62 per cent of the disposable income of single-parent households (in 2013) stems from paid work, while the corresponding figure for two-parent households is 76 per cent) (Statistics Sweden, 2016).

11.3.4. Who are the Poor Children?

Turning the perspective around, we can also ask: of those who are poor, how many belong to specific vulnerable groups? This, of course, depends not only on these groups' risks of being poor, but also on their relative size in the population. In Figure 11.8, we can see that child poverty has become more concentrated on vulnerable groups over time, with increasing shares of foreign-born, non-employed, and single parents. Figure 11.8 shows the composition of those in absolute poverty, but the trend and levels are similar for relative poverty. In 2013, 74 per cent of poor children lived with at least one non-employed parent, 61 per cent lived with at least one foreign-born parent, and 44 per cent lived with a single parent (obviously, these groups also overlap, which cannot be seen from the graph). At the end of the observed period, around 85 per cent of children in poor families were in either a single-parent or an immigrant-parent household.

11.3.5. Trends in Child Poverty Measured by Children's Own Economy

When studying child poverty using family income or material deprivation, we make an assumption about the equal distribution of economic resources within families, and furthermore we assume that children's economy is only determined by parents. Both these assumptions are theoretically problematic, even though family resources naturally are crucial for children. But to take child poverty to the child level requires data reported about children directly, and preferably reported by children themselves. Following the strategy set out for the Swedish Child-LNU study in 2000 (Jonsson and Östberg, 2010),

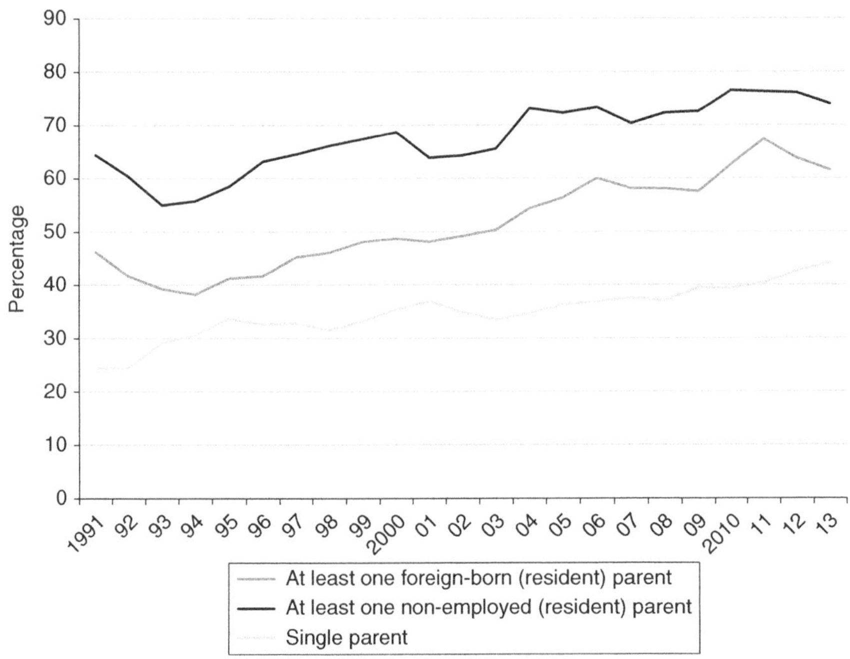

Figure 11.8. Composition of the group in absolute income poverty: proportion of all poor children who have 1) at least one foreign-born parent, 2) at least one non-employed parent, and 3) a single parent

Source: HEK.

Statistics Sweden started annual studies (Child ULF) of 10–18-year-olds in 2001, including some economic indicators (see Appendix B).

Figure 11.9 reports the proportion of children who say that they have their own room and their own TV, mobile phone, and computer. It also reports the proportion who responded 'often' to two questions about deprivation: whether they are unable to afford to buy things that their friends can buy, and whether they are unable to afford to take part in activities that their friends take part in. The proportion with their own room is quite stable, at 90–95 per cent, and the proportion with their own TV is also relatively stable, although there has been a slight decline since 2006. This decline co-occurs with a strong increase in the proportion with their own computer, and is probably more a reflection of technical development than of a worse economy, as computers are nowadays often used to watch movies and TV series. Similar evidence of technical development is provided by the increase in the proportion with their own mobile phone, going from just over 40 per cent to almost 100 per cent in just ten years.

The development of deprivation in terms of consumption and participation between 2002 and 2014 appears quite stable, or with perhaps a slight

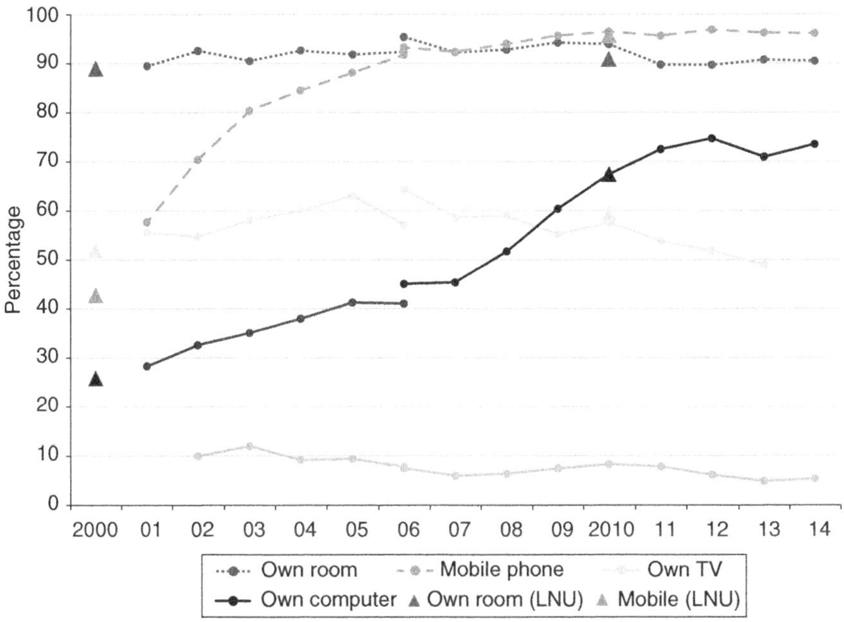

Figure 11.9. Percentage of children in Sweden with different material possessions, and in relative deprivation (self-reported)

Source: Child-ULF; Child-LNU.

improvement. It is interesting to note that this clashes with the increase in relative income poverty registered in Figure 11.2. This raises the question of the validity of the relative income measure, which also appears to be less predictive of social participation for adults (Mood and Jonsson, 2016). However, to evaluate this, we would probably need a longer time perspective—it is quite possible that the negative consequences of relative poverty need more time to take effect. Another possibility is that the reference group used by children is made up not of 'median kids', but of equally poor schoolmates or neighbours, which makes residential and school segregation a mitigating factor.

11.3.6. Child Poverty from the Children's Perspective: Does Parental Poverty Translate to Child Deprivation?

One reason that relative deprivation as experienced by children has not increased in spite of growing relative poverty may be that poorer parents allocate relatively more resources to children than do richer parents. It is therefore of interest to see how child deprivation varies with parental poverty. In Figure 11.10, we use matched parental and child data from the ULF survey

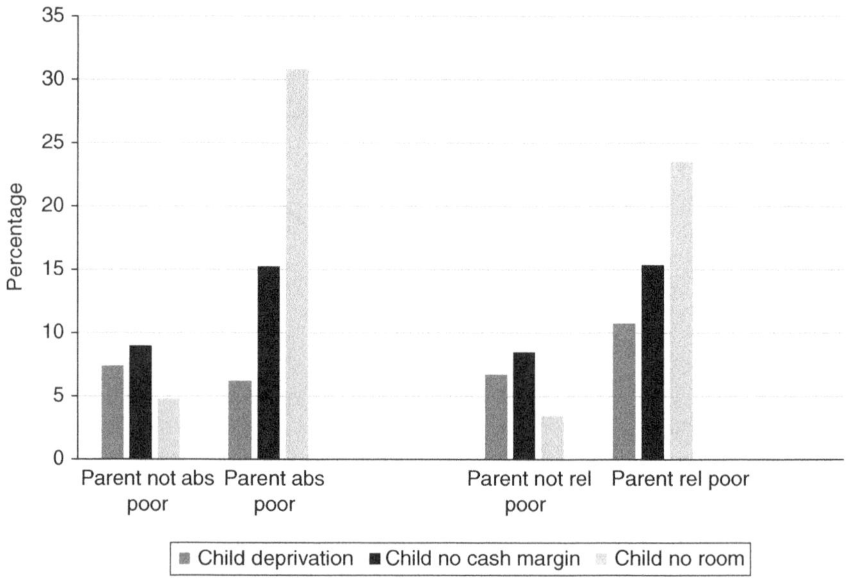

Figure 11.10. Percentage of materially deprived children in Sweden by parental absolute and relative income poverty

Source: ULF 2008–10.

2008–2010 (after which such matching is no longer possible) to study the association between parental poverty (absolute and relative, based on disposable family income and the same definition as above) and children's access to their own room, relative deprivation (having problems with both consumption and participation for economic reasons), and access to a cash margin (able to raise SEK 100/€11 by the following day, if needed).

Figure 11.10 shows that the children of poorer parents do indeed generally experience more deprivation than other children. In particular, 24–31 per cent of them lack their own room, whereas this is true of only 3–5 per cent of children of parents classified as non-poor. The mechanism is in this case quite clear: poorer parents tend to have smaller homes, largely because they are much more likely to live in apartments than in houses. Regardless of parental poverty status, the great majority of children do have access to a cash margin: only 8–9 per cent of children of non-poor parents lack this, and 15 per cent of children of poor parents. For relative child deprivation, the differences are very small; only in the case of household relative poverty is there any meaningful disadvantage experienced by children in poorer families. Overall, although there is an association between parental poverty and deprivation as experienced by the child, it is clear that this is far from a one-to-one relationship: most children of poor parents have a cash margin and can afford to consume and participate in activities on a par with their friends.

We have established that poverty risks are very high in immigrant and in single-parent families, when poverty is viewed from a household perspective. Is children's vulnerability also reflected in their own deprivation and everyday economy? In order to answer this question, we turn to data from the Swedish part of the Children of Immigrants Longitudinal Survey in Four European Countries (CILS4EU) project (Kalter et al., 2013), which is restricted to 14–15-year-olds but allows a more detailed look at child-reported deprivation by sub-groups, as it has a larger sample (N=5,025), with an oversampling of immigrant youth (see Appendix B). Design weights are used to allow generalization to the population of all 14–15-year-olds resident in Sweden in 2010–2011.

As expected, Figure 11.11 confirms that children in immigrant families lack their own room far more often than do 'majority' children: in single-parent families, 6 per cent of majority children lack their own room, compared to 22–25 per cent of children with an immigrant parent; and in two-parent families the difference is even larger, with 3 per cent of majority children lacking their own room, compared to 47 per cent of children who immigrated themselves (first-generation immigrant children). The situation appears to improve somewhat over time, because second-generation immigrant children (born in the host country to foreign-born parents) are less disadvantaged.

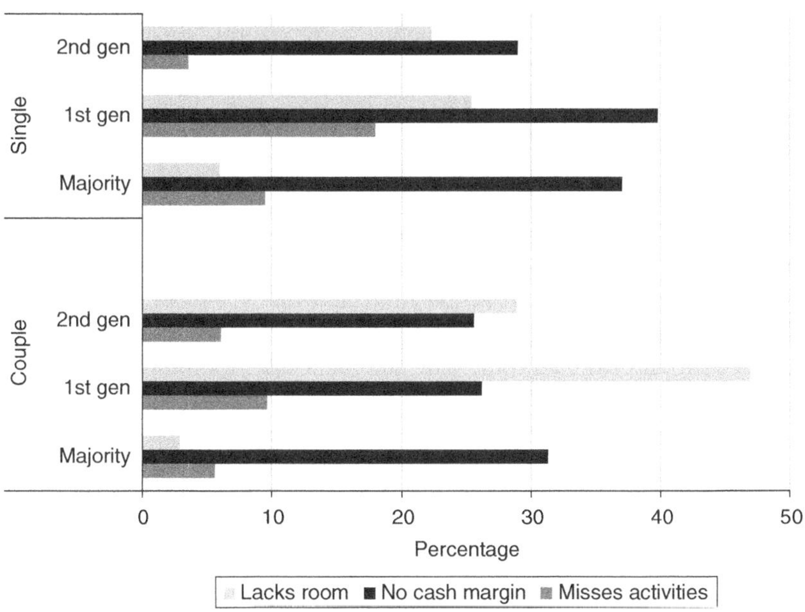

Figure 11.11. Child deprivation in Sweden, by parental family type and immigrant status

Source: CILS4EU Wave 1.

CILS4EU also asks about children's access to a cash margin, but to a larger amount (SEK 300/€33) than in the Child-ULF study referred to earlier, and in this case we see no systematic immigrant disadvantage. Supplementary analyses (not shown) suggest that immigrant parents actually tend to give their children larger amounts of spending money than do majority parents, despite their clearly worse family economy. Finally, there is also a question about missing out often on activities with friends because of a lack of money. Here we find a slight disadvantage for first-generation immigrant children, but no disadvantage for the second generation. As regards family type, the children of single parents have less access to a cash margin than do children in two-parent families, but deprivation in terms of lacking their own room is actually less common in immigrant single-parent families than in immigrant two-parent families, which probably reflects different family sizes.

11.4. POLICY AND POLITICAL DEBATE AROUND CHILD POVERTY

11.4.1. Responses, Retrenchments, and Reforms

The policy areas affecting children's economic situation are many and varied, from tax policy to school and social policy. Some reforms are directed towards children, and others affect them indirectly; furthermore some are responses to recessions and others are progressive, in the sense that the aim is to improve children's lives. We can distinguish between policies induced by austerity and those stemming rather from prosperity.

To start with some 'baseline', even at the beginning of the 1990s Swedish children had access to free schooling (including free cooked lunches, school nurses, and school psychologists), free dental care, and a universal child benefit amounting to around €80 per child per month, with an extra allowance for each additional child. Leisure-time activities were subsidized through economic support from both the state and the local communities for adult-led organizational activities (whether sport, cultural, political, or some other type), keeping the costs of membership and participation down for children (but with large variation across municipalities). For poorer families, the housing allowance, which helps with rents, was important; and for those below the poverty line social assistance would kick in—with the possibility of extra benefits for children's special needs. Parents could stay at home with their children for one and a half years on 80–100 per cent coverage of their salaries, up to a ceiling (which made losses for low-income earners less).

Following the deep recession in the first half of the 1990s, there was some retrenchment, both by the liberal–conservative government (1991–1994) and by the succeeding social democratic administration (1995–2006). Some concerned the household economy directly: unemployment and some other social benefits saw reduced replacement levels and decreased coverage (Regnér, 2000; Palme et al., 2002). At the same time, many public sector jobs were abolished. As a response to the fiscal crisis of the state, cutbacks in benefits were common across the Organization for Economic Co-operation and Development (OECD) bloc, and were actually more lenient in Sweden than in most other countries (Korpi and Palme, 2003). The more direct austerity measures for children included a reduction in child benefit (from SEK 750 to SEK 640/month) and the abolition of the extra child allowance for large families in 1996. In addition, there were cuts in the budgets for schooling and after-school care. Financial strain on the budgets of local municipalities furthermore had an (largely unknown) impact on the support for local organizations and their youth activities.

In 1998, when the economy recovered, the child benefits were restored and health care for those 0–18 was made free (in some regions this had been the case also earlier). Starting in 2002, there was a major reform making day care available for all children aged 1–6 at a heavily reduced cost, with at most three months waiting time. The maximum monthly fee was set at around €120 (similar to the child benefit) for the first child, and was reduced for the second and third child; day care was made free for the fourth child. Low-income earners, however, paid even less. A similarly generous scheme was introduced for after-school care. The child benefit was further increased in 2005, and in 2006 housing benefits were increased, and an extra child benefit for students with children was introduced.

The liberal–conservative government (2006–2014) continued the cuts in unemployment insurance benefits, as part of a general policy of promoting work rather than transfers or benefits: eligibility rules were tightened, fees were raised substantially, and replacement levels (as well as maximum benefit levels) were reduced, meaning that benefits lagged behind the increasing wage levels. Also the long-term ill saw a tightening of eligibility rules and reduced benefit levels. In addition, a five-step earned income tax reduction (introduced in 2007 to 2011) further increased the gap between those with and without employment. But the housing allowance was increased (2012 and 2014), and some earlier cuts to benefits were restored. Tax credits for cleaning services and construction work were introduced in 2008, increasing the demand for such services and hence potentially affecting employment levels. In 2014, a benefit (*Fritidspeng*) of SEK 3,000 (€310) per child per year for families on social assistance was introduced to promote poor children's participation in organized activities. This benefit was short-lived, however, as in 2015 it was abolished by the social democratic–green government (2014–).

This latest government has, however, implemented several reforms that are relevant to children (although none has yet made any imprint on our data).

Among these are free prescription drugs, free glasses for children, subsidies for holiday activities, and—on the household side—improved social and unemployment benefits, more generous benefits for those with long-term illness, and higher maintenance support for single parents. Social assistance benefit levels for families with children have also increased somewhat. The increase in unemployment benefits has been substantial and has made up for some of the cuts and the gradual erosion in benefit levels over the last two decades.

Overall, the (relative) poverty- and inequality-reducing impact of benefits and social insurances for families has decreased, at least since 1998 (the start year of the series; Försäkringskassan, 2015: 24, 47). The reduced impact holds for social insurance and universal benefits, as well as for means-tested benefits, but means-tested benefits have seen the largest reduction in impact, especially on relative poverty rates. This is as expected, because benefit levels have not increased at the same rate as earnings, and this is true in particular for means-tested benefits. Between 1998 and 2007, the impact of benefits and social insurance on the Gini coefficient more than halved; but since 2007, the impact on both inequality and relative poverty has been stable, in spite of rising rates of both (Försäkringskassan, 2015: 24, 47).

11.4.2. Discourse around Protecting Vulnerable Families/Children in the Policy Debate

In Sweden, child poverty has been high on the political agenda over the past five years. The rise in child poverty as a topic of political and media interest in Sweden is a fascinating example of how opinions can develop independently of actual conditions, and testifies to the power of today's large interest groups. In Figure 11.12 we see that the concept of 'child poverty' was hardly mentioned in the Swedish media during the deep recession of the 1990s, when poverty among children peaked at 17 per cent. In 2002, Swedish Save the Children published its first annual report on child poverty in Sweden, thereby establishing the concept (although it did not attract much interest until 2011). In 2011, studying the conditions until 2008, the organization could, for the first time, report an increase in child poverty, between 2007 and 2008. The increase was small (from 10.9 per cent to 11.5 per cent, defining poverty as having an income below the social assistance eligibility level or receiving social assistance) and the poverty level in 2008 was still lower than in 2006. It was also far lower than in 1991, before the recession. Nevertheless, the finding of an increase in child poverty was the cornerstone of a very efficient campaign, with the media and politicians from most parties uncritically accepting the picture of Sweden as a country with a large and growing problem of child poverty.

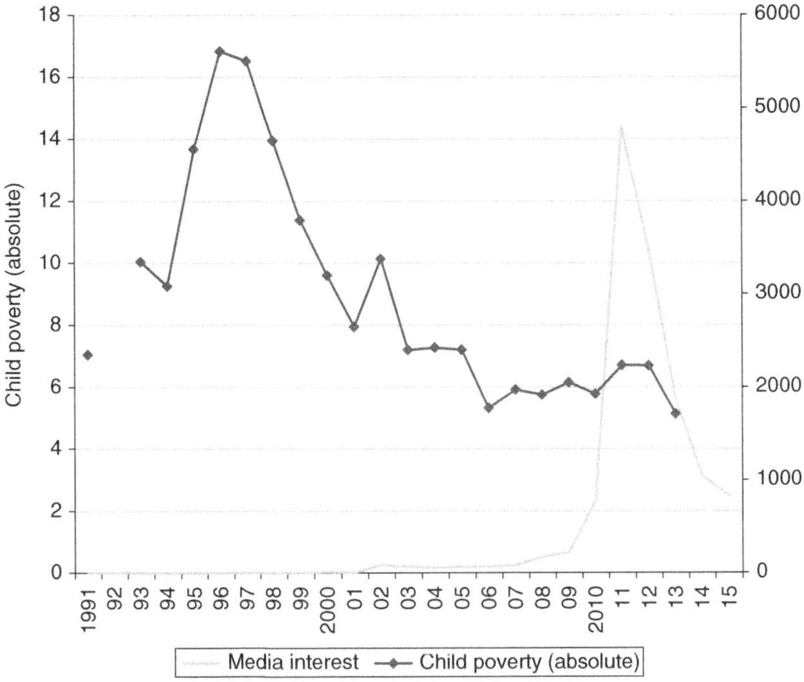

Figure 11.12. Instances of the term 'child poverty' (*Barnfattigdom/Barnfattigdomen*) in Swedish daily newspapers (1991–2015) and development of child poverty (absolute definition) in Sweden (1991–2013)

Sources: Media interest: Retriever Mediearkivet (25 December 2015); poverty: HEK, own calculations.

The campaigns evoked Dickensian images of material hardship, exemplifying child poverty with lack of warm shoes in winter, or with only being able to eat cooked food in school, and not being able to participate in school or out-of-school activities. Material deprivation of this kind is, however, extremely rare in Sweden, and in early 2013 the campaign suffered a backlash of criticism for exaggeration. Since then, interest has dampened somewhat, but child poverty is still frequently discussed, and the media are quick to pick up any news or claims on the topic.

The Swedish discourse on child poverty in the mass media and political debates can be characterized as a consensus that child poverty in Sweden is too high, with disagreement only on the emphasis on labour market solutions versus redistribution through benefits and social insurance as a means of solving the problem. Not surprisingly, the right-wing parties have emphasized labour market reforms, such as the introduction of tax credits on employment incomes in 2007, and the expansion of the low-skill, low-pay sector through tax credits on household work. The left-wing parties favour other labour market reforms, such as a right for part-time employees to work full time; but they are also more positive about redistribution as a means of combating child poverty. Insofar as moral arguments are ever raised, they are generally in terms of shaming other politicians or debaters for not doing or caring enough about child poverty. Behavioural arguments criticizing parents for lack of effort or responsibility are rare in the public debate.

There is still widespread acceptance, across the political spectrum, of the image that Sweden has a large group of children in severe material hardship, common examples being lack of food and warm clothes. This is surprising, given that in the latest measurement of child deprivation by EU-SILC (Eurostat, 2009), Sweden had the second-lowest child material deprivation rate of the twenty-eight countries in the study. For example, only around 0.1 per cent of children cannot afford to eat three meals a day, and 0.6 per cent report missing out on school activities for economic reasons. It seems that the very word poverty is stuck with connotations of severe material hardship, and it appears difficult for politicians and the public to accept a more nuanced view of what poverty can be in a wealthy society. One problem with this is that it is likely to lead politicians astray when it comes to suggesting reforms for improving the conditions of children who are economically the worst off.

11.5. CONCLUSIONS: IMPROVING OUTCOMES FOR CHILDREN

The recent Swedish macroeconomic history has brought two recessions: one that was extremely deep (around 1991–1996) and one more recent, which had a sudden impact on GDP in 2008–2009, but almost no repercussions for inequality (Björklund and Jäntti, 2012) or poverty (Jonsson et al., 2016). We have shown here that while absolute child poverty increased from 7 per cent to 17 per cent of children aged 0–18 between 1991 and 1996, the corresponding increase after the recent downturn was only from 6 per cent to 7 per cent between 2007 and 2011.

What lessons did we learn from the 1990s recession in Sweden? The 2–3 year lag with which the poverty levels increased following the macroeconomic crash suggests that automatic stabilizers, such as unemployment benefits, initially protected many from poverty. However, the severity and longevity of the recession eroded the economic buffers of families, as demonstrated by lagged effects on material deprivation. Our results for the 1990s indicate that even very comprehensive welfare state measures cannot cope with a sustained period of macroeconomic adversity. Moreover, they show that the recuperation could take time: it took around ten years for poverty rates to return to pre-recession levels, meaning that many experienced economic hardship during large stretches of their childhood.

Fortunes turned in Sweden, however. From around 2000 and onwards, real incomes increased across the board, and absolute poverty fell to levels even lower than before the 1990s recession. This is backed up by statistics on incomes, as well as on social assistance and material deprivation. We can say with some confidence that breadline child poverty is at a historical low, and that Swedish children have 'never had it so good' in a material sense.

At the same time, however, relative poverty has increased because of growing income inequality generally, including in the lower half of the income distribution. The last ten years have also seen a growing divide in the child population, with the children of two native-born parents having extremely low poverty risks, in contrast to the children of foreign-born and single parents. The notion of increasing relative poverty and a growing divide in the child population comes from our conventional analysis of the family economy (adjusted for household size and recalculated to per-child figures). This is of obvious importance to children, because parental income and material possessions are also shared by children—this goes especially for housing—and set limits on what can be transferred to children. But within these limits set by parental resources, the economy of children can and does vary a lot, and an analysis of child poverty should ideally also take this into account. We were able to use child-reported data to study trends in poverty and group differences in economic resources among children and adolescents, and the results are intriguing.

First, we find no trend towards increasing relative poverty between 2002 and 2014. Rather there is a weak trend in the opposite direction, which contrasts starkly with the development of relative poverty measured by household disposable income. Second, the emerging divide in poverty risks that stood out from our analysis of households, singling out the children of immigrants and lone parents as exceptionally vulnerable, appears to be much less profound in our analysis of adolescents' own resources. As far as we could measure economic resources at the child level, there were few clear group differences (access to one's own room is one, perhaps best described as located at the intersection between the household and the child level). It is likely that there are finer distinctions in consumption that we cannot cover (e.g. brands and models), but it appears plausible, given our data, that rather few children in vulnerable groups lack essential economic resources or lag far behind other children.

Why do we find results at the child level that do not correspond to what we find at the household level? Even if this probably has much to do with private redistribution within families, driven by an attempt by parents to compensate their children for the household's lack of resources, we believe that one can also invoke a welfare state explanation here. One reason why poorer parents can afford to support their children may be that such a large proportion of children's costs is covered by benefits, mostly in kind, but also supplemented by benefits in cash in terms of monthly child benefits. In Sweden, high-quality day care is affordable; cooked lunches are provided free of charge in day-care centres and schools; there are no direct costs of schooling at any level (except for course literature at the tertiary level); health-care is free up to the age of 18; and many leisure activities are subsidized, as is public transport.

Still, there are poor children who lag behind other children even in Sweden. Most serious studies suggest that the misery form of poverty—not being able to eat adequately, not having warm clothes or shoes, not being able to participate in school outings, etc.—is extremely rare, contrary to popular discourse and belief within political parties. In the EU-SILC study of child material deprivation (which unfortunately only contains parent-reported data), the proportion of children with unfulfilled basic needs barely exceeds 1 per cent in Sweden (Eurostat, 2009). The problem in countries like Sweden is rather with those children whose absolute standards of living are acceptable, but who lag behind others when it comes to consumption and participation. Such relative deprivation carries the risk of lowered self-esteem, shame, social rejection, and isolation—and, whether causal or not, these outcomes are indeed associated with both household poverty and a child's own poverty (Mood and Jonsson, 2015; Hjalmarsson and Mood, 2015; Plenty and Mood, 2016). We cannot rule out the possibility that the increased distance between the poor and median-income earners, in combination with stalling real income growth among the poorest, could mean that more children in the lowest-income families eventually lose ground when it comes to keeping up with their friends' consumption and more expensive habits.

How could child poverty be alleviated? We believe that the contours of child poverty in Sweden are such that the soup-kitchen type of response is not a viable strategy. Instead, it appears that lifting low-income groups to somewhat safer economic ground would have the potential of protecting economically disadvantaged children against social exclusion. Importantly, any reforms of this kind should in particular seek to target those at risk of long-term poverty. Most of those who become poor at any time recover swiftly, often without assistance and probably without any significant negative consequences. There is, however a group of persistently poor families (probably around 30–50 per cent of all poor families in a given year, cf. Jonsson et al., 2010; Mood and Jonsson, 2014; Mood, 2015) that is generally characterized by a very weak connection to the labour market.

More (reasonably paid) jobs for unemployed parents would obviously help many families, and so would reducing income inequality from the bottom. But while there is no inevitability in market income inequality, it is certainly difficult to reduce such inequality by policy, so that low earners can be lifted into the secure regions of the income distribution (cf. Atkinson, 2015, who shows that even with extremely radical, highly controversial, and entirely implausible policies, income inequality in the UK would not fall to current Swedish levels).

The poverty-reducing role of benefits and social insurances has decreased as their levels have lagged behind real earnings, and having a job has therefore become central to avoiding poverty. One straightforward way of shrinking the income gap between low and median earners would be to increase the levels and coverage of unemployment and sickness-related benefits. This would help the children of parents who are unemployed, on long-term sick leave, or who have been forced into early retirement. Although such reforms would help many vulnerable families, they would not be as efficient as before in targeting the most disadvantaged, because the composition of the group without work has changed over the past twenty years: it now contains a larger number who have not qualified for all social insurance benefits, as they have no (or only weak) connections to the labour market. Families in this group must rely on means-tested benefits, in particular social assistance, which is meant to be a short-term support; thus raised levels or a reformed structure of this kind of assistance have the potential to improve conditions for the poorest. Of course, the counter-argument is that raising any benefit levels will undermine incentives to work, and therefore prove counterproductive.

An alternative welfare state policy would be to raise the child benefit level. In Sweden, this benefit is universal, which means that it has relatively widespread support (Korpi and Palme, 1998); at the same time, it has the largest effect on the poorest. However, in order to make a real difference for this group, the total reform costs would be very high (Atkinson, 2015), and so the child benefit is a rather blunt instrument for alleviating child poverty.

Another possibility would be to focus not on the income of parents, but directly on children themselves. One principle could be to concentrate efforts on subsidizing those things that constitute the most tangible negative consequences of poverty for children. If we regard consumption and activities as the two major areas where poverty plays out (particularly for adolescents), then breaking down barriers in these areas should be a priority. However, it would seem that consumption is difficult to get at, as it is predominantly governed by the market, and the direct transfer of money is hardly possible to those who are not of age. Some things could be envisaged, perhaps, such as state, municipality, or school support for computers and Internet connections (in fact, most upper secondary pupils have their own computer at school, and via schools they are also connected to the Internet). The introduction of school uniforms—which is almost unthinkable in Sweden for historical and cultural reasons—would reduce costs for clothing.

All in all, it appears that one could be more optimistic about subsidizing children's *activities* rather than their consumption. For a long time in Sweden, both the state and the municipalities have provided economic support for clubs and organizations, based on membership and reported activities; as a consequence, membership fees have often been reduced to affordable levels. The generosity of this support does, however, vary across municipalities, and in many cases costs can still be a deterrent to participation. Of course, some activities also come with substantial equipment costs, and so free loans of equipment (e.g. musical instruments, skates, helmets) could also lower the economic threshold for participation. One benefit in this domain was the short-lived *fritidspeng* benefit, which explicitly targeted participation in activities (including membership and equipment) for children in families on social assistance. Another example is the new subsidy to municipalities that arrange free summer holiday activities for children (*sommarlovsstöd*). An additional way of supporting children's opportunities to take part in social activities would be to further subsidize public transportation, enabling them to attend activities and visit friends without having to depend on their parents' time and money. To avoid stigma, subsidies should either be universal (as is the case with *sommarlovsstöd*) or delivered in a way that does not disclose the subsidy to other participants or organizers (as was the case with *fritidspeng*).

As an important endnote, we want to emphasize the child perspective promoted in this chapter. If conventional poverty statistics are used as a guide, we become blind to many reforms that could make a big difference to the most vulnerable children. If only income-based poverty measures are used, any reform that targets the cost to families (e.g. provision of free prescription drugs and medical care) or that targets children directly (e.g. subsidized leisure and holiday activities) will not be identified as an improvement. In the worst case, improvements may even appear as an increase in poverty. This is the case, for example, with the poverty line used by Swedish Save the Children (which dominates the reporting in Sweden). It defines as poor those who are either below the social assistance eligibility limit or receive social assistance, meaning that more generous eligibility thresholds and social assistance benefits (as have just been introduced in 2016 to strengthen the economy of poor families) will lead to growing numbers of poor children, as more families become eligible. Only with a multidimensional approach to poverty that takes both families' and children's own conditions into account can we get a full understanding of what child poverty is and how best to combat it.

APPENDIX A: CHILD POVERTY BY AGE

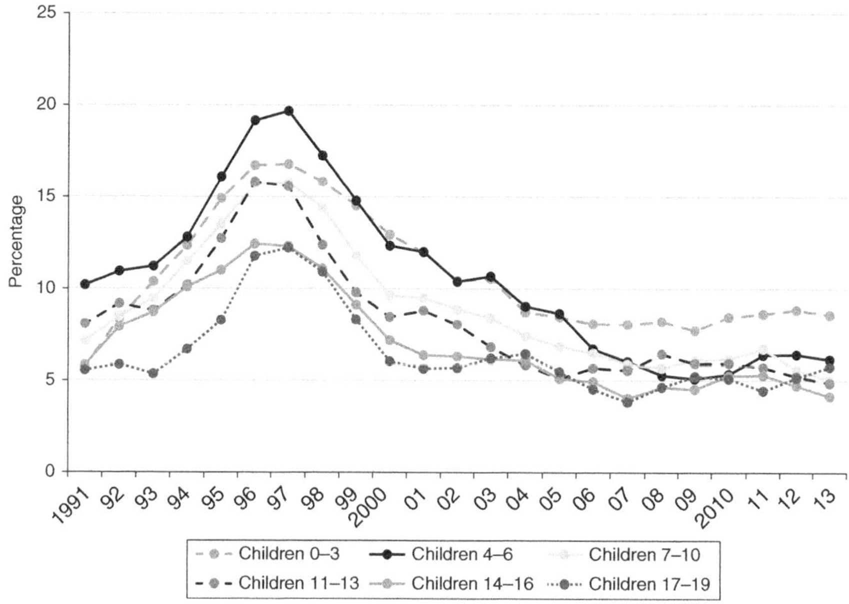

Figure 11.A1. Absolute poverty by child age (HEK), per cent

Note: Three-year moving average.

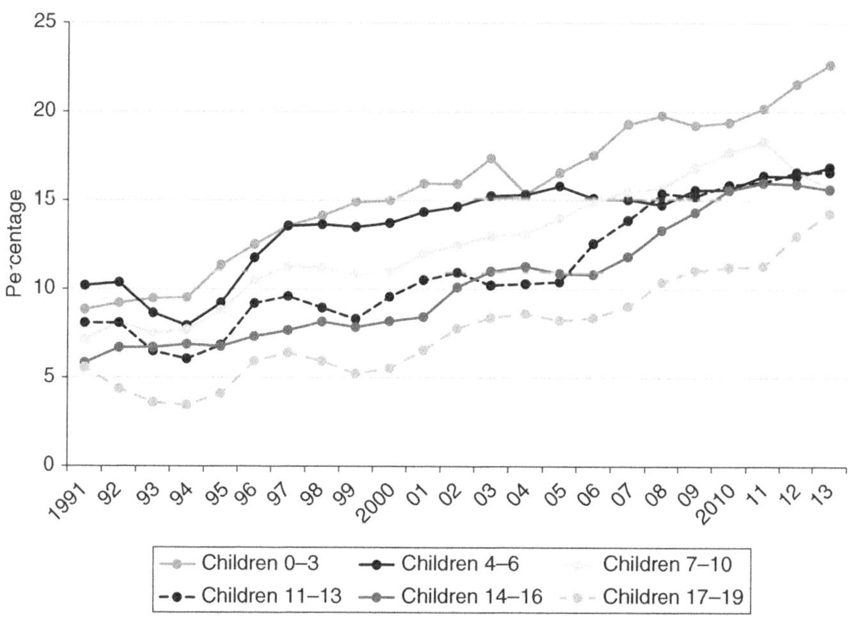

Figure 11.A2. Relative poverty by child age (HEK), per cent

Note: Three-year moving average.

APPENDIX B: DATA SOURCES

The following data sources are used in the analysis:

- **The Household Finances Survey** (HEK, Statistics Sweden) is an annual Swedish survey that has been running since 1975. The earliest comparable information in HEK pertains to 1993. However, in some cases, one can use a specially calculated value for 1991, and in these cases the value for 1992 is interpolated as the average of 1991 and 1993. Data are collected by phone interviews and cover, for example, household composition, housing, housing costs, childcare, employment, working time, occupation, and medical expenses.

The survey data are matched to register data on, for example, incomes, benefits, and taxes. The population consists of Swedish residents aged 18 years or over during the survey year, excluding people in institutions or in military service. Data are collected for the sampled persons and those in his/her household, and the sample size has varied between 10,000 and 19,000 households. The non-response rate has increased over time, reaching 35 per cent in 2010.

- **The income and taxation register** (IoT, Statistics Sweden) consists of register data on incomes, taxes, and benefits, and is available from 1968. In this report, IoT is the source of the income data in HEK, ULF/SILC, and LNU.
- **Living Conditions Survey** (ULF/SILC, Statistics Sweden) is a nationally representative survey that has been running since 1975, with an annual sample ranging between 6,000 and 8,000. ULF collects data on central components of welfare, such as health, economy, work, education, leisure activities, and safety. Non-response was between 20 per cent and 27 per cent between 1990 and 2008. Several changes in ULF took place in 2006–2008, affecting comparability over time. First, the data collection method changed from face-to-face interviews to phone interviews: until 2005, interviews were face to face; in 2006, 50 per cent of interviews were face to face and 50 per cent were by phone; and since 2007, all interviews have been conducted by phone. Another change was the integration with EU-SILC in 2008, which introduced new questions, and removed or revised several old questions.
- **Living Conditions Survey of Children** (Child-ULF, Statistics Sweden) is a survey covering children aged 10–18 whose parent has been interviewed in ULF/SILC (see above), with an annual sample of around 1,000 children. The survey started in 2001, using the same questions as Child-LNU (see below), but it was slightly modified in 2002. As in the ULF/SILC, the data collection method changed in 2005–2007; this affects comparability over time. Child-ULF contains self-reported data on children's health, school situation, leisure activities, and relations to friends, parents, teachers, and other adults. Data can be matched to parental data from ULF/SILC.
- **The Level-of-living Survey** (LNU, Swedish Institute for Social Research (SOFI), Stockholm University) is a panel survey that so far has been done in 1968, 1974, 1981, 1991, 2000, and 2010, with a sample that is representative of the adult Swedish population (approx. 5,000–6,000 respondents per survey). The face-

to-face interviews cover living conditions in a wide range of areas, including work, education, health, economy, leisure activities, housing, and political and civil participation. In 1991, the age span changed from 15–75 to 18–75. From the start, LNU has been a panel study, with replacement for young people and immigrants in order to make each cross-sectional survey representative of the Swedish population (each sample person represents 1/1000 of the population).

- **Child-LNU** (Swedish Institute for Social Research (SOFI), Stockholm University) is a survey that has been run in 2000 and 2010 covering children (10–18) whose parents were respondents in the LNU (see above). Children report on living conditions, such as housing, safety, social relations, school conditions, bullying, well-being, and economic and material resources. Sample size is approximately 1,000 per survey.
- **European Union Statistics on Income and Living Conditions (EU-SILC, Eurostat)** is an annual survey carried out since 2003 in the EU Member States. The 2010 survey included the twenty-seven member countries (Austria, Belgium, Bulgaria, Cyprus, Czech Republic, Denmark, Estonia, Finland, France, Germany, Greece, Hungary, Ireland, Italy, Latvia, Lithuania, Luxembourg, Malta, the Netherlands, Poland, Portugal, Romania, Slovakia, Slovenia, Spain, Sweden, and the United Kingdom), and also Croatia, Iceland, Norway, Switzerland, and Turkey. EU-SILC is representative of the population in each country and collects information on the respondents' social and economic situation, such as income, deprivation, social exclusion, and standard of living. The survey contains both cross-sectional and longitudinal data, and data are collected for individuals, but in some cases also for households. The Swedish data are collected by Statistics Sweden.
- **Children of Immigrants Longitudinal Survey in Four European countries** (CILS4EU, Mannheim Centre for European Social Research, Germany; Utrecht University and Tilburg University, Netherlands; Swedish Institute for Social Research (SOFI), Stockholm University, Sweden; Oxford University, England) is a longitudinal survey that started in 2010–2011 with approx. 19,000 14-year-olds in Sweden, England, Germany, and the Netherlands. The children are followed over time focusing on structural, social, and cultural integration during the formative teenage and young adult years. Data are collected on, for example, social relations, well-being, economy and work, education, leisure activities, attitudes, and religion, and the survey also collects data from teachers and parents. Schools with a high proportion of immigrants are oversampled, which makes the data particularly useful for analysing differences in child poverty between children of immigrants and children of majority country origin.

APPENDIX C: POVERTY AND ECONOMIC RESOURCES: VARIABLE DEFINITIONS

Household economic deprivation (ULF/LNU)

Indicator	Interview information
Lack cash margin by own means	Cannot raise a sum of money within a week through own assets or savings[a,b,c]
Lack cash margin entirely	As above, but cannot borrow money either[a]
Economic crisis	Has sometime during the last twelve months had a problem paying for food, rent, bills, etc.
Worried about the private economy	Often or sometimes worried about own or family economy

a. ULF 1980–2007. The sum required has been increased over time to compensate, approximately, for inflation: (1980–1981: SEK 5,000); (1982–1984: SEK 7,000); (1985–1987: SEK 8,000); (1988–1989: SEK 9,000); (1990–3: SEK 12,000); (1994–5: SEK 13,000); (1996–2003: SEK 14,000); (2004–7: SEK 15,000). In 2006, there was a methods change, from face to face to telephone, meaning that estimates for the pre- and post-2006 waves are not comparable.

b. LNU 2010: SEK 14,000.

c. ULF/SILC 2008–11: SEK 8,000; 2012–14: SEK 10,000. At the change from ULF to EU-SILC in 2008, both the sum and the formulation of the question changed, meaning that estimates up to 2007 and from and including 2008 are not comparable.

Household economic deprivation (EU-SILC)

Indicator	Interview information
Difficulty making ends meet	Difficulty or great difficulty in paying usual expenses
Afford to pay for holiday	Afford one week's annual holiday away from home
Afford unexpected expense	Ability to meet expense of 1/12 of 60 per cent of median
Arrears	Unable to pay rent, mortgage, utilities, or hire purchase on time due to financial difficulties during last twelve months
Material deprivation	Cannot finance at least three out of nine necessary consumer items or services (rent; heating; unexpected expense; eating meat, fish, or equal protein-based meal at least every second day; one week's vacation away; car; washing machine; TV; telephone)

Social assistance

Social assistance (SA) is a means-tested benefit given to those who lack sufficient income of their own to have an adequate living standard. The income limits for SA are set for different household types each calendar year by the government, and should reflect reasonable costs for food, clothes, shoes, household items, leisure activities/equipment, health, hygiene, newspaper, TV, and telephone. In addition, reasonable costs for housing insurance, electricity, travel, and union membership are judged for each household. Costs for special needs (e.g. dental care, glasses, childcare, and medicines) can also be covered. Our measure indicates whether or not the household has received SA some time during the year (irrespective of duration or sum).

Household income measures

The following measures are used:

- *Median income* is the income in the middle of the income distribution.
- *Disposable income* consists of income from work, capital, transfers, and benefits, while taxes are subtracted.
- *Equivalized disposable income* or *disposable income per consumption unit* adjusts the disposable income by an equivalence scale to reflect the needs as estimated by household size and composition. The equivalence scale used in the Household Finances Survey (HEK) is:

  1: one adult
  1.51: two adults
  0.52: first child 0–18
  0.42: later children 0–18
  0.60: children over 19 and other adults in the household

- *Real income*, reflecting purchasing power, is nominal income that is corrected for inflation (per consumer price index, CPI) in order to be comparable over time.

Household income poverty

Low income standard (absolute poverty)
The household's equivalized disposable income is below the threshold for low income standard. We use a CPI-adjusted standard developed to determine the levels of social assistance up until 1995, which was based on comprehensive calculations by the Swedish Consumer Agency. The standard is described in Jansson (2000) and is commonly used, as it is based on a rigorous assessment of living standards in different domains. A concern sometimes mentioned is that this measure may lose validity over time, such as when new 'socially necessary' products emerge (e.g. computers, tablets). However, when we replace this measure with more recent baskets, we get very similar results (primarily because basic consumption items constitute the bulk of all measures).

Relative poverty
The household's equivalized disposable income is below 60 per cent (or 50 per cent) of the median income in Sweden.

Children's economic deprivation (Child-ULF, Child-LNU)

Indicator	Information from interview
Material resources	Has the following: own room, own TV, own computer, own mobile phone
Cash margin	Can get SEK 100 (€9) (SEK 150 in Child-LNU 2010) by tomorrow, e.g. to go to the cinema, if needed
Participation	Could not afford to join friends for events, etc., several times during the last six months.
Consumption	Could not afford to buy things that s/he wanted, and that many of her/his age have, several times during the last six months

Children's deprivation (CILS4EU)

Indicator	Information from interview
Lacks room	Does not have own room in the primary home
Cash margin	Can get SEK 300 by the following day, if required
Miss activities	Often misses out on activities with friends due to a lack of money

REFERENCES

Atkinson, Anthony B. (2013). 'Reducing Income Inequality in Europe', *IZA Journal of European Labor Studies 2*, no. 12. doi:10.1186/2193-9012-2-12.

Atkinson, Anthony B. (2015). *Inequality: What Can be Done?* (Cambridge, MA: Harvard University Press).

Björklund, Anders and Markus Jäntti (2012). 'Country Case Study—Sweden'. In Stephen P. Jenkins, Andrea Brandolini, John Micklewright, and Brian Nolan (eds), *The Great Recession and the Distribution of Household Income* (Oxford: Oxford University Press).

Eurostat (2009). Statistics on Income and Living Conditions, Ad Hoc Module: Material Deprivation. <http://ec.europa.eu/eurostat/web/income-and-living-conditions/data/ad-hoc-modules>.

Eurostat (2015). 'At-risk-of Poverty Rate for Children by Country of Birth of Their Parents (Population Aged 0 to 17 Years) [ilc_li34]'. <http://appsso.eurostat.ec.europa.eu/nui/show.do?dataset=ilc_li34&lang=en>.

Försäkringskassan (2015). 'Barnhushållens ekonomi'. *Social Insurance Report 2015: 4* (Stockholm: Försäkringskassan).

Fritzell, Johan, Jennie Bacchus Hertzman, Olof Bäckman, Ida Borg, Tommy Ferrarini, and Kenneth Nelson (2014). 'Sweden: Increasing Income Inequalities and Changing Social Relations'. In Brian Nolan, Wiemer Salverda, Daniele Checchi, Ive Marx, Abigail McKnight, István György Tóth, and Herman van de Werfhorst (eds), *Changing Inequalities and Societal Impacts in Rich Countries: Thirty Countries' Experiences* (Oxford: Oxford University Press), ch. 27.

Gornick, Janet C. and Markus Jäntti (2011). 'Child Poverty in Comparative Perspective: Assessing the Role of Family Structure and Parental Education and Employment'. *LIS Working Paper No. 570* (Luxembourg: Cross-national Data Centre).

Gustafsson, Björn, Asghar Zaidi, and Eva Franzén (2007). 'Financial Poverty'. *International Journal of Social Welfare 16*, Supplement S1: pp. S67–S90.

Gustafsson, Björn (2013). 'Social Assistance among Immigrants and Natives in Sweden'. *International Journal of Manpower 34*, no. 2: pp. 126–41.

Halleröd, Björn and Daniel Larsson (2008). 'Poverty, Welfare Problems, and Social Exclusion'. *International Journal of Social Welfare 17*, no. 1: pp. 15–25.

Hassler, John (2010). 'Sweden in Past, Current and Future Economic Crises: A Report for the OECD Economics Department'. <http://hassler-j.iies.su.se/PAPERS/OECDSwedenAug2010.pdf>.

Hjalmarsson, Simon and Carina Mood (2015). 'Do Poorer Children Have Fewer Friends? The Role of Household and Child Economic Resources for Adolescent School-class friendships'. *Children and Youth Services Review 57*: pp. 201–11.

Jansson, Kjell (2000). 'Inkomstfördelningen under 1990-talet'. In Åke Bergmark (ed.), *Välfärd och försörjning*. SOU 2000:40. (Stockholm: Swedish Government).

Jonsson, Jan O., Carina Mood, and Erik Bihagen (2010). 'Fattigdomens förändring, utbredning och dynamik' [Poverty in Sweden: Trends, Scope, and Dynamics]. In *Social Rapport 2010* (Stockholm: Socialstyrelsen), ch. 3.

Jonsson, Jan O., Carina Mood, and Erik Bihagen (2016). 'Poverty Trends during Two Recessions and Two Recoveries: Lessons from Sweden 1991–2013'. *IZA Journal of European Labor Studies 5*, no. 3. doi: 10.1186/s40174-016-0051-8.

Jonsson, Jan O. and Viveca Östberg (2010). 'Studying Young People's Level of Living: The Swedish Child-LNU'. *Child Indicators Research 3*, no. 1: pp. 47–64.

Kalter, Frank, Anthony Heath, Miles Hewstone, Jan O. Jonsson, Matthijs Kalmijn, Irena Kogan, and Frank van Tubergen (2013). *The Children of Immigrants Longitudinal Survey in Four European Countries (CILS4EU): Motivation, Aims, and Design* (Mannheim: Universität Mannheim).

Korpi, Walter and Joakim Palme (1998). 'The Paradox of Redistribution and Strategies of Equality: Welfare State Institutions, Inequality, and Poverty in the Western Countries'. *American Sociological Review 63*, no. 5: pp. 661–87.

Korpi, Walter and Joakim Palme (2003). 'New Politics and Class Politics in the Context of Austerity and Globalization: Welfare State Regress in 18 Countries'. *American Political Science Review 97*, no. 3: pp. 425–46.

Mood, Carina (2011). 'Lagging Behind in Good Times: Immigrants and the Increased Dependence on Social Assistance in Sweden'. *International Journal of Social Welfare 20*, no. 1: pp. 55–65.

Mood, Carina (2015). 'The Not-very-rich and the Very Poor: Poverty Persistence and Poverty Concentration in Sweden'. *Journal of European Social Policy 25*, no. 3: pp. 316–30.

Mood, Carina and Jan O. Jonsson (2014). 'Poverty and Welfare among Children and Their Families 1968–2010'. *Research Report 2014/2* (Stockholm: Institute for Futures Studies).

Mood, Carina and Jan O. Jonsson (2015). 'Trends in Child Poverty in Sweden: Parental and Child Reports'. *Child Indicators Research 9*, no. 3: pp. 825–51.

Mood, Carina and Jan O. Jonsson (2016). 'The Social Consequences of Poverty: An Empirical Test on Longitudinal Data'. *Social Indicators Research 127*, no. 2: 633–52.

Organization for Economic Co-operation and Development (OECD) (2011). *OECD Economic Surveys: Sweden 2011* (Paris: OECD Publishing, 2011).

Palme, Joakim, Åke Bergmark, Olof Bäckman, Felipe Estrada, Johan Fritzell, Olle Lundberg, Ola Sjöberg, and Marta Szebehely (2002). 'Welfare Trends in Sweden: Balancing the Books for the 1990s'. *Journal of European Social Policy 12*, no. 4: pp. 329–46.

Plenty, Stephanie and Carina Mood (2016). 'Money, Peers and Parents: Social and Economic Aspects of Inequality in Youth Wellbeing'. *Journal of Youth and Adolescence 45*, no. 7: pp. 1294–1308.

Regnér, Håkan (2000). 'Ändrade förutsättningar för arbetsmarknadspolitiken?'. In Johan Fritzell (ed.), *Välfärdens förutsättningar: Arbetsmarknad, demografi och segregation*. SOU 2000:37 (Stockholm: Swedish Government).

Smeeding, Timothy M., Coady Wing, and Karen Robson (2009). 'Differences in Social Transfer Support and Poverty for Immigrant Families with Children: Lessons from the LIS'. In Elena L. Grigorenko and Ruby Takanishi (eds), *Immigration, Diversity, and Education* (London: Routledge).

Statistics Sweden. Table HE0103CC. 2016. http://www.statistikdatabasen.scb.se

Swedish Government Bill (Proposition) 1997/98:1, Appendix 6. '1990-91 års skattereform—en värdering'.

12

Impact of the Recession on Children in the United Kingdom

Jonathan Bradshaw, Yekaterina Chzhen, and Gill Main

12.1. INTRODUCTION

The global financial crisis hit the UK in 2007–8. The incumbent Labour government, led by Gordon Brown from 2007, responded with anti-cyclical policies intended to buoy up the economy and create jobs. However, in the general election of 2010, Labour lost its majority and a Coalition government comprising the Conservatives and the Liberal Democrats was formed. More recently, the 2015 general election saw the Conservatives elected with a small majority. Under the Coalition and now the Conservative governments, Labour spending has been blamed for creating not only a 'debt crisis' (Sparrow and Mulholland, 2010), but also a social protection system which 'trapped people in poverty and encouraged irresponsibility' (Cameron, 2012). The response to the crisis under the Coalition and Conservative governments has comprised austerity measures, largely achieved through cuts in public spending, which were positioned as necessary measures to redress national debt (Cameron, 2009). Thus the Conservative response was simultaneously presented as a painful political necessity that would nonetheless bear long-term gains, and as an ideological rejection of social protection, which was portrayed as resulting in irresponsible behaviours on the part of the poor.

Child poverty has been the focus of considerable policy and academic attention in the UK in recent decades. As such, it provides a valuable lens through which the impact of the crisis on children can be assessed. This chapter will provide background information on child poverty trends in the UK prior to the financial crisis. Trends in child poverty throughout the crisis will be examined. This will be linked to an analysis of the development of policy in line with the dual focus—on the perceived need for austerity and for a cultural shift in how social security is administered—as exhibited in Coalition and

Conservative policy and rhetoric. The development of policy responses will be examined in conjunction with an exploration of policy and popular rhetoric. Transmission mechanisms—that is, the methods by which policy changes may (or may not) have impacted child poverty rates—will be suggested. Finally, we draw conclusions about the likely future impacts of Conservative proposals on child poverty.

12.2. FINANCIAL AND ECONOMIC CRISIS

The UK enjoyed stable economic growth and low levels of unemployment between the end of the last recession in the early 1990s (when economic output contracted by 2 per cent over five successive quarters) and the outbreak of the global financial crisis in 2008. Over the period 2000–7, UK economic growth outpaced that of the EU-15, and both the total and the youth unemployment rates were below the EU-15 average.[1] Social protection spending remained stable, and family-related benefits increased somewhat as a share of total social protection expenditure, while public debt and deficit were kept in check, although not eliminated during the 'boom' years. However, as housing-related industries (construction, real estate, and finance) represented an increasing share of the economy, the UK was highly exposed to volatility in the global financial markets.

British banks invested heavily in the US housing market, so the first signs of a financial crisis surfaced as soon as the US mortgage-related securities were downgraded. Northern Rock, Britain's fifth-largest mortgage lender at the time, was the first to face problems of liquidity, in autumn 2007. It suffered a bank run, as investors began to withdraw their deposits, alarmed by rumours that the bank was at risk of collapse. Northern Rock turned for help to the government—which, having failed to find a buyer, nationalized the bank. A year later, several larger banks also ran out of money and were nationalized. Although the government ostensibly saved the banking system, banks limited their lending to the public, depressing housing demand, construction, manufacturing, and general levels of investment. Thus the UK financial sector both triggered and transmitted the economic crisis (Hills et al., 2010).

The UK fell into its deepest recession of the post-war period, as the financial crisis spilled over into the mainstream economy. Global output plunged at the same time, depressing demand for British exports in spite of sterling's depreciation, while the price of imports rose. UK economic output fell for five

[1] Unless otherwise indicated, all macroeconomic statistics cited in this section come from the UK Office for National Statistics. Direct comparisons with other EU countries are based on data from Eurostat.

consecutive quarters between Q1 2008 and Q3 2009, shrinking by more than 6 per cent in real terms. The main initial impact of the recession was felt in increased unemployment: working-age unemployment (16 and over) rose from 5.2 per cent in Q4 2007 to 7.9 per cent in Q4 2009, while youth unemployment (16–24) climbed from 13 per cent to 18.4 per cent. Economic productivity plummeted, with output per hour worked decreasing by 2.5 per cent over this period, while average earnings growth decreased from 4.4 per cent to 1.1 per cent.

The Labour government stepped in with radically anti-cyclical measures to limit the negative impact of the crisis on households and to jump-start the economy. In March 2009, the Bank of England slashed its interest rate to almost zero and started injecting £200 billion of newly created money into the economy through 'quantitative easing'. A host of fiscal and labour market measures were implemented, including the early uprating of benefits and an increase in the tax rate on higher incomes. There were no substantial cuts in benefits and services—in fact expenditure was sustained, while revenue fell. Having also bailed out the banks, the government increased its borrowing. Total net public debt ballooned from 36 per cent of gross domestic product (GDP) in Q4 2007 to 145 per cent of GDP in Q4 2008.

Although the UK economy avoided a double-dip recession, largely thanks to a timely and sustained government intervention during the crisis, real GDP did not recover to its pre-recession level of Q1 2008 until Q3 2013. Even as the recession was officially over in late 2009, the working-age and youth unemployment rates kept on rising until Q3 2011 and did not come down to their pre-recession levels until 2015. Meanwhile, real average earnings continued falling and are still (early 2016) below their pre-recession level after six years of economic growth. The prices of essentials—food, fuel, and private rents—have been increasing more rapidly than general inflation. The share of households with dependent children reporting difficulty in facing unexpected financial expenses increased from 32.4 per cent in 2008 to 42 per cent in 2010.[2] In a vicious circle of slow economic growth and stagnating disposable incomes, household spending remained weak in 2010–11, putting a brake on the pace of economic recovery.

Moreover, as the Conservative–Liberal Democrat (Coalition) government came to power after the 2010 general election, the country made a sharp turn from fiscal stimulus to austerity. Family-related benefits were some of the first to be cut in real terms. Thus, the economic crisis and the ensuing austerity affected households with children through several channels between 2008 and 2015. During the 2008–9 recession, rising unemployment and falling real earnings reduced households' ability to save and spend. Although the cut in

[2] Based on data from the EU-SILC reported by Eurostat (ilc_mdes04; last update on 15 March 2016).

the interest rate helped households with variable-rate mortgages, it did nothing to offset rising housing-related costs for renters and outright owners (Kamath et al., 2011). From 2010 onwards, cuts in benefits and services, as well as a rise in value added tax (VAT), put pressure on household finances, even as the economy was officially on the mend.

12.3. HOW DID CHILDREN FARE DURING THE CRISIS?

Analysis in this section is based on data from repeated cross-sections of the Family Resources Survey (FRS). This is a large, continuous, nationally representative household survey that collects information on the income and living conditions of private households in the UK. The FRS provides cross-sectional data for the EU Statistics on Income and Living Conditions (EU-SILC) from 2012 only, and so there are differences in the types of household variables available in the EU-SILC and earlier waves of the FRS.[3] For consistency with the official UK poverty statistics, but in a slight break from the rest of the chapters in this volume, we use 'dependent children' as units of analysis: those who are aged 16 or under, or who are 16–19 and are both unmarried and in full-time non-advanced education. The rest of the chapters define children as those under 18.

This section first describes long-term trends in child poverty rates and official targets before the financial crisis, and then investigates changes in the child poverty rates, risks, and composition between 2007–8 and 2013–14, the latest year for which comparable data are available at the time of writing.

12.3.1. Child Poverty in the UK before the Financial Crisis

Prime Minister Tony Blair's commitment in 1999 to eradicate child poverty by 2020 came two years after Labour achieved power in its landslide victory of 1997. The preceding Conservative governments had overseen a sharp rise in child poverty levels (Figure 12.1). In 1995–6, just prior to the Labour landslide, poverty rates among children in Great Britain, based on those living in households with an equivalized income below 60 per cent of the national median, had reached 25 per cent before housing costs (BHC) and 33 per cent after housing costs (AHC). These figures represented more than a doubling of the poverty rate since the Conservative victory of 1979, when child poverty rates stood at 13 per cent (BHC) and 14 per cent (AHC).

[3] For example, there is no information on migrant status or household work intensity (Eurostat definition) in the earlier FRS surveys.

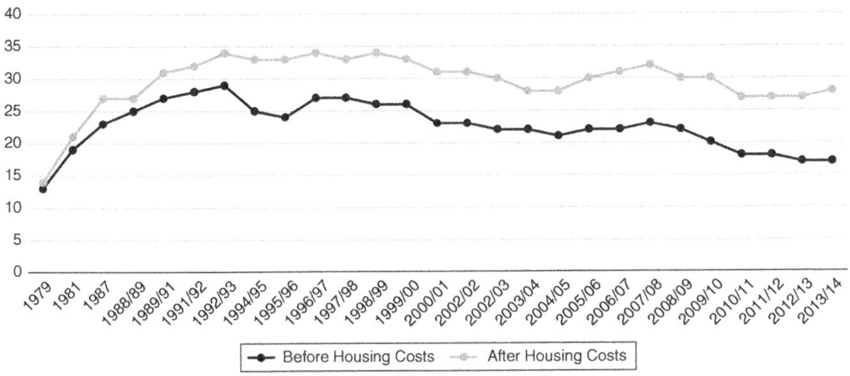

Figure 12.1. UK child poverty rate—below 60 per cent of the contemporary median (1979–2013/2014), per cent

Source: Department for Work and Pensions (2015: Table 4.1tr).

The Labour government invested heavily in anti-poverty policies to make progress towards eradicating child poverty by 2020. In addition to the introduction of a minimum wage, there were real improvements in child benefits and social assistance, and the introduction of tax credits. Spending on education, health, and childcare increased. There was also an institutional transformation in favour of children, culminating in the Child Poverty Act 2010, which established both clear targets and a Child Poverty and Social Mobility Commission (now to be changed to the Social Mobility Commission) to monitor progress. Meanwhile, the employment rate of men and women increased to record levels in the post-war period. As a result, the child poverty rate began to fall (Figure 12.1) and, on most indicators, child well-being improved (Bradshaw, 2011). According to internationally comparable estimates from the Luxembourg Income Study, the UK had by far the largest reduction in child poverty—of 11 percentage points—of any country in the Organization for Economic Co-operation and Development (OECD) between the mid-1990s and 2010.

12.3.2. Child Poverty in the UK after the Financial Crisis

The deep recession of 2008–9 did not translate into a rise in child poverty rates. Relative child poverty, based on 60 per cent of contemporary national median income (BHC), continued falling between 2007 and 2010. This is in part the result of median incomes—and therefore the poverty thresholds—falling during this period. However, it also shows that the fiscal stimulus in place at that time cushioned the impact of the economic crisis on households with children. Anchoring the poverty line at the start of the recession in 2007 and inflating it with retail price growth helps compare like with like by holding the poverty threshold constant in real terms. Anchored child poverty fell between 2007 and 2009, flat-lined for a year, increased by 2 percentage points between 2010 and 2011, and flat-lined again (Figure 12.2). As the recession was officially over and austerity measures started coming into force, progress in reducing relative child poverty stalled.

Average child poverty rates hide substantial variation by household characteristics. Table 12.1 disaggregates the rates of child poverty in 2007/8 and 2013/14 (using both a 'floating' and an anchored poverty line) by family type, household work status, number of dependent children in the household (one or two vs three or more), age of the youngest child, ethnicity of the household head, number of adults above pension age in the household, dependency ratio (the share of children and pensioners in the household), and government office region. Table 12.2 shows the composition of all children and poor children in the two periods, by household characteristics.

The relative child poverty rate decreased faster for lone parent than for couple families between 2007–8 and 2013–14, albeit from a much higher base (Table 12.1). The share of children in all income-poor, lone-parent families decreased by 11 percentage points—from 38 per cent to 27 per cent (Table 12.2). Most of this decline took place among those who are not in work, while the share of children in working-poor, lone-parent families increased. Couple families where no one works full time, as well as workless families, saw greater declines in child poverty than did families where both parents work full time. However, decreases in child poverty are smaller in

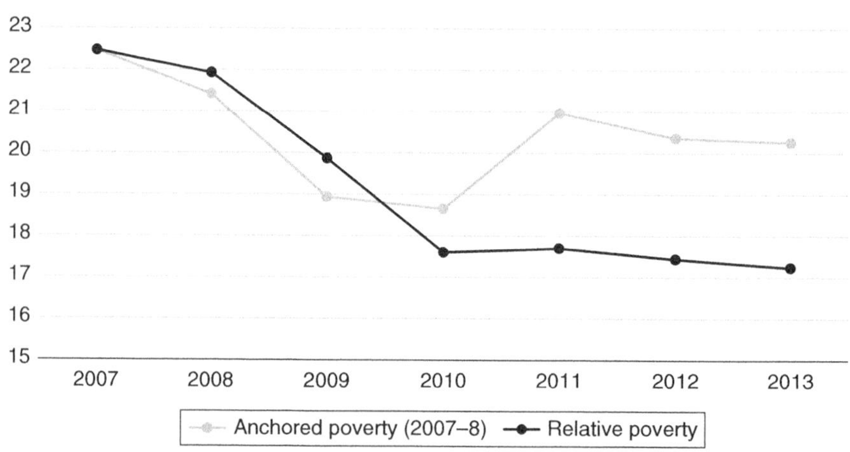

Figure 12.2. UK child poverty rate—below 60 per cent of the BHC median (2007/2008–2013/2014), per cent

Source: Authors' calculations using Family Resources Survey. Anchored poverty line uprated with the retail prices index.

Table 12.1. Percentage of children living in households in the UK with less than 60 per cent of median household income before housing costs, by family and household characteristics

	2007/8	2013/14	2013/14 anchored in 2007/8
At least one adult in the family in work	14.6	13.1	15.3
Workless family	58.2	37.0	44.1
Lone parent	35.8	19.0	23.3
In full-time work	10.6	9.2	10.5
In part-time work	24.2	16.0	18.3
Not working	54.4	26.6	34.0
Couple with children	18.2	16.2	18.8
Both in full-time work	3.6	2.9	3.8
One in full-time work, one in part-time work	4.0	4.8	5.9
One in full-time work, one not working	21.2	20.4	24.9
One or more in part-time work	56.3	41.2	46.3
Self-employed	23.8	22.7	25.1
Both not in work	65.5	55.8	62.7
One or two dependent children	18.2	15.3	17.8
Three or more dependent children	32.8	21.7	26.1
Age of the youngest child in the household			
0–5	25.1	17.0	20.7
6–11	20.3	16.1	18.5
12–19	19.7	18.3	20.5
White household head	19.8	15.2	18.2
Non-white household head	37.7	26.7	29.8
No pensioners in the household	22.2	16.9	19.9
One or more pensioners in the household	33.7	24.0	25.5
Dependency ratio 0.5 or below	16.4	15.0	17.3
Dependency ratio greater than 0.5	33.0	20.8	25.1
Government office region			
England	22.4	16.9	19.7
Wales	28.6	20.4	25.2
Scotland	19.5	14.1	16.8
Northern Ireland	23.1	23.0	27.0
All dependent children	*22.5*	*17.0*	*20.0*
N	7,527	6,142	6,142

Source: Authors' calculations using Family Resources Survey 2007–8 and 2013–14. Anchored poverty rates are calculated using the 2007–8 poverty line uprated with the retail price index. Dependent children grossing factor used.

magnitude if the same poverty line is used in both years, adjusted for inflation only. In fact, anchored child poverty increased for couple families that are either self-employed or have one person in full-time work, while the other either does not work or works part time.

Child poverty in households with three or more children declined using either poverty line, while the child poverty rate in smaller families remained stable (Table 12.1). The share of poor children in small families increased, but

Table 12.2. Composition of children living in households in the UK with less than 60 per cent of median household income before housing costs, by family and household characteristics (per cent)

	All 2007/8	Poor 2007/8	All 2013/14	Poor 2013/14	Poor (anchored) 2013/14
At least one adult in the family in work	82.0	53.4	83.7	64.5	64.1
Workless family	18.0	46.6	16.3	35.5	35.9
Lone parent	23.6	37.8	23.7	26.7	27.7
In full-time work	24.5	7.3	25.2	12.1	11.3
In part-time work	26.1	17.6	30.0	25.2	23.4
Not working	49.4	75.1	44.8	62.6	65.2
Couple with children	76.4	62.2	76.3	73.3	72.3
Both in full-time work	19.3	3.9	22.5	4.0	4.5
One in full-time work, one in part-time work	29.2	6.5	27.5	8.2	8.6
One in full-time work, one not working	22.2	25.9	21.4	26.9	28.3
One or more in part-time work	4.1	12.6	5.6	14.2	13.7
Self-employed	17.3	22.7	15.9	22.3	21.2
Both not in work	7.9	28.5	7.1	24.5	23.7
One or two dependent children	70.9	57.5	72.9	65.5	64.7
Three or more dependent children	29.1	42.5	27.2	34.6	35.3
Age of the youngest child in the household					
0–5	48.0	53.6	51.2	51.2	52.9
6–11	30.2	27.3	27.9	26.4	25.8
12–19	21.9	19.1	20.9	22.4	21.4
White household head	85.2	75.1	84.1	75.1	76.4
Non-white household head	14.9	25.0	15.9	24.9	23.6
No pensioners in the household	97.6	96.3	97.9	97.0	97.3
One or more pensioners in the household	2.4	3.7	2.1	3.0	2.7
Dependency ratio 0.5 or below	63.5	46.4	65.2	57.5	56.3
Dependency ratio greater than 0.5	36.5	53.6	34.8	42.5	43.7
Country					
England	84.3	83.9	84.6	83.8	83.4
Wales	4.8	6.1	4.7	5.6	5.9
Scotland	7.7	6.7	7.4	6.1	6.2
Northern Ireland	3.3	3.4	3.3	4.4	4.4
All dependent children	*100*	*100*	*100*	*100*	*100*
N	7,527	1,568	6,142	1,000	1,183

Source: Authors' calculations using Family Resources Survey 2007–8 and 2013–14. Anchored poverty rates are calculated using the 2007–8 poverty line uprated with the retail price index. Dependent children grossing factor used.

decreased for those in large families (Table 12.2). Poverty fell among children in non-white households, but the share of poor children in non-white households remained the same. Child poverty decreased for households with at least one pensioner, but very few children and poor children live in such households. While child poverty decreased in all regions on both measures, anchored poverty increased in Northern Ireland.

Reductions in child poverty were to some extent due to increases in parental work, although the biggest decreases in child poverty were concentrated among out-of-work households. There has been an increase in the labour supply of lone parents, although most of it was in part-time employment. The share of children in lone-parent families where the lone parent is out of work decreased from 49 per cent in 2007–8 to 45 per cent in 2013–14, while the share of children in lone-parent families where the parent works part time increased from 26 per cent to 30 per cent, with no change for full-time work (25 per cent). The proportion of children in workless couple families decreased from 8 per cent to 7 per cent, while the share of children living with both parents working full time rose from 19 per cent to 23 per cent. The share of children with one or more parents working part time increased from 4 per cent to 6 per cent. At the same time, there has been an increase in the share of poor children living in families where at least one adult works—from 53 per cent to 65 per cent over the same period. Two-thirds of poor children now live in working-poor families, suggesting that low pay, low wage growth, and under-employment, rather than joblessness, are the main drivers of poverty for households with children.

Child poverty actually fell for workless families, even using the anchored poverty line. The decrease in anchored poverty is much larger among non-working lone parents (from 54 per cent to 34 per cent) than among couple families (from 66 per cent to 63 per cent). Although, of all household types, workless couple families remain at the highest risk of poverty, fewer children and fewer poor children live in such families than in out-of-work lone-parent families (see Table 12.2). Figure 12.3 plots the distribution of real disposable household incomes for children living with out-of-work lone parents in 2007/8 and 2013/14. Disposable incomes of non-employed lone parents have increased in real terms, with a visibly lower share of children falling below the population-based poverty line. Since these lone-parent families receive no income from employment or self-employment, the increase is largely due to increased social transfers.[4] Indeed, mean equivalent benefit income grew by 11 per cent in real terms for out-of-work lone parents over this period, although it barely increased (by 2 per cent) for those below the anchored poverty line. Figure 12.3 illustrates that the increase in real disposable income has been larger in the vicinity of the poverty line than at the very bottom of the

[4] The amounts of 'miscellaneous' income and child maintenance payments from absent parents are too low to make much difference.

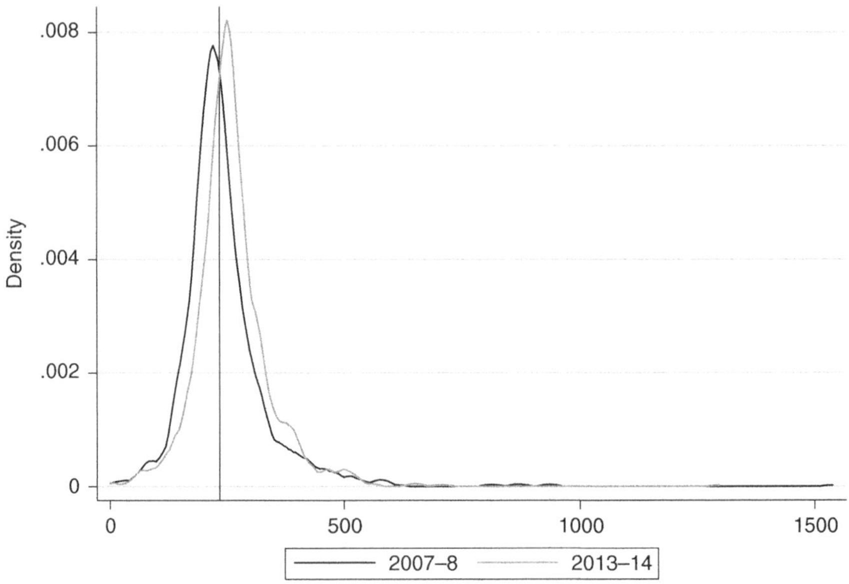

Figure 12.3. Density of weekly real disposable household income for children living with out-of-work lone parents, UK (2007–2008 prices)

Source: Authors' calculations using Family Resources Survey 2007–8 and 2013–14. The line is drawn at the 2007–8 population-based poverty line.

distribution, suggesting that the fall in the poverty rate for this household type was driven by increasing benefit incomes for those closer to the poverty line, many of whom were taken just above that line.

As noted above, the decline in real earnings during the recession and subsequent austerity period was combined with an increase in the cost of necessities. The importance of monitoring not only income (which represents an indirect measure of poverty or living standards) (Ringen, 1988), but also access to material resources (deprivation) was acknowledged in the Child Poverty Act 2010 targets, through the incorporation into two of these targets of deprivation indicators combined with income. The data also allow for a separate examination of levels of deprivation among children, compared to adults in households containing children. This analysis can offer important insights into the effects of the recession and austerity on child poverty, because previous research (e.g. Middleton et al., 1997; Main and Bradshaw, 2016) has found that adults in households with children who are managing on a limited income may sacrifice their own needs and go without necessities themselves, to ensure that their children do not miss out. Additionally, children in households suffering 'adult' deprivations are also likely to be missing out and feeling the effects of poverty, as many 'adult' items refer to household goods that relate to the decoration and repair of the household.

Table 12.3. Children in the UK lacking necessities in 2007–2008 and 2013–2014

Item	2007/8	2013/14	Chi²	
	%	%		
Outdoor space or facilities nearby where they can play safely	14.5	7.3	666.21	***
Enough bedrooms for every child over 10 of different sex to have his or her own bedroom	16.4	15.4	7.36	NS
Celebrations on special occasions such as birthdays, Christmas or other religious festivals	3.8	2.8	44.66	*
Leisure equipment (for example, sports equipment or a bicycle)	7.3	5.8	45.92	**
A holiday away from home at least one week a year with his or her family	31.7	36.1	107.57	***
A hobby or leisure activity	6.6	7.3	7.98	NS
Friends round for tea or a snack once a fortnight	7.2	8.1	14.13	NS
Going on a school trip at least once a term for school-aged children	5.1	5.5	3.58	NS
Play group/nursery/toddler group at least once a week for children of pre-school age	7.7	4.0	259.60	***

Source: Authors' calculations using Family Resources Survey 2007–8 and 2013–14. * $p < 0.05$, ** $p < 0.01$, *** $p < 0.001$, NS not statistically significant.

Table 12.3 shows the proportion of children lacking necessities, and Table 12.4 the proportion of adults living in families with children lacking necessities, in 2007–8 compared to 2013–14. Items are counted as lacking if parents report that children do not have the item because the household cannot afford it (answer options include: children have it; lack it because the parents cannot afford it; or lack it for another reason). The chi-square statistic presented in the fourth column of each table indicates whether the difference in the proportion lacking the items between the two years is statistically significant. Among the child necessities, no clear picture emerges. Many necessities have remained relatively stable—no significant differences are found in the proportions that do not have enough bedrooms, lack a hobby or leisure activity, cannot have friends round for tea, or cannot go on school trips. Modest decreases were found in the proportions that miss out on celebrations on special occasions and on leisure equipment. More substantial decreases were found in terms of lacking access to outdoor space and (for pre-school children) being unable to attend playgroup or nursery (both items saw the proportion lacking them halved between the two years). However, an increase of almost 5 percentage points was found in the proportion of children lacking an annual holiday.

The picture for adults living in families with children is less optimistic: deprivation rates have increased across the board and are statistically significant in all cases (Table 12.4). Over two adults in five (43 per cent) who live in a household with children cannot afford an annual holiday, up from 36 per cent

Table 12.4. Adults in families in the UK with children lacking necessities in 2007–2008 and 2013–2014

Item	2007/8 %	2013/14 %	Chi²	
Enough money to keep your home in a decent state of repair	16.60	18.58	35.18	**
A holiday away from home for one week a year, not staying with relatives	35.88	43.09	282.71	***
Insurance of contents of dwelling	16.44	20.27	126.68	***
Regular savings (of £10 a month) for rainy days or retirement	38.23	40.71	33.35	**
Replace any worn-out furniture	26.57	31.48	152.12	***
Replace or repair broken electrical goods such as refrigerator or washing machine	18.80	22.42	103.92	***
A small amount of money to spend each week on yourself, not on your family	29.75	35.58	200.82	***

* p<0.05, ** p<0.01, *** p<0.001, NS not statistically significant.

Source: Authors' calculations using Family Resources Survey 2007–8 and 2013–14.

in 2007–8; and almost as many (41 per cent) cannot afford savings of £10 per month, compared to 38 per cent in 2007–8. There were also increases in the proportion of adults living with children who were unable to maintain their home in a decent state of decoration, replace worn-out furniture, or replace or repair broken electrical goods. These deprivations will have an impact on the living standards of children, as well as adults, and will potentially lead to increased vulnerability to financial shocks in the future, as household resources deteriorate and simultaneously adults cannot save enough to maintain their living conditions.

This disparity between the findings relating to adult and child necessities suggests that the impact of the recession and austerity on poor families to date has been absorbed largely by adults acting protectively of the children in their families; but such sacrifices cannot sustain children's living standards indefinitely. This reflects the findings of previous research reported above: adults who live with children appear to prioritize the needs of those children over their own needs. However, as Chzhen et al. (2015) and Gabos et al. (2011) note, an alternative explanation may be that some parents understandably feel ashamed or otherwise reluctant to admit their difficulty in providing for their children, resulting in under-reporting of child deprivation compared to adult deprivation. A further consideration, as Ridge (2002) notes, is that children growing up in poor households tend to have a good awareness of the financial strains on their parents, so even if children are adequately shielded from material deprivation themselves, they may be sensitive to parental sacrifice in a manner that has an impact on their well-being. Thus this sacrificing behaviour on the part of adults living in households with children is likely to provide at best a partial and temporary shield from the effects of deprivation.

Linear regression was used to examine changes in deprivation levels for children and adults in 2007–8, compared to 2013–14. The results are presented in Table 12.5. Controlling for income poverty, family economic type, number of children in the household, age of the youngest child, ethnicity, gender, and UK country, the risk factors associated with higher deprivation levels remain broadly similar in 2007–8 and 2013–14 for both children and adults. This may reflect the time-lag between decreasing income and impacts on actual living standards noted by Gordon and Nandy (2012); ongoing monitoring is indicated to see whether the changing profile in terms of risk of low income is reflected in deprivation rates in the future.

The impact of all this on child well-being will take time to emerge. However, there is already evidence that child homelessness has increased sharply after a long period of decline, at a time when house building is at a very low level. Youth suicide rates are up, also after a period of decline (Bradshaw, 2016). There is some evidence that the subjective well-being of children has stopped improving (Children's Society, 2014). The Trussell Trust, the largest food bank organizer, says that 913,000 people got at least three days' emergency food last year—an increase of 163 per cent on the previous year—the best possible evidence of the collapse of the safety net. The number of nutritionally related admissions to hospital has risen (Taylor-Robinson et al., 2013). With so many health outcomes related to poverty, we can expect deteriorating health indicators (Wickham et al., 2016).

12.4. POLICIES

After the Coalition government came to power in 2010, the strategy changed from stimulus to austerity. The government decided to reduce the deficit by £81 billion by 2014–15. It chose to do this by planning to take 80 per cent from spending and 20 per cent from tax increases—though by 2015–16 it was to be 76 per cent (spending) to 24 per cent (taxes). The National Health Service (NHS) and the schools budgets were ring-fenced, while pensions were protected by a 'triple lock'—a guarantee to increase the state pension every year by inflation, average earnings, or a minimum of 2.5 per cent, whichever is highest. So the cuts had to come mainly from social security spending on the working aged. Child benefit was frozen; cuts were made in the real value of working age benefits and tax credits; limits were introduced on housing benefits in the private sector and a 'bedroom tax' was imposed in the public sector; and council tax benefits and the Social Fund were localized, resulting in further cuts. Useful benefits such as the Educational

Table 12.5. Linear regressions examining deprivation levels among children and adults in the UK in 2007–2008 and 2013–2014

	Child deprivation				Adult deprivation			
	2007/8		2013/14		2007/8		2013/14	
Income poor (<60% median BHC)	0.433	***	0.342	***	0.870	***	0.656	***
Family economic type (Ref: CP, both FT)								
CP: one FT, one PT	0.040	NS	0.065	NS	0.225	***	0.286	***
CP: One FT, one not in work	0.266	***	0.273	***	0.689	***	0.863	***
CP: One or more PT	0.676	***	0.516	***	1.247	***	1.552	***
CP: Self-employed	0.059	NS	0.036	NS	0.339	***	0.339	**
CP: Both not in work	1.036	***	1.134	***	2.198	***	2.722	***
LP: In full-time work	0.254	***	0.493	***	1.089	***	1.467	***
LP: In part-time work	0.598	***	0.612	***	1.618	***	1.971	***
LP: Not working	1.335	***	1.178	***	2.767	***	2.797	***
Number of children (Ref: 1)								
2	−0.005	NS	0.037	NS	−0.076	NS	0.029	NS
3+	0.292	***	0.363	***	0.382	***	0.395	***
Age group of youngest child (Ref: 0–5)								
6–11	0.054	NS	0.084	NS	0.054	NS	0.050	NS
12–19	0.130	**	0.293	***	0.124	NS	0.193	*
Ethnicity (Ref: white)	0.637	***	0.366	***	0.309	***	0.414	***
Sex of head of HH (Ref: male)	0.140	**	0.131	**	0.370	***	0.301	***
Age of HH (Ref: 35–44)								
16–24	0.280	**	0.137	NS	0.874	***	0.692	***
25–34	0.219	***	0.162	***	0.568	***	0.528	***
45–54	−0.022	NS	−0.124	**	−0.201	**	−0.331	***
55–59	−0.274	**	−0.102	NS	−0.693	***	−0.301	NS
60 or over	0.170	NS	−0.235	*	−0.219	NS	−0.221	NS
Country (Ref: England)								
Wales	−0.138	NS	−0.132	*	0.056	NS	−0.164	NS
Scotland	−0.036	NS	−0.086	*	−0.196	***	−0.212	**
N Ireland	−0.084	NS	−0.032	NS	−0.348	***	−0.188	*
Constant	0.069	NS	0.056	NS	0.537	***	0.794	***
R-squared	0.280		0.248		0.352		0.298	
N	6932		5676		7330		5905	

Notes: CP = couple parent; LP = lone parent; FT = full-time employed; PT = part-time employed; HH = household.

* p<0.05, ** p<0.01, *** p<0.001, NS not statistically significant.

Source: Authors' calculations using Family Resources Survey 2007–8 and 2013–14.

Maintenance Allowance and the Health in Pregnancy Grant were abolished. Table 12.6 outlines major policy changes since the 2010 Coalition government came to power, including more recent changes under the 2015 Conservative government.

Table 12.6. Timeline of policy changes in the UK since the financial crisis

2007–8	Onset of financial crisis
Q2 2008	Recession hits UK
October 2008	Three leading banks nationalized with £37 billion rescue package; heavy investment in UK financial system
January 2009	Bank of England cuts interest rates to 1.5 per cent; government announces second package of investment in banks
Q4 2009	UK comes out of recession
March 2010	Child Poverty Act 2010 receives Royal Assent, having passed through Parliament with cross-party support
May 2010	No clear winner in general election: Conservative–Liberal Democrat Coalition formed with David Cameron as Prime Minister
October 2010	Coalition announces large-scale public spending cuts—average cut of 19 per cent over four years for all government departments
Q1 and Q2 2012	Shrinking in UK economy marking return to recession
March 2012	Welfare Reform Act receives Royal Assent: —Benefits cap introduced —'Bedroom tax' introduced —Stricter sanctions for benefit claimants found to have breached rules introduced
December 2013	Government revises 2014 growth forecast from 1.8 per cent to 2.4 per cent
May 2015	General election returns Conservative majority government under David Cameron
July 2015	Welfare Reform and Work Bill proposed: —Repeal of much of Child Poverty Act 2010 —Lowering benefit cap —Four-year freeze on working-age benefit rates —Limiting support through Child Tax Credits/Universal Credit Additionally mentioned in the summer budget: —'Youth obligation' introducing stronger conditionality for 18–21-year-olds —Housing benefit scrapped for most 18–21-year-olds
January 2016	House of Lords defeats many components of the Welfare Reform and Work Bill, including repeal of the Child Poverty Act 2010 measures
March 2016	Welfare Reform and Work Act receives Royal Assent

Households with children were some of the main victims of austerity. The Child Poverty Action Group (2014) estimated that the failure to uprate child benefit by inflation since 2010–11 meant that the benefit had lost over 15 per cent of its value over the 2010–15 parliament, compared to its worth had it been uprated using the retail price index (RPI). In practical terms, this means that a family with one child lost £543 of support over the five years of Coalition government, and a two-child family sustained losses of £900. Moreover, the failure to uprate the child element of tax credits over the course of the parliament resulted in a reduction in their real value of 8.5 per cent. As a consequence, a family with one child lost £628 between 2010 and 2015, and a two-child family double this (£1,256). The rise in VAT from 17.5 per cent to 20 per cent in January 2011 squeezed household incomes further.

The Coalition government had promised fairness in its deficit-reduction strategy, but low-income families with children were hit hard. There have now been several analyses of the distributional consequences of austerity in the UK up to 2015 (Cribb et al., 2013; Office of the Children's Commissioner, 2013; Reed and Portes, 2014). They all show that it is the poorest families with children who have suffered the biggest losses in income, and that it is families with children who have suffered the largest cuts in services. The cuts have not only been regressive and hit families with children hardest, but they have also been spatially regressive, with the largest cuts in central government grants falling most heavily on local authority areas with the highest levels of child poverty (Beatty and Fothergill, 2013). Reed and Portes (2014) found that the combined effects of taxes and social security changes since 2010 had reduced the income of couples with children in the bottom income decile by 13 per cent. Universal Credit, the big and (initially) generally welcomed reform of social security that might have mitigated some of this increase in poverty, had it been implemented in 2013 as planned, is still mired in delay and has been undermined by cuts. At the time of writing (early 2016), it appears that Universal Credit may never emerge.

The Office for Budget Responsibility (2014) confirmed that the government had failed to achieve its target of eradicating the deficit by 2014–15. There were four main reasons for this. First, the economy began to grow later and more slowly than was hoped or planned—perhaps the result of pro-cyclical reductions in public spending after 2010. Second, living standards have been declining, with falling real wages and cash benefits. The growth in employment that has been witnessed of late was, until recently, dominated by the low-waged, and raised disappointing amounts of tax revenue. Third, the Coalition government had cut revenue by making tax cuts. Fourth, between 2008–9 and 2015–16, total public expenditure increased in nominal terms and also in real terms. Real spending on education has fallen slightly, and health spending has increased slightly. Spending on social protection has increased—as a result of increases in spending on pensions and disability benefits. Spending on family benefits has taken the biggest hit, suffering cuts of more than £6 billion in real terms between 2010–11 and 2014–15. Spending on families and children as a proportion of total social protection expenditure decreased from 12.6 per cent in 2010–11 to 9.7 per cent in 2014–15, while the share of old-age spending increased from 42.7 per cent to 45.9 per cent.[5]

Following the election of the Conservative government in 2015, the strategy was further revised. Total managed expenditure is set to fall to 36.5 per cent by 2020–1. This will take UK expenditure as a proportion of GDP below Japan's

[5] Table 5.2 'Public sector expenditure on services by sub-function, 2010–11 to 2014–15', HM Treasury Public Expenditure Statistical Analyses 2015 (last update 20 July 2015).

and to US-type levels.[6] If this is achieved, it will be the fourth-lowest level of national output since 1948. The total fall in real terms over the period of consolidation (2009–10 to 2019–20) is set to amount to £45 billion, with £10 billion coming in the four years from 2015. Only international development, health, and, in the next spending round, defence have been protected. Schools have been protected, but the education budget has fallen by 4 per cent. Local government will have been cut by 77 per cent by 2019–20. Capital spending is set to rise, with a substantial increase in 2020–1, but most of this will be in transport, while capital spending in many other areas is set to fall. The share of spending on older people and health will increase from 33.8 per cent in 1997–8 to 42.3 per cent in 2019–20 (Whittaker, 2015).

A new round of £11 billion cuts to working-age benefits was announced in summer 2015. All benefits and tax credits were to be frozen until 2020, and the benefits cap was to be reduced. These cuts would be partially offset by the introduction of a new increased national minimum wage (misleadingly named the 'national living wage'). This will add a premium to the existing and prospective national minimum wage for those over 25 of £7.20 from April 2016, rising to £9 by 2020, pegged to 60 per cent median earnings. The Child Poverty Act 2010 is to be amended to remove the duty on the Secretary of State to meet UK-wide child poverty targets. There will be a new statutory duty to publish an annual report on children in workless households in England and on the educational attainment of children in England at the end of Key Stage 4. The Social Mobility and Child Poverty Commission is renamed the Social Mobility Commission. The government eventually agreed to continue to publish the income-based poverty measures and has asked the Child Poverty Unit to draw up proposals for a set of 'Life Chances Indicators' (see CPAG, 2016).

Following the summer 2015 budget announcements, a number of analyses of their distributional consequences were published by organizations like the Resolution Foundation, the Institute for Fiscal Studies, and the Joseph Rowntree Foundation (Kelly, 2015; Finch, 2015a, 2015b; Elming et al., 2015; Hirsch, 2015; Cribb, 2015). These indicated that, despite the national minimum wage, under-25s, most families with children, and families at the bottom end of the income distribution would lose substantial amounts, while child poverty would increase by as much as 600,000 by 2020. More recent projections by the Institute for Fiscal Studies (Brown and Hood, 2016) predict that relative child poverty would rise from 17.8 per cent in 2015–16 to 25.7 per cent in 2020–21, increasing the number of poor children by 1.2 million and reversing most of the progress made since 1997–8.

[6] International Monetary Fund World Economic Outlook database, October 2015.

Following a defeat on the proposed cuts in tax credits in the House of Lords, the Chancellor of the Exchequer announced in the Autumn Statement on 25 November that he was abandoning some of the cuts to tax credits, in particular the reduction in the eligibility threshold and the increase in the taper. All the other measures remain: the freeze on cash benefit levels, the reduction in the income rise disregard, reduced eligibility for new claims (including loss of the family element and the limit being set at two children), and all the changes that were proposed to Universal Credit—including the reduction in the earnings disregard. The Chancellor also announced a new earnings floor for the self-employed (which assumes that they are earning the new minimum wage), tighter eligibility for child-care tax credits, and savings to housing benefit.

So some of the losses proposed for 2016 will be avoided. Losses that people actually experience will now depend on when (and if) they move onto Universal Credit. The Resolution Foundation estimates that average losses in 2020 will be £1,000 (£1,300 for families with children) and claims that the distributional consequences are heavily regressive (Whittaker, 2015).

The review above does not take account of the increasing tendency for policies to diverge in different countries of the UK. Thus in Northern Ireland, the Assembly never adopted the Welfare Reform Act 2012. The Northern Ireland (Welfare Reform) Act 2015 was only accepted with a £585 million fund to 'top up' UK welfare arrangements over a four-year period. This includes funding to boost tax credits and to ensure that tenants in Northern Ireland are not affected by the bedroom tax. A working group led by Professor Evason (2016) has set out proposals to mitigate the cuts in Universal Credit and other benefits in Northern Ireland. Scotland and Wales never abolished the Educational Maintenance Allowance. Scotland has already seen some devolution: Council Tax Benefit is now called the 'Council Tax Reduction' in Scotland. The Social Fund has been replaced in Scotland by the Scottish Welfare Fund, backed by extra resources. In Scotland, prescriptions and eyesight tests are not subject to means testing, as they are in England. The Scottish Government has also used schedule 5 of the Scotland Act 1998 to make discretionary housing payments available, and has announced funding measures that effectively abolish the bedroom tax. The Scotland Act 2016 gives the Scottish Government new powers to top up social security payments. Although these powers have not yet been extensively used in the context of the Scottish parliamentary elections in 2016, various bodies, including Child Poverty Action Group (CPAG) Scotland (2016), are calling for policies to be adopted to mitigate the impact of UK Government policies, including a higher rate of child benefit in Scotland.

12.5. SUMMARY: IMPROVING OUTCOMES FOR CHILDREN AND LEARNING FROM EXPERIENCE

This history of the UK since the recession illustrates what can be done and what can be undone, in relation to efforts to reduce and eradicate child poverty. To date, the story of the crisis in the UK is revealed by the absence of change in relative child poverty between 2007–8 and 2013–14. Though on the surface this could be interpreted as the state protecting children, a potentially much bleaker picture emerges in the context of a preceding decade of poverty reduction and cuts to welfare provision.

Prior to the recession, although the Labour government failed to meet its own child poverty targets in 2005 and 2010, rates of child poverty in the UK were decreasing. In this chapter, we have argued that such decreases were the result of a sustained and comprehensive package of redistributive public policies, designed to invest in and protect children. Even in the aftermath of the 2008 financial crisis, children's situations continued to improve. However, following the election of a Conservative–Liberal Democrat Coalition government in 2010, and especially following the Conservative majority government's victory in 2015, the policies put in place by the previous Labour government have been reversed. Rather surprisingly, this reversal includes substantial changes to the Child Poverty Act 2010, which in 2010 had received cross-party support. The gains made in terms of lifting children out of poverty have not yet been reversed—perhaps pointing to a protective effect of the redistributive policies in place at the start of the recession. However, progress has now stalled, and the evidence points to a strong likelihood of substantial increases in child poverty in the near future, with children and their families facing the risk of future economic shocks, while the safety net that had previously protected them is in the process of being dismantled.

Understanding the reasons for recent policy changes is necessarily a complex task. The near coincidence of the financial crisis (driving policy change for pragmatic reasons) and the election of a new government with very different ideas resulted in a situation where both pragmatic and ideological factors may have contributed to changes for children. However, it is possible to assess the extent to which children's needs are prioritized by comparing their status now not only to their position before the financial crisis, but also in relation to other social groups. The protection of pensioner incomes via the triple lock, at the same time as the incomes of families with children have diminished and legislation designed to protect them (such as the Child Poverty Act) have been weakened, suggests at least different priorities under the current government. Coalition and Conservative rhetoric sought to promote the idea that 'we're all in it together'; but the austerity policies have been shown to have had an unequal impact, focusing on raising money through cuts to social security, rather than by increasing, or even maintaining, tax revenue. Distributional analysis of the long-run impact of tax and benefits reforms, including the changes announced in the March 2016 budget, shows that lower-income working-age adults with children stand to lose the most between 2015 and 2019 (Hood and Johnson, 2016). While analyses of these policies and their effects are necessarily ongoing, it is clear that children have been major losers in the aftermath of the recession.

REFERENCES

Beatty, Christina and Steve Fothergill (2013). *Hitting the Poorest Places Hardest: The Local and Regional Impact of Welfare Reform* (Sheffield: Centre for Regional Economic and Social Research, Sheffield Hallam University).

Bradshaw, Jonathan (ed.) (2011). *The Well-being of Children in the UK*, 3rd edn (Bristol: Policy Press).

Bradshaw, Jonathan (ed.) (2016). *The Well-being of Children in the UK*, 4th edn (Bristol: Policy Press).

Browne, James and Andrew Hood (2016). *Living Standards, Poverty and Inequality in the UK: 2015–16 to 2020–21* (London: Institute for Fiscal Studies).

Cameron, David (2009). 'Conservative conference address, 8 October 2009', Transcript. <http://www.theguardian.com/politics/2009/oct/08/david-cameron-speech-in-full>.

Cameron, David (2012). 'Welfare speech', delivered at Bluewater, Kent, 25 June 2012. Transcript. <https://www.gov.uk/government/speeches/welfare-speech>.

Child Poverty Action Group (CPAG) (2014). 'Uprating and the Value of Children's Benefits'. Policy note 2. <http://www.cpag.org.uk/sites/default/files/CPAG-Uprating-childrens-benefits-policy-note-Dec-14.pdf>.

Child Poverty Action Group (CPAG) (2016). 'Life Chances Indicators CPAG Submission'. <http://www.cpag.org.uk/content/life-chances-indicators-cpag-submission>.

Children's Society (2014). *The Good Childhood Report 2014* (London: Children's Society).

Chzhen, Yekaterina, Chris de Neubourg, Ilze Plavgo, and Marlous de Milliano (2015). 'Child Poverty in the European Union: The Multiple Overlapping Deprivation Analysis Approach (EU-MODA)'. *Child Indicators Research 9*, no. 2: pp. 335–56.

Cribb, Jonathan (2015). 'Living Standards and Income Inequality'. Presentation on 16 July 2015, Institute for Fiscal Studies. <http://www.ifs.org.uk/uploads/publications/conferences/hbai2015/HBAI_Cribb.pdf>.

Cribb, Jonathan, Andrew Hood, Robert Joyce, and David Phillips. *Living Standards, Poverty and Inequality in the UK: 2013* (London: Institute for Fiscal Studies, 2013).

Elming, William, Carl Emmerson, Paul Johnson, and David Phillips (2015). 'An Assessment of the Potential Compensation Provided by the New "National Living Wage" for the Personal Tax and Benefit Measures Announced for Implementation in the Current Parliament'. *IFS Briefing Note BN175* (London: Institute for Fiscal Studies).

Evason, Eileen (2016). *Welfare Reform Mitigations Working Group Report* (Evason Report). <http://www.nicva.org/sites/default/files/d7content/attachments-articles/welfare-reform-mitigations-working-group-report.pdf>.

Finch, David (2015a). 'A Budget for Workers? The Impact of the Summer Budget on Work Incentives and Universal Credit'. Resolution Foundation briefing. <http://www.resolutionfoundation.org/wp-content/uploads/2015/07/Work-incentives-briefing.pdf>.

Finch, David (2015b). 'A Poverty of Information: Assessing the Government's New Child Poverty Focus and Future Trends'. Resolution Foundation briefing. <http://www.resolutionfoundation.org/wp-content/uploads/2015/10/Child-poverty-briefing.pdf>.

Gábos, András, Erhan Özdemir, and Terry Ward (2011). 'Material Deprivation among Children'. Research note of the Income Distribution and Living Conditions Network of the Social Situation Observatory (European Commission).

Gordon, David and Shailen Nandy (2012). 'Measurement and Methodologies: Measuring Child Poverty and Deprivation'. In Alberto Minujin and Shailen Nandy *Global Child Poverty and Well-being: Measurement, Concepts, Policy and Action* (Bristol: Policy Press).

Hills, Sally, Ryland Thomas, and Nicholas Dimsdale (2010). 'The UK Recession in Context: What Do Three Centuries of Data Tell Us?'. *Bank of England Quarterly Bulletin*, Fourth Quarter: pp. 277–91.

Hirsch, Donald (2015). 'Will the 2015 Summer Budget Improve Living Standards in 2020?'. Joseph Rowntree Foundation. <https://www.jrf.org.uk/report/will-2015-summer-budget-improve-living-standards-2020>.

Hood, Andrew and Paul Johnson (2016). 'Are We "All in This Together"?' Institute for Fiscal Studies. <http://www.ifs.org.uk/publications/8210>.

Kamath, Kishore, Kate Reinold, Mette Nielsen, and Amar Radia (2011). 'The Financial Position of British Households: Evidence from the 2011 NMG Consulting Survey'. *Bank of England Quarterly Bulletin*, Fourth Quarter: pp. 305–18.

Kelly, Gavin (2015). 'Will Wages Fix the Tax Credit Gap? Don't Budget for It'. Resolution Foundation. <http://www.resolutionfoundation.org/media/blog/will-wages-fill-the-tax-credit-gap-dont-budget-for-it>.

McKendrick, John H., Gerry Mooney, Gill Scott, John Dickie, and Fiona McHardy (eds) (2016). *Poverty in Scotland 2016: Tools for Transformation* (London: Child Poverty Action Group).

Main, Gill and Jonathan Bradshaw (2016). 'Child Poverty in the UK: Measures, Prevalence and Intra-household Sharing'. *Critical Social Policy 36*, no. 1: pp. 38–61.

Middleton, Sue, Karl Ashworth, and Ian Braithwaite (1997). *Small Fortunes: Spending on Children, Childhood Poverty and Parental Sacrifice* (York: Joseph Rowntree Foundation).

Office for Budget Responsibility (2014). *Economic and Fiscal Outlet.* Cm 8966 (London: Her Majesty's Stationery Office).

Office of the Children's Commissioner (2013). *A Child Rights Impact Assessment of Budget Decisions: Including the 2013 Budget, and the Cumulative Impact of Tax-Benefit Reforms and Reductions in Spending on Public Services 2010–2015* (London: Office of the Children's Commissioner).

Reed, Howard and Jonathan Portes (2014). 'Cumulative Impact Assessment: A Research Report by Landman Economics and the National Institute of Economic and Social Research (NIESR) for the Equality and Human Rights Commission'. *Equality and Human Rights Commission Research Report 94* (Manchester: Equality and Human Rights Commission).

Ridge, Tess (2002). *Childhood Poverty and Social Exclusion: From a Child's Perspective* (Bristol: Policy Press).

Ringen, Stein (1988). 'Direct and Indirect Measures of Poverty'. *Journal of Social Policy 17*, no. 3: pp. 351–65.

Sparrow, Andrew and Hélène Mulholland (2010). 'Gordon Brown Rejects David Cameron's Call for Immediate Cuts'. *Guardian* Online, 25 January 2010. <http://www.theguardian.com/politics/2010/jan/25/david-cameron-cut-deficit>.

Taylor-Robinson, David, Emeline Rougeaux, Dominic Harrison, Margaret Whitehead, Ben Barr, and Anna Pearce (2013). 'The Rise of Food Poverty in the UK'. *British Medical Journal*, no. 347: f7157.

Whittaker, Matthew (2015). 'O, Blessed Revisions: Fiscal Windfall and What to Do with It'. Resolution Foundation. <http://www.resolutionfoundation.org/wp-content/uploads/2015/11/SR2015.pdf>.

Wickham, Sophie, Elspeth Anwar, Ben Barr, Catherine Law, and David Taylor-Robinson (forthcoming, 2016). 'Poverty and Child Health in the UK: Using Evidence for Action'. *Archives of Diseases in Childhood*. doi:10.1136/archdischild-2014-306746.

13

USA Child Poverty: The Impact of the Great Recession

Christopher Wimer and Timothy M. Smeeding

13.1. INTRODUCTION: THE NATURE OF THE CRISIS—ORIGINS AND TRANSMISSION CHANNELS RELEVANT TO CHILDREN

The Great Recession (GR) was the most dramatic economic downturn the USA has experienced in more than six decades. Tumbling stock and housing markets erased more than $15 trillion in national wealth in 2008, or nearly 10 per cent of real total national financial assets, the largest drop on record since 1945. As financial markets and the rest of the economy slowed to a halt, real gross domestic product (GDP) did not grow in 2008 and fell by 2.6 per cent in 2009, again the largest decline in six decades. In addition, by 2011, housing prices had dropped by 30 per cent since their 2005 peak (Kowalski and Shachmurove, 2011), and in many areas of the country prices have not yet recovered to their 2007 level. Employment in the United States fell by more than 8 million (5 percentage points) between January 2008 and December 2009, only finally recovering in September 2014 (United States Department of Labor, 2015). Moreover, the number of unemployed rose to a peak of 15.6 million in October 2009. Overall, by 2011 the Great Recession had resulted in over $7,300 in forgone consumption per person (or about $175 per person per month) (Lansing, 2011).

According to the latest data derived from the monthly Current Population Survey (CPS), median annual household money income in November 2015 was $56,746, in November 2015 dollars, finally recapturing the ground lost since the beginning of the recession in December 2007, when it was $56,714, but still short of previous peaks since January 2000 (Figure 13.1). The median income recovery thus took almost eight years—and an unemployment rate of 5 per cent—to get back to the same real median income level as in late 2007.

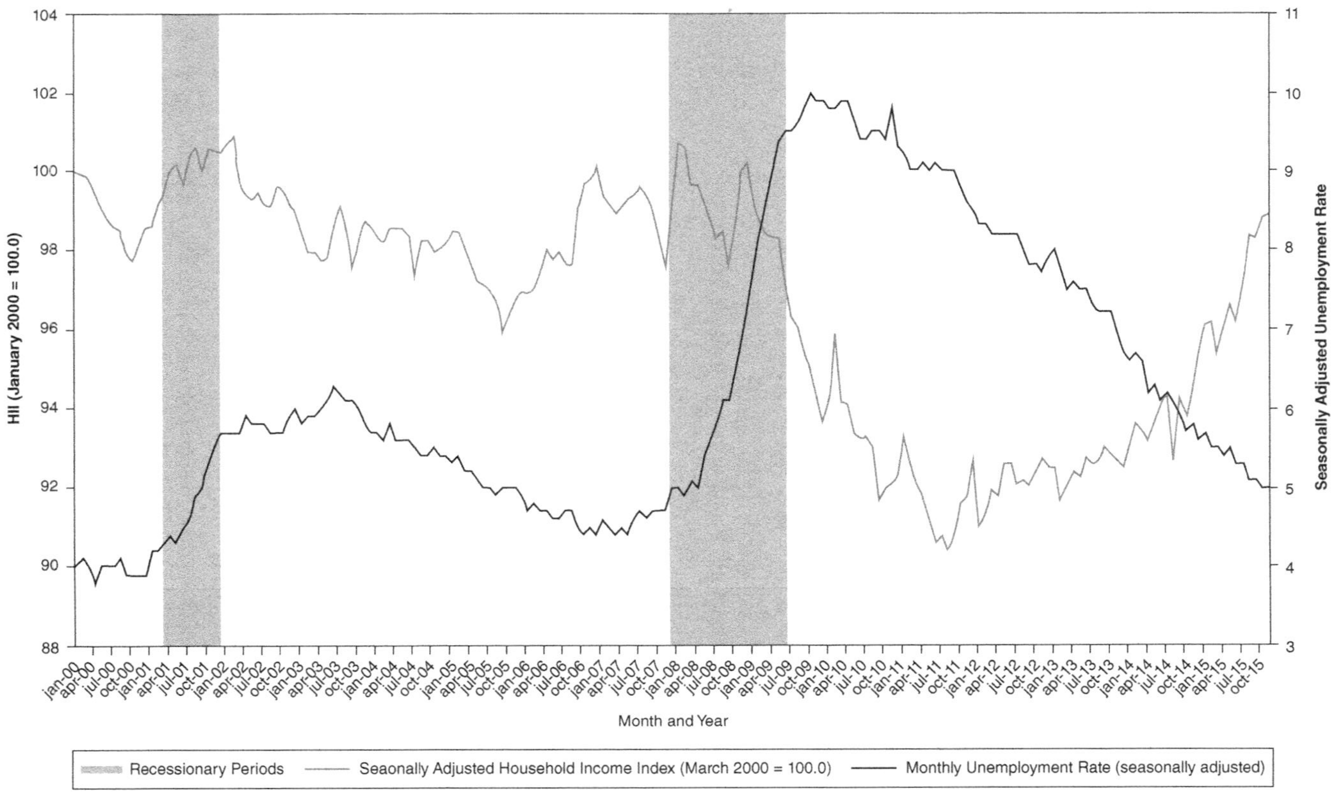

Figure 13.1. US median household income index (HII) and unemployment rate by month (January 2000 to November 2015)

Source: Sentier Research (2016).

A somewhat broader measure of employment hardship—which, as well as the unemployed, includes both marginally attached workers (including those with part-time jobs who want full-time work) and discouraged workers who have dropped out of the labour force—only declined from 16.1 per cent in August 2011 to 9.9 per cent in November 2015. This broader measure suggests that the GR's negative effects on employment were larger for less-skilled than for better-skilled workers (Bitler and Hoynes, 2016). Indeed, employment and real wages for unskilled younger men have been particularly stagnant throughout the recovery (Ross and Svajlenka, 2015; Thompson and Smeeding, 2013).

Flat and falling real hourly wages at the bottom and the middle of the distribution, alongside marked growth at the top, have produced a surge in wage inequality in the US, with the Gini index and the P90/P10 and P90/P50 ratios reaching thirty-year highs. After adjusting for taxes, transfers, and household size, the P90/P10 ratio for net, equivalized income among non-elderly households for each of these inequality measures climbed sharply, mainly because of income growth at the ninetieth percentile (Thompson and Smeeding, 2013).

Money income poverty increased during the Great Recession, but the official poverty rate for all households remained below the levels reached during the economic downturns of the early 1980s and early 1990s. For households with younger heads (under 34) and for childless households (with heads under 55), the official poverty rate reached a thirty-year high. More importantly, since 2007 public transfers rose and taxes declined, as a share of income across the distribution, indicating that public policy has softened the impact of the GR on household well-being and poverty, as measured using the new Census's Supplemental Poverty Measure (SPM); research has extended the SPM measure back to the late 1960s (Fox et al., 2015; Wimer et al., 2016; Haveman et al., 2015).

Average household size has also increased across the income distribution since 2007, particularly among the lowest-income groups; this suggests that households are opting to live together—or stay together—as a mechanism for coping with poor job opportunities. Even with this movement (which reduces poverty as measured, due to economies of scale), money income poverty and inequality rose among the non-elderly during and just after the Great Recession (Thompson and Smeeding, 2013; DeNavas-Walt et al., 2013).

13.2. POVERTY: CONCEPTS, ESPECIALLY FOR CHILDREN

The fundamental concept of poverty concerns itself with people who have too few resources or capabilities to participate fully in society. As Blank (2008,

p. 243) reminds us, 'poverty is an inherently vague concept, and developing a poverty measure involves a number of relatively arbitrary assumptions'. Ultimately, social scientists need first to establish the breadth and depth of the social phenomenon called 'poverty' before they can meaningfully analyse it and explore its ultimate causes and remedies.

Official modern poverty measurement began as an Anglo-American social indicator. But nowadays 'official' measures of poverty (or measures of 'low income') exist in over a hundred countries, and for the European Union as a whole (Guio, 2005). The United States (DeNavas-Walt et al., 2013) and the United Kingdom (Department for Work and Pensions, 2016) have long-standing 'official' poverty series. The official US measure, developed by Mollie Orshansky in 1963, relies on poverty defined only in terms of money income. Money income is a crucial resource for US families with children. Of course, there are other important kinds of resources, such as social capital, wealth, non-cash benefits, early childhood education, primary education, and access to basic healthcare, all of which add to human—especially children's—capabilities (Coleman, 1988). These resources are available more or less equally to all people in many rich societies, regardless of their money income. But in nations like the US, where one has to pay almost full cost for young child health and education services, these costs reduce well-being by limiting people's capacity to participate fully in society.

Various factors increase economic insecurity, reduce human capabilities, and increase poverty, especially for US families with children. These include inadequacies in childcare and early childhood education, the high cost of healthcare, large inequalities in the neighbourhoods in which people live, racial and ethnic discrimination, neighbourhood violence, low-quality public schools and other social services, lack of good jobs, and job instability. For example only 70 per cent of 4-year-old US children participate in publicly subsidized early childhood education, thus leading to lower school readiness and worse school outcomes for younger children in the US than in Australia, Canada, and the United Kingdom (Bradbury et al., 2015). These aspects of child poverty in terms of services are not counted in the construction of European or international relative poverty rates.

The US is also fairly unique in comparing money income to an absolute poverty threshold—a threshold that was developed more than five decades ago. In the broadest sense, all measures of poverty or economic need are relative, because context is important to the definition of needs. The 2014 US 'absolute' money income poverty threshold was about $20,000 for a family of three, while half of median income (a common relative poverty standard in the United States and elsewhere) was approximately $29,500 for a family of the same size. If we use the European 60 per cent of median income, this figure increases to about $35,500. The US's new SPM, which is based on the cost of a set of core necessities, averaged out in 2014 at approximately

$23,000 for a family of three. It is imperative that these different 'need' standards be understood, as we measure poverty in different ways in this chapter.

A fully relative measure of poverty changes mechanically with changes in median income, while an absolute measure changes only with prices. The income elasticity of the poverty line is therefore between zero for the absolute measure and one for the fully relative measure. In some countries, such as the United States, the SPM measure of poverty has become 'quasi-relative', as the poverty line advances only with the living standards of the bottom part of the distribution and not the whole distribution (Short, 2012; Johnson and Smeeding, 2012). Ravallion and Chen (2011) refer to these as 'weakly-relative measures', which have the feature that the poverty line will not rise proportionately to the median or mean, but will have an income elasticity greater than zero, but less than unity.

Absolute and relative poverty measures tell different stories about living standards and material deprivation. Increasingly, the idea of 'anchored' poverty measures have become important and can be employed to indicate both relative (or weakly relative) and absolute poverty trends within a given nation. Anchored poverty measures begin with the same fully or weakly relative measure in one year (t) and then compare relative poverty in some future year (say year $t+10$) or some past year (say year $t-10$) to poverty measures against a poverty line that has been changed only for prices between year t and year $t+10$ or $t-10$. These measures are especially useful in periods of rapid expansion or contraction of an economy (such as during the Great Recession), when relative poverty may not change much, but absolute poverty does change due to the economic growth or contraction (Atkinson et al., 2002; Smeeding, 2006; 2016; Johnson and Smeeding, 2012; OECD, 2013; Fox et al., 2015; Wimer et al., forthcoming).

Any absolute poverty line is also, therefore, an anchored poverty line. The difference is that an anchored poverty line can be updated to any period that is policy relevant, given the analysis. The absolute (or anchored) US Orshansky poverty line for the 1960s was about the same as a fully relative half median income measure at that time (Fuchs, 1967). The United States has anchored its 'official' poverty measure at this same point ever since. Now, more than fifty years later, the US poverty line is fixed at a level that is equivalent to about 30 per cent of median income (rather than 50 per cent, as at the outset in the early 1960s). Hence, analysts prefer to anchor their US poverty studies at a semi-relative line (Smeeding, 2006; Johnson and Smeeding, 2012; Wimer et al., in press). Of course, one can make an anchored poverty analysis by setting any relative poverty line as the base, as we do in this chapter.

Here, for the sake of simplicity and breadth, we focus on the 'headcount' measure of poverty, the share of people who fall below some definable point on the income distribution—here 60 per cent of median income. Because headcount measures are more easily understood, compared, and implemented than other, more complex measures, we rely mainly on these measures in the pages that follow.

13.3. DATA, MEASURES, AND METHODS

13.3.1. Data

To measure child poverty in the United States, we rely on the primary data source for measuring poverty and inequality in the US—the CPS Annual Social and Economic Supplement (ASEC). This is a nationally representative household survey conducted primarily in March every year, and it collects information on resources during the previous calendar year. Thus, the 2015 CPS ASEC collected information on resources during the 2014 calendar year. In recent years, the CPS ASEC has collected detailed income information on approximately 200,000 individuals per year. We use CPS ASEC data from 2006 to 2015, covering the calendar years 2005 to 2014. This ensures that we have income and poverty data from well before the economic crisis of the Great Recession to five years into the recovery. In the United States, the Great Recession is dated to between December 2007 and June 2009, though the unemployment rate did not improve dramatically until well into 2010, and real median (money) income did not recover until late 2015 (Figure 13.1).

We use a more comprehensive definition of income (resources) than is employed in official poverty statistics. Official poverty statistics (and median household income, as shown in Figure 13.1) rely on a definition of income that includes only pre-tax cash resources. Such a definition has become increasingly outdated over time. In the United States, both 'near cash' in-kind food and housing benefits and after-tax resources have become more important components of low-income families' resources (e.g., the Supplemental Nutrition Assistance Programme (SNAP) or the Earned Income Tax Credit (EITC) discussed in section 13.4.2). For families with children, these benefits are supplemented by school meals programmes and by the Women, Infants, and Children (WIC) programme, which covers critical categories of food for low-income pregnant women and mothers of young children. In addition to in-kind nutrition assistance policies, low-income families also benefit from housing assistance programmes and in-kind energy assistance. Housing assistance programmes in the US are limited in scope, reaching less than one eligible family in four; they take the form of either public housing units or housing assistance vouchers (Desmond, 2016). Though families wait for long periods of time to receive housing benefits, the monetary value of such assistance, when received, is quite large. Energy assistance benefits, on the other hand, are fairly small in monetary terms, but they do help low-income families meet their regular utility payments. The cross-national data used by the Organization for Economic Co-operation and Development (OECD) and the Luxembourg Income Study (LIS) to evaluate poverty in a harmonized framework use this income definition in their relative poverty calculations. The SPM also uses these same income components and adjusts for childcare and healthcare expenses, and for the regional cost of housing; all of this affects US poverty. But none of these adjustment are included in the cross-national literature on poverty (Smeeding and Thévenot, 2016).

13.3.2. Measures

We begin by looking at recent trends in child poverty according to the US Supplemental Poverty Measure. The SPM differs substantially from purely relative European measures, but reflects current wisdom among poverty experts in the United States (Citro and Michael, 1995; Interagency Technical Working Group, 2010; Johnson and Smeeding, 2012). The SPM uses a so-called 'quasi-relative' threshold, in contrast to the absolute threshold embodied in the official US poverty statistics and the relative poverty thresholds common in European nations. The SPM's quasi-relative thresholds are based on five years of consumer expenditure data for a core basket of goods and services deemed necessary—food, clothing, shelter, and utilities—plus a small multiplier (0.2) to account for other necessities.

These thresholds, which vary by housing tenure (renters, owners with mortgages, owners without mortgages) and geographic cost of living, are then compared against a more comprehensive definition of resources, here post-tax resources plus the monetary value of in-kind near-cash benefits. Importantly, non-discretionary expenses (such as medical, work, and childcare expenses) are then subtracted from available resources in order to ascertain whether a family has enough resources to meet routine expenses. This accounting is important for the United States, though it still likely underestimates the cost of child services like childcare or early childhood education, as low-income families cannot afford to spend much on such services. Were costs normatively adjusted by the true cost of a high-quality childcare programme, such as those subsidized heavily in Europe, child poverty would rise substantially in the United States. But the reality is that low-income working parents, especially single parents, earn very low wages and cannot afford high-quality care. Hence out-of-pocket expenses are low, and care tends to be given by family or friends in the absence of such resources.

The SPM provides a framework with which to assess the elements that drive trends in poverty in the United States, and also a tool to see whether trends would differ if one did not include resources from government policies and programmes. Such trends are derived by 'zeroing out' resources stemming from government policies and programmes, and then reassessing what poverty trends would look like if only pre-tax, pre-transfer resources were included in the definition of income. These 'counterfactual' estimates allow us to gauge the impact of the Great Recession on labour and capital income, ignoring behavioural responses to the presence or absence of government programmes.[1]

We also consider alternative definitions of income and poverty when examining the status of children before, during, and after the economic crisis. In our primary measure, and in concert with other chapters in this volume, we look at relative poverty. In each year from 2006 to 2015 (for calendar years 2005 to 2014), we calculate a weighted median total household income. Household income is measured here as post-tax plus in-kind resources. Children are then deemed poor if their total household resources fall below 60 per cent of a given year's median.[2] This is a relative poverty measure that is closest in spirit to measures calculated in other countries. We use the OECD's equivalence scale to standardize the measure for differences in family size and composition.[3]

We also consider an 'anchored' poverty measure. The anchored measure treats the poverty threshold as absolute, and is set in 2008 (for calendar year 2007), based on median income. Using an anchored measure shows how changes in income and resources operate independently of changes in the income distribution that might have been influenced by the economic contractions of the Great Recession. We derive median income in the 2008 CPS (for income in calendar year 2007), and then calculate poverty thresholds forward and backward using changes in inflation—in this case, using changes in the Consumer Price Index for All Urban Consumers Research Series (CPI-U-RS), the United States Census Bureau's preferred inflation measure for calculating changes in earnings and income inequality. Because trends are broadly similar, we then focus primarily on the purely relative measure when looking at demographic breakdowns in recent poverty trends before, during, and after the Great Recession.

[1] United States research suggests that these responses are small in the aggregate (Ben-Shalom et al., 2011; Moffitt, 2016).

[2] Remember that the 60 per cent of median threshold is 75 per cent higher than the official US poverty line and more than half again as large as the SPM line.

[3] In analyses (not shown) we also calculated poverty rates using the square root of household size as the equivalence scale, which generally resulted in higher child poverty rates.

13.4. RESULTS

We begin by looking at trends in child poverty using the SPM, the most up-to-date poverty measure currently being released by the US government. We harness data that calculate the measure back before the official release for 2009 and 2010 (Short, 2012; Fox et al., 2015). The SPM allows poverty trends to be documented both with and without the inclusion of resources stemming from government policies and programmes. Thus, in Figure 13.2 we show child poverty trends using two different definitions of resources. First, we show trends based on pre-tax, pre-transfer resources (so without the inclusion of resources either from in-kind programmes like SNAP or housing assistance programmes, or from after-tax programmes like the EITC or Child Tax Credit (CTC)). Second, we show trends based on post-tax, post-transfer resources—i.e. after taking into account resources from the programmes mentioned above. These trends also reflect a measure of resources where medical, work, and childcare expenses are subtracted from income, and also reflect a lower poverty threshold for those who own their home without a mortgage.

Without taxes and transfers, poverty rates among children would have risen by over 4 percentage points between 2005 and 2014 (from 23.5 per cent to 27.7 per cent; Figure 13.2). This translates to a rise in child poverty of about 18 per cent. But using a fuller measure of resources that includes after-tax income and in-kind benefits, child poverty remained essentially flat, at 16.6 per cent in

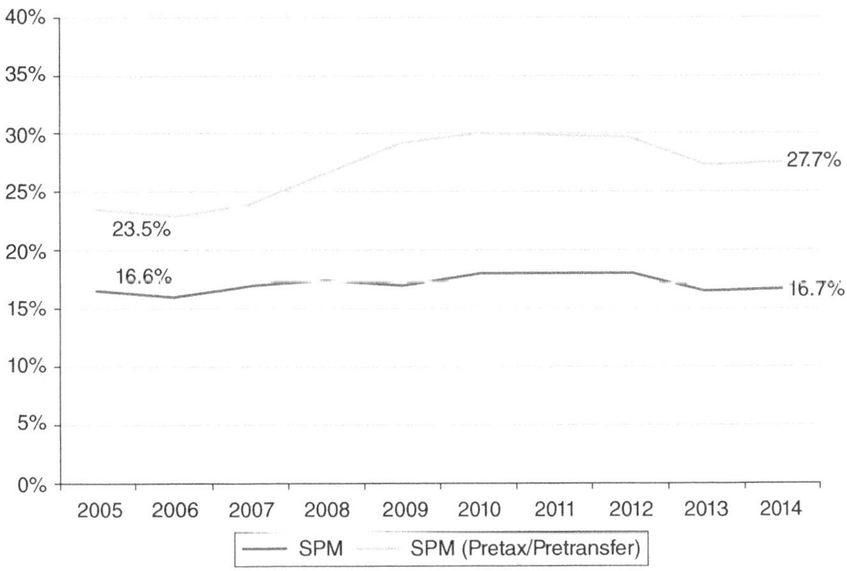

Figure 13.2. Child poverty in the United States using the Census Supplemental Poverty Measure (SPM) (2005–2014)

2005 and 16.7 per cent in 2014. Child poverty did rise to a high of 18.1 per cent in 2011 and 2012 following the height of the crisis; but without resources from government policies and programmes that figure would have reached nearly 30 per cent. Government policies and programmes, then, reduced child poverty at the height of the crisis by over a third when evaluated at the SPM poverty threshold. Even in 2014, government policies and programmes reduced child poverty by over 40 per cent, from 27.7 per cent to 16.7 per cent. The SPM thus shows the degree to which government programmes were successful in the United States in ameliorating child poverty amidst one of the greatest economic downturns in recent memory (Fox et al., 2015). Though we do not show them here, the trends for working-age adults and the elderly—and by extension for the whole US population—were also largely flat over the time period considered here.

The SPM, despite its advantages over official poverty statistics, still stands at odds with how most other advanced democracies measure poverty: namely using a fully relative poverty measure, whereby incomes are measured relative to a fixed percentage of the median. In order to compare trends to other countries in this volume, we thus adopt such an approach to measuring child poverty in the remainder of this chapter. We first consider a purely relative measure, comparing income in each year to a poverty line defined as 60 per cent of median size-adjusted or equivalized income. To allow comparison with the SPM estimates in Figure 13.2, we show relative poverty rates with a pre-tax/pre-transfer definition of 'market income' resources and a definition of resources that includes all taxes and transfers. Note that for both definitions, medical, work, and childcare expenses are not deducted from income—if they were, the poverty levels among US children displayed in Figure 13.3 would be higher still. The results are similar to the SPM results in Figure 13.2, with pre-tax/pre-transfer child poverty increasing from 30.8 per cent in 2005 to an apex of 35.1 per cent in 2010, before trailing down to 33.3 per cent in 2014, the end of our series. The results in Figure 13.3 show some key differences from those under the SPM in Figure 13.2, however. While in both series, taxes and transfers have kept child poverty rates from rising as much as they would have done in the absence of such taxes and transfers, Figure 13.3 shows that when one sets the poverty line higher and in alignment with standards in other advanced democracies, the US safety net does much less in both absolute and relative terms to reduce child poverty. For example, in 2014 policies and programmes reduced SPM child poverty rates by 11 percentage points. In the same year, policies and programmes reduced relative child poverty rates by just 6.6 percentage points. Both are major and meaningful reductions in child poverty, to be sure; but the juxtaposition highlights the fact that social benefits are smaller and more targeted in the United States, and thus do less to bring people very far up the income distribution.

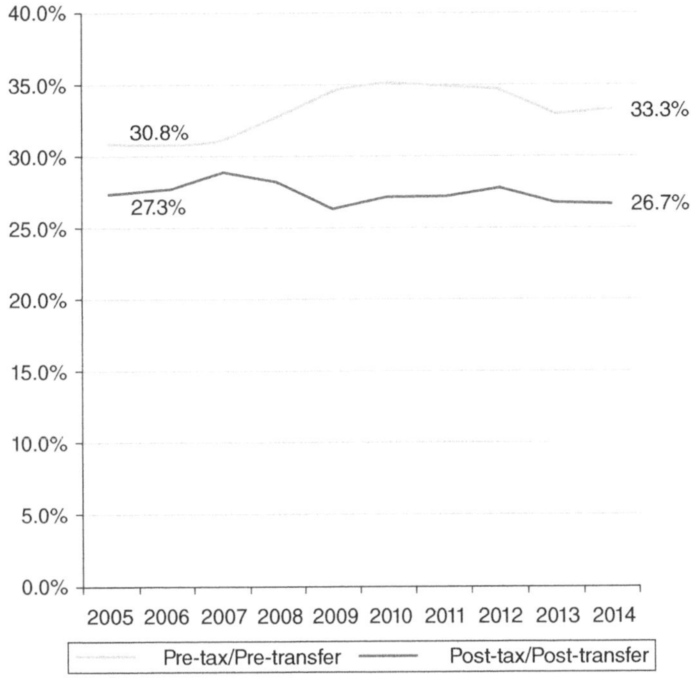

Figure 13.3. Trends in relative child poverty rates in the US before and after counting taxes and transfers (2005–2014)

Relative poverty measures have been criticized, however, for potentially distorting trends in times of rapid economic change, such as the Great Recession. This is because, if median income changes very rapidly, year-to-year changes are likely to be driven not only by changes in underlying incomes, but also by changes in the resultant poverty thresholds, which mechanically move with median incomes. In Figure 13.4, then, we show child poverty rates according to two definitions. The first is the purely relative measure shown in Figure 13.3 (with income including taxes and transfers), whereby disposable income child poverty is assessed against 60 per cent of the median each year. The second measure is based on 60 per cent of median income, but measured in 2008 (for calendar year 2007). This poverty line is then tracked backward and forward over time using the CPI-U-RS. This is therefore an 'anchored' poverty series, based on absolute incomes measured in 2008, right before the onset of the Great Recession.

Figure 13.4 shows that relative and anchored child poverty rates were largely flat between 2005 and 2014, although anchored child poverty rates rose somewhat over time (from 27.9 per cent to 30.2 per cent) reflecting the effects of the recession on family incomes at or near the poverty line, while

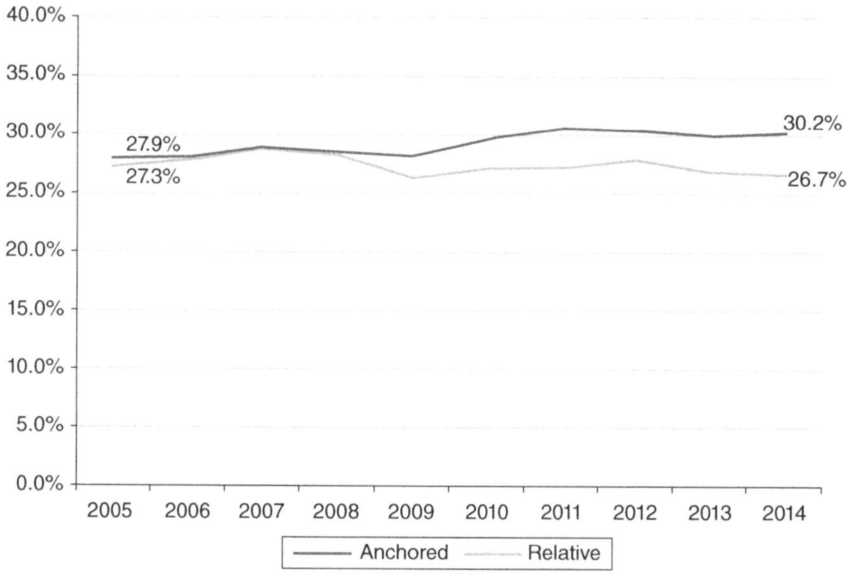

Figure 13.4. US child poverty rates using an anchored vs relative poverty threshold (2005–2014)

relative rates did not change much, if at all (27.3 per cent to 26.7 per cent over the same years). This is most likely because median incomes stagnated and fell slightly over the years of the crisis, leading relative poverty rates to stay roughly the same over the period. As measured against pre-recession median income levels, child poverty rates actually increased slightly over the period, suggesting that inequality also expanded at the bottom of the distribution, despite the decline in median money income shown in Figure 13.1.

13.4.1. Relative Child Poverty by Demographic Characteristics

In the remainder of this chapter, we focus on child poverty as measured using the relative poverty rate, in keeping with other countries' methodologies. Table 13.1 shows overall trends in children's relative poverty levels by a number of key demographic characteristics examined across chapters in this volume. We define the pre-recession period as 2005–7, the recession period as 2008–10, and the post-recession period as 2011–14. Note that the Great Recession in the US ended officially in 2009, but we include 2010 in the recession period, since unemployment levels remained high long after the recession's end, and actually peaked in 2010. The first row of the table shows what we saw in Figure 13.3: that relative child poverty rates have been fairly stable over the three periods, at a shade over 27 per cent.

Table 13.1. Child poverty rates in the US before, during, and after the Great Recession

	Pre-recession	Recession	Post-recession
All children	27.9%	27.2%	27.1%
Married	20.2%	19.6%	19.2%
Cohabiting	37.8%	39.8%	38.2%
Single	48.6%	45.4%	45.5%
0–5 years	31.8%	30.8%	29.9%
6–11 years	27.6%	26.6%	27.3%
12–17 years	24.5%	23.6%	24.1%
1–2 children	21.2%	20.9%	21.1%
3+ children	39.0%	37.0%	36.9%
1 working-age adult	49.2%	45.0%	44.4%
2 working-age adults	22.0%	21.2%	21.7%
3+ working-age adults	29.1%	30.7%	29.6%
0 pensioners	27.7%	26.9%	26.9%
1+ pensioner	32.8%	30.0%	29.3%
Low dependency	17.1%	18.3%	18.4%
Moderate dependency	20.7%	21.0%	21.3%
High dependency	39.3%	36.6%	36.3%
Northeast	23.5%	21.6%	21.8%
Midwest	24.9%	24.8%	23.9%
South	31.3%	30.1%	30.3%
West	28.8%	28.0%	28.2%
Metropolitan	27.0%	26.3%	26.2%
Non-metropolitan	33.1%	31.0%	31.8%
US-born	24.5%	23.4%	23.6%
Foreign-born	37.9%	37.1%	35.5%

The first panel of Table 13.1 shows child poverty rates for children in married, cohabiting, and single families. For all groups, child poverty rates are relatively stable across the three periods, despite the economic upheaval in the wider economy. Children in single-parent households actually see a decline in poverty of about 3 percentage points from pre- to post-recession, while the rates for children in married and cohabiting families are flatter. The second panel shows poverty rates by child age. Again, for all groups we see that poverty rates are fairly flat across the three periods. For young children, who have the highest poverty rates among US children, the rates decline from 31.8 per cent in the pre-recession period to 30.8 per cent in the recession, and 29.9 per cent in the post-recession period. Children aged 6–11 show similar patterns, with poverty rates hovering around 27 per cent across all three periods. Adolescents aged 12–17 have the lowest poverty rates among children, at around 24 per cent, but again we do not see much change across the three periods.

The third panel shows trends by family size. Once again, there is little evidence of a clear trend, though we do see that the small overall drop in child poverty across the period from Figure 13.3 seems to be driven by large families. For families with one or two children, poverty rates across the three periods are almost completely unchanged. For larger families, though, poverty drops by about 2 percentage points from pre-recession to during the recession and after. Thus, larger families have higher poverty rates in general, but their poverty rates have converged somewhat with families with only 1–2 children. The next panel shows child poverty rates by the number of working-age adults in the family. As we would expect, children in families with only one working-age adult have the highest rates (at nearly 50 per cent), but these declined from over 49 per cent in the pre-recession period to about 45 per cent in the recessionary and post-recession period. Trends for families with two or three and more working-age adults were much flatter. In combination, these two panels of Table 13.1 show that declines in poverty were largest for those with only one working-age adult but multiple (three or more) children. As we will discuss below, these families were a target of policy intervention in response to the Great Recession.

The next panel of Table 13.1 shows trends in poverty rates by the number of pensioners, here defined as the presence of an adult aged 65 or older. Children living with an older adult are more likely to be poor across all three periods, but among both groups child poverty rates decline across the three periods. This mirrors trends for other demographic groups above, where we find essentially flat trends in child poverty across the periods before, during, and after the crisis. The next panel shows child poverty rates by the so-called 'dependency ratio', which is defined as the total number of children and elderly household members, divided by total household size. The panel shows that child poverty rates are highest when the dependency ratio is highest. Children in 'high-dependency' households have poverty rates of nearly 40 per cent, compared to about 17 per cent in 'low-dependency' households. In terms of trends, however, we see no clear patterns, with child poverty rates mostly flat over the period. If anything, we see a drop in poverty in high-dependency families, which may reflect the increased investment in policy response to the recession among families with children.

The next two panels show child poverty rates across the crisis according to where children live. The US is often broken down into four broad regions: the Northeast, Midwest, South, and West. Child poverty rates are historically highest in the South and West, and lower in the Northeast and Midwest. This is true in the pre-recession, recessionary, and post-recession periods. Across the board, however, child poverty rates are flat to somewhat down across all regions. For instance, child poverty rates in the Northeast dropped from 23.5 per cent to 21.8 per cent from pre- to post-recession, and child poverty rates fell from 31.3 per cent to 30.3 per cent across the same period in the South. These declines are not dramatic, but they do show that there are no major increases in child poverty in the US associated with the recession across geographic regions. The same is true of the next panel, where we break down trends in child poverty rates by urban (metro area) and rural (non-metro area) status. In both types of areas, child poverty rates are not much different during and after the recession than before. Finally, in the last panel of Table 13.1, we show child poverty rates by 'nativity'—that is, whether the child is US or foreign born. As we would expect, US-born children have, on average, lower poverty rates in each period (about 12 percentage points lower). However, for both groups of children, overall poverty rates are more or less flat, if anything declining over the periods covered. Thus, across almost all demographic groups we see no major evidence of increases in child poverty associated with the crisis. If anything, for most groups poverty decreased by a small amount during and after the crisis. What might account for these surprising trends in the US, which has historically been considered a laggard when it comes to anti-poverty policy? In the next section, we discuss the US policy response to the crisis.

13.4.2. Understanding Impacts on Children: The US Policy Response to the Great Recession

Section 13.4.1 of this chapter showed that trends in child poverty in the US have been largely favourable, given the extent of the economic crisis. These facts are puzzling, if one accepts the widespread assumption that the US is a laggard when it comes to providing anti-poverty relief to its most vulnerable citizens, including those with children. So what explains the lack of any major impact of the crisis on child poverty rates? In this section, we discuss the policy response to the Great Recession, which we argue largely explains the stable child poverty rates shown above. We argue that a unique political moment in the US allowed stabilizers to be both deployed and expanded to mitigate the effect of the crisis on child poverty, though these stabilizers are now under threat in the current political moment.

One would expect automatic stabilizers to mitigate income losses from the Great Recession without policy change. Aggregate spending on targeted (income-tested) safety-net programmes indicates that (with one exception, the Temporary Assistance to Needy Families (TANF) programme) the social safety net provided significant support to households affected by the recession, especially those with children (Figure 13.5).

In the years just before (and then during and after) the Great Recession, three means-tested transfer programmes in the social safety net stand out as cushioning the blow for the poor—the US food subsidy programme, popularly known as 'Food Stamps' and now as the Supplemental Nutrition Assistance Program (SNAP), the refundable Earned Income Tax Credit (EITC), and the

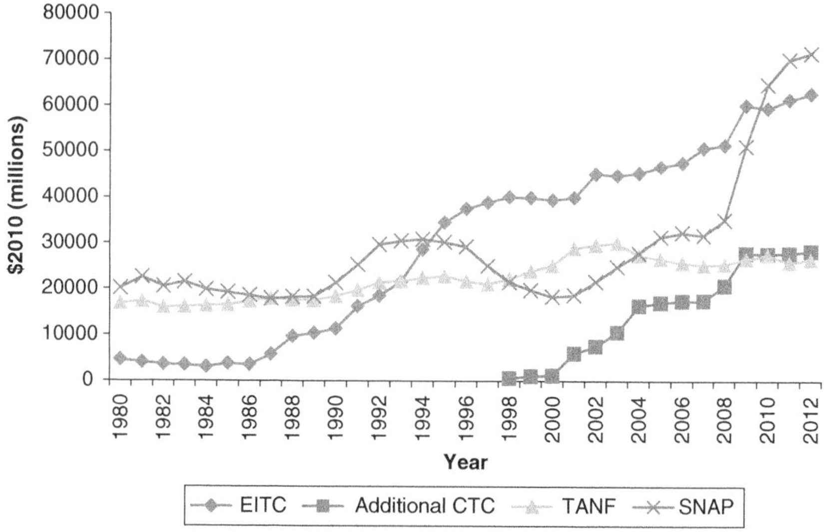

Figure 13.5. Trends in real spending in the US on selected safety-net programmes (1980–2012)

Additional Child Tax Credit (ACTC), which is the refundable portion of the Child Tax Credit. These programmes disproportionately benefit low-income working families with children (Fox et al., 2015; Moffitt, 2015). From 2000 to 2012, real spending on these programmes grew by 290 per cent, 59 per cent, and over 2,200 per cent respectively.[4] In contrast, real spending on cash welfare—the Temporary Assistance for Needy Families (TANF) programme—remained flat, reflecting the transformation of the safety net away from cash-based assistance to one more reliant on refundable tax credits and in-kind food assistance (Hardy, 2016; Moffitt 2013; 2015b; Ziliak, 2011). In 2011, for instance, Food Stamp expenditure amounted to $72.8 billion, and more than one person in seven in the US received benefits from SNAP (Tiehen et al., 2016; Hardy et al., 2016).

The EITC supplements the wages of workers who do not make much money throughout the year, through the provision of a refundable tax credit. The amount depends on how much the worker makes and how many children he or she has. The original goals of the EITC were to reduce poverty, while increasing employment. The credit provides help to the working poor, and by making work more remunerative, it also increases the incentive for people to join the labour market. These incentives were particularly important in the late 1990s, when labour markets were strong and TANF cuts were deep.

[4] The rapid growth in the CTC was due to provisions of the American Recovery and Reinvestment Act of 2009 (ARRA) that enabled 'Additional' refundable CTCs to go to families with earnings of $3,000 a year or more in 2009. Thus, rapid growth of the CTC for low earners added to the effectiveness of the CTC (CBPP, 2016).

Effectively, then, welfare reform turned the welfare poor into the working poor (Schoeni and Blank, 2000).

The ACTC is also very important, as it allows those who make $3,000 a year or more to receive a refundable tax credit of up to $1,000 per child. These benefits all come in one cheque at tax time, and are sometimes also supplemented by zero income tax withholding and by supplemental state EITCs, which are piggybacked onto the federal EITC. As Figure 13.2 shows, the total of federal and state EITCs, the CTC, and the ACTC was almost $90 billion in 2012.

In addition to the built-in stabilizers already on the books in 2008, the American Recovery and Reinvestment Act 2009 (ARRA) was passed in February 2009 and contained many provisions that further expanded the social safety net. The Food Stamp maximum benefit was increased by $25 per person per month (this provision expired in October 2013). ARRA 2009 also expanded the EITC to include a more generous schedule for families with three or more children, reduced taxes through the introduction of the Making Work Pay Tax Credit (providing up to $400 per worker), and extended the CTC with the ACTC. In 2014, the maximum refundable tax credit for someone with no qualifying children was $496 in EITC. For someone with three or more qualifying children, the maximum was $6,143 in EITC and another $3,000 for the CTC. The total cost of these expansions was over $200 billion in 2009 (Thompson and Smeeding, 2013).

The maximum duration of Unemployment Insurance benefits was also extended to ninety-nine weeks during the Great Recession by the ARRA, far beyond the normal maximum of twenty-six weeks (Rothstein, 2011). Both extended and emergency programmes provided expansions to Unemployment Insurance (UI) before and with the ARRA. First, in June 2008 Congress enacted the Emergency Unemployment Compensation programme, which (eventually) raised maximum UI benefit durations to ninety-nine weeks. With passage of the 2009 ARRA, Congress extended these benefits. In 2010, in the depths of the Great Recession, about $70 billion were paid out under the emergency UI programme, in addition to the $69 billion paid for regular and extended benefits: a total of $139 billion. The ARRA also raised the weekly UI benefit by about $20 (Rothstein, 2011). But these programmes ended in 2012 and 2013 when the extensions ran out. Moreover, they mainly helped middle-class families to maintain their standard of living, as the work histories of the official and SPM poor do not generally qualify most of them for UI (Smeeding et al., 2011).

By contrast, the SNAP, EITC, and CTC programmes have not declined by much (if at all) since the end of the Great Recession. That is because low-skill, irregular, and short-term jobs that pay relatively low wages have been prevalent in the US economic recovery. For example, employment opportunities paying at or below $13.33 an hour constituted 22 per cent of job losses and

44 per cent of jobs recovered since 2010 (Jaimovich and Siu, 2012; NELP, 2014). If these jobs continue to represent post-recession longer-term opportunities for workers, the safety net might take on a more permanent role as a wage supplement for the working poor (Hardy et al., 2016). Indeed, outlays on SNAP are forecast by the Congressional Budget Office (2015) to remain high, at roughly $75 billion annually in nominal dollars between 2015 and 2025. At the same time, spending on EITC and CTC are forecast to cost $94 billion annually in nominal dollars by 2017 and beyond, as the ARRA expansions of the two credits have now been extended indefinitely (CBPP, 2016). However, it is unclear whether the expanded protections for low-income families that stabilized child poverty rates in the crisis will live on: SNAP has repeatedly been a target for budget cuts, despite the fact that it is one of the most successful US anti-poverty programmes, with effects on the poverty rates of families with children that are even larger than those generated by refundable tax credits (Tiehen et al., 2016).

Public spending on other social services, including health, education, and childcare, were also important during the GR. While only a small amount of extra support for childcare and early childhood education was put through, and on a matching basis, in 2009 the US passed the Affordable Care Act (ACA), which has rapidly expanded health insurance coverage in the United States, principally for the poor via the Medicaid system, which had added six million poor or near-poor people to its rolls by the end of 2015. It is important to note that while such services do not fall within the standard measure of relative income poverty in rich nations, their effects do show up in the US's SPM, where reductions in childcare costs and lower out-of-pocket expenses for healthcare help reduce poverty (Sommers and Oellerich, 2013).

More generally, children's budgets in the federal system are composed of the means-tested entitlements above, plus discretionary amounts for public housing, childcare, and educational services, among other programmes. These programmes are now subject to automatic cuts by congressional budget rules (Isaacs et al., 2015). In contrast, non-means-tested entitlements for the elderly, social retirement, and health insurance (Medicare) are not subject to sequestration and are scheduled to grow very rapidly with the ageing of the baby boomers, thus adding to the pressure to cut discretionary benefits for families with children even more in coming years.

In summary, the United States continues to suffer from high levels of child poverty, with targeted work supports and food subsidies being the major anti-poverty tools expanded during the Great Recession. While refundable tax credits have been extended, SNAP benefits have been rolled back as economic recovery has taken hold in the United States. The US is also a country that relies extensively on targeted programmes. While the combined programmes of interest—SNAP, the EITC, and the CTC—provide help to the working poor, and especially to working-poor families with children, they taper down rapidly as incomes increase and do little to aid families whose members are unable to work. As our results show, they have done more to lift people above a fairly low poverty line (by international standards) than to lift people above a higher and more widely used poverty line.

13.5. LESSONS LEARNED FROM THE US EXPERIENCE

In this chapter, we have documented recent trends in US child poverty rates before, during, and after the Great Recession. We first showed child poverty rates using the US's new Supplemental Poverty Measure, which represents the latest thinking on how to measure income poverty using a so-called 'quasi-relative' poverty concept in the United States. Using this measure, we saw that, without resources from government policies and programmes, child poverty rates would have increased fairly dramatically following the Great Recession. But once resources from such policies and programmes are included in the definition of income, child poverty rates remain remarkably flat—this despite one of the worst economic cataclysms (in fact, *the* worst) of recent decades. It is important to note that the poverty lines in the SPM are about 40 per cent of median income, and are hence far below the 60 per cent of median standard used in Europe and in the larger study of which this chapter is a part.

We then used a similar income concept (post-tax/post-transfer resources) to examine changes in relative poverty—a concept more closely in line with other advanced democracies, at 60 per cent of median poverty, with no adjustments made for the costs of working, childcare, or healthcare (as in the SPM). Moving to this approach generally leads to higher poverty rates among US children, but (as with the SPM) in virtually no groups of children did the Great Recession coincide with large spikes in child poverty. To be sure, many important gaps in child poverty rates persist—but by and large the Great Recession does not appear to have exacerbated these gaps. Indeed, what is quite remarkable is just how little rise in child poverty we see across the figures presented here, despite the fact that unemployment roughly doubled and the consequences of the economic downturn were so widely felt. We take these results to mean that the American safety net—even if it is commonly thought to be a patchwork of programmes that pales into insignificance when compared to what is in place in many other advanced democracies—largely did its job by US standards (Figures 13.2 and 13.4), and to a lesser extent by European standards (Figure 13.3). Certainly, child poverty rates in the United States remain unconscionably high. And there is much more that could be done to reduce these rates in the future. But we can take some small comfort from the fact that these policies and programmes seem to have prevented a bad situation from getting much worse. Of course, just because child poverty rates as measured here have remained flat, that does not mean children aren't suffering more *below* the poverty line. Indeed, some distressing new work (Shaefer and Edin, 2013; Edin and Shaefer, 2015; Jencks, 2016) suggests an alarming rise in so-called 'extreme poverty,' or those living on under $2.00 per day. Helping those who are so disconnected as to fall under such a level of deprivation should be a top priority for public policy in the United States.

We conclude by noting that income poverty measures, however defined, tell just one part of the story of what has happened to children in the United States, and there is much more to learn. Unlike Europe, which regularly measures hardship and social exclusion (Marlier et al., 2007), these are not part and parcel of the US poverty measurement framework. We do know that children in the United States have experienced increases in material hardship due to the recession, though again the safety net seems to have blunted what would have been a more substantial rise (Pilkauskas et al., 2012; Smeeding and Thévenot, 2016). And the stressors associated with the recession may also have contributed to increases in so-called harsh parenting (Brooks-Gunn et al., 2013). Some effects on children may only be uncovered over the longer term, however, as the devastation wrought on families' market incomes plays out in the lives of already vulnerable children.

REFERENCES

Atkinson, Tony, Bea Cantillon, Eric Marlier, and Brian Nolan (2002). *Social Indicators: The EU and Social Inclusion* (Oxford: Oxford University Press).

Ben-Shalom, Yonatan, Robert A. Moffitt, and John Karl Scholz (2011). 'An Assessment of the Effectiveness of Anti-poverty Programs in the United States'. *NBER Working Paper 17042* (Cambridge, MA: National Bureau of Economic Research).

Bitler, Marianne and Hilary Hoynes (2016). 'The More Things Change, the More They Stay the Same? The Safety Net and Poverty in the Great Recession'. *Journal of Labor Economics 34*, no. S1: S403–S444.

Blank, Rebecca M. (2008). 'Presidential Address: How to Improve Poverty Measurement in the United States'. *Journal of Policy Analysis and Management 27*, no. 2: pp. 233–54.

Bradbury, Bruce, Miles Corak, Jane Waldfogel, and Elizabeth Washbrook (2015). *Too Many Children Left Behind: The US Achievement Gap in Comparative Perspective* (New York: Russell Sage Foundation).

Brooks-Gunn, Jeanne, William Schneider, and Jane Waldfogel (2013). 'The Great Recession and the Risk for Child Maltreatment'. *Child Abuse and Neglect 37*, no. 10: pp. 721–29.

Center on Budget and Policy Priorities (CBPP) (2016). 'Policy Basics: The Child Tax Credit'. (Washington, DC: Center on Budget and Policy Priorities.)

Citro, Constance F. and Robert T. Michael (eds) (1995). *Measuring Poverty: A New Approach* (Washington, DC: National Academies Press).

Coleman, James S. (1988). 'Social Capital in the Creation of Human Capital'. *American Journal of Sociology 94*, Supplement: S95–S120.

Congressional Budget Office (CBO) (2015). 'The Effects of Potential Cuts in SNAP Spending on Households With Different Amounts of Income'. CBO. <https://www.cbo.gov/sites/default/files/114th-congress-2015-2016/reports/49978-SNAP.pdf>.

DeNavas-Walt, Carmen, Bernadette D. Proctor, and Jessica C. Smith (2013). 'Income, Poverty, and Health Insurance Coverage in the United States: 2012'. *Current Population Reports P60-245* (Washington, DC: US Census Bureau).

Desmond, Matthew (2016). *Evicted: Poverty and Profit in the American City* (New York: Crown).

United States Department of Labor (2015). 'BLS Statistics of Unemployment and Employment'. <http://www.bls.gov/bls/unemployment.htm>.

Department for Work and Pensions (2016). 'Households Below Average Income'. UK Government. <http://research.dwp.gov.uk/asd/index.php?page=hbai>

Edin, Kathryn J. and H. Luke Shaefer (2015). *$2.00 a day: Living on Almost Nothing in America* (New York: Houghton Mifflin Harcourt).

Guio, Anne-Catherine (2005). 'Income Poverty and Social Exclusion in the EU25'. *Statistics in Focus 13/2005* (Luxembourg: Official Publications of the European Communities, 2005).

Fox, Liana, Christopher Wimer, Irwin Garfinkel, Neeraj Kaushal, and Jane Waldfogel (2015). 'Waging War on Poverty: Poverty Trends Using a Historical Supplemental Poverty Measure'. *Journal of Policy Analysis and Management 34*, no. 3: pp. 567–92.

Fuchs, Victor R. (1967). 'Redefining Poverty and Redistributing Income'. *The Public Interest 8*: pp. 88–95.

Hardy, Bradley L. (2016). 'Income Instability and the Response of the Safety Net'. *Contemporary Economic Policy*. DOI: 10.1111/coep.12187.

Hardy, Bradley L., Timothy M. Smeeding, and James P. Ziliak. 'The Changing Safety Net for Low Income Parents and Their Children: Structural or Cyclical Changes in Income Support Policy?' *Working Paper* (Washington, DC: American University, 2016).

Haveman, Robert, Rebecca Blank, Robert Moffitt, Timothy M. Smeeding, and Geoffrey Wallace (2015). 'The War on Poverty: Measurement, Trends, and Policy'. *Journal of Policy Analysis and Management 34*, no. 3: pp. 593–638.

Interagency Technical Working Group (2010). 'Observations from the Interagency Technical Working Group on Developing a Supplemental Poverty Measure'. <https://www.census.gov/hhes/povmeas/methodology/supplemental/research/SPM_TWGObservations.pdf>.

Isaacs, Julia, Sara Edelstein, Heather Hahn, Ellen Steele, and C. Eugene Steuerle (2015). Kids' Share 2015: Report on Federal Expenditures on Children in 2014 and Future Projections (Washington, DC: Urban Institute).

Jaimovich, Nir and Henry E. Siu (2012). 'The Trend is the Cycle: Job Polarization and Jobless Recoveries'. *NBER Working Paper 18334* (Cambridge, MA: National Bureau of Economic Research).

Jencks, Christopher (2016). 'Why the Very Poor Have Become Poorer'. *NY Review of Books*, June 9, 2016.

Johnson, David S. and Timothy M. Smeeding (2012). 'A Consumer's Guide to Interpreting Various US Poverty Measures'. *Fast Focus 14* (Madison, WI: Institute for Research on Poverty).

Kowalski, Tadeusz and Yochanan Shachmurove (2011). 'The Financial Crisis: What Is There to Learn?' *Global Finance Journal 22*, no. 3: pp. 238–47.

Lansing, Kevin J. (2011). 'Gauging the Impact of the Great Recession'. *FRBSF Economic Letter 2011-21*.

Marlier, Eric, A. B. Atkinson, Bea Cantillon, and Brian Nolan (2007). *Facing the Challenges: The EU and Social Inclusion* (Bristol: Policy Press).

Moffitt, Robert A. (2013). 'The Great Recession and the Social Safety Net'. *Annals of the American Academy of Political and Social Science 650*, no. 1: pp. 143–66.

Moffitt, Robert A. (2015). 'The Deserving Poor, the Family, and the US Welfare System'. *Demography 52*, no. 3: pp. 729–49.

Moffitt, Robert A. (2016). 'Multiple Program Participation and the SNAP Program'. In Judith Bartfeld, Craig Gundersen, Timothy M. Smeeding, and James P. Ziliak (eds), *SNAP Matters: How Food Stamps Affect Health and Well-Being* (Stanford, CA: Stanford University Press).

National Employment Law Project (NELP) (2014). 'The Low-wage Recovery: Industry Employment and Wages Four Years into the Recovery'. *NELP Data Brief*, April 2014 (New York: NELP).

Organization for Economic Co-operation and Development (OECD) (2013). 'Crisis Squeezes Income and Puts Pressure on Inequality and Poverty: Results from the OECD Income Distribution Database (May 2013)'. <http://www.oecd.org/els/soc/OECD2013-Inequality-and-Poverty-8p.pdf>.

Pilkauskas, Natasha V., Janet Currie, and Irwin Garfinkel (2012). 'The Great Recession, Public Transfers, and Material Hardship'. *Social Service Review 86*, no. 3: pp. 401–27.

Ravallion, Martin and Shaohua Chen (2011). 'Weakly Relative Poverty'. *Review of Economics and Statistics 93*, no. 4: pp. 1251–61.

Ross, Martha and Nicole Prchal Svajlenka (2015). 'Worrying Declines in Teen and Young Adult Employment'. <http://www.brookings.edu/research/papers/2015/12/16-declines-in-teen-and-young-adult-employment-ross-svajlenka>.

Rothstein, Jesse (2011). 'Unemployment Insurance and Job Search in the Great Recession'. *Brookings Papers on Economic Activity 43*, no. 2: pp. 143–213.

Schoeni, Robert F. and Rebecca M. Blank (2000). 'What Has Welfare Reform Accomplished? Impacts on Welfare Participation, Employment, Income, Poverty, and Family Structure'. *NBER Working Paper 7627*. National Bureau of Economic Research. DOI: 10.3386/w7627.

Sentier Research (2016). 'Household Income Trends, 2016'. <http://www.sentierresearch.com/reports/Sentier_Household_Income_Trends_Report_March2016_04_28_16.pdf>

Shaefer, H. Luke, and Kathryn Edin (2013). 'Rising Extreme Poverty in the United States and the Response of Federal Means-tested Transfer Programs'. *Social Service Review 87*, no. 2: 250–68.

Short, Kathleen (2012). 'The Research Supplemental Poverty Measure: 2011'. *Current Population Reports P60-244* (Washington, DC: US Census Bureau).

Smeeding, Timothy M. (2016). 'Poverty Measurement'. In David Brady and Linda M. Burton (eds), *The Oxford Handbook of the Social Science of Poverty* (Oxford: Oxford University Press).

Smeeding, Timothy M., Irwin Garfinkel, and Ronald B. Mincy (2011). 'Introduction: Young Disadvantaged Men: Fathers, Families, Poverty, and Policy'. *Annals of the American Academy of Political and Social Science 635*, no. 1: pp. 6–21.

Smeeding, Timothy M. and Céline Thévenot (2016). 'Addressing Child Poverty: How Does the United States Compare With Other Nations?' *Academic Pediatrics 16*, no. 3 Supplement: S67–S75.

Smeeding, Timothy M. (2006). 'Poor People in Rich Nations: The United States In Comparative Perspective'. *Journal of Economic Perspectives 20*, no. 1: pp. 69–90.

Sommers, Benjamin D. and Donald Oellerich (2013). 'The Poverty-reducing Effect of Medicaid'. *Journal of Health Economics 32*, no. 5: pp. 816–32.

Thompson, Jeffrey and Timothy M. Smeeding (2013). 'Country Case Study—USA'. In Stephen P. Jenkins, Andrea Brandolini, John Micklewright, and Brian Nolan (eds), *The Great Recession and the Distribution of Household Income* (Oxford: Oxford University Press).

Tiehen, Laura, Dean Jolliffe, and Timothy M. Smeeding (2016). 'The Effect of SNAP on Poverty'. In Judith Bartfeld, Craig Gundersen, Timothy M. Smeeding, and James P. Ziliak (eds), *SNAP Matters: How Food Stamps Affect Health and Well-Being* (Stanford, CA: Stanford University Press).

Wimer, Christopher, Liana E. Fox, Irwin Garfinkel, Neeraj Kaushal, and Jane Waldfogel (2016). 'Progress on Poverty? New Estimates of Historical Trends using an Anchored Supplemental Poverty Measure'. *Demography 53*, no 4: 1207–18.

Ziliak, James P. (2011). 'Recent Developments in Antipoverty Policies in the United States'. *Discussion Paper 1396–11* (Madison, WI: Institute for Research on Poverty).

14

Learning the Lessons: Enhancing Capacity to Protect Children

Brian Nolan, Bea Cantillon, Sudhanshu Handa, and Yekaterina Chzhen

14.1. INTRODUCTION

This volume has presented a set of in-depth analyses of the impact of the economic crisis and subsequent recession on children in eleven Organization for Economic Co-operation and Development (OECD) countries, selected to cover a wide range in terms of their initial conditions and the way the crisis played out. Each chapter has highlighted some important lessons for the country in question from the outcomes examined and the policies described and assessed. In this concluding chapter, we stand back, drawing on these country-level analyses to bring out broader conclusions and lessons for how children can be better protected from bearing the brunt of such crises in the future.

14.2. LEARNING FROM DIVERSE COUNTRIES AND COUNTRY EXPERIENCES

Drawing general lessons from these country experiences is not a straightforward exercise, because the impact of the crisis and recession on children will have differed across them for a variety of reasons.

First of all, countries were very differently placed as the crisis struck. This was the case in terms of the extent and nature of child poverty itself: countries differed substantially—not just in the initial level of child poverty, as conventionally measured, but also in terms of its correlates, the characteristics of the families affected, and which groups were most vulnerable. This also applied to the strength and capacity of the social protection system, and of the economy and welfare state more broadly, to cushion the impact on children of a major economic downturn.

Second, *trajectories* before the crisis also differed considerably. Sweden continues to provide an example of how low child poverty can be attained. However, since the 1990s families with children have experienced a long trend towards increasing relative poverty. Despite the growth of employment and incomes and high levels of social spending, Belgium and Germany also experienced an increase in child poverty in the better years before the crisis. In these highly developed welfare states, the redistributive impact on poverty rates has declined since the 1990s, in consequence of a declining benefit adequacy for vulnerable families. The UK and Ireland provide examples of how successful packages of anti-poverty policy—including the minimum wage, improvements in child benefits, social assistance, tax credits, and increasing spending on education, health, and childcare—can be implemented.

Third, to talk of the impact of 'the crisis' obscures the crucial consideration that the macroeconomic 'shock' itself differed greatly across countries, both in its initial impact and in the way it subsequently played out. This variation is clear from comparison across the eleven countries of the extent to which unemployment rose and wages fell, how much average incomes declined, how long high unemployment and depressed incomes persisted, how badly banks were hit and the consequences for governments, borrowers, and savers, whether property and asset prices also collapsed, whether an external 'bailout' of the country was required, and so on.

Finally, policy choices then also varied and different decisions were made in response to the way the crisis hit and evolved, as new and pressing needs emerged, which affected outcomes for children. At the same time, of course, resources became highly constrained where public budget deficits soared, and so the constraints were very real and have to be to the fore in any assessment. Within those constraints, which included external pressures from the financial markets, there was some space for domestic choices, but the worst-affected countries were very substantially constrained by the external bailout programmes that they needed.

Considering each of these in turn, the variation in levels of child poverty across the eleven countries as the crisis struck is evident from the overview chapter and subsequent case studies. Measured against a relative income standard, the percentage of children in households with incomes below 60 per cent of the median just before the onset of the crisis ranged from about 13–15 per cent in Sweden and Germany, 17–18 per cent in Belgium and Ireland, 20 per cent in Hungary, 23–24 per cent in Greece, Italy, and the UK, and about 27 per cent in Spain and the USA. Taking the perspective of relative income poverty, we must, of course, be aware that this measure has inherent conceptual and methodological shortcomings. This relative poverty indicator would be unaffected in an economic downturn if poor families with children in each country did not suffer more than those in the middle of the income distribution (which in many countries is *not* what we observe) even though their living standards declined. It has been emphasized throughout the volume that these purely relative income poverty measures need, of course, to be seen in the context of the very substantial differences in average income levels and living standards across these countries when the downturn struck. Average gross domestic product (GDP) per capita in purchasing power terms in 2008 was highest in the USA, with Sweden and Ireland next highest (though Ireland was artificially boosted by profits remitted abroad by multinationals operating there). Belgium, Germany, and the UK were at similar levels to each other, at around four-fifths of the US figure. Italy, Japan, and Spain were closer to 70 per cent of the US level, with Greece below that and Hungary well below half that level.

So both the average level of income and its distribution crucially affect living standards for children. For the nine case-study countries that are members of the EU, this is captured (at least to some extent) by the variation in rates of material deprivation being reported by the households in which children live, using the harmonized measure included in the EU's suite of social inclusion indicators. There one sees the percentage of children who were in households reporting such deprivation ranging from only 6 per cent in Sweden to 14–16 per cent in Belgium, Germany, and Spain, 17–18 per cent in Ireland and the UK, 19 per cent in Greece and Italy, and 39 per cent in Hungary.

The differences in initial levels of GDP per head are also highly relevant to the capacity of the social protection system to cushion the impact of a macroeconomic shock on children. The level of social spending is also key: its overall scale as a proportion of GDP as the crisis hit was highest in Belgium, Germany, Italy, Sweden, and the UK; followed by Greece, Hungary, Ireland, and Spain; and lowest in Japan and the USA. The composition of social spending and its coverage and structures were also central to its responsive capacity, as is brought out in the variety of country experiences. Hungary, for example, had a relatively high level of family/child-related expenditure compared to other EU countries; Italy, on the other hand, had almost 60 per cent of its social transfers going on pensions. The mainly categorical system in Italy also left substantial groups unprotected (or inadequately protected), and this was compounded by the underdevelopment of family policy and the absence of a national minimum income scheme. Geographic/regional variation in entitlement and support is a significant issue in some countries, such as Italy, Spain, and Greece, as well as the USA. The trajectory of economic growth in the years preceding the crisis also matters: among the hardest-hit countries, for example, the exceptionally rapid growth seen in Ireland, Greece, and Spain contrasts with the stagnation in Hungary and Italy, and this will have affected both household and state capacity to cope with recession. Some countries improved their poverty-reducing capacity; others did not. Finally, the state of the public finances as the crisis struck also served as a more binding constraint on action in some countries than in others, in terms of both fiscal deficits and the level of national debt: this in turn reflects *inter alia* macroeconomic developments in the decade or more up to this crisis.

The differential impact of the crisis by country was also made clear from the outset of this volume, in the overview presented in Chapter 2 and in the detailed descriptions in the country chapters. Each of the countries studied suffered some decline in GDP per capita, but the scale and duration of that decline and the way in which it impacted on the labour market differed greatly.

At one end of the spectrum, Germany saw an initial decline of about 5 per cent in GDP per capita, but it recovered rapidly, so that by 2014 GDP per capita was 8 per cent over its pre-crisis level; unemployment showed little increase and by 2014 was lower than in 2007. Belgium had a lower initial decline in GDP per capita, but was only back to its pre-crisis level in 2014, when unemployment was still above its 2007 level.

In Hungary, Japan, Sweden, the UK, and the USA, GDP per capita fell by 5–7 per cent at the onset of the crisis, and by 2014 had recovered to about the 2007 level; unemployment was then higher than it had been pre-crisis, except in Japan. By contrast, Spain saw GDP per capita fall by 9 per cent, with only a slight recovery from that by 2014, while unemployment more than doubled (from an already high level).

Ireland and Italy experienced initial declines of 12–13 per cent in GDP per capita, but their subsequent fortunes diverged, with Ireland seeing some growth return, while Italy suffered further decline; both saw a pronounced rise in unemployment, though Ireland saw this decline somewhat in 2013–14.

Finally, Greece is an extreme case, where GDP per capita fell by a stunning 25 per cent; by 2014 it had not recovered at all. Meanwhile, like Spain, unemployment more than doubled, to over 50 per cent. The finance and wealth-related aspects of the crisis also differed across countries, with the collapse in asset values and in credit much more serious in some (such as Hungary, Ireland, Spain, the UK, and the USA).

So the countries studied here represent a diverse set in terms of the scale and nature of the macroeconomic 'shock' they experienced; this has to be to the fore in learning from them. It is worth noting, though, that even in a country such as Belgium, where the impact on economic growth and unemployment was relatively modest, the decline in GDP growth was the most marked since the Second World War. For the USA, where employment fell by more than 8 million (5 percentage points) by the end of 2009, the Great Recession was clearly the most dramatic downturn experienced since the Great Depression. Some countries—notably Sweden, Hungary, Italy, and Japan—had also experienced waves of austerity or recession in the years up to the crisis, while others (such as Ireland, Greece, and Spain) had seen exceptionally high growth. Across the rich countries, the Great Recession represented a real test of the capacity to protect children in the face of a severe economic shock.

14.3. THE VARYING IMPACT OF THE CRISIS ON CHILD POVERTY

The impact of the crisis and subsequent recession on child poverty was similarly diverse. Against an income threshold held fixed in purchasing power through the crisis (rather than moving—often down—with the median), Sweden saw a decline in child poverty; Belgium and Japan had an initial increase, but then a decline; there was a modest increase in Germany; a slightly greater one in the UK and the USA; and increases that were much more marked in Hungary, Ireland, Italy, Spain, and especially Greece. In Spain, the anchored poverty rate for children was well over a third by 2014. Greece once again represents an even more extreme case, with child poverty using the anchored threshold going up from the already very high figure of a fifth to over half of all children. (Measured against a relative income standard, which is less suitable in a context where average/median incomes fell, the percentage of children in poor households was little changed in Germany, Ireland, Italy, and the USA; fell in the UK; fluctuated in Japan; and was higher in 2014 than 2007 in Belgium, Sweden, Hungary, Spain, and Greece.)

These changes in poverty measured in terms of real incomes (that is, adjusted for price changes) were broadly consistent with the levels of material deprivation reported by the households in which children live. Those levels fell in Germany, Japan, and Sweden; rose initially in Belgium and then fell back; and went up markedly in Hungary, Ireland, Italy, Spain, and especially Greece. In Italy, for example, the percentage of children living in households that could not afford at least four out of nine items considered necessary for a decent life soared from 9 per cent in 2008 to 17 per cent in 2012 (though it then fell back somewhat). While it is very difficult to capture the impact on children themselves, several countries were able to look at indicators that related to them. In Italy, for example, the percentage of households that could not afford new clothes for the children rose from 6 per cent to 12 per cent. In Spain, there was some increase in the proportion reporting inability to afford activities and celebrations for the children, having their friends around, school trips, etc. Parents clearly do their best to shield their children from the worst effects of financial problems, though the stresses involved for the adults may often be visible to the children and have an impact on them.

14.4. RESPONDING TO THE CRISIS

The response by governments to the crisis covered a very wide range of policy levers and varied with their circumstances. At the macroeconomic level, both automatic stabilizers and designedly anti-cyclical measures were extremely important—the latter including, for example, the explicit fiscal stimulus implemented in countries such as Germany and the USA, and subsequently monetary policy bringing interest rates to remarkably low levels by unprecedented measures in the USA, UK, the Eurozone, and Japan.

The main focus in this volume has not been on the macroeconomic response—either initially or as the crisis played out—though that has been hotly debated in terms of both the balance between fiscal and monetary policy and the scale of the 'austerity' measures imposed in many countries, in the form of public expenditure cuts and tax increases. The point to emphasize here, as is clear from the country cases, is that these cuts and tax increases often played a major role in the impact that the crisis had on the living standards of families and children. Economic mismanagement, which created the conditions in which the financial crisis could occur and could have such serious consequences, must shoulder much responsibility for what followed.

More proximately, the labour market is seen—from all the country cases—to have been central to the transmission of the impact of the crisis to households with children. In many of the countries studied, increasing child poverty was closely linked to an increase in the proportion of those households with little or no employment. In Spain, for example, by 2013 these accounted for 15 per cent of all households; and 14 per cent of all children lived in such households. In some countries, the poverty rate also increased for these households; but the dominant influence on the overall poverty rate was most often the increase in the number of such households, as employment rates fell at the individual and the household level. The poverty rate for children in households with little or no employment is generally remarkably high: again in Spain, by 2012–14 it was as high as 86 per cent, set against an anchored poverty threshold. As well as rising unemployment, many employees who remained in work saw their gross earnings fall, while some self-employed people suffered very sharp drops in income from the market. It is also important to note that in a considerable number of countries (for example, Belgium, Ireland, Italy, Hungary, and Spain) labour market outcomes meant that the crisis disproportionately increased poverty among specific risk groups that already faced exceptionally high rates—notably those with low levels of education, single parents, and a migrant background. In some countries, notably Italy and Spain, children in large families also continued to face a particularly high risk. Equally important, however, is the observation that child poverty is not only a problem of having parents with low qualifications or little work: as a general rule, it is not an isolated phenomenon, but is spread quite widely across the population.

In this context, we must highlight the importance of measures directed at keeping workers in or attached to their jobs as the crisis hit. This was central to the strategy adopted in Germany and Belgium as GDP fell, in particular through the short-term work programmes that were already in place, but where entitlement and coverage were substantially increased to cope with the crisis. (Public works programmes to directly provide employment were also implemented in some countries, such as Hungary from 2010.) It is true that the scale of the macroeconomic shock—as well as the policy discourse on the drawbacks of 'passive income support' which prevailed before the crisis—would have made it much more difficult for some other countries to follow such an approach. Nevertheless, some important lessons may be drawn from the way in which the measures themselves were framed and implemented, and from the institutional context that allowed this to be achieved. The importance of building the tripartite institutions and relationships required to underpin such a coping response to hard economic times should be emphasized. It is also noteworthy that, by contrast, some of the worst-affected countries, such as Italy, Greece, and Spain, introduced measures to reduce employment protection, for example by making contract termination easier, reducing the cost of dismissals, extending the probationary period for new workers, and giving firms the chance to opt out of collective agreements. Whatever the merits of such policies in the medium to long term, implementing them in the depths of recession increased precariousness. Again there are important lessons for the future—if nothing else, then for the timing of such reforms.

14.5. THE CENTRALITY OF SOCIAL PROTECTION

With falling incomes from the market the core consequence of the crisis, all the case studies emphasize the central role that social transfers played in cushioning the immediate impact on household disposable income and on child poverty. The extent to which declining income from employment and self-employment has an impact on disposable income and living standards depends on the income protection system's ability to replace lost income. This, in turn, is a reflection both of the comprehensiveness of the social protection system (how many of those facing income falls are covered) and of its relative generosity (the extent to which, for those covered, the lost market income is replaced).

In terms of acting as a buffer for families as the crisis struck, the income protection system was clearly more robust and effective in some countries than in others. As noted, in some countries the social fabric became stronger before the crisis, while in others there was a deterioration in the poverty-reducing capacity of the welfare state well before the crisis struck. A substantial initial cushioning effect is evident from the case studies of countries such as Sweden and Belgium (although in these countries the effect was less strong than it would have been if the poverty-reducing capacity of social protection had not been affected before the crisis), as well as Ireland and the UK (at least partly due to the increased effectiveness of the social fabric before the crisis).

However, as well as in countries conventionally regarded as having systems with broad coverage, the cushioning impact of social protection was important in the US, Italy, and Hungary. In Hungary, the level of child poverty would have been more than twice as high without working-age cash social transfers. In the US, the immediate impact of the sharp increase in unemployment on families with children was limited, because the social safety net provided significant support. This was especially through 'Food Stamps' (renamed the Supplemental Nutrition Assistance Program a decade ago), with more than one person in seven in the USA receiving benefits from that programme by 2011. The Earned Income Tax Credit (EITC) and the Additional Child Tax Credit served to supplement the income of the working poor, but did not help the jobless poor. The US is also notable for low social spending and for having no universal child allowance or income floor for all children. Some distressing new work suggests an alarming rise in so-called 'extreme poverty' (those living on under $2.00 per day).

Japan is unusual in the limited extent of social protection transfers for working-age households. Greece, Italy, and Spain also have less comprehensive, more fragmented social protection systems than their northern European counterparts. By way of illustration, in Spain, by 2012 only 64 per cent of the registered unemployed received unemployment benefits. The high poverty rate for the rapidly rising number of households with low work intensity in those countries reflects the fact that, as the Spanish chapter concludes, 'the social insurance system that protects children when their parents are out of the labour market is neither sufficiently generous nor adequately comprehensive'. Despite that, the existing schemes, combined with the redistributive action of families, did play a shock-absorber role with respect to the initial impact of the crisis on households. Particularly in Mediterranean countries, family solidarity played a role in mitigating the impact of unemployment on poverty, at least for a time.

Some countries, such as Belgium, Spain, the UK, and the USA, also sought to minimize the impact of unemployment or reduced working hours on disposable incomes by increasing levels of unemployment benefit and/or social assistance, at least for a time, before fiscal consolidation became the priority. In Spain, for example, the amount of means-tested child benefit for young children more than doubled, while maternity leave became more generous and a one-off universal child benefit payable at birth was introduced.

In the US, the American Recovery and Reinvestment Act 2009 significantly expanded the social safety net: the Food Stamp maximum benefit was increased, EITC was made more generous for families with three or more children, taxes were reduced through the Making Work Pay Tax Credit, and child tax credits were expanded. The maximum duration of Unemployment Insurance benefits was also extended to ninety-nine weeks, far beyond the normal maximum of twenty-six weeks. As a consequence, the American safety net—which, as the case study puts it, 'is commonly thought to be a patchwork of programmes that pales into insignificance when compared to what is in place in many advanced democracies'—did effectively serve to limit the rise in child poverty as unemployment rose, according to the USA's own poverty measure.

14.6. SOCIAL PROTECTION AND SOCIAL SPENDING AS THE CRISIS UNFOLDED

While the cushioning effect of social protection was key in the immediate aftermath of the financial crisis, the extent to which countries could maintain that buffer beyond the initial onset depended very much on the severity of the recession and on whether fiscal pressures—as perceived externally or internally—required urgent major 'correction'. Ireland, for example, is among those countries assessed externally (including by the EU and the OECD) as having a social transfer system that is relatively effective in bringing households, including those with children, up to conventional poverty thresholds. However, the level of support provided at the outset of the crisis could not be maintained as it unfolded.

The same is true of Spain, and of course Greece, the most extreme case. The impact of the austerity measures imposed was then most evident in these hardest-hit countries (where yawning public deficits necessitated an external bailout), as well as in Hungary (which had already had recourse to the International Monetary Fund in 2008) and Italy. They were more severely constrained in the choices open to them than countries that were less seriously affected and not subject to such a degree of external oversight.

On top of the direct impact of the crisis on the labour market, the cuts in cash transfers and the increases in direct and indirect taxes, introduced in the interests of fiscal correction, had a profound effect on families with children. National strategies differed enormously. In Italy, Spain, and Greece, there was a strong acceleration of the pension reforms, allowing for a gradual shift towards active-age spending. In Italy and Spain, unemployment benefits became more universal, while new, categorical and targeted social assistance benefits were introduced. In some cases, new measures were also put in place that specifically targeted families with children (e.g. the Italian 'Bonus bebè'). In others, however, existing child-related benefits were cut (e.g. the halving of the means-tested Spanish child benefit).

The UK is one of a number of countries where political shifts saw major changes in strategy in the course of the recession, with severe cuts in social spending from 2010. Working-age transfers bore the brunt, while pensions were protected (via 'triple-lock' indexation). Households with children were thus among those most seriously affected, and those on lower incomes suffered the largest falls in income. Japan saw major reform and expansion in universal child benefit around the same time. This was partly funded by cuts in the income tax deduction for child dependants (though there was a subsequent roll-back, reflecting the political swing).

Hungary also saw a shift in political ideology and strategy a few years after the onset of the crisis: in this instance there was a shift from family allowances to family tax benefit, as well as cuts to social assistance. As a consequence of a strong shift towards workfare, conditionality, and activation policies, the poverty-reducing capacity of the Hungarian social protection system decreased dramatically. In Italy, by contrast, there was some progress towards more universal coverage of income support in unemployment to cover previously unprotected workers.

In assessing the overall impact on children of the cuts in public spending and the increases in taxes and charges (often lumped together under the label 'austerity'), one has to bear in mind a counterfactual: what would the outcomes have been had 'fiscal correction' taken a different path? This is hotly debated and there is little sign of consensus emerging in many countries—though in the extreme case of Greece, it is widely thought that the scale of spending cuts imposed has been counterproductive, even from a medium-term growth perspective, and carries with it very high costs. More generally, though, one can also focus on how the burden of adjustment was distributed and whether different choices could have been made in that respect.

Here one can point to many instances where the cuts in cash transfers actually implemented were more damaging to children than the available alternatives. In the case of Hungary, for example, cuts in social assistance meant that the poverty-reduction impact of cash benefits declined. In the UK, which had reduced child poverty via redistributive policies in the previous decade, the change in strategy and associated benefit cuts from 2010 meant that children lost out. In Ireland, working-age and child-focused income transfers were cut, while those for the over-65s were mostly protected.

This also applies to social spending more broadly, with cuts in expenditure on public services a very important feature of the recession's impact on families with children. In Spain, for example, large education spending cuts from 2012 led to an increase in class sizes and a retrenchment of the special educational supports that targeted children from disadvantaged backgrounds (these also suffered resource cuts in Ireland). Healthcare spending was likewise cut and charges were increased, while waiting times lengthened. Meanwhile in Italy, the social budget allocated by the centre to the regions for the provision of services was drastically reduced, particularly in the area of social care. In Greece, there was a rise in the costs associated with access to a range of public services, including healthcare.

This trend was not confined to the hardest-hit countries: in the UK, for example, low-income families with children also suffered from cuts to local services, especially because the reductions in central government grants fell most heavily on local authority areas with the highest levels of child poverty. Again, this reflects very real constraints, but also choices about priorities.

In a context where poverty is now often higher in childhood than in old age, the way in which family/child-focused social spending is treated vis-à-vis pensions is an aspect that cannot be ignored, especially as the proportion of older people in the population grows. In the US, for example, non-means-tested entitlements for the elderly, including healthcare, are scheduled to grow very rapidly with the ageing of the 'baby boomers', thus adding to the pressure to cut discretionary benefits for families with children. More broadly, inter-generational differences in wealth have been growing, notably in the UK and the US, with access to housing a particular challenge for younger cohorts. The central choices involved should not be reduced to privileging children or older people, however. Instead, the challenge is to keep stable the relative positions of the young and the old, to put in place a social safety net that provides basic adequacy for all and to make sure that it continues to do so in hard times.

14.7. TACKLING CHILD POVERTY AND PROMOTING PROTECTIVE CAPACITY FOR THE FUTURE

Thinking in those terms, the country experiences analysed here bring out the importance of building a coherent 'social fabric'. In most cases, this implies increasing social transfers, while protecting work incentives. Experience over the longer term across the rich countries demonstrates that adequate income protection is central to tackling child poverty, but is not enough on its own. There is, however, no denying the tensions and trade-offs involved, as demonstrated by the Hungarian case. The measures that are required to address child poverty effectively, over and above the social safety net, would also add greatly to the protective capacity in future recessions.

Countries such as Greece, Japan, Italy, and Spain, with their fragmented social transfer systems and substantial gaps in their safety nets, can certainly learn from the success of other countries in achieving high coverage rates with (different) combinations of social insurance, and means-tested and universal payments. Reliance on contributory social insurance for 'standard workers' and their families leaves major gaps in coverage; a broad social assistance scheme acting as a social safety net of last resort is a minimum requirement (and something the worst-hit countries sought to address even in the depths of the crisis). More generally, in a deep recession it is imperative that systems are able to cope effectively with large numbers of unemployed people who exhaust their insurance-based benefit. This is something with which many countries struggle. This applies not only to the coverage of the means-tested safety net, but also to its adequacy. As some countries have shown, though, an extension of insurance entitlement in such circumstances can potentially be an important policy tool. Providing adequate social protection for the self-employed is also often problematic: Spain, for example, has sought to address this by introducing new unemployment insurance for those self-employed people who had been making social insurance contributions but had ceased their activity for economic reasons.

The experience of the US points to the importance of adequate wages. Low wages and falling wages, with no increase in the minimum wage, were hallmarks of the US non-response. Hence unemployment fell, but poverty fell by much less, as incomes continued to be inadequate. Minimum wages also have an important indirect impact: adequate minimum in-work incomes and adequate minimum out-of-work incomes indeed tend to coexist.

Child benefits/family allowances have an important role to play, and in the countries with neither a universal child benefit nor an effective and comprehensive income-based family payment, that is a significant gap to be addressed. Quite a few countries continue to debate the role of universality versus selectivity, and of cash transfers versus tax deductions in their child-focused payments. Experience before and through the crisis demonstrates how politically challenging it can be to maintain a well-directed, adequately resourced and effective structure. While not a panacea, adequate child-focused payments, with a balance between selectivity and universality, are a key, potentially powerful element in the overall social safety net for working and non-working families alike. Italy can serve as an illustration of the point that the redistributive efficiency of existing child-related income transfers (allowances and tax deductions) is often much less than it could be.

This is, of course, also true more broadly: the poverty-reducing impact of current social protection and social spending could often be increased. Progressive taxation and a higher degree of efficiency can be achieved through better design of cash benefits and in-kind services, rebalanced towards the poor and vulnerable. The specifics will depend on the details of the system architecture in the particular country, and means testing has a role to play in the provision of the basic safety net; but better direction of resources need not entail wholesale reliance on income testing. Rather, a combination of universal, social insurance-based, and means-tested provision of income support, with spending on education and health directed most towards those with the greatest need rather than the already well-resourced, can address child poverty more effectively in reasonably good times and can also serve as a much more effective buffer when economies are in recession. The Hungarian experience might be an example of how a shift in focus from the poor to the middle classes contributes to increased poverty rates.

It is also essential for social spending to be appropriately aligned with labour market policy, in order to address the structural problems of low education and other factors that underpin low labour force participation (particularly among mothers) and household worklessness. The successful activation and integration of such households into the labour market—including, for example, lone parents and those from minority or migrant backgrounds—is key. A coherent strategy encompassing social protection, the labour market, education, and childcare is required. Minimum wages, social assistance and unemployment benefits, in-work income support, child-focused income transfers and affordable childcare, and activation should all play a central role in this strategy. Enabling and supporting those parents (particularly mothers) who have lower levels of education to work is central to their children's living standards and prospects. Constraints (e.g. inadequate or expensive childcare) on mothers' labour market participation must be addressed, particularly in low-income households. It is also important to equip young people with the right skills to participate fully in society and make a successful transition to further/higher education, and from school to work and independent living.

A final lesson that must be drawn is that even the best-designed and resourced social support structures would struggle to cope with recession of the severity experienced by the worst-hit countries in the crisis. The conclusion reached in the Greek chapter—that 'the depth and duration of the Greek crisis, including mass unemployment, would have posed insurmountable challenges to any welfare state, even the most advanced'—is unarguable. Indeed, the experience of Sweden in its recession of the early to mid-1990s underlines the point. The consequences of misguided macroeconomic and regulatory policies will be very real for families and children, even with strengthened social safety nets, and that must also be at the core of the lessons learned from the crisis.

14.8. LEGACIES OF THE CRISIS AND PUTTING CHILDREN FIRST

The recession brought on by the financial crisis, meriting its label of 'Great Recession', continues to have its macroeconomic effects, but also entails a highly challenging legacy in many of the countries of the developed world. Unemployment remains particularly high in some, and its scarring effects on the future prospects of those affected are a major concern. While some countries may be emerging from the crisis with their labour market institutions and social protection systems strengthened, or with reforms that hold out the prospect of improvement under way, other countries are pursuing reductions in employment protection and security and in social transfers that will leave families more vulnerable. Cuts in social spending more broadly run the risk of deepening health and educational divides and making child poverty more intractable.

Disappointing child poverty trends before, during, and after the crisis point to the failure of policy mixes. In order to reduce poverty, countries must not only develop effective employment policies but also ensure adequate protection. Clearly employment policies are important, but not sufficient. Today, minimum income protection for jobless households falls short of the poverty line—in particular for families with dependent children—even in the most generous settings. Jobs for low-skilled people are under pressure (in terms of both number and pay), and so is social protection in case of inactivity. In many countries, the institutions of the welfare state remain ill-equipped to deal with the labour force participation of mothers and with single-parenthood, while the poverty-reducing capacity of social spending is much weaker than one might expect. The success of poverty reduction depends on jobs at the lower end of the labour market, on the distribution of these jobs across households with different work intensity, and on properly designed social protection systems.

This implies an increase in social benefits and services for households below the median, at the same time as work incentives are protected. Clearly, enhancing poverty reduction presents an extremely difficult challenge in terms of both the overall financial and operational capacity of the welfare state, and its redistributive strength. The experience of some countries shows, however, that a move towards a decent safety net and adequate child benefit packages, while expensive, is not altogether impossible, provided the policy design is coherent and efficient. In addition, social action and investment in children's capabilities as a response to the persistence of poverty, the concentration of disadvantage in multicultural urban areas, and the pressures on the low-skilled segments of the labour market should be regarded as powerful supporting pillars of structural social policies. The importance and value of locally embedded civil society and place-based social work should not be underestimated, especially when it targets children's activities.

The case studies analysed in this volume have brought out the varying extent to which child poverty has been on the national policy agenda through the crisis. In some countries, child poverty did not traditionally figure on the political agenda as a major concern, but it has received greater attention since becoming more visible during the crisis. Despite all the challenges and constraints associated with the macroeconomic legacies of the crisis, this represents an opportunity to press for the strategies required both to address child poverty effectively and to protect children against the worst effects of future crises.

Index

'Tables and figures are indicated by an italic *t* and *f* following the page number.'